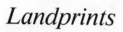

Landprints

Also by Walter Sullivan:

Black Holes: The Edge of Space, the End of Time
Continents in Motion
We Are Not Alone
Assault on the Unknown
Quest for a Continent

NYT **Times** BOOKS

WALTER SULLIVAN
LANDPRINTS

On the Magnificent American Landscape

To those who rejoice in the world below, above, and around us,
who see "sermons in stones," and who are inspired by the
sweep of our panoramas and their history.

Published by TIMES BOOKS,
The New York Times Book Co., Inc.
130 Fifth Avenue, New York, N.Y. 10011

Published simultaneously in Canada by
Fitzhenry & Whiteside, Ltd., Toronto

Library of Congress Cataloging in Publication Data

Sullivan, Walter.
  Landprints.

  Includes index.
  1. Geology—United States. I. Title. II. Title: Landprints.
QE77.S84   1984   557.3   83-45035
ISBN 0-8129-1077-X

Designed by Betty Binns

Manufactured in the United States of America

84 85 86 87 88 5 4 3 2 1

ACKNOWLEDGMENTS

This book, dealing, as it does, with a very wide range of subjects, could not have been written without the generous help of many specialists. Those who reviewed parts of the manuscript include: Walter Alvarez, University of California, Berkeley; Victor R. Baker, Peter J. Coney, and William R. Dickinson, University of Arizona; Clark Blake, Jr., Robert L. Christiansen, Warren Hamilton, David L. Jones, Kenneth Pierce, and Eugene G. Robertson, U.S. Geological Survey; Norman Berg, American Farmland Trust; Kenneth Bergman, National Weather Service; Eric S. Cheney, University of Washington; Gordon P. Eaton, Texas A&M University; Richard P. Goldthwait, Ohio State University; Leo Hall, University of Massachusetts; John Fraser Hart, University of Minnesota; Robert D. Hatcher, Jr., University of South Carolina; James V. Hines, III, U.S. Army Corps of Engineers; Peter R. Hooper, Washington State University; Nelson Jarmie, Los Alamos National Laboratory; Sheldon Judson and Franklyn B. Van Houten, Princeton University; John B. Lyons, Dartmouth College; Charles Merguerian, Hofstra University; Ralph Moberly, University of Hawaii; James W. H. Monger and Raymond A. Price, Geological Survey of Canada; William D. Pattison, University of Chicago; Orrin H. Pilkey, Duke University; John Rodgers, Yale University; and Eugene Shoemaker, California Institute of Technology and U.S. Geological Survey.

Photographs and other material were provided by many institutions and individuals, including some of those cited above. In addition to those credited beneath their photographs I am particularly indebted to: the Agricultural Stabilization and Conservation Service, U.S. Department of Agriculture in Salt Lake City; that department's Office of Governmental and Public Affairs and its Soil Conservation Service in Washington; Nicholas M. Short and his colleagues at the Goddard Space Flight Center in Maryland; Christopher S. Scotese and his coworkers at the University of Chicago; Jeppesen Sanderson, Inc., in Denver; Canada's National Air Photo Library in Ottawa; and the Space Science and Engineering Center at the University of Wisconsin. At the U.S. Geological Survey in Reston, Virginia, Frank Forrester, Robert Johns, Donovan Kelley, Gail Wendt, and Wil. J. Dooley were particularly helpful, as well as John A. Shanton of the Survey's National Cartographic Information Center there. Further aid was provided by Gerald C. Schaber in the Survey's Flagstaff office; Edna King in its Menlo Park, California, office; its Photographic Library in Denver; its EROS Data Center in Sioux Falls, South Dakota; its glaciology office in Tacoma, Washington; and by Raymond C. Douglass at the U.S. National Museum in Washington.

I owe a special debt of gratitude to Lyman Abbott and the University of Hawaii Press for generously providing many illustrations. Material was also provided by such individuals as: Tanya M. Atwater of the University of California, Santa Barbara; Robert E. Bergstrom and Richard H. Howard, Illinois Geological Survey; Michael B. E. Bograd, Mississippi Department of Natural Resources; Barbara Borowiecki, University of Wisconsin, Milwaukee; Charles E. Chapin, New Mexico Bureau of Mines and Mineral Resources; Lee Clayton, Wisconsin Geological and Natural History Survey; Horace R. Collins, Ohio Department of Natural Resources; Donald Currey, University of Utah; James F. Davis, California Department of Conservation; Robert I. Davis, New Hampshire Department of Resources and Economic Development; R. F. Diffendal, Jr., Nebraska Geological and Natural Resources Surveys; D. G. Edward, Air Canada; C. Elachi and Don Harrison of the Jet Propulsion Laboratory, Pasadena, California; John R. Everett and colleagues at the Earth Satellite Corp., Chevy Chase, Maryland; W. L. Fisher, University of Texas; Philip M. Glick, Chevy Chase, Maryland; C. G. Groat, Louisiana State Geologist; S. L. Groff, Montana Bureau of Mines and Geology; David P. Harper, New Jersey Geological Survey; C. W. Hendry, Jr., Florida State Geologist; Wallace B. Howe, Missouri State Geologist; Y. W. Isachsen, New York State Geological Survey; Preston McGrain, Kentucky Geological Survey; Charles J. Mankin, Oklahoma Geological Survey; Jack E. Oliver, Cornell University; Pete Packett, Florida Department of Agriculture and Consumer Services; John B. Patton, Indiana State Geologist; H. Wesley Peirce, Arizona Bureau of Geology and Mineral Technology; Jean C. Prior of the Iowa Geological Survey; Sid Quarrier, Connecticut Geological Survey; R. A. Robison, University of Kansas; Jon Roethele, Michigan Department of Natural Resources; Ross G. Schaff, Alaska Department of Natural Resources; Earl A.

Shapiro, Georgia Department of Natural Resources; Joseph A. Sinnott, Massachusetts State Geologist; Dorothy M. Skillings, Michigan Department of Natural Resources; Arthur A. Socolow, Pennsylvania Department of Environmental Resources; Dann J. Spariosu, Lamont-Doherty Geological Observatory; and Alan-Jon W. Zupan, South Carolina Geological Survey.

A special word of thanks is due John S. Shelton of La Jolla, California, who provided many of the aerial views. Others have also been particularly helpful. Pamela Flynn typed a large part of the manuscript. My colleagues at *The New York Times* and the staff of Vantage Art, Inc., were responsible for the drawings, and Andrew Sabbatini prepared most of the maps. The book was designed by Betty Binns and Karen Kowles. Finally, my wife, Mary, edited the entire book with her usual skill and provided the title.

CONTENTS

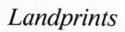

Landprints

1 THE GREATEST SHOW ON EARTH

Human history has its great epics—the Teutonic legends of gods, fire, magic, and gold made famous by Richard Wagner, the sagas of Iceland, the heroic myths of ancient Greece, and numerous grand scenarios from Asia, Africa, and Polynesia. But nothing in man's history or imagination can hold a candle to the true account of how North America came to be formed.

It is a tale of continental collisions, incredible lava floods leading to animal stampedes that defy the imagination, volcanic explosions that are to the 1980 eruption of Mount Saint Helens as a bomb to a hand grenade. Much of this history is laid out for all to see. Some of it—the rise of mountains perhaps higher than the Himalayas, and their gradual erosion—took place in slow motion. But some occurred with catastrophic abruptness in ways no living human being can appreciate in terms of personal experience.

Written on the land are scars left by deluges of mixed water, ice, and boulders whose flow must be reckoned in cubic miles per minute. Strange patterns of the landscape, such as the parallel drumlins of Wisconsin, are puzzling unless one knows they are the handiwork of a mile-high ice sheet that also produced Nantucket and Martha's Vineyard off Massachusetts and New York's Long Island.

Such wonders as the Grand Canyon are not the only remarkable features of the American scene. The East and Gulf coasts are embraced by a chain of barrier islands more extensive than anywhere else on earth. They bear witness to dynamic processes that are constantly reshaping the frontier where continent meets ocean.

The histories written on the land are also those of continuing human endeavor—constructive and destructive—taming the rivers, as at Grand Coulee and Hoover dams, and reshaping the agricultural landscape in efforts to save the soil. The changes in use of the land are everywhere evident, from the farmlands of the West to the expanding suburbs of our cities. The traces of the past are there to be seen, from pioneer trails to the twisting streets of the early city centers.

This book is designed to help the reader share the excitement and wonder of these epic tales. No matter where on the continent one lives, the traces of at least some of them lie close at hand, if one knows how to read them. Rocks freshly exposed in cuts along the interstate highways record much of the continent's dramatic history. The motorist can see the rock-warping agony of continental collisions or past flooding of the region by lava outpourings, making travel on segments of such transcontinental highways as the Trans-Canada Highway or Interstates 40, 70, 80, or 90 a voyage into the earth's past. Not only is this true in the scenic West but in the more subdued landscape of the East, as through New England on Interstate 91. The journey can be a deeply moving experience when the landscape is seen in the context of its history. That history is written not only in towering mountains or exposed cuts and cliffs of tortured rock, but in more lowly clues. By deciphering gravels, sands, silts, and muds spread over the earth as ancient mountains eroded, it has been possible to reconstruct their majestic past. As John Rodgers at Yale University, dean of Appalachian geologists, likes to point out: What one sees in the East is largely not what has been pushed up, but what has been worn down.

Much of the continent's history, from Alaska and the Canadian Arctic to Mexico, can be most fully appreciated from the air, including the full sweep of landscape visible from above 30,000 feet. On a clear day a transcontinental flight can indeed be ''the greatest show on earth.''

Only the lucky ones, however, enjoy a window seat flying across the continent on a cloudless day, and even fewer ever look down from earth orbit, but those perspectives can be experienced in photographs, a number of which are included in this book. The early chapters tell, in terms of the revolutionary new concept of a dynamic, ever-changing earth, how the mountains, volcanoes, and other natural features of the American scene came to be formed. Some of the hypotheses are so new that they are still controversial. Subsequent chapters discuss other handiworks of nature—rivers, scars left by the ice ages and by the ''Age of Winds.''

Later chapters concern man-made features such as the great checkerboard imprinted on the landscape by efforts to parcel out the land equitably (and pay off the national debt of the fledgling United States), as well as the various farming patterns designed to save the land from destruction. In suburbia revolutionary changes can be seen in the making.

The book has been inspired in part by the author's experience of flying across virtually all parts of the continent as well as many motor trips, transcontinental and otherwise. Included, as well, is a chapter on the extraordinary landscape of the Hawaiian Islands. What has made the adventures far richer and more meaningful has been witnessing the recent scientific revolution in understanding how the continent came to be as it is. Preparation of the book has been aided by the generous help of many government and academic specialists in geology, urban development, and agricultural practice. The author's hope is that the following pages will convey some of the wonder and excitement to be enjoyed in traveling across the American landscape. In the back of the book are itineraries and a map to aid in identifying features along the more heavily traveled air routes.

2 THE GRENVILLE COLLISION–
LAYING THE FOUNDATIONS OF
THE ADIRONDACKS, THE BRONX,
AND THE GREAT SMOKIES

The history of explosive or prolonged volcanic eruptions and of slow agony within the crustal rocks that built North America has been one of repeated collisions between continents and of rifting as the continents were torn apart to form new seas between them. Chains of volcanic islands that arose between these land masses were swept up in the collisions. Slivers of other continents were captured and incorporated into the American landscape. American slivers were stolen by the retreating continents.

It is a history reckoned in hundreds of millions of years—a time scale difficult to appreciate for those accustomed to thinking in terms of decades and centuries. One of the earliest documented collisions occurred more than a billion years ago. If one thinks of a billion years in terms of the airline distance between New York and Baltimore (157 miles) a century is only one inch. In that early collision a land mass of uncertain identity apparently came out of an ocean off what is now the East Coast and plowed into the continent's eastern rim, thrusting sea-floor rocks up to form new mountains and generating widespread eruptions. That battle was like the one between India and Asia that even today is raising the Himalayas faster than erosion can wear them down.

Geologists refer to it as the Grenville orogeny, or period of mountain-building (named for the town of Grenville, west of Montreal). If, as seems likely, great mountains were raised along the East Coast, wind, rain, and frost action (during the hundreds of millions of years that followed) wore them down to insignificance. Their remnants, however, are visible in a broad band west of the Saint Lawrence River. It extends as far north as Labrador and as far west as the Grenville Front, from Lake Huron to Labrador, beyond which the bedrock changes abruptly to the much older rocks surrounding Hudson Bay. The ancient bedrock covering most of eastern Canada —the Canadian Shield, including the Grenville region—has been weathered and ground down by flowing ice and much of it is covered with only meager topsoil. The first view of America, for air travelers from Europe, is typically the stark landscape of Labrador with its vivid evidence of scouring by repeated ice sheets, its long lakes and trackless wilderness. It is primeval geology laid bare—almost as awesome as a panorama of great mountains, for the ice has served as surgeon to peel away all else

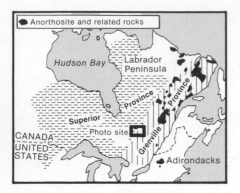

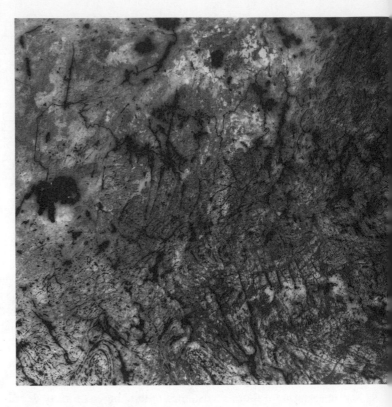

The border area between the Grenville Province (lower right) and Superior Province (upper left) as viewed from Landsat more than 400 miles overhead. The Grenville terrain was severely deformed by a continental collision more than one billion years ago. The far older Superior Province is relatively smooth. The area, indicated on the accompanying map, is a somewhat barren part of northern Quebec. (NASA photo)

and let us see a landscape utterly unlike that along most air routes. Nowhere farther south is one likely to see so much bare rock, so many faults, fjords, even astroblemes —the remnants of craters formed by the impact of giant meteorites long ago.

In few regions is there uniformity over so vast an area as the Canadian Shield. Some of the oldest rocks in the world, formed more than three and a half billion years ago, lie on the southern edge of the shield in Minnesota. South of that, on the Central Plains, the deposits left by ancient seas, partially reworked by winds, ice, and flowing water, have hidden whatever history the older bedrock may have to tell, but both regions have clearly been spared geologic upheavals for a very long time.

The effects of the Grenville collision have been traced as far south as Mexico and may also exist in Europe, notably Norway, implying involvement of that continent. Some of the rocks formed then—granites and gneisses—are exposed as "domes" at such sites as Chester, Vermont; Pelham, Massachusetts; Pound Ridge, New York; the Bronx, New York; the Baltimore-Washington area; and near Philadelphia. Granite forms only at great depth in the earth from a fully mixed pudding of molten rock that cooled extremely slowly, allowing its chemical constituents to segregate themselves into multicolored crystals large enough to give that rock its speckled appearance. Gneiss derives from material that had a more complicated history and solidified into a layered structure. The so-called Fordham gneiss of the Bronx, its alternating dark and light bands formed 980 million years ago, according to one determination, can be seen at many locations—for example, in crags overlooking the Harlem River at 161st

Street and Sedgwick Avenue. The Towson Dome can be seen where the Baltimore Beltway, north of that city, begins turning from east to southeast and climbs onto the dome.

It was about 700 million years ago that the continents began separating. What drove them apart is uncertain, although it is agreed that some sort of heat-driven motions within the earth were responsible. Such motions would be like those in a burbling pot where some delicious concoction rises in the center, sinks down the sides, is reheated, and rises again. One proposal is that the continents were carried away from one another by one or more "plumes" of molten rock rising from deep within the earth along the line of cleavage. The best modern example of such a plume would be the intermittent upsurging of molten rock beneath Iceland. Some of it erupts on the island's surface as highly fluid lava, forming miniature seas of the dense, dark rock known as basalt. It is such upwelling, according to the hypothesis, that is splitting Iceland apart, forming the rift along its centerline within which the world's first parliament was held in A.D. 930. That rift is a segment of the cleavage along the mid-Atlantic Ridge marking where the entire ocean is being split apart, widening the distance between Europe and America at a rate of two inches per year. The rising, spreading plume of molten rock beneath Iceland, combined with the action of similar plumes farther south—under the Azores and Tristan da Cunha—are said to be responsible for the separation. An alternate view, however, is that heat-generated movements elsewhere within the earth are pulling—rather than pushing—the ocean apart.

Separation of North America from the continent with which it had been mated, following the Grenville collision, produced violent eruptions along much of the East Coast. Between South Mountain, on the Pennsylvania-Maryland border, and Mount Rogers, near the common corner of Virginia, North Carolina, and Tennessee, there were outpourings of lava on a vast scale. It has been estimated that more than 7,000 cubic miles of it flooded that region. The deposit at Mount Rogers is two miles thick. That mountain, rising 5,720 feet above sea level, is Virginia's highest, but its high elevation is of more recent origin, as is that of the Blue Ridge system, including South Mountain on the Pennsylvania border and Catoctin Mountain, its sister ridge to the southeast. They were produced by a radical folding of the landscape during the later collision that produced the Appalachian mountain ranges. It was on Catoctin Mountain in Maryland that Franklin D. Roosevelt established a secret hideaway, later known as Camp David. The parallel ridges of Catoctin and South Mountain are shaved-off remnants of a single, gigantic arch whose crown towered over what is now Middletown Valley, between the ridges. Several of these features are identified in the map on page 15.

Whether it was a plume or some other force that split the continents apart, it cracked open their crusts, allowing molten basalt to well up in many places. Such lava erupting onto or near the surface cooled too fast to form large, visible crystals, such as those in granite, and remained instead a homogeneous-looking, dark rock. Some of the erupting basalt forced its way horizontally between layers of the crust, hardening into great, buried "sills," some of which were later uncovered by erosion. The Hudson River Palisades are the uncovered edge of a giant basalt sill far more recently

*When hot lava cools and solidifies into basalt, it shrinks, fracturing into
columns that are often six-sided. The top of this deposit, near Grand Coulee,
was near the surface and cooled rapidly, breaking into smaller fragments.
(Ruth and Louis Kirk)*

formed. When basalt cools it tends to fracture into tall, hexagonal columns, as evident
in the cliffs of the Palisades. Five hundred yards south of where Tennessee Highway
91 crosses the Virginia border it cuts through columnar basalt spread by the earlier
outpourings. Their remnants are visible from northwest Newfoundland along the
Appalachians past the Blue Ridge Mountains into Tennessee and Georgia.

Along Skyline Drive in Shenandoah National Park these basalts cap many of the
highest summits, and some are columnar, though not on the grand scale of the
Palisades. On Mount Marshall they form a succession of terraces on one of which
both Skyline Drive and Browntown Valley Overlook were built. Similar layers,
folded upright on the side of that mountain, stand as a dozen or more benches,
separated by cliffs and debris slopes, visible from the crest of Stony Man above
Skyland Lodge.

As the other continent retreated, it left behind an American coastline that probably
ran from Vermont, past New York City, Philadelphia, and Baltimore, then southward
along the eastern side of what is now the Blue Ridge system to Alabama. The once
magnificent Grenville Mountains eroded away. Their debris spread east and west,
filling a basin formed by rifting along the North Carolina–Tennessee border. As the
basin's floor subsided, sand, gravel, clay, and other material accumulated to a depth
of seven miles—a deposit destined to become the Great Smoky Mountains in the next
continent-continent collision.

A vast sedimentary apron also extended scores of miles into the widening ocean, its outer edge sloping gently down to abyssal deeps of the newly formed ocean floor. After millions of years the situation in many respects resembled that along the eastern seaboard of today which, too, has long been spared continental onslaughts. The sediment now on the continental shelf and on the slope descending to the oceanic depths has accumulated to thicknesses of many miles, some of it enriched with oil-forming organic remains. In one regard, however, the offshore environment then was basically different from the current one. The climate was tropical and the ocean teemed with tiny creatures whose shells rained to the bottom, forming deep limestone accumulations. At times the sea reached as far inland as Texas and Minnesota, forming the limestones found there today. The offshore deposits were later thrust across the coast, crushed and folded to form limestones and marbles that are quarried from Vermont to Alabama.

The one region where rocks from the Grenville period provide scenic landscapes is in the Adirondack Mountains of New York State. The core of those mountains, rising to their summit in Mount Marcy, is formed of anorthosite, a bluish-gray "mystery rock" with crystals of labradorite that glisten iridescent in sunlight. Its pebbles have been the inspiration for the name of the Opalescent River, a source of the Hudson. Whereas other rocks of which the earth is formed—such as basalt, granite, gneiss, and the various sedimentary rocks—have been generated throughout the planet's history, anorthosite was produced only prior to 600 million years ago. When specimens from the lunar highlands were brought home by the Project Apollo astronauts, a

To obtain a profile of structures deep within the earth, five vibrator trucks of the Consortium for Continental Reflection Profiling (COCORP) are stationed forty feet apart, and the platforms under them are lowered until pressed firmly against the ground. Piston systems on each truck set them vibrating in unison, transmitting the vibrations to the ground. More than 2,000 geophones, spread along six miles of highway, record the vibrations after they have traveled different routes through the earth. The convoy then moves ahead and repeats the process. (Cornell University)

number of them proved to be anorthosite, indicating that the process responsible for producing that material on earth was also active early in the moon's history.

Seen from the air the narrow lakes of the Adirondacks, such as the thirteen-mile stretch of Long Lake, seem to lie preferentially along a southwest-northeast axis, but there is no systematic folding like that of the Appalachians. The mountains boast the most awesome precipice east of the Rockies—the east face of Wallface Mountain, soaring 1,300 feet above Indian Pass alongside the headwaters of the Hudson River. Tributaries of that river have cut spectacular canyons, such as High Falls Gorge followed by Route 86 between Lake Placid and Wilmington, and Ausable Chasm farther downstream.

A startling clue to what may have lifted the Adirondacks has come from a new technique that can chart layered structures within the earth to depths of several miles. It is a form of seismic, or vibrational, probing developed for oil prospecting. Fifteen-ton trucks jack themselves up on platforms to apply their weight firmly to the ground, then shake the landscape at a variety of frequencies. The vibrations, after penetrating deep into the earth, are recorded along a line of stations. So sensitive is the technique that it must be used as far as possible from sources of "cultural noise"—earth tremors from superhighways, railroads, factories, etc. A number of such surveys have been done by an alliance of academic, oil-company, and government scientists called COCORP (Consortium for Continental Reflection Profiling), and one of them, across the Adirondacks, has detected a succession of layered deposits a dozen miles beneath those mountains. This could mean that the entire upper block was shoved over sedimentary deposits during the Grenville collision, but it has also been suggested that the layers are successive volcanic instrusions that have lifted the mountains—and may still be doing so. From laboratory tests it has been shown that some Adirondack rocks could have been formed only under pressures that exist at depths of fifteen miles or more. Perhaps, in the Grenville collision, one continental plate was piled onto the other, forming a double-thick crust much of which has now eroded away. Or it may be that the rocks now forming Mount Marcy were brought up in some other way. Small earthquakes recorded almost daily, especially around Blue Mountain Lake, and some surveys indicate the mountains are still rising—by one estimate three times faster than the Swiss Alps. One proposal is that the Adirondacks, as well as the Black Hills of South Dakota and the Ozarks of Missouri, too far from coastlines to be obviously related to continental collisions, owe their existence to "hot spots" in the earth's interior.

If the uplift of the Adirondacks continues long enough, they could become one of the great mountain ranges of the world. None of the great ranges now in existence, however, are formed of such ancient rocks. As in the Alps and Himalayas, their rocks are young, chiefly bulldozed from ocean floors. The Adirondacks, having had their day in the sun, are more likely to succumb gradually to the onslaughts of winter cold and summer storms.

3 A CAVALCADE OF CONTINENTS

After the Grenville collision and breakup of the continents to form a new ocean, the stage was set for the long sequence of events that shaped the present landscape of eastern North America. Scattered around the world at that time were landmasses ancestral to the continents of today, but very different in composition.

They were not yet inhabited by animals, much less people to name them, for life existed only in the seas, but the landmass destined to become the nucleus of North America is now referred to as Laurentia. In terms of today's geography it also comprised an odd assortment of other continental fragments. In addition to Greenland, according to a reconstruction by scientists at the University of Chicago, they included Scotland, coastal Norway, that part of Siberia facing Alaska across the Bering Strait, and even lonely Spitsbergen, now far out in the Arctic Ocean.

Laurentia then lay on the equator, tilted so that what is now its Arctic region faced east. To its south, in terms of today's compass directions, lurked a giant continent, Gondwanaland, consisting of all the present southern continents (Africa, Antarctica, Australia, and South America), plus Florida, India, Tibet, and the region embracing Turkey, Iran, and the Arabian Peninsula.

Far across the sea off what is now eastern North America was Baltica, formed of the lands now encircling the Baltic Sea: Scandinavia, European Russia, Poland, and northern Germany. Southern Britain, Spain, France, and central Europe may have formed a landmass called Armorica (from the Latin for Brittany) then glued to the African part of Gondwanaland, along what is now the Mediterranean coast of Africa. Most of Siberia and the rest of Asia were broken into pieces adrift on the far side of the earth.

This reconstruction of land distribution 550 million years ago, as well as of the motions and collisions that followed, has been made possible chiefly by the measurement of magnetism trapped in rocks that, at various times and places in this eruptive history, cooled from a molten or high-temperature state. When certain types of rock cool, they become imprinted with the magnetic field of the earth existing at the time and place of cooling. It is as though tiny compasses indicating both the vertical and horizontal components of the earth's magnetism at that location were frozen in place.

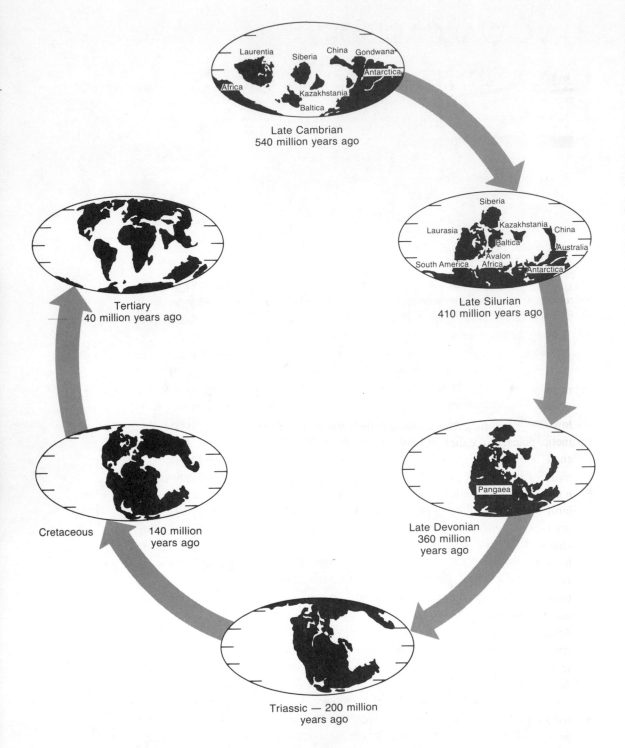

The cavalcade of continents that led to the formation of North America, as reconstructed by C. R. Scotese of the University of Chicago.

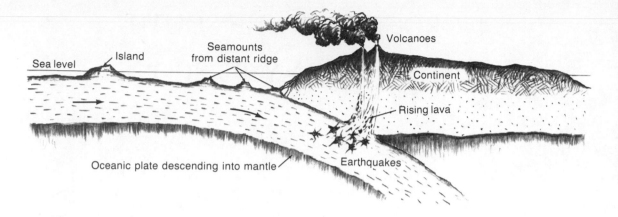

Sea level · Island · Seamounts from distant ridge · Volcanoes · Continent · Rising lava · Oceanic plate descending into mantle · Earthquakes

Continental motions, past and present, are believed driven by heat-generated flow of semi-molten rock within the earth. In this schematic view, sea floor carried by such flow descends under the advancing front of a continent, causing earthquakes, and at a critical depth some of it melts and rises into volcanoes. Periodically, seamounts and islands, riding the sea floor, are plastered against the continental rim.

From analysis of such rock samples it is possible to determine in what direction, from that location, the North or South Magnetic Pole lay at that time. Furthermore, the up-or-down tilt of the magnetism indicates the latitude of the site—its distance from the magnetic poles. At either of those poles the magnetic field is vertical. On the Magnetic Equator it is horizontal. As one moves from the equator toward one of the poles, the tilt becomes increasingly vertical. By measuring the magnetism in rocks from many stages of geologic history and from as many regions as possible, scientists in Europe, North America, and the Soviet Union have been able to piece together a history of land movements that until the 1980's would have defied credulity.

What helped make such an account believable was the accumulation of evidence, in the 1960's and 1970's, that the world's geography is in constant flux. Some oceans, like the Atlantic, are being split apart along mid-ocean rifts, constantly increasing their width as molten rock wells up to form new sea floor. Since the surface area of the spherical earth remains constant, the Pacific Ocean must shrink as the Atlantic grows. In other words, the spreading of the Atlantic pushes Eurasia and America toward one another on the opposite side of the globe. The volcanically active island arcs, such as Japan and the Aleutians, as well as the volcanic coastlines of the Pacific Northwest and of Central and South America, mark zones where Pacific sea floor is descending into the depths of the earth to compensate for new sea floor created along the mid-Atlantic rift and along spreading zones in the Pacific.

The record of past continental movements is far from complete and will certainly be revised by future researchers. Nevertheless, for the first time it provides a coherent account of how the East Coast features came into being.

4 OROGENY IN THE SOUTH–
PUSH GIVES WAY TO SHOVE

Using the world of today as a guide to the past, one can see now that the Appalachians were formed by collisions from the east, following closure of an ocean that preceded the Atlantic. Particularly striking in the southern Appalachians is the uniformity of the parallel zones resulting from this process.

Bordering the ocean, from New Jersey to Alabama, is the Coastal Plain—essentially a continuation of the submerged continental shelf that, thanks to the current level of the sea, is dry land. At times, as between the last two ice ages, much or all of the Coastal Plain was submerged. During the ice ages, when sea levels dropped radically, a large part of the continental shelf as well as the Coastal Plain was exposed.

Inland of that plain is the Piedmont, a foothill plateau whose name is derived from Italy's Piemonte (''foot of the mountains'') region. Its outer edge is the fall line where the Piedmont drops to the Coastal Plain, marking the limit of oceanic attack on the landscape. It played a key role in the siting of American cities, for it is there that rivers flowing to the Atlantic have their last (and often their biggest) waterfalls or rapids. These offered to early settlers a source of industrial power and also often defined how far upstream their ships could sail. Hence such cities as Philadelphia, Wilmington, Baltimore, Washington, Richmond, Columbia, Augusta, and Macon were built on the fall line.

Overlooking the Piedmont and forming the backbone of the Appalachians are the Blue Ridge and its extensions, paralleling the coast for almost 2,000 miles from Georgia to the Long Range of Newfoundland. Their continuation beyond Newfoundland was torn away when the continents separated to form the present Atlantic but survives in the mountains of Scotland, coastal Norway, and even Spitsbergen. The Blue Ridge itself runs from northern Georgia into Pennsylvania. Southwest of Roanoke, Virginia, it splits into two spurs. The part nearest the coast continues to be called the Blue Ridge. The inland spur broadens and reaches its highest elevation in the magnificent Great Smoky Mountains of Tennessee and North Carolina. Between those spurs, in the Black Mountains of western North Carolina, Mount Mitchell rises 6,684 feet above sea level—highest summit in the Appalachians.

Structurally the Blue Ridge extends northeast into Pennsylvania as South Mountain, then, after a gap, continues as a sequence of ridges from Reading, past

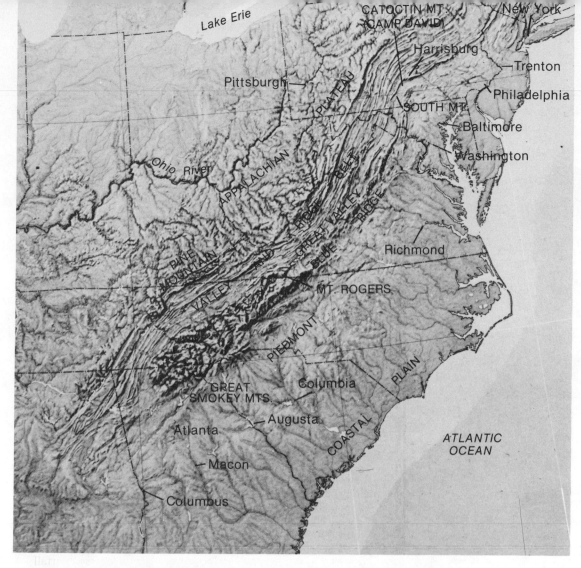

The East Coast and southern Appalachians. The fall line passes through Philadelphia, Baltimore, Washington, Richmond, Columbia, Augusta, Macon, and Columbus.

Bethlehem and across northern New Jersey to traverse the Hudson River in the Bear Mountain-West Point area. The formation runs north through the Housatonic and Berkshire highlands of western Connecticut and Massachusetts to become the Green Mountains of Vermont and the Notre Dame Mountains of Quebec. From Virginia north and northeast the Blue Ridge is five to ten miles wide, rising steeply from the Great Valley, which lies along its northwest flank, separating it from the next parallel zone—the many-tiered folds of the Valley and Ridge Province of the Appalachians.

The Great Valley, five to ten miles wide, reaches from New York State to Alabama. It has different local names: Wallkill Valley in New York, Kittatinny Valley in New Jersey, Lehigh and Lebanon valleys in Pennsylvania, continuing as the Cumberland Valley into Maryland, the Shenandoah Valley in Virginia, then on through the valley of the Tennessee River in eastern Tennessee to the Coosa Valley of Georgia and Alabama. Cradled between its walls are Poughkeepsie, Easton, Allentown, Harrisburg, Hagerstown, Staunton, Roanoke, and Knoxville. Some geologists

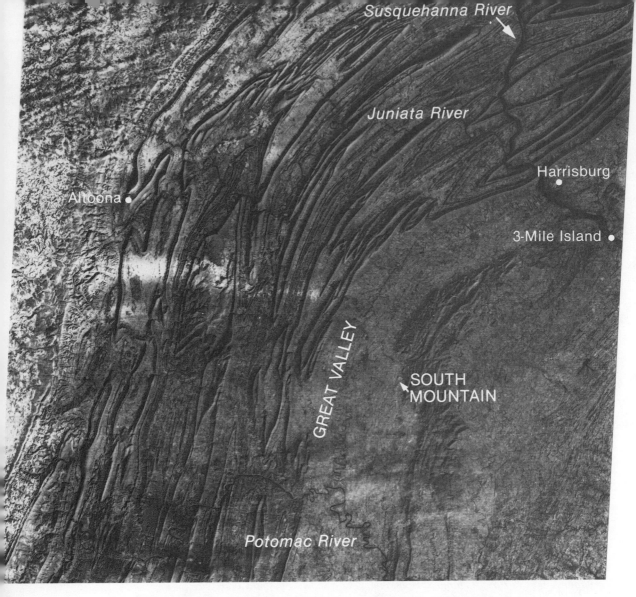

The Susquehanna River cuts across Appalachian folds, highlighted by low sun angle in this Landsat image. The folds form "noses" whose converging ridges represent the two sides of a single giant fold much of which has eroded away. (NASA)

consider the middle Hudson and Lake Champlain valleys to be its northern continuation. When pioneers first headed west many of them chose to settle in the Great Valley, made fertile by the limestone that protrudes through its green fields, rather than struggle across the mountains beyond. When Stonewall Jackson drove north in the 1860's he logically chose the Shenandoah Valley. It led the Confederates as far north as Pennsylvania, but ultimately to their defeat at Gettysburg.

Beyond the Great Valley the long ridges of the Valley and Ridge Province, when viewed from the air, are one of the wonders of American topography. Running from Pennsylvania to Alabama, they are spaced six to ten miles apart and so uniform that they seem man-made. One of them, Clinch Mountain, extends 140 miles from Tennessee into Virginia, rising 4,705 feet above sea level near its northeast end. It is

1

2

3

*How the Appalachian folds
may have evolved: Flat-
lying sediments (1) were
compressed from the east
(2) and eroded to a level
plain (3). Rivers then cut
valleys in the less erosion-
resistant layers (4), leaving
ridges formed of the hardest
material. Some ridges and
valleys converge, forming
"noses," as shown below.*

4

cut by only one stream. Another ridge, 200 miles long, is known in New York State as Shawangunk Mountain, in New Jersey as Kittatinny Mountain, and in Pennsylvania as Blue Mountain. Although cut at the Delaware Water Gap and a few other places, it is clearly a continuous feature.

These ridges have resulted from the erosion of great parallel folds formed as though a stack of rugs had been compressed. After their erosion the edges of the most resistant layers were left as ridges. The more easily worn zones, such as those of limestone, were carved into valleys.

One of the most striking elements of this "province," especially in Pennsylvania, is the manner in which rivers have cut through the ridges to form scenic water gaps— gorges in some cases 1,000 feet deep. North of Harrisburg the Susquehanna has carved out five such gaps, registered as a national natural landmark. Farther east the long ridge known as Blue Mountain is crossed by both the Schuylkill and Lehigh rivers. How rivers cut their way through the ridges has long been debated. One theory is that after the landscape had been crumpled into parallel folds, it was eroded down to a level plain across which major rivers such as the Susquehanna found their way.

Tributaries to those streams then began cutting into this plain, following the paths of least resistance—the most easily eroded surfaces remaining from the original folds, such as those formed of limestone. As a result the valleys of today have no relationship to those of the original folding. They delineate the long, narrow soft regions and the ridges are edges of the hard ones. Some geologists question whether the region was ever totally flat. Nevertheless, that the ridges and valleys no longer represent the original folding is obvious in the tilt of rock layers along many of the roads across them.

Innermost of the belts is the Appalachian Plateau, northwest of the Valley and Ridge Province. It extends from New York's Catskill Mountains to Alabama. Parts are flat, like a true plateau, but elsewhere millions of years of water action have carved systems of branching valleys out of the flat surface. The valleys in the Pittsburgh area, cut by the converging Allegheny and Monongahela rivers and their tributaries, are precipitous and deep, but the relatively uniform height of the rolling country around them indicates that they have been eroded from a plateau. Farther south, in West Virginia and Kentucky, the plateau, seen from the air, resembles the waves of a disordered sea. In eastern Kentucky, for example, the valleys are uniformly about 500 feet deep. Being V-shaped, their floors offer little room for farming.

The belt is considered a plateau because, even though deeply eroded, its rock layers remain horizontal rather than being folded as in the neighboring Valley and Ridge Province. The mountains carved out of this great plateau begin, at its northeast end, with the scenic Catskills, whose highest summits rise more than 4,000 feet above sea level. Other ranges from Pennsylvania through Ohio, West Virginia, Kentucky, and Tennessee to Alabama include the Poconos, Alleghenies, and Cumberlands. Spruce Knob in the Alleghenies of West Virginia, rising 4,860 feet above sea level, is the highest point on the plateau. To the southwest, where Virginia, Kentucky, and Tennessee meet, is the Cumberland Gap through which wave upon wave of pioneers headed west.

Before the concept of continental drift became plausible, geologists devised a variety of theories to explain the strikingly parallel folds and other structures of the southern Appalachians. Some proposed that they were produced by shrinkage of the earth's crust. Others thought that there must have been a catastrophic shove—or series of shoves—from the direction of the Atlantic. One suggested explanation was a series of colossal offshore volcanic explosions.

The explanation now generally accepted begins with gradual closure, starting some 500 million years ago, of the ocean between the three continents of Laurentia (North America-to-be), the supercontinent of Gondwanaland (including Africa), and Baltica (destined to become northern Europe). Along one or more fronts in that ocean, as is now occurring in the Pacific, the sea floor began descending into the earth's interior, and chains of volcanoes arose over the descending rocks as they heated up. From the study of contemporary volcanic chains it is known that when a descending slab of water-saturated sea floor several miles thick reaches a depth of sixty miles or more, part of it melts and forces its way upward to erupt in a line of volcanoes. As the ancient sea shrank, one or more chains of volcanoes arose far from the Laurentian

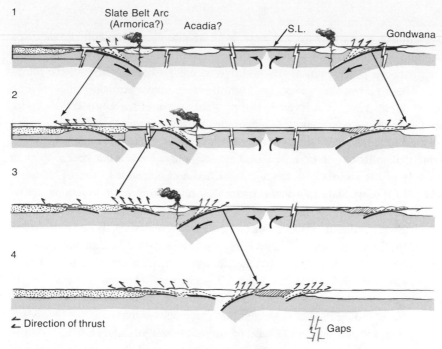

1 Slate Belt Arc (Armorica?)   Acadia?   S.L.   Gondwana

2

3

4

⤴ Direction of thrust   Gaps

Hypothetical stages in the closing of the ancestral Atlantic Ocean. (These and the diagrams on page 24 are adapted from "The COCORP seismic reflection traverse across the Southern Appalachians" by F. A. Cook, L. D. Brown, S. Kaufman, and J. E. Oliver, in AAPG Studies in Geology, no. 14, 1983, pp. 34-37.)

1. Between 500 and 800 million years ago: opening of the ocean along a mid-ocean ridge. An arc of volcanic islands (possibly Armorica) destined to become the Carolina Slate Belt and another continental fragment, Acadia, are carried toward North America. Sea floor descending beneath the Slate Belt islands produces volcanic eruptions.
2. Between 400 and 500 million years ago: The Slate Belt collides with North America. Shrinkage of the ocean pushes sea floor under the Acadian fragment, producing additional eruptions.
3. Between 320 and 400 million years ago: Acadia is welded onto the continent and additional eruptions occur as sea floor begins descending under the continent.
4. Between 225 and 320 million years ago: The European-African part of Gondwanaland collides with North America.

shore, either along an arc of Aleutian-type islands or on continental land, such as the rim of the African part of Gondwanaland or an archipelago like New Zealand.

The situation can be likened to the landmass that will probably arise as Australia, currently drifting north, sweeps up Indonesia and plasters those islands against Southeast Asia. In that ancient ocean the volcanoes that erupted as it first began to shrink were apparently distant from America, because in the region now occupied by the Blue Ridge—then near the rim of the continent—no ash thrown up during that period is to be found.

As Africa drew closer, however, sea floor apparently began plunging into the depths of the earth near the coast, giving birth to new volcanoes in the Piedmont from Maryland south. The most catastrophic eruptions, some 450 million years ago, spread volcanic debris over most of the eastern United States and Ontario. Because the surviving ash becomes increasingly thick toward eastern Tennessee, the volcanoes were probably in the Carolinas.

The Piedmont is paved, here and there, with granite thought to be the residue of monumental structures, known as batholiths, formed in the heart of volcanic zones and then exposed by erosion, as has occurred in the Yosemite Valley of the Sierra Nevada. These granites, however, far from towering above the landscape (as they may have done), have been leveled. During final stages of the continent-continent collision they were also transported many miles northwest from their ''roots'' in the earth's crust to locations where they are now quarried for building material.

During that collision one or more island arcs or volcanic zones that had formed on the far side of the shrinking ocean were crushed and embedded in the Piedmont, forming the Carolina Slate Belt that runs for 400 miles from central Georgia across the Carolinas into southern Virginia and the Charlotte Belt that flanks it on the inland side. Both are formed of debris from ancient volcanoes, material exposed in the more deeply eroded Charlotte Belt having been more severely altered by heat and compression and probably revealing much of the ''plumbing'' beneath the volcanoes. Analysis of volcanic remains from these belts has shown the material to be strikingly similar, chemically, to that currently formed by eruptions in the Aleutian Islands.

While several geologists had suspected that these belts were vestiges of an island arc that had originated on the far side of the ancestral Atlantic, it was a chance discovery in 1982 that provided convincing evidence. Sara L. Samson, a geological graduate student at the University of South Carolina in Columbia, was on a field trip

Left: This trilobite, Paradoxides paradoxissimus *(Wahlenberg), from Sweden is similar to those found at East Coast sites thought to be of "alien" origin.*

Right: This Zacanthoides *trilobite specimen from Utah is typical of the native American species. (Both examples courtesy of R. A. Robison, University of Kansas)*

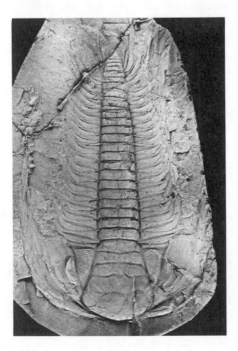 

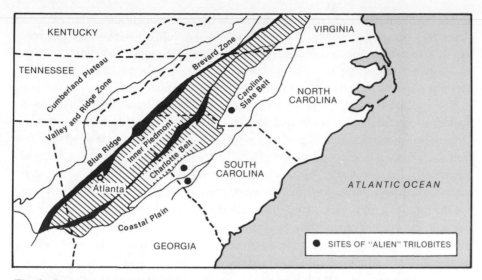

The finding of "alien" trilobites at three sites confirmed that the Carolina Slate
Belt arrived from across an ocean.

near Batesburg mapping one of the bodies of granite, or plutons, that had pushed up
into the slate belt deposits, then been eroded to ground level, when she saw a stone
the size of a hand on which there seemed to be a fossil imprint. She showed it to
Donald T. Secor, a professor of geology at the university, who recognized the imprint
as that of a trilobite head.

Trilobites, now extinct, were the most numerous inhabitants of shallow waters
fringing the ancestral Atlantic. They were many-segmented creatures, possessing a
complex—but symmetrical—pattern of legs and antennas. Some were smaller than a
fingernail, resembling the pill bugs (sow bugs or wood lice) exposed when one
overturns a stone. Others were as big as a human foot. They were among the earliest
members of the arthropods—the great phylum or basic division of the animal king-
dom that now includes the crustaceans and insects. Their remains are abundant in
sedimentary rocks laid down under shallow coastal waters several hundred million
years ago, then incorporated into nearby continents. Countless species evolved in
various parts of that ancient ocean and are grouped by geologists into more than 1,000
genera.

The specimen retrieved by Sara Samson led to an intensive search of the area, and
hundreds of trilobite fragments were discovered, not only in loose-lying stones, but
embedded in the solid bedrock. At least five species were found, but what created a
sensation among geologists was the fact that they included members of the genus
Paradoxides, which had been native only to the far side of the ancestral Atlantic.

It was not the first such discovery. A youth named John Brattain, skipping stones
into a North Carolina stream, had found a stone with two curious imprints and for
several years had used it as a doorstop. Then, perhaps inspired by his high school
course in earth science, he took it to Joseph St. Jean, professor of geology at the
University of North Carolina in Chapel Hill, who recognized the imprints as clearly
those of *Paradoxides*. Brattain tried to lead the geologists to where he had found the

stone, but all efforts to find more specimens failed. As evidence of alien terrain it was interesting but not convincing. A second find, on the edge of the slate belt overlooking the Coastal Plain on the Carolina-Georgia border, was reported in 1981 by a group of geologists including Dr. Secor, but it was too poorly preserved for precise identification. Sara Samson's find was therefore the clincher.

The specimens were examined by a leading authority on trilobites, Allison R. Palmer of the Geological Society of America, who had originally been skeptical of proposals that sections of the East Coast were of "foreign" origin. He described Sara Samson's finds as "really exciting stuff." They are, he added, "very definitely un-American." He questioned, however, the tendency of some geologists to say flatly that the slate belt and Charlotte Belt were once part of Africa. If, as seems likely, they are the ruins of a former island arc, there is still no clue as to where they lay when the ocean began to close, apart from their being on its European-African side. The ocean may not have been two-sided in the manner of the present Atlantic but surrounded by a quite different arrangement of landmasses.

The most intensely studied trilobites of the European-African realm have come from Czechoslovakia, Poland, and southern Europe. Those collected in Africa have not been described in sufficient detail to enable a specialist like Allison Palmer to determine whether the Carolina species were more closely related to those of Africa or Europe.

Early in the debate on "alien" pieces of the American landscape Palmer had been won over to the view that parts of Newfoundland had come from afar, based on his study of trilobites there in combination with their associated geological formations. Not only were the fossils like those found in England, but the rock formations were similar. "It is the whole picture," he said, "that is convincing." It was such evidence as well that originally led J. Tuzo Wilson of the University of Toronto, in 1966, to make the then-revolutionary proposal that a predecessor of the Atlantic Ocean had closed, crushing the East Coast to produce the Appalachians, and had then reopened. He cited a long-standing puzzle: that shallow-water fossils in ancient deposits along the coast from Rhode Island to Newfoundland are similar to those from the far side of the Atlantic—not to those of North American creatures of that period. Likewise fossils of similar age from the coastal region of Norway as well as from northwest Scotland and northern Ireland are of American—not European—affinity. Wilson's now generally accepted explanation was that the Norwegian coast and part of Scotland and Ireland were part of North America torn loose when Europe, Africa, and America broke apart with formation of the present Atlantic. Likewise, the Canadian-New England seaboard was originally Moroccan—or, as some now suspect, joined to Spain and other parts of Europe.

Robert D. Hatcher, Jr., of the University of South Carolina has seen rocks like those of the Carolina Slate Belt near Casablanca in Morocco, and he points out that similar fossils also occur in Spain and France. He does not take this as evidence that the slate belt volcanics originated on the European-African side of the ocean, but that all these areas are part of a former subcontinent that today has fragments as well in Newfoundland, southeastern New England, Wales, and other parts of Europe.

Flanking the Carolina Slate Belt to the northwest is the Inner Piedmont, 60 miles wide and running 400 miles from the western Carolinas southeast across central Georgia (including Atlanta) to Alabama. It is separated from the Blue Ridge by the Brevard Zone, one of the most debated features of American geology. Named for Brevard, North Carolina, through which it passes, it is only a half mile to four miles wide. In some sectors its more easily eroded material has formed long, straight valleys, and like the San Andreas Fault of California, it can be seen from the air and even from earth orbit. It is crossed by U.S. Highway 64 some three miles west of Rosman in western North Carolina, and its western edge can be seen if one turns south a short distance on County Road 1139 (a former section of U.S. 64). Intense deformation near the zone is evident on U.S. Highway 76 in South Carolina fifteen miles west of Westminster. The zone skirts Atlanta to the west, its graphite schists visible along that city's peripheral highway. The Brevard Zone marks emergence at the surface of a deep-seated interface where two very different structures have slipped against one another, grinding, crushing, and altering what lay between.

Douglas Rankin of the U.S. Geological Survey proposed in the mid-1970's that the Brevard Zone marks the leading edge of an African Plate that pushed over the basement of North America, past the earlier edge of the continent. This could mean that virtually the entire Piedmont, including Atlanta, was once "African." Not all geologists have accepted this hypothesis. While Hatcher has used geologic and geophysical data to conclude that such a foreign origin was true of the slate belt and Charlotte Belt, he has balked at extending the "African" invasion as far as the Brevard Zone.

If inhabitants of the Inner Piedmont find startling the idea that they are living on alien land, they can take comfort from seismic probing, which seems to show that beneath the intruding sheet is the original bedrock of North America. It is remarkable that this deep rock apparently remained flat and undisturbed as the layers above it were shoved scores of miles inland. Anyone who has had the disquieting experience of watching a glass slide of its own accord across an almost level table and crash to the floor can better appreciate how layers of landscape can slip over a lubricating layer.

The material initially thrust over the rim of North America some 450 million years ago was that which, while that ancestor of the Atlantic Ocean was growing, had accumulated and solidified on the coastal sea floor to thicknesses of several miles. Following that, slabs of sedimentary rock formed in deep water beyond the continental shelf were pushed on top of the shallow-water deposits already thrust onto the continent. The onslaught continued for several tens of millions of years until, with direct collision imminent, sections of deep ocean basement were pushed on top of the sedimentary slabs.

There was a basic change in the damage being wrought, once the converging continents came "eyeball to eyeball," their bedrock in direct collision. During the approach phase the intervening sea floor descended into the earth, sweeping its load of island arcs against the continent, crushing the hinterland and generating volcanic activity there. But once the collision occurred, continental rocks were too light and buoyant to sink into the depths. They had to fight it out on the surface, as is occurring in the Himalayas, severely crumpling and folding the landscape. It is hard to imagine

Evolution of the southern Appalachians.

1. Between 500 and 600 million years ago: The East Coast faced a stable ocean. Sediments from erosion of the continent spread far out to sea. Limestone formed on flooded parts of the continent and continental shelf.

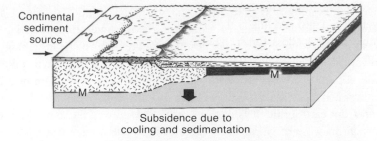

Continental sediment source

Subsidence due to cooling and sedimentation

2. Between 400 and 500 million years ago: The offshore deposits were shoved against the coast, forming mountains whose erosion carried sediment in the opposite direction, to an inland sea.

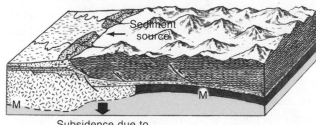

Sediment source

Subsidence due to thrusting and sedimentation

3. Subsequent collisions added new terrain and shoved earlier formations inland, leaving the situation found today.

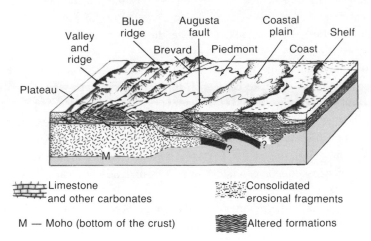

Valley and ridge   Blue ridge   Augusta fault   Coastal plain   Shelf
Brevard   Piedmont   Coast
Plateau

Limestone and other carbonates

Consolidated erosional fragments

M — Moho (bottom of the crust)

Altered formations

deformation on so huge a scale. Some folds were pushed completely over on their sides so that older layers lay over younger ones. The result was a mighty mountain range, largely built of sea-floor slabs, but that now has been eroded to its bedrock core—the Blue Ridge ranges.

Motoring across those ridges is a journey into the past, notably along highways such as U.S. 33 and 250, which cut across Skyline Drive atop the main ridge, plunge into Shenandoah Valley, then up over the folded rock layers of Massanutten Mountain and into the ranges beyond. In spring it is a journey forward and backward in time, seasonally speaking, as one climbs from late spring (laurel and rhododendron in full bloom) through mid-spring (dogwood) to early spring (the road banked with lavender redbud) and finally the heights with only white blossoms of the serviceberry visible in the leafless forest. The sequence is then reversed on the descent. At the same time the many-layered, folded remains of a vast sea floor pass in review: sandstone, flaky shale, limestone, and crumbly brown siltstone.

The folding is hard to decipher, for the original folds were far higher and, in some cases, folded over upon one another. Erosion of softer material and survival of more resistant layers have left a topsy-turvy situation in which Massanutten Mountain is formed of material that was at the bottom of a trough. Driving across the ridges one sees layers rising out of a valley wall toward a crest that once stood over the neighboring valley. Along Skyline Drive one can see beds of erosion-resistant white quartzite standing vertically, its sawtooth ridges and sharp pinnacles soaring above the greenery.

The Pine Mountain overthrust seen from space by Landsat. For emphasis it has been printed darker in this U.S. Geological Survey image. Pine Mountain lies along the northwest (top) side of the overthrust, which continues northeast along the Kentucky-Virginia border. Its left boundary is the Jacksboro Fault, with Knoxville near its south end.

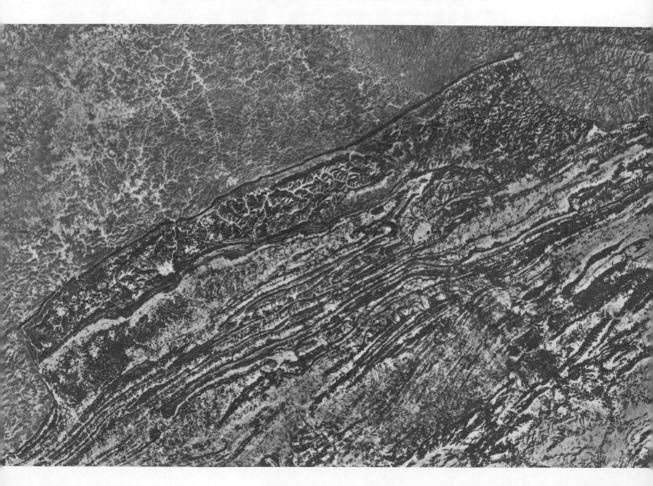

John Rodgers of Yale University, a leader in efforts to decipher how the Appalachians came to be, has pointed out that in Pennsylvania the effect was chiefly to produce folds, but farther south, notably in Tennessee, the layers were pushed over one another, stacking like shingles or roof tiles. Ten major thrust sheets are piled in the Knoxville area.

From aloft, particularly in space photographs, the most obvious thrust is the Pine Mountain Overthrust (also known as the Cumberland Overthrust Block)—an enormous slab of sedimentary rock 125 miles long and 25 miles wide, bounded on the northwest by Pine Mountain and on the southwest by the Jacksboro Fault, which meets that mountain at right angles. This slab looks from space like a 25-mile-wide flap or lapel laid across the landscape. Interstate 75, running northwest from Knoxville, closely follows the edges of this block. It first runs close to the Jacksboro Fault southwest of Norris Lake, whose multiple, snaking arms lie within the overthrust block. A couple of miles northwest of the entrance to Cove Lake State Park the highway begins climbing onto the thrust block, passing nearly vertical rock beds before reaching the relatively flat-lying sandstones, shales, and siltstones that cover the thrust itself. After the highway swings northeast it follows the crest of Pine Mountain for ten miles, then descends into Elk Valley and briefly runs along the front of the fault block before reaching the Kentucky line.

The effects of Tennessee's multiple overthrusts are evident along many highways—for example where Interstate 40, west of Knoxville, passes Ozone and the Crab Orchard Mountains. Similar evidence of past crushing is exposed where Central Avenue runs north from the center of Knoxville into Sharp Ridge Memorial Park, as well as at Bull Run Ridge nine miles north of the city on Interstate 75, or near Cove Lake State Park, where that highway climbs the front of the Pine Mountain thrust block near a strip-mining area. The exposed beds there are almost vertical. Thirty miles west of Knoxville, where U.S. 70 crosses the Clinch River, concentric folds are visible in shale exposed in a large cut opposite the TVA plant at Kingston. Spectacular folds can be seen along Interstate 75 some seventeen miles north of Chattanooga.

Another revealing highway is U.S. 129, which skirts the south edge of the Great Smokies, then, after entering Tennessee from North Carolina, skirts Chilhowee Lake, passing the intersection of the Foothill Parkway. The latter runs eighteen miles along the crest of Chilhowee Mountain overlooking the Valley and Ridge Province to the northwest. Near the lake U.S. 129 passes exposures of rock layers that were sharply folded and tilted onto their sides. Elements of the tortured western flank of the Blue Ridge can also be seen at Chilhowee Dam, near the west end of the lake. South of the Smokies, near the Georgia border, U.S. 64, after crossing the Brevard Zone at Rosman westbound, cuts through Chunky Gal Mountain—part of the Blue Ridge system, near Shooting Creek—and, after entering Tennessee, passes other dramatic exposures west of Ducktown.

In final stages of the great collision sheets of sedimentary rock on the Appalachian Plateau were shoved farther and farther west, some of them almost as far as the Ohio River. The layers over which some of these sheets slipped are exposed in cross section on Tennessee Highway 8, two miles west of its junction with U.S. 127, thirty miles northwest of Chattanooga. The wrinkling of the Valley and Ridge Province, as seen along Interstate 40, ends near Crossville, west of the Crab Orchard Mountains and about seventy miles west of Knoxville.

Prior to these final thrusts a radical transformation had taken place. Plants and then animals had colonized the land. The Appalachian zone was very different from today. Inland from the newly formed mountains, in the zones destined to become the plateau as well as the Ridge and Valley Province, was a broad, flat region of densely vegetated swamps bordering a shallow sea that covered the heartland of the continent. The region, then lying along the equator, was hot and humid. It must have been much like the southwest coast of western New Guinea (Irian), whose deltas and tropical swamps, interwoven with meandering streams, extend from horizon to horizon.

The conditions were ideal for the initial stages in formation of coal. The stagnant, oxygen-poor swamp waters inhibited decay, allowing vegetable matter to accumulate as thick beds of peat. Periodically these were buried as the inland sea invaded the land, burying its swamps in mud and sand. Even after compression the interlayered deposits of coal, sandstone, siltstone, or shale were still 2,000 feet thick—in the analogy of one geologist "like a thick book with every twentieth page made of black paper." Oil formation is usually associated with marine deposits and that may explain why today's oil and gas fields from Pennsylvania to Kentucky lie along the northwest Flank of the coal belt, in a region frequently submerged by a shallow sea.

It was Africa's final push from the east that helped complete the requirements for fossil fuel maturation. This was the "Alleghenian" phase, between 230 and 280 million years ago, following what may have been a pause in the battle between continents. It was this that rumpled the thrust sheets west of the Blue Ridge like carpets on a rigid floor, forming the folds of the Valley and Ridge Province. In Pennsylvania the folds running through Scranton and Schuylkill County, as well as one west of Roanoke, Virginia, were so severely squeezed and heated that the peaty deposits within them evolved into anthracite or "stone" coal—the most extensive such deposits in the world. The plateau, from Pennsylvania to Alabama, was less radically folded and squeezed, so the coal beds there are of the bituminous or soft coal variety. In the mid-eighteenth century Pennsylvania's first coal mine began operating on Duquesne Heights, overlooking Fort Pitt across the Monongahela River in what is now downtown Pittsburgh. The coal seams that it exploited helped make that city one of the world's foremost producers of steel and extended across western Pennsylvania, southeast Ohio, and northeast West Virginia, although not always at accessible depths. It was, however, largely the anthracite of eastern Pennsylvania that fueled the American industrial revolution. Shiploads of Irish and Polish immigrants were transported to the mining centers by train directly after their Ellis Island reception. During World War I, when American industry was working at peak capacity and was still fueled chiefly by coal, there were 329,000 men at work in the Pennsylvania coal fields.

Motorists crossing Pennsylvania from west to east on Interstate 80—the Keystone Shortway—enter the Bullion-Clintonville oil field soon after crossing into the state from Ohio and before reaching Clintonville (Exit 4). Pumping jacks are in operation on both sides of the highway at Mile 33 and additional oil fields are crossed between there and the exit for Knox (Exit 7). Then, for one hundred miles, the highway crosses beds of bituminous coal. Some fifty of them are stacked, one upon the other, although only at key locations has tilting brought them within reach of underground or surface mining. Active and reforested strip mines are first visible at Mile 48. A number of strip mines are passed in the Clearfield County sector, notably between Mile 116 and Mile 134. Then, in road cuts across the great folds of the Valley and Ridge Province, radical warping of the sedimentary beds becomes evident.

Where highways and rivers cut deeply into the plateau near Pittsburgh, the flat layering of that region is dramatically exposed. On the other hand, Interstate 81, sometimes called the Penn-Can Highway because it links Pennsylvania with Canada, traverses most of the state's anthracite fields between Harrisburg and Scranton, where the folding is particularly obvious.

The full scope of the thrusting produced by Africa's impact was not evident until the 1980's, following development of the vibration technique in which trucks shake the ground to chart layered structures deep within the earth. One survey was done across Georgia and southern Tennessee by the COCORP consortium of university and oil-company scientists, whereupon others followed—one across North Carolina and northeast Tennessee, another across much of Virginia. Such surveys and deep oil-prospecting wells have done for Appalachian geology what Alpine tunnels did for geology in Europe. The numerous railroad and highway tunnels through the Alps revealed to what an extent they are formed of sea-floor slabs shoved hundreds of miles inland and heaped or folded atop one another.

The surveys in the southern Appalachians confirmed what Robert Hatcher had proposed earlier, based on surface, gravity, and magnetic data, namely that under what appeared to be the ancient bedrock of the Blue Ridge were stacks of sedimentary rock layers resembling those in the plateau region and the Valley and Ridge Province to the northwest. It became evident that the entire Blue Ridge Mountain zone and at least part of the neighboring Piedmont had been pushed as much as 150 miles inland, burying a coastward extension of the Valley and Ridge Province and plateau. In places this overthrust layer, as much as six miles thick, covers sedimentary slabs close to four miles in thickness.

The significance of those deeply buried sediments was not lost on the oil companies, since oil extracted from similar deposits on the plateau had already built great fortunes. In 1859 the first oil well in the world was drilled on Oil Creek, near Titusville, Pennsylvania, and in that region, during the closing years of the nineteenth century, John D. Rockefeller began building the Standard Oil Company and its many offshoots. As of 1982 there were still 18,000 producing oil wells and 22,000 gas wells in that region.

5 THE HIMALAYAS IN NEW ENGLAND

The events that produced the northern Appalachians—north of New York City— had many similarities with those in the South, although the resulting parallel zones are not so clearly defined. In both regions the Appalachian mountain-building sequence has counterparts in Africa, Scotland, and Scandinavia. In the Trondheim area of Norway sea-floor slabs have been pushed several hundred miles inland. Volcanic remains are evident there, as well as in northwest Africa. It is a wonderful, one-world history that has left similar imprints on such diverse regions as Connecticut, Spain, Morocco, and Mauritania.

Geologists, based chiefly on work in the northern Appalachians, have divided formation of the mountain system into three great phases, although there may not have been a time when there was total respite along the entire front. It was during the initial, or Taconic, phase, between 450 and 470 million years ago, that slabs of sea-floor rock were thrust onto the continent, forming a mountain range probably comparable with the Himalayas, whose core survives as the Blue Ridge ranges from Newfoundland to Georgia. The second, Acadian phase, between 360 and 400 million years ago, takes its name from Acadia, the former French colony in Nova Scotia and New Brunswick, where its effects are very evident. It may have occurred when promontories of the African landmass first made contact with their American counterparts, and sea floor began plunging under the coastal rim, causing volcanic eruptions there instead of on offshore island chains. In the final, Alleghenian phase, from 250 to 300 million years ago, Africa, having first hit in the north, produced the extraordinarily symmetrical folds of the Valley and Ridge Province farther south.

The Taconic phase can be likened to that which would occur if closure of the Pacific Ocean brought Japan toward the West Coast. Sea floor descending under Japan would generate extensive eruptions in those islands, as it does today. Then, as the islands neared the coast, they would sweep up the deep accumulation of sediments on the intervening ocean floor and thrust them onto the land, forming a mountain range of monumental stature.

Incredible as it may seem, after such mountains had been formed, some 460 million years ago, parts of those in western Massachusetts, Connecticut, southern

New York, and New Jersey slid—or were pushed—tens of miles westward into a shallow sea covering New York and Pennsylvania. Some of this range survives in the Taconic Mountains along the eastern border of New York.

An oddity of special interest is Stark's Knob, a forty-foot tower of black rock near the west bank of the Hudson and a little more than a mile north of Schuylerville, New York. It was used as an artillery emplacement by General John Stark during the battles south of Saratoga that led to the surrender of General John Burgoyne and proved a turning point in the War of Independence. The rock is lava that erupted under water and therefore cooled rapidly into pillowlike lumps. Presumably it was formed as the Taconics were being born and was carried with them westward. The Berkshire, Housatonic, and Hudson highlands, from Massachusetts through Connecticut, across southern New York into northern New Jersey, may be "stumps" of the mountains that were raised, tilted, and slid westward.

There is no question that the original mountains were on a monumental scale. Mud and sand from their erosion first spread over New York State and Pennsylvania. Then, as the mountains grew, such material crossed a third of the continent, forming the Maquoketa shale along the Mississippi River in Iowa and reaching as far south as Tennessee. Shales and limestones laid down beneath what was an inland sea are

Relics of the evolution of the northern Appalachians. (Adapted from Peter Robinson and Leo M. Hall in "The Caledonides in the USA," p. 78)

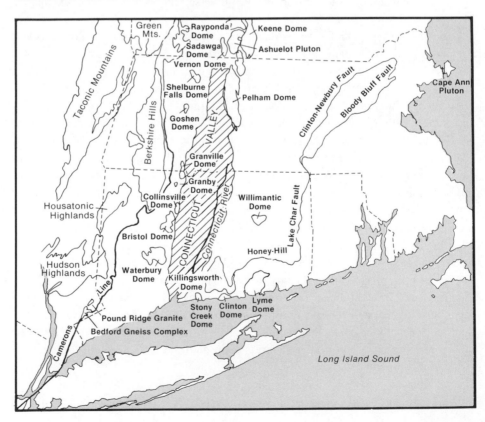

exposed in road cuts and gorges all along the south shore of Lake Ontario. They were subsequently capped by durable dolomite, a stone derived from the shells of countless sea creatures but, unlike its cousin limestone, relatively hard. When, 10,000 years ago, retreat of the last ice sheet allowed the Great Lakes to begin draining down the Saint Lawrence Valley, a great waterfall formed at Niagara. The falls cascade over a rim of dolomite, but they gradually undermine the shale beneath it. This, over the last ten millennia, has created the Niagara Gorge in whose walls the limestone and shale are exposed.

In the 1950's Eugene N. Cameron of the University of Wisconsin delineated an abrupt change in geology along a line that parallels the east side of the highlands in western Connecticut, skirting Torrington on the west. It has now been extended north into Massachusetts along the east flank of the Berkshires and south across Westchester County into New York City along White Plains Road, west of Bronx Park. Although more hidden than the Brevard Zone of the Piedmont, the line (a zone 50 to 300 feet wide) shows ample signs of crushing, compression, and slippage. Along parts of it the movements involved plastic deformation, rather than cracking, that could have occurred only under the heat and pressure at depths of eight miles or more—testimony to the extent of erosion there.

Formations to the west of Cameron's line largely consist of rocks that apparently remained from the continent's earlier coastline as well as greatly altered remnants of the shallow-water material shoved in front of an advancing island arc. Everything to the east of this line is thought to be of exotic, oceanic origin—the leading edge of a slab derived from deep-sea sediments laid down on the outer slope of the continent's original margin. In the process of being shoved inland this material became buried as much as ten miles underground. There it was altered into the rock known locally as Manhattan schist and became plastic enough for folding into extraordinarily complex patterns. One recent autumn day Charles Merguerian of Hofstra University and Leo M. Hall of the University of Massachusetts allowed me to accompany them as they debated the origins of these formations. They focused special attention on a schist exposure west of Riverside Drive at 165th Street in Manhattan. The rock there records a complex history of repeated, widely spaced episodes of intense folding and alteration. Amidst the folds are light-colored veins of coarse crystals intermingled with black tourmalines (not of gem quality) and glittering mica. Much of the ledge is densely studded with garnets. Its subtle north-west-trending grooves testify to far more recent activity—the passing of a great ice sheet. It is hard to believe this material formed as sediment on the surface of a sea floor, was buried eight miles down, and rose again to be exposed after prolonged erosion of what lay above it.

It is on Manhattan schist that most of New York's towering buildings rest. That forming Washington Heights and the other heights in Manhattan is massive, with little evident layering. It towers as a mighty wall alongside the High Bridge sector of Harlem River Drive. Structurally above it, Merguerian has identified another slab of schist, distinctly layered and rich in garnets that he believes underlies much of lower Manhattan. It can be seen at the southeast corner of Central Park and in Riverside Park along the Hudson shore, including the outcrop at 165th Street. Also east of the Hudson River extending from Yonkers into the Bronx and northward beyond White

Plains, as well as in Pound Ridge to the northeast, are great masses of pink gneiss that are about 570 million years old, distinctive from the more ancient Fordham gneiss of the Bronx and Westchester formed during the Grenville orogeny 1,100 million years ago. Both of the gneisses are resistant to erosion and underlie the higher ridges in southeastern New York.

Another relict of the upheavals that laid the foundations of New York City is the mass of green rock (serpentine) traversed by the Staten Island Expressway. It is a characteristic sea-floor rock that in its finest form is verd antique, a widely used decorative material that resembles a green marble but originated far beneath the sea floor. This rock and another like it on Interstate 287 near Port Chester were transported to those locations during development of Cameron's line.

East of the Connecticut Valley a chain of gneiss "domes" from Long Island Sound to as far north as the Rangeley Lakes of Maine are believed to be roots of island-arc volcanoes that erupted somewhere off the coast but were driven ashore and are now surrounded by the debris of their own eruptions as well as deposits from the ocean in which they lay. They are called domes because of their internal structure even though they have largely been leveled by erosion. Another series of much older domes flanks the Connecticut Valley to the west—near Waterbury, Bristol, Collinsville, and Granby as well as Granville, Massachusetts. The one near Waterbury is cut by Route 8, and in the gorge of the Naugatuck River the complicated folding and thrusting the rocks have suffered is easily seen from a passing car.

During the Acadian phase—the final stages of collision when sea floor descending under the continent rather than under an island arc was fueling continental volcanoes—eruptions occurred in Maine, from Mount Katahdin (that state's highest summit) and Traveler Mountain in Baxter State Park, to Chaleur Bay on the coast of northeast New Brunswick. At Traveler Mountain it is evident that almost 10,000 feet of volcanic rock was laid down. It is hard to believe that this serene Maine wilderness was once the scene of such intense volcanic paroxysms.

Before the shrinking ocean finally closed in on Maine the Aroostook County area was covered by a sea whose floor accumulated alternate layers of lime and clay. The resulting "ribbon limestone" has made Maine one of America's chief producers of potatoes. To explain these deposits, some of which seem to have been laid down in deep water, it has been proposed that an ocean basin opened briefly during this period and then closed again.

In the initial, or Taconic, phase volcanic rock that had erupted in mid-ocean to form the floor of the annihilated ocean was driven onto land, some of it surviving along the east flank of the Green Mountains. Beneath them, during the later great collision (the Acadian phase), granite crystallized in a manner that, laboratory tests have shown, can occur only under a mountain mass several miles thick. This beautifully homogeneous, brightly colored, and sparkly rock, now laid bare by erosion, notably near Barre, Vermont, has been used for structures throughout the Northeast.

Another volcanic chain, many believe, came from far across the sea, riding a continental sliver or archipelago called Avalon, some of which survives in the Avalon Peninsula, where Newfoundland's capital city, St. John's, is located. Other remnants

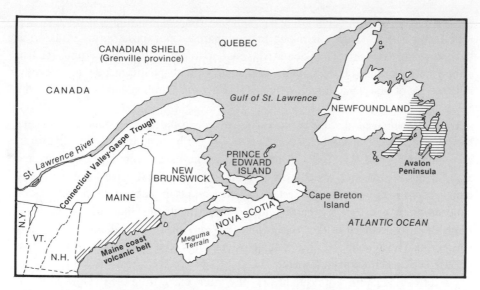

Alien components of the northern Appalachians. The Meguma deposits in Nova Scotia may have come from African rivers.

of Avalon, as defined by the occurrence of "un-American" fossils, form northern Nova Scotia, the coastal parts of New Brunswick, Maine, New Hampshire, Massachusetts, Rhode Island, and easternmost Connecticut, and possibly the Carolina Slate Belt. Since Avalon may have originated close to—or attached to—Africa, it has been proposed that the 30,000-foot-thickness of sediments covering most of southern Nova Scotia were delivered by great rivers flowing out of northwest Africa.

While the most dramatic product of the final, Alleghenian, phase of Appalachian evolution is the Valley and Ridge Province from Pennsylvania south, it also affected the entire length of the system. Seismic surveys—one by ground vibrators of the COCORP consortium from southern New Hampshire across Vermont into New York and another by a Canadian group across Quebec—indicate that in the north the entire coastal landscape, with its newly formed mountains, was pushed west, although apparently to a lesser degree than in the south.

Squeezing, kneading, heating, and compression along the entire length of the Appalachians helped produce important mineral resources. It converted limestone transported onto land from the continental shelf into marble now quarried in locations from Vermont to Alabama. Some deposits are exploited for their structural beauty— notably in Vermont—but less high-grade marble is used as a source of lime for fertilizer, mortar, or sewage disposal. The troughs occupied by many rivers and long lakes owe their existence to the presence of easily eroded marble on their floors. This is the case with the Housatonic River and Candlewood Lake in northwest Connecticut and the valleys dammed for New York City's reservoirs in Westchester County. The Inwood marble of southern New York State, 2,000 feet thick under White Plains, has made Manhattan an island, for it underlies both the East and Harlem rivers. That is why in Manhattan, Harlem, and the area of upper Broadway near the Harlem River are low compared with neighboring Morningside Heights, Washington Heights, and Fort Tryon Park. Strangely wrinkled Inwood marble lies exposed in Isham Park, at the corner of Isham Street and Seaman Avenue, two blocks from the terminal (207th Street) station of the A train in north Manhattan. Other deposits include the Cockeysville marble of Maryland, the Murphy marble of North Carolina and Georgia, and the Sylacauga marble of Alabama.

It has become clear that the process whereby ocean shrinkage produces mountains has generated some of the richest ore deposits on earth, such as the gold, silver, tin, zinc, and copper of the Andes. Metal-rich deposits have recently been discovered along zones of sea floor spreading where they have been extracted from the newly emplaced rock by superheated water that then erupts in submarine geysers. Such concentrations can then be carried into coastal mountains like the Andes. This probably also occurred in the Appalachians. While most of the deposits have long since eroded away with the great mountains that embraced them, the East Coast was once America's chief metal resource.

For a time the entire world production of chrome came from the Piedmont area of southern Pennsylvania and Maryland. It was first found in about 1810 at Bare Hills, near Baltimore, on property owned by the Tyson family, which soon monopolized its production. In 1827 Isaac Tyson, Jr., noticed that a cider barrel on a farm wagon in Baltimore's Belair Market was chocked with black stones that he recognized as chromite ore. He found the source, near Jarrettsville, which became the second largest chromite mine in the United States. Its output was only exceeded by the Wood Mine in Lancaster County, Pennsylvania.

In 1608 Captain John Smith, exploring Chesapeake Bay, found iron in clays along the Patapsco River estuary, but iron manufacture did not begin in that area until 1681. By then a blast furnace had been operating in East Haven, Connecticut, for two decades. In 1734 iron was found near Salisbury, in the northwest corner of that state, and was also mined at nearby Roxbury. The Salisbury smelters produced the high-quality iron needed for railway wheels. According to one account, during the nineteenth century, ''no reputable railroad would have any other than chilled Salisbury iron wheels under its cars.'' From such deposits, during the American Revolution, came iron for the chain that was suspended on logs across the Hudson at the current location of the Bear Mountain Bridge to block British naval vessels from sailing up the Hudson. The chain failed to stop the British and a later replacement was never challenged. During the eighteenth and nineteenth centuries in Maryland alone there were fifty-five furnaces smelting local iron, but eventually the East Coast deposits could not compete with the richer ones discovered in Michigan and beyond.

In 1705 copper was found west of Hartford and was mined there until 1741. In nearby Simsbury, beginning in 1737, a blacksmith named Joseph Higley minted copper coins that circulated widely in Connecticut as ''Granby coppers.'' On the eve of the American Revolution the copper mine's underground galleries were converted into Newgate Prison (named for the infamous one in London) and after General Washington's Boston campaign a contingent of Tory prisoners was sent there to be incarcerated in damp, cold misery. The mine served this purpose throughout the war, although most of the prisoners are said to have escaped. The prison was closed in 1827.

Farther south the Piedmont helped enrich the fledgling United States after a gold nugget weighing a fabulous seventeen pounds was found in 1799 on the Reed Plantation in Cabarrus County, North Carolina. Soon a number of gold strikes had been made in a zone from the District of Columbia along the Carolina Slate Belt and Inner Piedmont to east-central Alabama. The discoveries were a boon to the impoverished young republic, which, from 1831 to 1857, licensed two Carolina jewelers, Christian Bechtler and his son, to mint gold coins. They were issued in denominations of $1.00, $2.50, and $5.00. Needless to say, gold coins of that value at today's prices could be counted only under a magnifying glass.

For a number of decades before the Civil War the Carolinas and Georgia were the country's chief gold producers, and there were dozens of mines in the Piedmont. One on Neabsco Creek in Virginia was only eighteen miles down the Potomac from Washington. Unfortunately for those seeking to balance the current national budget, most of those mines are exhausted. The gold-producing zone also yielded copper, lead, silver, and zinc.

There are occurrences of iron, manganese, and other metals along the full length of the Appalachians. Some, such as the small deposits of bog iron in New England, were concentrated by water action after the recent ice ages, but others were formed, as were those in the Andes, by the mountain building itself. The Thetford mines midway between Quebec City and the northern tip of New Hampshire were long the world's chief source of asbestos. Their huge open pits provide a striking view for air travelers. Although Thetford is now separated from the sea by part of Quebec and the full width of Maine, it is believed to be a large chunk of deep ocean floor and underlying mantle thrust up onto the continent.

Today asbestos is out of fashion because of its association with cancer. Most of the eastern gold fields are probably mined out. The iron deposits cannot compete with those—however depleted—in Minnesota. Copper is still mined in northern Nova Scotia, and there is renewed prospecting for oil and gas, as well as for gold and for various metallic sulfur compounds. Nevertheless, it will be a long time indeed before another continental collision builds new mountains and deposits fresh minerals along the eastern seaboard.

6 THE FINAL BLOW–
FLORIDA ARRIVES,
YUCATAN DEPARTS

The most sensational proposal regarding evolution of the northern Appalachians has come from analysis of the magnetism in ancient rocks from the northeastern part of the continent. It appeared that during the coal-forming period, 250 million years ago, when closure of the ancestral Atlantic was almost complete, the latitude of the region, known as Avalon, whose fossils indicate a distant origin, was 1,000 miles farther south relative to the rest of North America. Specimens from road cuts in such eastern Massachusetts communities as Andover, Ayer, Belmont Hill, Dedham, Gloucester, Lexington, Lincoln, and Peabody were collected by Patrick M. Hurley and his colleagues at the Massachusetts Institute of Technology. Others extracted rock specimens near Eastport at the northeastern extremity of the Maine coast as well as from Nova Scotia and Newfoundland. Multiple samples from each site were analyzed, and in virtually all of those that were more than 250 million years old the indicated direction and distance to the North Magnetic Pole put them a thousand miles down the coast relative to the rest of the continent at that time. It appeared that coastal Maine lay in the latitude of Georgia!

The latitude of the main body of North America on which this startling hypothesis was based had largely been determined by magnetic measurements on Catskill Mountain deposits, since that region was presumably part of the mainland. The findings, made by Dennis V. Kent and Neil Opdyke of Columbia University's Lamont-Doherty Geological Observatory, were soon confirmed by Rob Van der Voo and his colleagues at the University of Michigan.

If the magnetic clues are valid—and some geologists are skeptical of so radical a displacement—something must have given the sliver of land known as Avalon a tremendous shove northward during the final coming together of Laurentia (North America), Baltica (parts of Scotland and northern Europe), and that part of Gondwanaland composed of South America and Africa, perhaps including, as an appendage of Africa, the region (Armorica) destined to become England and southern Europe. It has been suggested that Gondwanaland was responsible for pushing Avalon a thousand miles north.

The geologists whose magnetic analyses indicate such a northward movement have pointed to a series of north-south faults, or linear breaks in the earth's crust, along which slippage could have occurred. The faults are widely thought to mark where Avalon became welded onto New England. Among them is the Clinton-Newbury Fault that closely follows Boston's outer circumferential highway, Interstate 495, from northeast of Worcester through Lowell, Lawrence, and Haverhill. Some motion could also have occurred along the parallel Bloody Bluff Fault closer to Boston. The proposed zone of slippage farther south, from Massachusetts across eastern Connecticut, is known most widely as the Lake Char Fault—a shortened version of its full name, which is as difficult to squeeze onto a map as it is to pronounce. It is named for a body of water in Massachusetts called (from its Indian name) Lake Chargoggagogg-manchauggagoggchaubunagungamaugg. The fault continues south into Connecticut along Route 52, which becomes the Connecticut Turnpike, then curves west and south toward Long Island Sound as the Honey Hill Fault. Tortured rocks, in some cases folded as though in a jelly roll, are visible along Route 52 in road cuts north of the Sutton Road crossing in Massachusetts, alongside the underpass at Exit 2 and at the Wilsonville Road exit. Connecticut east of those faults (shown in the map on page 30) may therefore have been part of Avalon.

Whether this was true of the Carolina Slate Belt is more doubtful. That region

Intricate folds along the Lake Char Fault, exposed along Route 52 north of the Massachusetts-Connecticut line. These and related faults appear in the map on page 30. (Photo by the author)

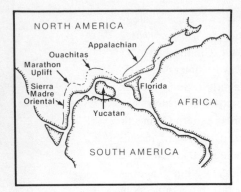

South America may have driven Yucatan and Florida against North America, according to J. F. Dewey and J. Pindell (left, top). D. V. Kent and D. J. Spariosu believe the Acadia-Avalon fragments may have approached from the south (left, bottom).

Right: The Ouachita Mountains in southeast Oklahoma, viewed here from space, were formed by tremendous pressure from the southeast. The Canadian River flows from the upper left margin into Eufaula Lake at the top, which drains to the right and off the top of the picture into the Arkansas River. South of the mountains is the heavily farmed valley of the meandering Red River, which enters the bottom of the picture on the left and forms Oklahoma's border with Texas. It is joined, west of Hugo, by the Muddy Boggy and Clear Boggy rivers, flowing in from the Northwest. Hugo Lake is northeast of that confluence. Indian Nation Turnpike runs west of Eufaula Lake and south across the mountains, traversing the Red River west of Hugo Lake. (GEOPIC processing of Landsat data by Earth Satellite Corporation)

carries the same alien fossils as the New England rim and could therefore be considered part of Avalon. Yet there is geologic evidence that it was welded onto the continent long before Avalon's alleged slippage. The University of South Carolina group believes the slate belt joined the continent about 400 million years ago, whereas the Avalon landscape farther north is not said to have arrived until 150 million years later.

Likewise in New England some parts of Avalon have been intruded by formations that do not seem to fit the proposed timetable of its movement. Some geologists therefore believe New England and the Maritime Provinces of Canada are composed of several alien lands that were swept together (and, in some cases, rotated) during closure of the ancestral Atlantic.

Still not adequately explained are the massive blocks of granite that, to a large extent, define the rugged, deeply indented coastline of Maine. These granites were formed during a prolonged period of the ocean's shrinkage, possibly as the roots of volcanoes or as the products of compression, deep burial, and heating during continent-continent collision. They are younger that those along the Connecticut River Valley, which appear to be remnants of an oceanic island arc formed soon after the ocean began closing. The coastal granites extend as far as Connecticut and account for such venerable monuments as Cadillac Mountain on Mount Desert Island off the

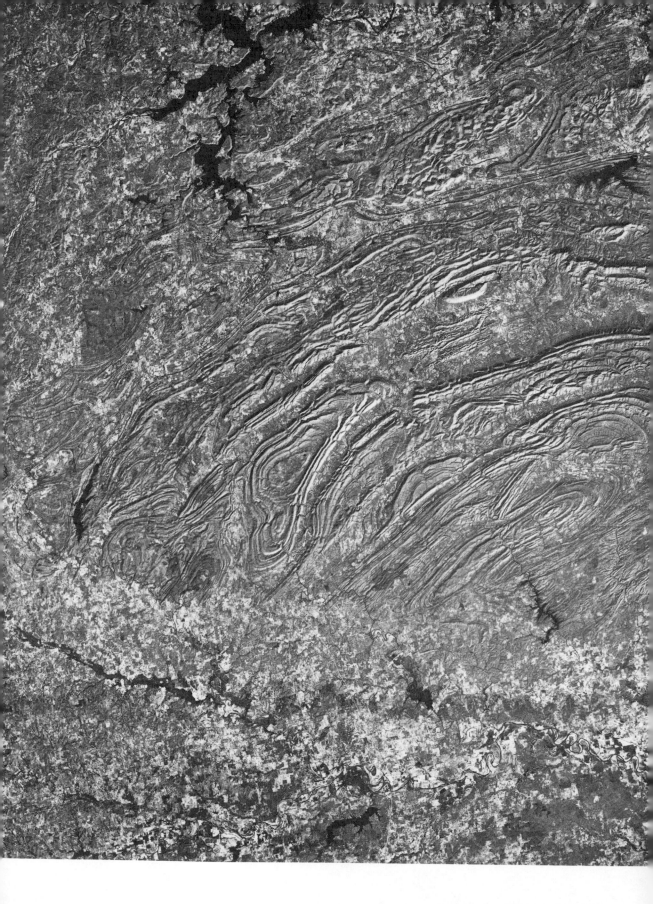

Maine coast as well as other coastal islands: Grand Manan, Vinalhaven, Matinicus, and Monhegan. From rocky beaches and almost 200 granite quarries in Maine—especially those handy to water transport—came many of the cobbles that still pave streets in eastern cities. Vinalhaven's granite built the imposing Custom House at the south end of Manhattan.

Even if Avalon was not transported 1,000 miles north during final closure of the ocean, as implied by the magnetic evidence, a colossal shove from the south must have occurred to explain other long-standing enigmas of the American landscape: the manner in which Florida joined the continent and the origin of the Ouachita Mountains that run west from Little Rock, Arkansas, into Oklahoma. Holes drilled through the deep sediments of the Suwannee Basin of northern Florida and southernmost Georgia have penetrated rock laid down 350 to 450 million years ago bearing fossils of an African affinity. The magnetism of the rock also indicates that its latitude was then similar to that of Africa. Thus Florida and the southern fringe of Georgia seem to have been linked to Gondwanaland and could have been glued onto North America by the impact of that giant continent. Magnetic evidence from South America shows that it, as part of Gondwanaland, was moving steadily north before the collision.

Although the Ouachitas have many similarities with the Appalachians, their direction, or strike, is so different that it would appear they could not have been produced in the same manner. They were formed 300 million years ago, near the termination of Appalachian mountain-building. Some sixty oil wells drilled recently in Arkansas and Mississippi, between the two mountain systems, have provided hints of a buried link. The great push that added Florida to the continent could also have produced the Ouachitas and their seeming continuation southwest across Texas to the Marathon Highlands, the Glass Mountains (now traversed by U.S. 90), the magnificent mountains in Big Bend National Park on the Rio Grande, and the Sierra Madre Oriental of Mexico. West of the Marathon Highlands the oil basins of west Texas seem to have been formed in much the same way as those on the inland side of the Appalachians.

In 1982 a bold hypothesis was advanced by John F. Dewey and James Pindell of the State University of New York at Albany. It stated that the Ouachitas were pushed up, not by South America, but by Yucatan, which was shoved as a giant wedge into the lower Mississippi Valley between Alabama and Texas. Yucatan, they proposed, had been an independent plate that on the opening of the Caribbean withdrew to become part of Central America. By injecting it into the Mississippi cleft they were able to fit all the continents tightly together without a gap. If their hypothesis is correct, it means that all the oil-bearing sediment of the Gulf Coast, extending from the lower Mississippi Valley, across the coastal plain of Texas and out under the Gulf—some of it ten miles thick—has accumulated in the 150 million years since Yucatan withdrew. Before that someone walking from Alabama to Texas would have had to cross what later became the land of the Mayas. There were no people around then to take such a hike, but some of the giant dinosaurs may, in fact, have done just that.

7 THE GREAT RIFTING

The outpourings of lava that occurred in much of eastern North America 700 million years ago, when the continents tore apart after the Grenville collision to form the ancestral Atlantic Ocean, are no longer much in evidence. But after that ocean closed, producing the Appalachians, the more recent splitting that gave birth to the Atlantic Ocean of today left marks familiar to almost anyone living along the East Coast.

As the landscape was stretched, rift valleys like those now found in East Africa formed from Nova Scotia to Florida. They were typically several hundred miles long, ten to fifty miles wide, and of great depth. One survives as the Connecticut River valley in Massachusetts and Connecticut, reaching Long Island Sound at New Haven (rather than at the mouth of that river). Another, the Newark Basin, extends from Tappan Zee on the Hudson River across northern New Jersey. Lying along its northwest flank in New Jersey are Pompton Lakes, Great Piece meadows, and Great Swamp National Wildlife Refuge. It southwest side, from the Hackensack meadows, follows the path of the railroad from Newark to Trenton. The chain of such features continues to the Gettysburg Basin in Pennsylvania, the Culpeper Basin of Maryland and Virginia, and the Dan River Basin in Virginia and North Carolina. Similar valleys lie hidden beneath sediments farther south and offshore on the continental shelf, as in the Baltimore Canyon area now being drilled for oil.

As in East Africa and Lake Baikal in Siberia, long narrow lakes of very great depth formed in these valleys. Over millions of years, as the valley floors subsided, vast amounts of sediment accumulated there to depths of 15,000 feet or more. The sediment survives as sandstone or shale, much of which has eroded to color the land red. At numerous points along Interstate 91, from New Haven north to Vermont, the highway cuts through these deposits. A particularly durable form of this sandstone, known for its color as brownstone, was quarried at many sites along the Delaware, Connecticut, and Hudson rivers to be shipped by barge for construction of the brownstone houses on many streets in New York and elsewhere.

In 1802 a farm boy named Pliny Moody found large, three-toed footprints in solidified mud near South Hadley, Massachusetts. Since dinosaurs were unknown, they were assumed to have been the prints of a giant bird, but are now regarded as the world's first discovery of dinosaur tracks. Since then tens of thousands of such footprints, large and small, as well as the imprints of fish, ripples left from the floors of lakes they inhabited, and even raindrop marks from downpours many millions of years ago, have been discovered in the Connecticut Valley—some uncovered when passage was being cut for I-91 north of Holyoke—and others have been found in the Dan River Basin of North Carolina.

Despite these clues to the past environment, it is hard to conjure up a complete picture of what it was like during that great rifting. The pulling apart of the continents was a long-drawn-out procedure and for several million years the dinosaurs enjoyed a peaceful existence in the rift valleys. Some 200 million years ago, however, the continents finally split apart along what is now the outer edge of the continental shelf. Life for the dinosaurs became perilous. The valley floors opened and lava came pouring out. In some cases, as in the earlier rifting, it was fluid enough to flood large areas before hardening into basalt. Elsewhere it penetrated layers of weakness in the flat-lying sedimentary deposits, forming broad horizontal sills of buried rock (diabase—similar to basalt but formed by slower cooling). The most famous, of course, is the sill whose edge stands as the Palisades along the west shore of the Hudson River. It was originally 1,000 feet thick. That it was intruded underground, rather than erupting onto the surface, is evident, for example, in the cut made for Interstate 95 west of the George Washington Bridge near the Englewood golf course. Sandstone on top of the sill was baked when the molten rock intruded beneath it. As it cooled, the rock of the Palisades, like that of other sills and lava flows, fractured into vertical columns several feet in diameter and six-sided or polygonal, giving those majestic cliffs their special appearance.

This sill and others like it are exposed because they were tilted up toward the east. Their east-facing, upturned edges form a succession of ridges farther south in New Jersey—Rocky Hill, Sourland, Cushetunk, Round, and Baldpate mountains. Two outcrops, Snake Hill and Little Snake Hill, rise as volcanic islands from the Hackensack meadows and are seen by all who travel from New York to Newark Airport. Soon after passing the first toll station on the New Jersey Turnpike the highway

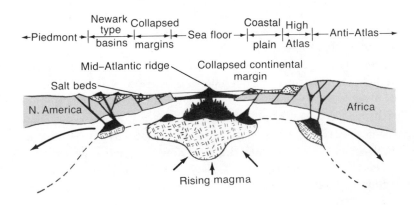

Reopening of the Atlantic 185 million years ago created rift valleys and lava outpourings, and gave birth to the mid-Atlantic Ridge. (Adapted from "Separation of Morocco and Eastern North America: A Triassic-Liassic Stratigraphic Record" by W. Manspeizer, J. H. Puffer, and H. L. Cousminer, in Geological Society of America Bulletin, *vol. 89, 1978, p. 914.)*

climbs over the shoulder of Snake Hill—the "high point" of an otherwise not very scenic journey—and its graffiti-covered rocks are also visible from Amtrak trains.

To the east, in Connecticut, there are matching sills that look like dislocated samples of the Palisades. They form East Rock and West Rock that hem in New Haven, their west-facing cliffs exposed because they were tilted up toward the west. The Wilbur Cross Parkway tunnels through West Rock near a cave, which in the seventeenth century sheltered two fugitives, Edward Whalley and his son-in-law William Goffe, who were sought by British authorities because they had sat on the High Court of Justice that condemned Charles I to death. Sympathetic farmers fed them, and three of New Haven's avenues are named for them and their fellow regicide, John Dixwell. Some geologists believe West Rock and the Palisades are remnants of the same sill whose central region, now eroded away, was lifted by internal forces.

The same humping could account for the uptilting toward the east of lava flows that erupted onto the surface in New Jersey and the tilting in the opposite direction of those that flooded southern Massachusetts and Connecticut. The chief remnants of the flows in New Jersey are the parallel ridges of the Watchung Mountains, reaching more than thirty miles from Paterson to Somerville. During a period of two million years, three separate episodes of volcanic eruption buried the landscape in basalt. After each period the basalt was covered by sediment before the next outpourings. The first succession of lava flows was 650 feet thick, followed by an intermission in which 600 feet of sand and mud accumulated on top ot it. The next eruptions added 850 feet of basalt, subsequently topped by 1,200 feet of sediment before final eruptions added a third layer that was also buried. The deposits remained covered until the tilting of the land and erosion finally brought them into view.

The three basalt edges of this layer cake now stand as concentric ridges. The one on the southeast, known as First Watchung Mountain, towers over Paterson. It is traversed by Highway 46 at Great Notch and has been extensively quarried there and throughout the region for its homogeneous "trap" rock that makes excellent crushed stone. (The term "trap" derives from the Swedish for "step." The successive lava flows, as in the extensive Deccan Traps of India, often leave steplike deposits.) Part of the Watchung lava erupted into lakes, producing the bulbous "pillow lavas" in Paterson's Upper New Street Quarry. Second Watchung Mountain is beyond that ridge, to the northwest. The rim of the third, originally uppermost flow appears beyond as a chain of ridges: Packanack Mountain, Hook Mountain, Riker Hill, and Long Hill.

Because the sequence of outpourings in Connecticut and Massachusetts was so similar to that in New Jersey, it is possible the lava flows were identical, forming basalt seas like those visible on the moon. Three great episodes of eruption are evident in the uptilted, west-facing edges of the flows from Long Island Sound to the Holyoke Range north of Springfield. Their remnants include Saltonstall Ridge, crossed by the Connecticut Turnpike west of the East Haven toll station, the Hanging Hills of Meriden, and Talcott Mountain, which parallels the Connecticut Valley west of Hartford and is cut by the Farmington River Gorge at Tariffville. The lava flows form many of the ridges seen from Interstate 91, notably where it climbs over the

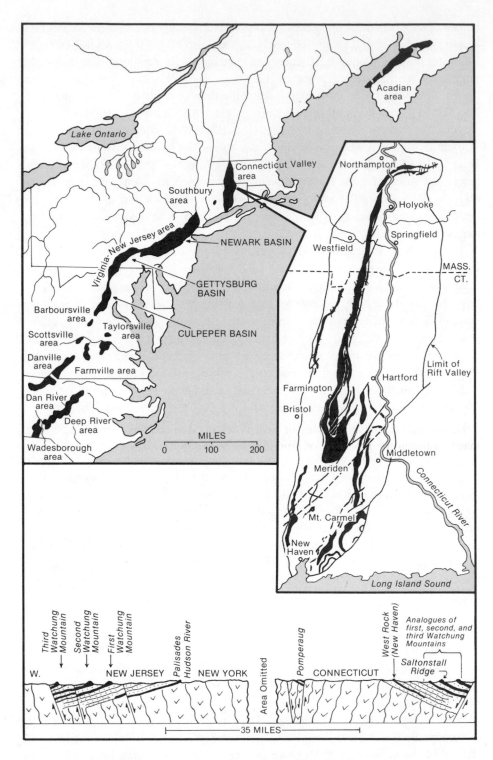

Scars of the Great Rifting. Lava outpourings are shown in black. (New Jersey-Connecticut cross section from Walks and Rides in Central Connecticut and Massachusetts *by Chester R. Longwell and Edward S. Dana. New Haven, Connecticut: Tuttle, Morehouse and Taylor, 1932.)*

shoulder of Higby Mountain near Meriden. The earliest of the flows, like that which produced the First Watchung Mountain, erupted into water, producing pillow lavas. The exposed basalt cliffs, with enough iron to "rust" and turn reddish, tend to be columnar, like the Palisades. Chunks produced by their disintegration where I-91 crosses Higby Mountain look like so many building blocks. Smaller-scale flows are evident between Woodbury and Southbury in the Pomperaug Valley of western Connecticut.

Similar sequences of lava eruptions and sill intrusions occurred in other troughs from the Bay of Fundy to the Gettysburg Basin and beyond. Sills at Gettysburg played a fatal role in the great battle there. The Union soldiers occupied high ground—the Round Tops, Cemetery Ridge, and Cemetery Hill—but were unable to dig in because they were on a sill so near the surface that entrenching was impossible. When the Confederates attacked in what came to be known as Pickett's charge, the casualties of the defenders were heavier than those of the attackers even though the Confederates had to cross open ground. In the battle the Union army lost 23,000 who were killed, wounded, or missing compared with about 20,000 for the Confederates.

Unlike the northern formations, those in the South were not scraped clean by the recent ice ages, and signs of the great rifting tend to be deeply buried. Nevertheless, holes drilled through surface deposits near Charleston, South Carolina, have penetrated alternate layers of basalt and red sediment at depths of several thousand feet. The drilling was done by the U.S. Geological Survey in search of clues to what caused the earthquake that severely damaged the city in 1886. Such relicts of the rifting are encountered in wells as far south as northern Florida.

Dating and chemical analyses of lava flows in Morocco have shown a striking match between the timetable of eruptions there and those of North America as the continents split apart. Eruptions in Morocco's Atlas Mountains coincide in time and chemistry with the lava flows of the Watchung Mountains, Palisades, and Holyoke Range, and the sediments in the Atlas also look like their North American counterparts. In both regions ten million years elapsed after the onset of rifting before eruptions began to make life miserable for the dinosaurs.

8 PISTON PLUTONS–BIRTH OF THE WHITE MOUNTAINS

Geologic maps of central New Hampshire show several extraordinarily circular, or semicircular, mountain ranges formed immediately preceding and during the rifting that gave birth to the present Atlantic Ocean. Their origin was long debated, particularly since earthquakes sometimes originate under or near one of them—the Ossipee Mountains. Like other such features in the White Mountains, the Ossipee formation, nine and a half miles in diameter, is enclosed in a cylindrical shell formed of concentric walls, or dikes, of volcanic rock. The dikes (formed chiefly of a coarse, granitelike rock called syenite) vary in width from two inches to fifty feet and extend deep into the earth, flaring away from the central formation. Within them is a mass of granite.

The Ossipee Mountains, west of the lake of that name, are far from the grandest of the White Mountains, although one, Mount Whittier, is high enough to have a chair lift. Their remarkable circular geometry is evident only from the air or on topographic maps. They have, however, been intensively studied on behalf of the Boston Edison Company to assess earthquake threats that might influence design and licensing of Pilgrim II, the second reactor planned for the utility's nuclear power plant at Plymouth. Two quakes on December 20 and 24, 1940, were centered at the town of Tamworth, on the north edge of the Ossipee formation. Chimneys, weakened by the first quake, collapsed during the second one, their bricks falling to the roofs and sliding to the ground. The crusted snow on surrounding fields broke into half-inch cracks running in all directions.

Circular or oval features like the Ossipee structure also occur in Australia, Nigeria, Norway, and Scotland. It is believed that they were formed when the roof of a chamber filled with molten rock (magma) perhaps a dozen miles below the surface either was pushed upward by a surge of high pressure in the chamber or collapsed after a pressure drop, allowing the overlying cylinder of crust to sink into it. Either process would create a cylindrical plug, or "piston," surrounded by fractures through which lava could erupt, then solidify into the circular dike wall. In some cases there have been repeated up-and-down piston motions as volcanic activity revived and subsided. Because the region between dike walls narrows toward the top, however,

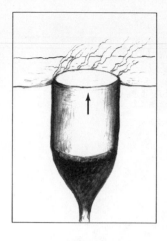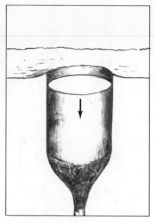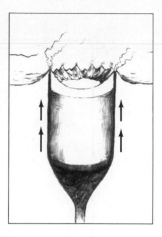

A schematic representation of how "piston plutons" are formed. Pressure of lava filling a deep volcanic chamber, on the left, pushes a "piston" upward. As the chamber empties of lava, center, the piston sinks. Repeated eruptions, on the right, then push lava up around the piston, forming a "ring dike."

the central plug cannot rise much above its original position. Molten rock rising around the plug floods the region inside the dikes, forming a massive "pluton" of erupted rock, such as the granite and gabbro in the center of the Ossipee structure.

Creation of the White Mountain "piston plutons," between 110 and 228 million years ago, marked the end of volcanic activity in eastern North America. The foundations of those mountains had been laid 450 million years ago, when initial closing of the ocean ancestral to the modern Atlantic produced volcanic activity that buried the region now forming western New Hampshire under 5,000 feet of debris. When the big squeeze came, these deposits were folded and invaded by molten granite, then worn down before the final collision folded the landscape. Mud, sand, limestone, and other sediments laid down on the floor of an earlier inland sea were altered into the black-and-white banded gneiss now forming most of the higher summits of the Presidential Range.

The mountains created then, some 380 million years ago, are not those traversed today by the Appalachian Trail. They, too, were worn away as the region slowly rose, leaving only a high plateau. Laboratory tests have shown that rocks now exposed on the mountains crystallized under eight miles of material. During the next 200 million years those eight miles eroded away (at 1.9 feet every 10,000 years). Even 180 million years ago the present route of the Appalachian Trail was at least three miles below the surface.

As the continents split apart and the Atlantic Ocean began to form, new eruptions built volcanoes over the region. The piston formations indicate some of their locations. None is evident in the Presidential Range, although the hearts of those mountains were intruded by individual dikes and great masses of granite, such as those, farther west, in the ice-polished cliffs of Cannon Mountain that tower above the famous Old Man of the Mountain rock formation in Franconia Notch. A huge volcano, however, must have arisen north of the Presidentials where there is now a circular complex of ring dikes eleven miles wide. Dikes on the east side of this structure, eight miles long, form the Crescent Range and are the best exposed of the

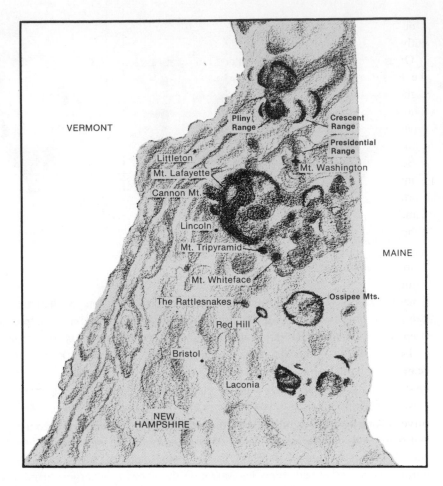

complex. Those on the opposite side, to the west, embrace the Pliny Range. Originally they may have been full circles. An even longer dike encloses the northern half of
the Pemigewasset Wilderness. It runs for twenty miles from north of Big Coolidge
Mountain northward along the ridge that parallels U.S. 3 on the east; then, before
reaching Mount Lafayette, curves northeast to the Twin Mountains, past Mount Hale,
and down the west side of Crawford Notch. West of Mount Hale it is more than a mile
wide, but for most of its length it is a half mile or less in width. The remainder of this
giant structure, enclosing the southern half of the Pemigewasset Wilderness, has
never been traced.

Similar but smaller structures form mountains familiar to hikers and skiers. They
include Tripyramid at the head of Waterville Valley, Red Hill on Squam Lake, and
the Belknap Mountains, site of the Gunstock Ski Area on the south side of Lake
Winnipesaukee. Although the slopes of these features are densely forested, one
geologist found more than a hundred dikes at Red Hill. Across Squam Lake from Red
Hill are the Rattlesnakes, twin 1,250-foot summits that I myself climbed a score of
times before realizing the strange manner of their birth as piston plutons. Crescent-
shaped dikes enclose Mount Ascutney, one of the westernmost outposts of the White

Mountains on the Vermont side of the Connecticut River. Its central cylinder apparently rose and subsided a number of times.

Once volcanic activity finally ended and erosion did its leveling best, the area of the Presidential Range seems to have been a rolling plain more than 10,000 feet higher than the present summits. Since then repeated ice ages, racing streams, and the wild winds, blizzards, and freeze-thaw cycles that have given Mount Washington its reputation as home of "the worst weather in the world" have eroded that plateau into a hiker's—or skier's—paradise.

Some geologists have proposed that the White Mountain eruptions manifested a plume of molten rock rising from deep in the earth that, as the Atlantic expanded and North America moved west, produced the Montreal hills, for one of which that city is named, then the White Mountain eruptions, and finally the New England Seamounts, a thousand-mile chain of submarine volcanoes reaching out into the North Atlantic from off Cape Cod. Some of their peaks, more than thirty of which have been charted, rise at least 13,000 feet above the sea floor. Like the Hawaiian chain, the seamounts would have been "squirted out" by the plume one by one as North America and the floor of the western Atlantic passed over it. Using various radioactive decay processes as stopwatches, geologists have analyzed volcanic specimens from the various White Mountains to determine how much time has elasped since the rocks cooled at each site. This has provided a wide range of ages for the eruptions, spread over one hundred million years, that do not become progressively older to the west, as would be expected from the plume theory.

Nevertheless a possible link with the chain of seamounts has been uncovered by surveys done for the Boston Edison Company. They have identified a circular feature that seems very similar to the Ossipee formation under the sea a few miles off Cape Ann, thirty-five miles northeast of Boston. Magnetic and gravity surveys were conducted by plane and, in some cases, by boat. Magnetism of the Ossipee piston proved unusually high as was gravity exerted by its central pluton. This was taken to mean the formation (formed 110 to 115 million years ago) was younger than the other White Mountain volcanic features and could explain why it was still a source of earthquakes. The feature off Cape Ann has similar magnetic and gravitational properties and may have been the source of the two largest earthquakes that have shaken New England: those that struck Boston in 1727 and again in 1755.

According to a contemporary account of the 1727 quake, which was felt as far away as Philadelphia, it was evident as ". . . a noise like a storm of Wind at a distance gradually increasing to that of a roaring of a foul chimney afire, and at its height resembling the rattling of 20 or more carts unloading great stones." Those who were in the streets, the account continued, "say that the Stars seemed to them to dance before they perceived the shock, so that the undulation of the Earth was in some degree begun before the shock was attended to. . . ."

The next quake, in 1755, was felt from Nova Scotia to Maryland and was described by Professor John Winthrop of Harvard University in a report to the Royal Society of London, based on his own observations (he was in bed) and those of a neighbor who was out of doors. The neighbor reported that "he was obliged to run and catch hold of something, to prevent being thrown down. The tops of two trees close by him, one of which is 25, and the other 30 feet high, he thinks waved at least ten feet. . . .'' When this motion stopped, Winthrop assumed the quake was over. ''But instantly, without a moment's intermission,'' he wrote, ''the shock came on with redoubled noise and violence; though the species of it was altered to a tremor, or quick horizontal vibratory motion, with sudden jerks and wrenches. The bed, on which I lay, was now tossed from side to side; the whole house was prodigiously agitated; the windows rattled, the beams cracked, as if all would presently be shaken to pieces.''

According to another account, ''In some parts of the country, particularly at Pembroke and Scituate, about 25 miles S.E. from hence, there were several chasms or openings made in the earth, from some of which water was issued, and many cart-loads of a fine whitish sort of sand. . . . The vessels in our harbours were so shaken, that it seemed to those that were in them, as if they were beating on the bottom. . . . Large numbers of fish of different sorts, both great and small, came up to the surface of the water, some dead, and others dying.''

What has happened before may occur again. The scientists conducting the Boston Edison study concluded that, while it is not known whether such piston plutons as the Ossipee formation will produce a really large earthquake, severely damaging quakes are unlikely in most of New England. In January 1982, after completion of that study, an earthquake centered at a hamlet called Gaza ten miles west of the Belknap Mountain piston was felt from Quebec to New York. It did slight damage in nearby Laconia and in more distant towns, such as White River Junction in Vermont. It seems to have occurred on a fault unrelated to the Belknap structure and many New England earthquakes originate far from any such formation.

9 HOW THE WEST
WAS MADE

Although the West holds by far the most dramatic landscapes of the continent—the towering cliffs of El Capitan at Yosemite, the symmetrical and deceptively serene volcanic peaks of the Cascades, the glacier-sharpened monuments of the Canadian Rockies, and the majestic Grand Canyon, to name only a few—how they came to be is only now beginning to be understood. It makes an epic even more incredible than that of East Coast history—as grand in its scope as the resulting landscape is magnificent. And it is basically different, as becomes evident from a glance at the map. The Appalachians form a relatively narrow series of zones parallel to the coast. The western mountains are spread across a region 1,000 miles wide. They are far younger and some, such as the Grand Tetons, are still growing.

The coasts differ because they were formed by two very different processes. In the East it was primarily the monumental collisions of vast continents. In the West, North America, like a continent-sized bulldozer, swept up a succession of island arcs (like Japan), mid-ocean island chains (like Hawaii), wandering continental fragments, and submarine plateaus. Over a period of 150 million years, ending 15 million years ago, they were plastered, layer upon layer, against the westward-driving continent; then the northward motion of the Pacific floor tore them into more than one hundred slivers and chunks, which were smeared along the western rim of the continent. Some were pushed as far north as Alaska, which caught them, one by one, like a giant catcher's mitt. The process was like the collision of large ice floes with the shore of a swift-flowing stream. The floes are broken up, swept along, rotated, and mixed to form a maze of fragments like that mapped by geologists in the West—more than fifty of them in California alone—some of which may have journeyed to this continent from latitudes in the Southern Hemisphere now occupied by Samoa and Peru.

Thus much of Alaska, western Canada, and the United States west of a line from Montana through Idaho, Nevada, and northern Arizona is "alien"—a collage of bits and pieces that geologists refer to as "terranes" (as opposed to the more general term, "terrain"). Although they now lie cheek to jowl, each is formed of rocks whose composition, fossils, and magnetic "memory" of past movements indicate a history and original homeland unrelated to those of its neighbors, from which it is separated

Left: During the great Alaskan earthquake of 1964, the sea floor drove under the coast, raising Hanning Bay, on the southwest shore of Montague Island, as much as sixteen feet and producing this raised scarp. (U.S. Geological Survey)

Right: Hypothetical plate motions that assembled western North America. Double lines mark zones of plate separation like the one currently down the mid-Atlantic. Plate motions over the Hawaiian "hot spot" account for the Emperor Seamounts and the Hawaiian Islands. (Adapted from David Engebretson and other sources)

by faults and sutures. Along some of the boundaries between terranes the collisions built mountain ranges. Elsewhere—perhaps because the collisions were oblique—the terranes were not much altered. The ages of "stitching granites" formed along the sutures indicate when the "docking" occurred.

Assembly of these terranes from earlier fragments and their sweeping up by North America resulted from changing motions in the floor of the great ocean west of the continent, as well as from westward movement of the continent itself. Today almost the entire Pacific floor north of the equator is a single plate, moving inexorably northwest relative to the plates around it. The rim of California from Point Reyes southward has been captured by that plate, and its northwest motion causes periodic earthquakes and slippage, chiefly along the San Andreas Fault. This motion continues, in rare but sometimes devastating earthquakes, to wrench the landscape of southeastern Alaska, distorting and shifting the coastal terranes (chiefly along suture zones where they first became amalgamated to their neighbors). It continuously thrusts the sea floor under southern Alaska, resulting in many minor earthquakes, as well as an occasional great quake, such as in the one in 1964 that destroyed parts of Anchorage and many other communities.

The plate motions that assembled western North America, including Alaska, were very different from those of today. The floor of the ocean west of the continent was subdivided into several plates moving away from one another in different directions, carrying with them an overburden of island arcs, continental fragments, seamounts, and submarine plateaus much like those currently scattered across the Pacific Ocean.

The record of these motions can, to some extent, be reconstructed from the "footprints" of former plate motions. The most dramatic record is provided by the Hawaiian chain and its continuation, as the Emperor Seamounts, to the northwest corner of the Pacific Ocean. Tuzo Wilson's proposition that the Hawaiian chain

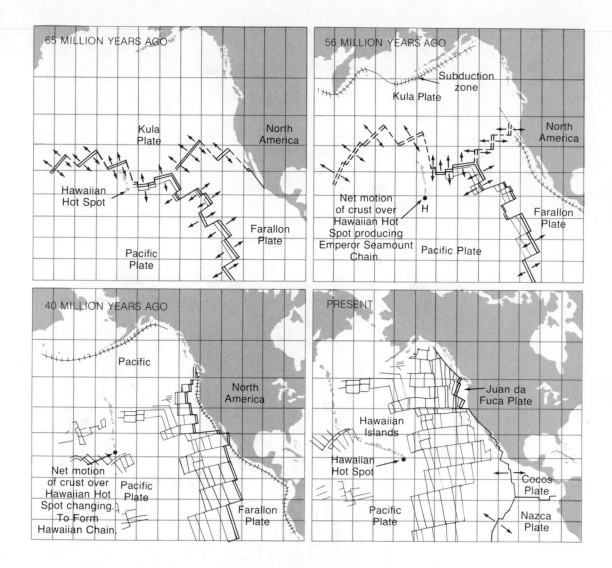

marks the path of the Pacific Plate over a deeply rooted "hot spot" has now been amply confirmed. The big island of Hawaii is being carried away from the volcanic source that feeds its volcanoes—Mauna Loa and Kilauea—and eruptions have begun to build a new island still farther southeast. In the opposite direction rock dating has shown each of the islands to the northwest to be older, for each passed over the hot spot longer ago. Most striking is the "elbow" at the point where submerged remnants of the Hawaiian chain meet the line of submerged Emperor Seamounts. The latter were obviously produced by the same hot spot and the elbow marks the time, forty million years ago, when—almost instantaneously, geologically speaking—motion of the sea floor there changed from north to northwest.

The footprints of plate motion that have been most useful, however, are magnetic patterns imprinted on the sea floor as it is manufactured along mid-ocean ridges. One can think of the ocean floor along a ridge in terms of an ever-spreading highway that grows by the eruption of new pavement along a crack down its centerline. For a certain time all the new pavement is colored white, forming a white zone that grows continuously wider on each side of the crack. Then black pavement begins to erupt through the crack, forming a black zone that splits the white pavement formed earlier. The latter is pushed farther and farther from both sides of the centerline. Production then returns to white, splitting the black, and so forth, over and over. The result will be parallel zones of black and white pavement on either side of the road, their widths varying according to the duration of each phase of white or black production. The resulting pattern of wide and narrow stripes on one side will be a mirror image of the pattern on the other side.

Magnetic maps of the sea floor are also colored in alternating black and white bands to represent zones of abnormally intense or weak magnetism. Actually, of

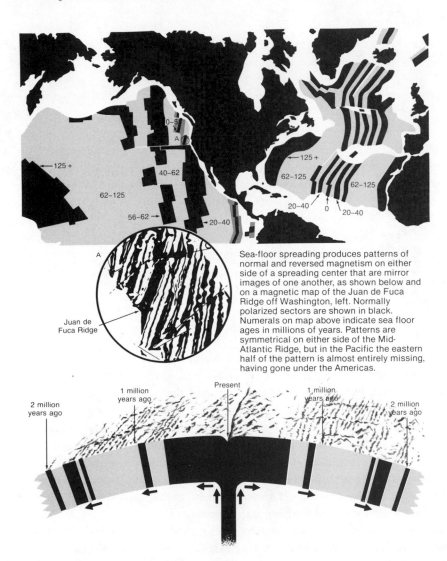

Sea-floor spreading produces patterns of normal and reversed magnetism on either side of a spreading center that are mirror images of one another, as shown below and on a magnetic map of the Juan de Fuca Ridge off Washington, left. Normally polarized sectors are shown in black. Numerals on map above indicate sea floor ages in millions of years. Patterns are symmetrical on either side of the Mid-Atlantic Ridge, but in the Pacific the eastern half of the pattern is almost entirely missing, having gone under the Americas.

course, basalt formed along the mid-ocean spreading centers is all the same drab color, but the zones alternate between opposite magnetic polarities. The reason is that, as the sea floor forms, it becomes imprinted with the magnetism of the earth in force at that time. Over millions of years the polarity of this magnetism has flipped many times. With each flip a compass needle that previously pointed toward one magnetic pole would then point in the opposite direction. The timetable of these magnetic reversals has been irregular, producing on the floors of all oceans the same alternating sequence of broad or narrow magnetic zones. Because this history of magnetic reversals has been well established, it is possible, merely from magnetic mapping, to estimate quite closely when each area of sea floor was formed.

This has shown the oldest sea floor to be in the Mariana Basin of the western Pacific, having formed about 160 million years ago along one or more ridges that have been partially overridden by the westward drive of North America. Returning to the analogy of a spreading avenue, the Pacific floor of today is only one half of the street. Where is the other half? It appears that an area comparable with the entire North Pacific has been swept under North America. No wonder the landscape of the West looks as though it had been built by giants. Not even Atlas and the other Titans had at their disposal the forces that have driven an entire ocean floor under the continent, producing its grandest scenery.

Until the 1980's it was assumed that the process primarily responsible for building the western landscape, and that of other coasts facing a shrinking ocean, such as the Andes, was simple "subduction"—compression of the continent by descent of sea floor under its rim, addition to the continent of material scraped off this descending sea floor, as well as volcanic activity over the descending plate. Yet some geologists found it difficult to explain in this manner the slice-against-slice structure either of the Andes or the North American West.

One school of thought now believes that subduction of deep sea floor beneath a continent can proceed for millions of years without much effect on the continent, apart from volcanic eruptions above the descending plate, until mid-ocean islands or other land areas riding on the sea floor are driven against the coast. This implies that formation of the West has been episodic, occurring chiefly when the great bulldozer ran into new lands—some of which may formerly have lain on the far side of the ocean or in the Southern Hemisphere.

Others regard the chaotic mixture, or "mélange," of sea floor material within which some terranes are embedded as scrapings continuously peeled off the Pacific floor while it was burrowing under the coast. William R. Dickinson of the University of Arizona believes compression continues, whether or not islands are smashing into the continent. He cites evidence that the Andes are continuing to be deformed, presumably in response to pressure from the west caused by underthrusting of the Pacific floor. He, along with Warren Hamilton of the U.S. Geological Survey and others, believes both processes have played a role—the sweeping up of islands and other bits of land, as well as prolonged subduction of deep-sea floor. In any case the Pacific continues to be a shrinking ocean and it appears that millions of years hence Hawaii, the Marianas Islands, the Philippines, and Japan may all be crushed against Asia—Taiwan having become physically (as well as politically) united with China.

At first this revolutionary concept of the world did not win many converts, but many geologists now believe all the continents are collages or amalgams of bits and pieces, slivers and globs, that have repeatedly been assembled, juggled, and reassembled to form a succession of continents. Europe, 500 million years ago, did not exist—at least in anything like its present form. The lands now forming Asia were scattered around the world as at least a dozen blocks. The theory marks a revolution in understanding of the earth comparable with that of the 1960's, when the reality of continental drift (now referred to as plate tectonics) became accepted. As Alfred M. Ziegler of the University of Chicago has put it, theories of how the landscape came to be "will have to be totally rethought."

Some terranes incorporated into the West seem to have moved at speeds greater than those of any plates today—as much as ten inches per year. Dickinson has pointed out that when the earth was young the rate of radioactive decay within its interior was far greater than now. The chief source of such radioactivity is disintegration of three radioactive elements found in most rocks—thorium, uranium, and potassium 40. The resulting heat is believed to produce the churning motions within the earth that cause movements of the surface plates. As those elements have been depleted by decay, the heat production has waned, and it has been calculated that heat generation may once have been five times greater than today.

More than once, Dickinson believes, all the major landmasses were glued together and the rest of the planet was covered by one vast ocean. The lands then broke apart into fragments that, in some cases, drifted thousands of miles before rearranging themselves into new continents. "Without this insight," he admonished his fellow geologists in 1977, "we can all too easily err on the side of conservatism for the Pacific region, just as our colleagues once did in other contexts for the Atlantic region." As in the case of the Appalachians, he said, the truth may prove stranger than fictions that "seem more comfortable by being more familiar." However outrageous some of these ideas may have appeared in 1977, they are now widely accepted.

10 THE GRAND ASSEMBLY

Decipherment of how slivers and fragments of faraway lands became incorporated into western North America has required remarkable geologic detective work, unraveling a history of volcanic eruptions of incredible scope, sleuthing geologic, magnetic, and fossil clues to an ever-changing geography. With conquest of the polar regions virtually complete, one might assume that exploration of the earth has come to an end. But a new kind of exploration has evolved and its findings seem as extraordinary to contemporaries as the discovery, early in this century, of warm-climate plant fossils near the South Pole.

When, in the early 1960's, Warren Hamilton was working in the mountains of western Idaho, he saw a remarkable resemblance between rocks there and those of the Aleutian Islands. Yet he hesitated to suggest that this region, 350 miles inland, had once been an arc of volcanic islands. He wrote later of his 1963 report on the region: "I lacked the guts then to speculate in print on how the rocks got attached to Idaho."

An early synthesis of the new findings was published in the November 27, 1980, issue of *Nature* by three of those involved in deciphering the evidence: Peter J. Coney of the University of Arizona, David L. Jones of the U.S. Geological Survey, and James W. H. Monger of the Geological Survey of Canada. They spelled out how individual terranes had been identified in terms of their distinctive fossils, geology, magnetic record of past movements, and faults separating them from their neighbors.

The first addition to the continent apparently came about 330 million years ago, after several hundred million years in which the Pacific Coast, then running from Montana to Arizona, resembled the East Coast of today. A vast apron of sediments had accumulated to seaward, but its peace was broken when an enormous shove from the west pushed an eight-mile-thick slab of deep-sea floor—perhaps including scraps of oceanic crust—eastward one hundred miles over the coastal formations. Not only did this resemble what happened in the east but seems to have occurred during a period when North America (including Greenland) was being squeezed from several sides, producing mountains in the Appalachians, east Greenland, and on the ocean-facing sides of islands in the Canadian Arctic.

The eastern limit of the slab thrust over the West Coast is evident in mountains of central Nevada—the region between the Rockies and Sierra Nevada known as the Basin and Range Province. In Antler Peak, nearby areas of Battle Mountain, and the 10,000-foot Roberts Mountains are rocks derived from an oceanic basin. That great thrust of the distant past was followed, about 100 million years later, by a second in which deep-sea rocks were pushed east close to 100 miles, burying much of the original thrust and ending in what is now the Sonoma Range, a short distance west of the earlier advance. This thrust, 230 million years ago, coincided with collisions on the East and Gulf coasts that produced the Alleghenies and Ouachitas, so events on the opposite coasts may have been related. The ocean off the West Coast was closing and either the continent was squeezed from several sides or the shove from the east pushed America westward.

In any case there is no doubt that 150 million years ago, as the Atlantic reopened, the continent began pressing westward, overriding the Pacific floor and adding to the continent another terrane—a chain of volcanic islands now embedded in the Klamath Mountains of California and the Sierra Nevada along the California-Nevada border. Much of the land west of Interstate 395 that skirts the eastern flank of the Sierras—85 percent of California—was added by this and subsequent accretions, although mixed with the alien terranes may be land that originated along the American rim. As the sea floor descended under the continent it generated volcanoes whose roots survive as some of the mighty towers of granite visible the entire length of the Sierras and Klamath mountains, most notably at Yosemite. The granites are progressively younger (from 125 to 88 million years) toward the east side of the range, tracing eastward progress of the sea floor burrowing beneath them. Whereas it has been possible, by the magnetic record in their rocks, to trace the wanderings of other terranes before they joined North America, so far this has not been possible in the Sierras because such records were wiped out by the heat of subsequent volcanism.

Following "arrival" of that terrane, other ones large and small, some of them "prefabricated" from diverse sources before they reached North America, were swept up one after another, torn apart, rolled northward, and finally embedded in what is now the region from California to Alaska. The dates when they collided with one another can often be found by measuring the extent to which uranium has decayed to lead since cooling of the stitching granites that formed in the suture zones.

The most exotic of all were terranes that, some argue, may have traveled from as far as Australia or Asia. One of the largest, known as the Cache Creek Terrane, lies between the Canadian Rockies and the Coast Mountains of British Columbia, but fragments of similar origin are scattered from Alaska to California. They have been identified in the North Fork area of the Klamath Mountains and one lies west of Sonora, California—almost within sight of Yosemite and so far inland that it obviously was an early arrival. The Cache Creek Terrane takes its name from a town on the Trans-Canada Highway. Interlayered with its fossil-bearing marine sediments are volcanic layers such as would be found by digging deeply into a mid-Pacific atoll or Bermuda. In 1950 it was realized that the fossils there were "un-American." They were fusulinids—tiny, amoebalike animals—belonging to species that, some 300 million years ago, were native to the coastal waters of lands once tropical and now forming Japan, Indonesia, Malaysia, and parts of China. Their shells, of intricate

The major western terranes. (Derived in part from an article by P. J. Coney, D. L. Jones, and J. W. H. Monger, in Nature, vol. 288, 1980, p. 330. Copyright ©1980 by MacMillan Journals Limited. Reprinted by permission.)

This fusulinid, Nagatoella orientis (top), is from Amador County, California, but resembles specimens from Japan.

This fusulinid, Paraschwogerina (bottom), from Nevada, is typical of "native" American fossils. (Both illustrations from U.S. National Museum; (magnification 10-fold)

spiral design, abound in sedimentary rocks of that period. Their American cousins occur widely throughout Texas, Nevada, Kansas, and points in between, belonging, however, to a completely different family from those in the Cache Creek Terrane. Fossils in the latter zone have been transported across the Pacific Ocean by plate movements, with the result that distinctive and once far-separated fossils occur in formations that now are nearly contiguous.

The Stikine Terrane, the longest sliver of all, extends from the Alaskan border almost to the state of Washington and includes the Stikine Range of British Columbia. Its magnetism points to an origin 900 miles farther south.

Tuzo Wilson, who had proposed that alien fossils on the East Coast could be explained if the Atlantic had once closed and opened again, made a similar suggestion in 1968 regarding the Pacific. Perhaps, he said, Asia and North America were once joined and then split apart, leaving a bit of Asia behind. This, however, would not explain the mix of terranes from many sources now identified in the West. Furthermore, if Asia was not assembled in its present form 250 million years ago, some of its constituents may have been rubbing elbows with the Cache Creek Terrane far from either continent but somewhere near the equator. Those lands would then have dispersed, most joining Asia, but this one captured by North America.

West of the Sierras is the Great Valley of California, whose Sacramento and San Joaquin valleys produce fruits and vegetables found in every American supermarket. It is filled with a deep accumulation of sediments, but magnetic and gravity measurements have persuaded some geologists that beneath them lies a suture zone where a new terrane docked against the Sierras 130 million years ago, having also traveled from afar. Most of the bedrock is buried, but along the western side of the valley it emerges as pillow lavas and other ocean-floor rocks that formed in low latitudes, according to their imprinted magnetic "compasses."

West of the Great Valley are the Coast Ranges, produced by prolonged subduction of Pacific floor, including the capture of alien terranes. Debate continues as to how much of this material, known collectively as the Franciscan assemblage, came from the offshore trench and other elements of a local subduction process and how much was of truly exotic origin.

The assemblage includes the Yolla Bolly Terrane, scattered from the Yolla Bolly Mountains near the Klamath ranges in the north to the region east of Monterey, formed of rocks from an ancient sea floor as well as sandstones that some believe came from the granites of a distant continent. This terrane, which includes Tiburon Peninsula, protruding from Marin County into San Francisco Bay, Angel Island off its tip, and Mount Hamilton, fifty miles southeast of San Francisco (whose summit is capped by the famous Lick Observatory), is believed to have arrived ninety million years ago.

Wrapped around the Yolla Bolly Terrane is a mélange—a chaotic mix of ocean sediments, fossil-bearing cherts (flinty rocks), and volcanics that seem to have gone through a great geologic blender. Indeed, the complex history of this region shows in its landscape, whose contours are chaotic, though softened by time into rolling hills that shine green after rains but otherwise are tan, marked off by ribbons of willow and eucalyptus. Around San Francisco Bay at least eight individual terranes have been identified. One, forming the towering Marin headlands at the north end of the Golden Gate Bridge, consists of mid-ocean sea floor that, for 100 million years, lay far enough out in mid-ocean to accumulate sediments free of continental material. If one scrambles up and down slopes near the highway interchange north of the bridge, one can see layer upon layer of cherts rich in the skeletons of tiny marine radiolaria as well as other fossil-bearing sediments. The bottom layer is 180 million years old, whereas the age of the cherts at the top is 94 million years, completing a record of almost 90 million years of placid oceanic environment. The formation lies immediately on pillow lavas marking the original sea floor. The pillows can be seen in remarkable profusion from the lighthouse at Point Bonita on the north side of the Golden Gate.

This terrane, which also includes Twin Peaks, overlooking San Francisco, docked with the mainland about 53 million years ago.

Embedded within the Franciscan assemblage are terranes no larger than a city block—islands in a sea of chaotic material (mélange) scraped from the down-going plate. Such is the Laytonville Terrane on Route 101 in northern California. It seems to have acquired its magnetic imprint in the latitude of Peru and Tahiti during the period, ninety-five to ninety-eight million years ago, when a steady rain of tiny foraminiferal and radiolarian shells was building up its thirty feet of limestones. Yet only forty million years later, according to present estimates, it was becoming incorporated into the California landscape. Some geologists question whether it could have moved north so fast. The tilt of its inborn magnetism has been taken to indicate formation at 17 degrees south latitude. But if the magnetic field of the earth then was of opposite polarity, that would put it at 17 degrees north latitude. Walter Alvarez and his colleagues at the University of California in Berkeley, who have studied the terrane, note, however, that it was formed during a period when there apparently were no magnetic reversals, leaving little doubt about polarity of the earth's magnetism. Only if this chunk of landscape had been turned completely upside down might the indication of a Southern Hemisphere origin be deceptive. That unlikely turn of events seems to have been ruled out by a microscopic study of its successive fossil layers showing that the oldest ones lie on the bottom. As Alvarez has put it, "The Laytonville results are something of a puzzle. An original latitude of about 17 degrees north would fit well into the emerging picture of plate motions, but the only way we can reasonably interpret our measurements is as indicating a latitude of 17 degrees south." Another answer to the paradox, favored by Dickinson at the University of Arizona, is that the terrane arrived much later than has been assumed.

Scattered along the present California coast are pieces of the last terranes to be captured, including the one called Salinia, whose granitic rocks and overlying sandstones, spread along 300 miles of coast, seem derived from Mexico or even from another continent. Most of the terranes are slabs only a few miles thick—"flakes" scraped off the floor of the Pacific as it descended under the continent. Salinia, on the other hand, arrived atop its original basement, having moved more than a thousand miles north. It forms the primary terrane of the Coast Ranges, being separated in the east from the Franciscan assemblage—the jumbled fruits of sea-floor subduction—by the San Andreas Fault. Along California's scenic Highway 1 it includes Bodega Head and Point Reyes, northwest of San Francisco, and sections of the coast from Half Moon Bay, south of that city, past the Gabilan Range overlooking the Salinas Valley (from which Salinia takes its name) to San Luis Obispo. Salinia is bordered on the west by the sea or by more Franciscan-like rocks. Cliffs of the Big Sur coastline are partially formed of a conglomerate—cemented-together pebbles, cobbles, and other material—derived from the underlying Salinia granites. Point Sur itself, however, is a slice of Franciscan material. California 1 snakes perilously along this deeply indented shoreline, clinging to slopes that drop precipitously to the pounding surf—one of the world's most dramatic battlegrounds between land and sea.

Many of these terranes were rotated clockwise during emplacement, as though acting like ball bearings between the continent and north-drifting terranes. Hence, while it has been possible to estimate in what latitude a terrane once lay from the tilt of its imprinted magnetism and its polarity (whether it points up or down), the magnetism is of no value as an indicator of where it lay on that latitude line, in part because the terrane may have rotated during its journey.

While California was being assembled, other terranes were drifting north into the Alaskan "catcher's mitt." Of these none had a more remarkable history than Wrangellia, whose remnants now lie as much as 1,700 miles apart. The largest includes Alaska's Wrangell Mountains and part of the region south of the Alaska Range. When Wrangellia was driven north against the underbelly of Alaska, the collision greatly deformed the landscape now exposed in the most magnificent scenery of North America—the more recently uplifted mountains of the Alaska Range. Their loftiest summit, Mount McKinley (some prefer to call it Denali), rises higher above the land around it than any mountain on earth. In the 1930's, as a seventeen-year-old, I tried to see it when the train to Fairbanks stopped overnight at Curry, southeast of the range. In the perpetual daylight of an Alaskan summer night a friend and I climbed a hill behind the lodge and when we reached the summit our hearts sank—nothing but clouds to the northwest. But then we looked up, and above the clouds, soaring toward the zenith, towered the most magnificent monument of snow and rock I have ever seen.

Some 1,900 miles to the southeast a lonely chunk of Wrangellia has been deeply cut by the Snake River, forming Hells Canyon along the border between Oregon and Idaho. The river, now dammed, enables jet-boaters to ride through the deepest, narrowest gorge on the continent. Large chunks of that terrane also line the Pacific Coast of Canada—Vancouver Island, the Queen Charlotte Islands, and Canada's Coast Mountains, whose gigantic blocks of granite are among the most massive such formations on earth. Other bits of that terrane are farther south—in the Wallowa and Matterhorn mountains east of La Grande, Oregon, and a couple of pieces only a few miles wide at the northern end of the Blue Mountains, northeast of Walla Walla, Washington.

Wrangellia seems to have originated more than 300 million years ago as a mid-ocean arc of volcanic islands. They were tropical, and this was the end of the Carboniferous (coal-forming) Period, when many lands were covered with fern forests and other vegetation very different from that of today. How wonderful it would be if we had film coverage of that lost world! Our only clues to its vegetation are in the rocks.

The volcanoes of Wrangellia died about 290 million years ago and sank beneath the sea, where, for a few million years, they accumulated shallow-water shales, sandstones, and fusulinid-bearing limestones. Those little creatures were not of the "Asian" variety found in the Cache Creek Terrane and so, while both were in warm latitudes, Wrangellia was presumably closer to North America. After some tens of millions of years vast outpourings of lava covered its marine deposits, building a volcanic pile that rose above sea level as one of the world's most massive accumulations of basalt. It reached a thickness of 20,000 feet and a volume estimated at almost one hundred cubic miles. These eruptions may have been related to the process that sent Wrangellia on its northward march. It was then far from any continent, for the sediments preserved in its rocks contain no continental silt or sand. During its journey Wrangellia amalgamated with terranes that evolved into some of Alaska's most scenic regions, such as the one forming the Alaska Peninsula, scene of the great 1912 eruption that destroyed the Katmai volcano and left as its memento the Valley of Ten Thousand Smokes. Others—the Chugach and Prince William terranes, comprising most of Kodiak Island and the Kenai Peninsula—also bear magnetic clues to a southerly origin, as does the Alexander Terrane. The latter, possibly a continental fragment, includes much of southeast Alaska and the Alexander Archipelago, whose towering islands enclose the Inside Passage, whereby ships reach Ketchikan and Alaska's capital city of Juneau. In the 1930's I rode a ship through its fog-shrouded fjords and sounds, and since radar had not been invented, the captain kept in mid-channel by periodically blowing his whistle to make sure the echoes came simultaneously from both walls. Rocks formed 150 million years ago by the suturing together of the Alexander and Wrangellia terranes during their northern journey would now be hidden by later deposits were it not for recent upheaval of the landscape that has formed the Saint Elias Range. The suture runs close to Mount Logan, Canada's highest mountain and second highest on the continent.

Several terranes are crowded into this region, dominated by Mount McKinley, including the Chulitna and Yukon-Tanana terranes. (National Park Service)

The most straightforward interpretation of magnetism frozen into the rocks of Wrangellia indicates that the region originated near 15 degrees south latitude. While this does not call for such rapid northward motion as that attributed to the far smaller Laytonville Terrane, some geologists suspect it was at 15 degrees north. In that case, however, Vancouver Island must have rotated enough to turn its north end to the south. When, some eighty-five million years ago, the Wrangellia-Alexander amalgam hit the coast to the south it may have done so obliquely, which would explain why its flat-lying formations have been little altered. After sliding northwest it finally docked against the Yukon-Tanana Terrane of central Alaska, also suspected of having come from another continent. Between them were trapped bits and pieces such as the thirty-mile-long Chulitna Terrane, whose tortured formations bear witness to yet a different history. After these marriages the process did not end. To this day pressure and rifting continue to alter the landscape, winning out over the softening effects of weather and time.

The most dramatic evidence of more recent rupture of the landscape is a deep gash that cuts northward for 250 miles across the coastal mountains. It passes near Juneau, its seaward end occupied by a long fjord known as Chatham Strait and farther inland by Lynn Canal, which terminates at Skagway, gateway to the Klondike and Yukon in gold rush days. On those special days when skies over this rainy region are clear, those on Seattle-Anchorage flights can readily understand why this extraordinarily straight feature is called a "canal," although it was not dug across a flood plain but cuts through high mountains. Because the rocks on each side of it are completely discordant it clearly marks where lateral slippage has occurred. Estimates of how much the oceanic side has been dragged northwest relative to the continental side range from a dozen to several hundred miles. Some geologists trace this fault in a sweeping curve that passes behind the ice-capped Saint Elias Range and then along Alaska's highest mountains in the westward-trending Alaska Range. Slippage along part of it may have reactivated the suture between Wrangellia on the south and the Yukon–Tanana Terrane on the north.

The evolution of northern Alaska was very different from that of the southern part of the state. It is widely believed that a continental plate embracing the Brooks Range and the lowlands flanking it to the north and south, as well as the northwest edge of Canada's Yukon Territory, was originally attached to the Canadian Arctic Archipelago and (as shown in the map on page 59) swung counterclockwise to its present position, rotating about a pivot point in the Mackenzie River delta. This would have provided the setting in which the North Slope oil deposits accumulated. As this terrane, known as the Arctic Alaska Plate, swung away from the Canadian Arctic islands, it left behind the deep basin of the Beaufort Sea. To the south it overrode sea floor, forming the Brooks Range and its ore deposits. As in other areas of continental collision, mountain ranges, such as the Endicott Mountains, seem to have been formed as the Yukon Valley was compressed one hundred miles or more. In swinging into position against the continent the plate also compressed the Alaska-Canadian border region, forming the Mackenzie Mountains.

In a 1977 symposium on "The Relationship of Plate Tectonics to Alaskan Geology and Resources," organized by the Alaska Geological Society with a number of oil

Sandstones, Argillite Marine fossils (170 million years old)

Limestones and Pillow basalts (180 million years old)

Red beds (190 million years old)

Sandstones, Argillite Marine fossils (170 million years old)

The complex history of the Chulitna Terrane is exposed in these folded and tilted layers. (D. L. Jones et. al. Geological Professional Paper 1121-A, Reston, Virginia: U.S. Geological Survey, 1980.)

specialists in attendance, this emerged as the leading hypothesis. It was pointed out by the keynote speaker, C.C.S. Davies, vice-president of the Sohio Petroleum Company, that rocks in the Brooks Range are typical of those formed on a continental shelf, such as one that would have existed along what is now the south side of the range when it was attached to the Canadian Arctic islands and facing an ocean to the northwest.

Others told the symposium of magnetic measurements that seem to confirm such rotation, beginning about 150 million years ago. As the northern edge of the plate pulled away from the Canadian islands, there would have been conditions similar to those that produced abundant oil accumulations along parts of the African and North American coasts as the Atlantic Ocean began opening. These would have included rapid sedimentation, high heat flow from below, and formation of geologic structures in which oil could accumulate.

While the proposed rotation of northern Alaska has wide support, Davies reminded the meeting that "much study remains to be undertaken before the geology of Alaska is really understood."

11 CALIFORNIA–
THE FINISHING TOUCHES

While California is an amalgam of numerous swept-up terranes and sea-floor accumulations, its mountains are the children of relatively recent upheavals. Until thirty million years ago the coast was being underthrust by a section of Pacific floor called the Farallon Plate for the cluster of islands off the entrance to San Francisco Bay. This presumably produced a coastal trench in the sea floor like the one now off Chile and Peru. It also crushed and underthrust the coastal region, tilting the former sea floor to stand vertically, as at Point San Pedro in San Mateo County, where thick, upright layers of dark shale are set off by intervening, light-colored sandstones.

Some fifteen million years ago there were intense volcanic eruptions in the Coast Ranges of California (not to be confused with the Coast Range in Washington and Oregon or the Coast Mountains of British Columbia and southeast Alaska) and their formation continued into the Ice Age Epoch of the past two million years. In fact much of the coastline has continued to rise into recent times, as evident in steplike successions of raised beaches such as the thirteen terraces that rise to a height of 1,300 feet on the coastal side of the Palos Verdes Hills between Los Angeles and the sea. Dating of seashells from those beaches has shown them all to be young—formed during the past million years or so. This was a period of successive ice ages and large sea-level changes, but most of them involved a lowering rather than a raising of present levels. None could explain a beach now 1,300 feet above the sea. The southwest shore of San Clemente Island, seen from the air, shows a succession of terraces, each 20 to 100 feet higher than the one below it. California's Highway 1 between Carmel and Big Sur runs atop a wave-cut terrace now 190 feet above the sea. Along this coast past Point Sur the sea continually cuts into the recently arisen cliffs, carving out islets and sea stacks—narrow columns of rock also found along other sectors of the West Coast.

The onslaught of the Farallon Plate intensely deformed the mélange of the coastal Franciscan assemblage. Yet to the east, in the Sierra Nevada, one finds almost exclusively uplift—and on the grandest imaginable scale. As the mountains rose, the eroding away of ten miles or more of surface material has exposed granitic roots of the ancient volcanic arc that, 150 million years ago, docked with the continent there.

The Southwest from space. (Landsat mosaic by Agricultural Stabilization and Conservation Service, U.S. Department of Agriculture)

Above: The eastern escarpment of the Sierra Nevada, almost two miles high, seen from Owens Valley, California. (U.S. Geological Survey)

Right: The towering granite batholiths of Yosemite. (National Park Service)

Below: Steplike marine terraces mark the uplift of San Clemente Island. (John S. Shelton)

More recent granite structures form the magnificent batholiths at Yosemite and elsewhere in the Sierras. Someone flying or driving across the region is unlikely to see many rocks that are not granite. The entire range, 350 miles long and 60 miles wide, has been lifted and tilted to the west, forming steep escarpments that rise 9,000 feet along its eastern front. The cliffs plunge into slopes of erosional debris (talus) along a fault that shows the mountains are still rising.

On the west the slopes are gradual, as in Yosemite Valley, and rivers flowing westward off the range have helped fill the Great Valley with 25,000 feet of sediment. Gold-bearing quartz was intruded into the western foothills of the Sierras, producing the Mother Lode that extends from Mariposa north to Nevada City. It was the discovery of gold along the South Fork of the American River that led to the gold rush of 1848.

The process that raised the Sierras may also have lifted and tilted the Peninsular Ranges, which for 750 miles form the spine of Baja California, then follow the coast for 140 miles north toward Los Angeles. As was the case with the Sierras, their mountain building probably began more than fifty million years ago but did not reach its climax until the past few million years. Like the Sierras, the Peninsular Ranges have been tilted westward, forming great escarpments on the east and gradual slopes to the west, as is dramatically evident when one crosses from San Diego to Yuma on Interstate 8.

As the Farallon Plate, some thirty million years ago, gradually "committed suicide" by vanishing under the continent, the plate beyond it that now forms the North Pacific floor came into contact with the edge of the continent (as shown on page 53). First touching in the south, the zone of contact gradually migrated up the Mexican and California coasts, tearing loose part of the continent to form the peninsula of Baja California, the Gulf of California (which is still slowly widening), and the San Andreas Fault, which with its sister faults extends from the Gulf of California northwest to Cape Mendocino, where it turns abruptly west under the sea. Ever since then the region west of those faults has been dragged northwest by the drift of the Pacific Plate. The total displacement may be several hundred miles.

Such motion accounts for most of California's earthquakes, close to thirty of which, between 1812 and 1983, caused damage. Typically land to the west of the faults slips northwest relative to that on the east. The great 1906 quake that destroyed part of San Francisco was centered in the region where Tomales Bay, which fills an elongated trough along the fault, separates the continental plate from Point Reyes, riding the Pacific Plate. Slippage displaced a road crossing the south end of the bay by twenty feet. Lines of trees were offset thirteen and fourteen feet. Altogether, fault movements in 1906 broke the surface for 200 miles, from San Juan Bautista, near Hollister, north to Point Arena, beyond which the fault follows the coast under water. Near Hollister is a winery of the Almaden vineyards that was inadvertently built across a section of the fault. Small slippages there are frequent and those parts of the building separated by the fault are sliding out of alignment at a couple of inches per year, requiring periodic repairs. Amid the barrels of wine scientists have installed various instruments to record activity on the fault.

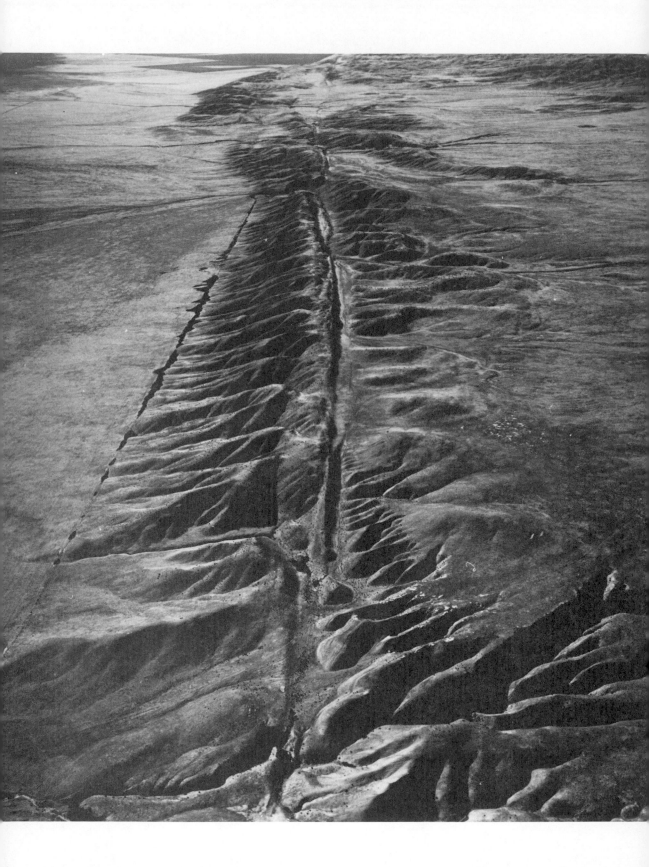

On the seaward side of San Francisco the fault runs beneath new real-estate developments in Daly City and down the center of the peninsula south of that city, cradling two long lakes that parallel Interstate 280. In arid regions farther south the long, linear trace of the fault is clearly visible from the air, and older rivers crossing the fault perform a marked dogleg to maintain contact with their displaced channels. Cumulative displacements along the fault are so great that the terrain on one side of it is sometimes mountainous whereas across the line it is flat. The relationship is as incongruous as it would be if New York's financial district east of Broadway were shifted northward until it faced farms and forests west of the avenue.

The Hayward Fault, parallel to the San Andreas but east of San Francisco Bay, passes directly under the University of California stadium in Berkeley. In 1836 an earthquake on this fault ruptured the surface along the base of the Berkeley Hills from Mission San Jose to San Pablo. Another one in 1868 produced twenty miles of faulting from San Leandro, on the southern edge of Oakland, to Warm Springs.

One concern is that movement along the San Andreas Fault seems to have been locked for more than a century by a bend in its otherwise straight path where it passes the Garlock Fault, which skirts the north edge of the Mojave Desert. A great earthquake occurred there in 1857, centered at Fort Tejon where Interstate 5 crosses the Tehachapi Mountains over Tejon Pass, but no large quake has occurred since then. The mountains there run almost at right angles to the San Andreas and parallel to the Garlock Fault, suggesting that the Garlock Fault and the mountains are products

Left: The San Andreas Fault traverses the Carrizo Plain southwest of Bakersfield. (U.S. Geological Survey)

Right: Motion along the San Andreas Fault has offset this river to the right. (Robert E. Wallace, U.S. Geological Survey)

Above: The San Andreas Fault cuts across Daly City, south of San Francisco. Beyond, Upper and Lower Crystal Springs reservoirs lie along the fault. (Robert E. Wallace, U.S. Geological Survey)

Right: The Coast Ranges of California southeast of Monterey. (GEOPIC processing of Landsat data by the Earth Satellite Corporation)

of the same process. Displacements along the San Andreas during the 1857 quake were extreme. The two sides of the sector between Fort Tejon and Parkfield appear to have slipped thirty feet relative to one another. Farther south the displacement was about ten feet. A quake of that magnitude today would be devastating. Fort Tejon is only fifty miles from Los Angeles, and the sector of the San Andreas skirting San Francisco also appears locked and accumulating stress.

Not all California earthquakes are of this type. Some occur when drag by the Pacific Plate drives a section of landscape, such as the Los Angeles basin, under land to the northwest. This process, over the last few millions of years, appears to have produced the east-west Transverse Ranges north of Los Angeles—the San Gabriel,

Salinas

San Benito River

SAN ANDREAS FAULT

Soledad

Greenfield

Big Sur

SANTA LUCIA RANGE

Salinas River

San Lucas

San Ardo

Jolon

San Antonio Reservoir

PACIFIC OCEAN

Lake Nacimiento

San Simeon

Paso Robles

MILES

0   20

Estero Bay   Morro Bay

California coastline and Santa Ynez Mountains viewed with imaging radar on the space shuttle Columbia *in November 1981. (Jet Propulsion Laboratory)*

Santa Susana, and San Bernardino mountains, the Santa Monica Mountains, their seaward extension as the Channel Islands off Santa Barbara, and the Santa Ynez Mountains rising behind Santa Barbara. Just as the San Andreas Fault bends near Fort Tejon, so does the coastline to the south, and there may be a relationship. Because the fault is hindered from smooth slippage, the Transverse Ranges may be receiving the brunt of pressure caused by the northwesterly drive of the Pacific Plate. The effects of compression can be seen throughout those ranges.

West of Santa Barbara, where U.S. 101 turns north across the Santa Ynez Mountains, an awesome series of tilted sea floor layers with a combined thickness of several thousand feet can be seen. They are especially evident on the north side of the mountains below Buellton. Where the highway follows the coast west of Santa Barbara those same south-tilting layers form the southern faces and crests of the range. These deposits are part of the Stanley Terrane—sediment-laden ocean floor that formed about 150 million years ago relatively near to the equator, then was broken up and tilted as it was driven against the continent. Closer to Los Angeles, where U.S. 101 cuts the southern side of the Santa Monica Mountains, the highway is flanked by a wall of layered marine shales gleaming white with diatom shells. The San Diego Freeway crosses those mountains west of Beverly Hills through extensive

Santa Barbara

Oxnard

N

exposures of slates bearing fossils that lived in the seas some 150 million years ago. Both from the air and from California Highway 14, as it crosses the western end of the San Gabriel Mountains, the landscape is jagged with protruding sandstone layers, all dipping toward the south as further evidence of great compression. These are components of the Tujunga Terrane, which forms much of the mountain range and seems of alien origin. Where the highway descends through Soledad Canyon the banded outcrops are of the ''mystery rock'' anorthosite, typical of the Adirondacks and the lunar highlands.

The most forceful recent example of Transverse Ranges uplift was the San Fernando earthquake of February 9, 1971, which severely shook the entire region north of Los Angeles. Most of the fifty-eight people killed were in two hospitals that had been built in the foothills of the San Gabriel Mountains north of San Fernando. Forty-nine died in a relatively old Veterans Administration Hospital. The new medical center of the Olive View Hospital had been dedicated only a month earlier and was designed to be earthquake resistant. Although the main building was offset two feet and suffered major damage, only three lives were lost. The twelve columns supporting the roof over an ambulance shelter collapsed and the ambulances were all crushed. No one was in them, but the hospital's ability to cope with casualties was

GARLOCK FAULT

MOJAVE
DESERT

TEJON
PASS

SAN ANDREAS FAULT

SAN GABRIEL MOUNTAINS

Santa Monica

Malibu

N

Long Beach

*The Los Angeles area from space. (GEOPIC processing of Landsat data by the Earth
Satellite Corporation)*

paralyzed. At the intersection of the Golden State Freeway and Foothill Boulevard three overpasses collapsed, one of them falling on a truck and killing its two occupants. Another person died in the collapse of an old building in downtown Los Angeles.

The reservoir-keeper who lived below Lower Van Norman Dam, a massive earth-fill structure, was asleep when the first shaking began. "I tried to get out of bed," he reported later, "but couldn't until the worst of it was over. I made a quick check of the family and a quick check of the house, then dressed and went to check the dam. When I got to the main road going to the top of the dam, I could see, through the dust, an irregularity of the crest. . . . I drove to the top of the dam and around the west abutment and saw the damage to the face. It was hard to believe what I saw." Although damaged, the dam held. Had it broken, part of San Fernando would have been swept away. As it was, the city's water system was almost entirely inoperative, and water tunnels through the mountains were displaced in ways that reflected uplift of the range. Surveys showed that the land within an ellipse six miles long centered near the Olive View Hospital, in a matter of seconds or minutes, had risen as much as five feet. South of that zone land subsided, suggesting that perhaps, as the Transverse Ranges have risen, the Los Angeles Basin has subsided, accumulating the 30,000 feet of sediments that have made it a rich source of oil and gas.

The deformation that produced the rows of hills in the basin bent the sediment layers upward, producing "traps" where oil and gas could accumulate. Extracting such fuel has deflated the land, in some cases lowering it below sea level. The Wilmington area of Los Angeles County subsided twenty-eight feet until oil companies were required to pump seawater down the wells to replace what was removed.

Beginning in the 1960's surveys seemed to show that across the San Gabriel Mountains from Los Angeles the area astride the San Andreas Fault near Palmdale was swelling ominously. It became widely publicized as the Palmdale Bulge, but some geologists questioned accuracy of the surveys and in any case no relationship to an earthquake threat was immediately evident.

Nevertheless, the virtual certainty of recurring earthquakes in California has gradually become accepted. In 1928 an eminent geologist said that "the accumulative weight of data substantiate beyond a doubt my deduction that Los Angeles is in no danger of a great earthquake disaster." Five years later nearby Long Beach was hit by ten to twenty seconds of violent shaking. Poorly attached cornices, parapets, and other ornamentation rained down on those who fled their homes. Many were injured and 120 died. The damage was close to $50 million. It was soon thereafter that California began imposing stringent building codes regarding parapets and other structures vulnerable to shaking.

Much of California planning has assumed that earthquakes there occur chiefly along well-established faults. The Coalinga quake of 1983 demonstrated the fallacy of that assumption. It inflicted heavy damage so far from any fault known to be active that the community was taken completely by surprise. Clearly much remains to be learned before it becomes possible confidently to assess local earthquake hazards.

12 THE GREAT
LAYER CAKE

Some experiences suffer from too great anticipation. Ecstatic description all too often leads to subsequent disappointment. Nevertheless, those who for the first time stand on the rim of the Grand Canyon are inevitably ill prepared for what they see. One cannot find anticlimactic something that cannot be adequately described. The viewer is overwhelmed not only by the dimensions of the scene, but by the panoply of history, spanning hundreds of millions of years, writ in the horizontal layers of pink, brown, gray, and ocher.

The stage for this awesome display was first set by a very long period of sediment accumulation while the region was low enough to be flooded repeatedly by the sea. Then, during the so-called Laramide Revolution, which, to a large extent, made the mountain states what they are today, the land was subjected to pressure from the west. Finally, relatively recently, it was raised to form the Colorado Plateau, a roughly circular region covering large parts of Colorado, Utah, Arizona, and New Mexico.

It was into that plateau in northwest Arizona that the Grand Canyon was carved, exposing formations produced by prolonged accumulation in an environment very different from that of today. Earlier collisions to the west had raised high mountains in Nevada. East and north of the plateau, chiefly in Colorado, the "ancestral Rockies" had been formed, possibly by the pressure of South America against the Gulf Coast. This produced two parallel ranges, one following the present path of the Front Range, the dramatically abrupt wall of mountains that first greets the westbound traveler. The second belt extended from the Uncompahgre Plateau of western Colorado to where, in the southeast of that state, the remains of those earlier mountains have been buried by volcanic eruptions that produced the magnificent San Juan Mountains.

For millions of years sand, silt, and mud that had been eroded from the earlier mountains was spread across great inland seas covering most of the continent's interior. They extended from the Gulf of Mexico to Hudson Bay and what is now the Arctic Coast. The flooding apparently occurred when the ocean basins became shallower as sea floor rose along volcanically active ridges where oceanic plates were being pushed asunder. The effect was to inundate much of the land. Initially, within this continental sea, no fish swam and over it no birds flew, for such creatures had not yet evolved, but within its waters proliferated tiny creatures whose shells rained to the bottom, accumulating and consolidating into deep deposits of limestone. At times, reckoned in millions of years, the water receded, and muddy river deltas, lake bottoms, and coastal wetlands hardened into shale. As layer was heaped upon layer they recorded the evolution of fish, amphibians, and finally huge dinosaurs. Sometimes the land became arid, perhaps when changing world geography or newly arisen mountains cut off sources of moist air. Some of the resulting sands were wind-sculpted into dunes. Once buried, the sand and dunes formed white and brick-red sandstones later carved into some of the world's most dramatic landscapes.

The debris spread east across the plains states, mixing with organic sediment on the sea floor to provide the source material for numerous oil fields. In the Andarko Basin north of the Wichita and Arbuckle mountains of Oklahoma (formed at the same time as the Ancestral Rockies) the accumulation exceeded 30,000 feet. Similar deposits formed in west Texas, Wyoming, Utah, and Arizona. As far east as Minnesota, Iowa, and Kansas this prolonged period of sedimentation lasted until the crust of western North America began to be buckled by the Laramide Revolution.

The western shores of the inland sea retreated eastward, toward the centerline of the continent, leaving behind them swampy coastal plains. Because the continent was then equatorial, those plains became covered with dense rain forests whose remains now form some of the world's most extensive coal deposits. They reach from Canada, Montana, and North Dakota as far south as Arizona and New Mexico. On the Colorado Plateau in northeast Arizona, for example, coal reserves beneath Black Mesa are estimated at more than 21 billion tons, with 1 billion within range of strip mining. From a 14,000-acre lease on tribal lands there, the Peabody Coal Company is extracting about 12.5 million tons a year.

The manner in which the history of this region has been preserved in the flat-lying beds of the Colorado Plateau, now displayed in the Grand Canyon and other eroded areas, is a wonder of the American landscape, revealing successive episodes of the earth's history that were played out on a vast scale as life and the earth inexorably evolved to the world of today. Because the cycles of inundation and desiccation affected the entire region, the same history can be read in the many-colored layers of cliffs from Utah and Colorado to New Mexico. They appear in the canyons, buttes, and pinnacles of the numerous national parks of that region (Arches, Bryce Canyon, Canyonlands, Capitol Reef, Mesa Verde, Grand Canyon, and Zion) and many other areas, such as Colorado National Monument west of Grand Junction, where water has cut deep into the landscape.

Riding down the Colorado River today is like an inside voyage through the earth's bloodstream, but it is a very different experience from that of John Wesley Powell, who had lost an arm in the Civil War at the battle of Shiloh, but turned geologist and, despite his handicap, led a historic expedition of nine men down the canyon in 1869. They started in four boats at the Green River Station of the newly built Union Pacific Railroad, but as their supplies ran low and fearsome rapids lay ahead, three of the party decided to climb the walls of the canyon to the plateau. Powell and the others safely emerged from the lower end of the canyon to be greeted by Mormon settlers, but the other three were killed by Indians.

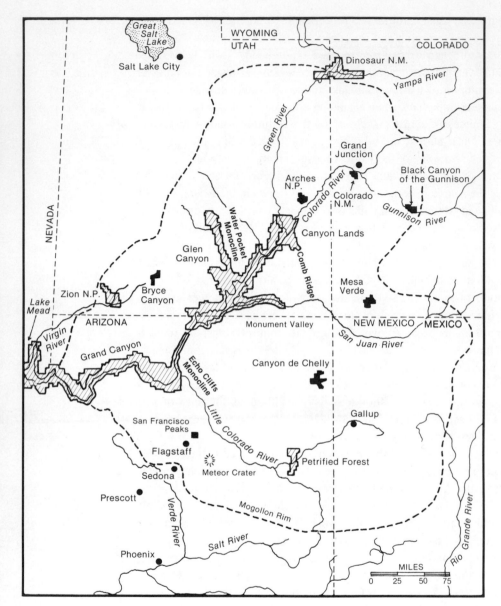

Left: The Colorado Plateau.

Right: The Colorado River flowing through Grand Canyon. (U.S. Geological Survey)

While seeing the canyon at close range is an overwhelming experience, only when flying over it at high altitude can one see its entirety. Nowhere else is the power of running water more dramatically displayed. The river has removed thousands of cubic miles of rock from the canyon as well as many layers of deposition from the plateau, 10,000 feet of which have been carried away. Part of this material now fills the Imperial Valley of California, west of the river's mouth. Until upstream dams trapped the sediment, the river's abrasive burden helped cut the canyon and its color inspired the Spaniards to call the river Colorado from their word for "reddish."

The very deepest part, the Inner Gorge, is a narrow V cut into granites 1.7 billion

years old. They are surmounted by lava flows and marine limestones formed from the remains of the countless tiny blue-green algae—primitive, single-celled marine organisms from an early stage in life's evolution. An ancient landscape carved in these beds is now buried under a mile and a half of layers the lowest of which, visible in the canyon walls as the Tonto Platform, accumulated 600 or 700 million years ago from coastal sands, mudflats, and lime. Plants and animals had not yet colonized the land, but the deposit contains the remains of trilobites—those segmented creatures of ancient seas that were among the earliest multicelled animals. As with other layers whose exposures in the canyon are sloping, the shale forming the middle layer of the

Tonto Platform is more easily eroded than the canyon's cliffs of limestone and sandstone. In the walls of the canyon such vertical cliffs alternate with the sloping deposits of shale, mudstone, or siltstone to produce the steplike appearance so characteristic of this and other formations in the area.

In the eras that followed, fish began to evolve, but that part of the record is missing in the canyon, possibly because the surface was exposed to erosion. Above the Tonto Platform and this historical gap rise the cliffs of Redwall limestone, towering as high as the Washington Monument. This strikingly uniform limestone tells of a wide, placid sea that covered this area for millions of years as tiny shells settled onto its bottom, burying the fossils of sea lilies and primitive fish. The Redwall limestone, which is actually gray but has been stained bright red by iron oxide washed down from the Supai Formation above it, is found under various local names from Alberta to Arizona and even into Mexico's Sonora.

The Supai's 800 feet of sedimentary rock contain impressions of fernlike plants and the footprints of early amphibians, some of whom are known only from their tracks since their skeletons have never been found. Above that is the Hermit shale, apparently deposited on a broad, marshy coastal plain, holding the remains of numerous species of fern and cone-bearing shrubs as well as the tracks of salamanderlike animals. Elsewhere the same deposit has yielded the bones of such fearsome reptiles as the ten-foot dimetrodon with a tall, spiny sail on its back. It is thought to have been the dominant carnivore of that region 250 million years ago.

And so it goes, layer upon layer, epoch upon epoch. The Coconino sandstone, forming a 300-foot cliff in the canyon walls, is a deposit of windblown sands and dunes that can be seen over a vast area of the Colorado Plateau. While the region was then desertlike, it was not devoid of life. The footprints of at least twenty-seven animal species have been found in that layer. Unlike beach sands that are a mix of many-sized particles, those of the Coconino sandstone were winnowed by the wind to relatively uniform size. Also widespread over the region is the Kaibab limestone, whose erosion-resistant rock forms the canyon's rim. It can be traced from Las Vegas, Nevada, across the plateau to southern Utah and beyond New Mexico into the oil-bearing formations of Texas.

If one travels from the canyon ninety miles south to the rim of the plateau, then descends Oak Creek Canyon to Sedona—a spectacular drive—the same history can be seen in the canyon walls: Kaibab limestone crowning the wind-carved Coconino sandstone and, below it, the more easily eroded redbeds of the Supai Formation. Emerging from the canyon at Sedona, one enters a region dominated by huge, freestanding blocks of the plateau that, thanks to their lids of hard rock, have resisted the erosion that has reduced the surrounding region to an arid plain. Each of these monuments is a masterpiece of unique design, yet each repeats the same history. Some have been eroded into groves of towering pinnacles. Others stand intact as giant blocks. Camped at an isolated spot east of Sedona in 1982 my wife and I were surrounded by this multicolored landscape, first under the changing light of a setting sun. Then (after a night under an unbelievable multitude of stars) the same Wagnerian landscape was reversely illuminated by sunrise.

Marking the edge of the plateau north of Sedona is the Mogollon Rim (locally pronounced *muggy-own),* a 300-mile east-west series of escarpments, here and there buried by massive lava flows. The rim marks the transition between two very different provinces of Arizona. To the north is the high plateau, sparsely inhabited, often cold, covered with scrub growth, but forested with ponderosa, piñon pine, and juniper on higher slopes or where the rim itself pushes up passing air masses, causing them to precipitate rain. By contrast the southern region, with 95 percent of Arizona's population, is hot desert country—broad, dry basins prickly with columnar saguaro cactus, aglow at night with such booming centers as Phoenix and Tucson, and set off by widely spaced ranges whose ruggedness has not been softened by frequent rains.

All of the rocks displayed in the Grand Canyon were laid down during or before the Permian Period, which ended 230 million years ago, the more recent layers having been eroded away after the plateau was raised. Although the plateau has remained relatively undeformed, it is gently tilted upward toward the north where layers more recent than the ones surviving at the canyon break the surface in a succession of cliffs. This is called the Grand Staircase, its steps known by their colors. First, north of the canyon, are the Chocolate Cliffs, formed of Moenkopi shale laid down 220 million years ago directly on top of the Kaibab limestone. It extends at least 300 miles north—as far as Flaming Gorge, where the Green River is dammed at the Wyoming-Utah border.

Next, in northernmost Arizona, are the more prominent Vermilion Cliffs, whose brilliantly red sandstone rests on the darker Chinle Formation. The latter, in northeast Arizona, is 1,200 feet thick and extends at least as far north as central Colorado. Its shales have yielded heavy-bodied amphibians as well as early dinosaurs, and the Petrified Forest in eastern Arizona was also preserved by that formation. The next step to the north, the White Cliffs, is the exposed edge of a "fossilized desert"—the

	Grand Canyon	Zion	Canyonlands	Mesa Verde	Bryce Canyon
Tertiary Period 10–65 million yrs ago					Wasatch Fm
Cretaceous Period 65–135				Mesaverde Fm / Mancos Shale / Dakota Ss	Kaiparowits Fm / Wahweap Ss / Straight Cliffs Ss / Tropic Shale / Dakota Ss
Jurassic Period 135–180		Carmel Fm / Navaho Ss	Morrison Fm / Summerville Fm / Curtis Fm / Entrada Ss / Carmel Fm / Navaho Ss	Morrison Fm / Summerville Fm / Curtis Fm / Entrada Ss	Winsor Fm / Curtis Fm / Entrada Ss / Carmel Fm / Navaho Ss
Triassic Period 180–230		Kayenta Fm / Wingate Ss / Chinle Fm / Moenkopi Fm	Kayenta Fm / Wingate Ss / Chinle Fm / Moenkopi Fm	Older rocks not exposed	Older rocks not exposed
Permian Period 230–280	Moenkopi Fm / Kaibab Ls / Toroweap Fm / Coconino Ss / Hermit Shale	Kaibab Ls / Older rocks not exposed	Cutler Fm		
Pennsylvanian Period 280–310	Supai Fm		Rico Fm / Hermosa Fm		
Mississippian Period 310–345	Redwall Ls				
Devonian Period* 345–400	Temple Butte Ls		Older rocks not exposed		
Cambrian Period 450–600	Muav Fm / Colorado River / Bright Angel Shale / Tapeats Ss				
Precambrian Era 600 and earlier	Vishnu Schist				

*Rocks of Ordovician and Silurian age are not present in the Grand Canyon.

Fm = Formation   Ls = Limestone   Ss = *Sandstone*

Navaho sandstone that stands exposed in the walls of Glen Canyon on the Colorado River (partially filled by Lake Powell). It also forms Rainbow Bridge, now reached from that lake by boat up what the Indians call *Nonnezoshi-biko*—"canyon of the rainbow turned to stone." That stone arch—275 feet long and 290 feet high—is said to be the world's largest natural bridge.

Also carved out of Navaho sandstone are the magnificent structures of Zion National Park on the eastern edge of the plateau, resting on the more colorful Vermilion Cliffs sandstone. Finally, at the head of the Grand Staircase in Utah are the Gray Cliffs and Pink Cliffs, the latter a lime-rich siltstone formed on the bottom of a

Left: Zion National Park. (National Park Service)

Right: A natural arch in Canyonlands National Park. (National Park Service)

great freshwater lake. From it have been eroded the incredible forests of pinnacles, spires, and columns forming Bryce Canyon in south-central Utah—actually not a single canyon but a maze of ravines on the plateau edge. Its wild structures are tinted in delicate shades of red, pink, and cream—gentle coloration rare in geology.

At Canyonlands National Park in southeast Utah, where the Green River joins the Colorado, the plateau has been deeply etched into the most complex and diverse landscape of all, bearing such names as the Maze and the Land of Standing Rocks. From the air or from vantage points such as Green River Overlook and Dead Horse Point it is hard to believe this is the earth and not the setting for a *Star Wars* drama or the surface of some lifeless, deeply eroded planet. In particular the view calls to mind those parts of the Martian landscape apparently carved by catastrophic floods when that planet was wet.

Particularly striking are the crosshatched cleavages that have produced such extraordinary features as the Needles and Grabens. In places these patterns of deeply fractured rock look as though someone baked a huge, crumbly, reddish cake, then cut it lengthwise into countless slices and, occasionally, cut it crosswise. A short distance up the Colorado, water has eaten holes though the thinner slices of such formations, producing at least fifty-five stone spans in Arches National Park.

From Dead Horse Point one can look across the Colorado River toward Island in the Sky, a great mesa rising like a giant Tibetan fortress between the converging Colorado and Green rivers. Exposed in the mesa's massive cliffs is part of the record written on the Grand Staircase: the Moenkopi shale (hardened floodwater mud) covered by the fossil-rich Chinle Formation with Navaho sandstone on top.

In Monument Valley on the Arizona-Utah border, where the plateau was humped into a dome, then severely eroded, a similar message can be read in the walls of

Merrick and Mitchell buttes, named for two prospectors who in the 1880's ignored warnings from the Indians not to enter their sacred valley and were killed. Merrick Butte is capped by Chinle layers on top of Moenkopi shale and other formations.

Monument Valley is very different from other deeply eroded parts of the plateau. Its spires, mesas, and castellated crags, instead of being crowded together, are scattered across vast expanses of the Navaho reservation. Many stand alone and go by such descriptive names as Camel Butte, Elephant Butte, the Rooster, the Big Chair, the Thumb, and the tall, slender Totem Pole. On occasion the Navahos gather at night alongside the Totem Pole to chant and dance around a great bonfire.

Raymond Carlson, who for a time edited the famous pictorial magazine *Arizona Highways,* visited the valley before it was penetrated by true roads. He first viewed it at sunset: "The monuments and spires were tall, regal fingers of burnished sandstone, almost ghostly in appearance, and the shadows they cast were long, long shadows, so long they seemed to flow off the very edges of the earth. The scene was unreal, strange, and unearthly. It would not have been surprising to the beholder to see a dinosaur or some other prehistoric monster come hobbling along scratching his back on the towering spires."

The grandeur of this landscape has not escaped the attention of filmmakers. It was a favorite of John Ford, who produced at least three films there: *Stagecoach,* the original *Fort Apache,* and *She Wore a Yellow Ribbon.* In the higher levels of Monument Valley structures are formations that still cover large parts of the West. The Dakota sandstone, first identified in northeast Nebraska in 1862, is evident throughout the mountain states and at least as far east as Kansas. It was within its upper layers that the great coal deposits of Black Mesa were laid down on the eve of the Laramide Revolution, eighty million years ago. Coal is also found in a widespread formation visible, for example, in the colorful cliffs of Mesa Verde National Park in southwest Colorado under whose overhangs prehistoric Indians built their famous cliff dwellings.

Many uranium deposits have been found within sandstones and shales of the Morrison and Chinle formations, such as the one that made Charles A. Steen an "instant millionaire" in the 1950's. Although he was regarded by some specialists as a crackpot, his unorthodox prospecting located extensive uranium deposits in the Chinle Formation of southeast Utah. His flamboyant life-style in a mansion that he built overlooking the nearby uranium boom town of Moab became legendary. In 1957, to celebrate the fifth anniversary of his strike, he is said to have entertained 8,800 guests. By 1973, however, he had been bankrupted by federal claims for back taxes and other difficulties.

The Morrison Formation—a source of dinosaur bones in Colorado and Utah—as well as the Chinle deposits extend northeast into Nebraska and southeast across New Mexico to the Llano Estacado, or "Staked Plain," a vast tableland, not as lofty as the Colorado Plateau, which is capped with Dakota sandstone and spans the Texas–New Mexico border. Its western edge is marked by the long Mescalero Escarpment. Two west Texas cities, Lubbock and Amarillo, are on the plain, which is famous for dust storms whose wind-driven grains can ruin the paint finish on a car.

The region's name is said to derive from the sixteenth-century Spanish expeditions

Canyon de Chelly. (National Park Service)

that penetrated the Southwest in search of the Seven Cities of Cibola, whose streets allegedly were paved with silver and gold. After one expedition into Zuni country had been massacred, Coronado led a heavily armed force to capture Zuni, New Mexico, only to find that it and the other fabled cities were pueblos of adobe huts and dusty streets. A side expedition discovered the Grand Canyon, and when a party set out across the flat and featureless Llano Estacado, it allegedly used stakes, as do explorers of polar ice caps, to find its way back.

Part of the Colorado Plateau in northeastern Arizona, while barren, is so colorful that it is called the Painted Desert. Gazing on its arid wasteland one finds it hard to believe the area was once heavily forested, but the Petrified Forest bears witness to an era millions of years ago when this region was a moist lowland, shaded by 200-foot pines beneath which roamed long-snouted, crocodilian reptiles. The great trees fell, were entombed by flood silt, and then lay for millions of years as hundreds of feet of sediment and volcanic ash accumulated above them. Groundwater extracted silica from the ash and deposited it inside the cellular structure of the logs, where it formed crystals of white quartz, rose quartz, and amethyst. Iron oxides provided yellow, red, and purple hues. The wood of the logs was converted into many-colored gem collections. After erosion exposed the petrified logs, the Navaho thought them to be legs of Yietso, their mythological giant. Settlers carted off large quantities, which were made into ornaments and peddled or ground into abrasives. Part of the deposit, however, is now protected as a national park.

13 THE SOUTHWEST REDESIGNED

One of the most stubborn mysteries in geology has been how activity along the Pacific Coast—descent under the edge of the continent of a vast area of Pacific floor known as the Farallon Plate—could account for mountains overlooking Denver, 1,000 miles inland. Nor was it clear, until recently, why this was followed by large-scale stretching of the entire region between the Southern and Central Rockies on the east and the Sierra Nevada on the west. Still debated as well has been the final raising of the Colorado Plateau like the floor of a giant freight elevator, with virtually no crumpling.

There is little doubt that the Laramide Revolution, initiating formation of the modern Rocky Mountains, began eighty million years ago as the North Atlantic began to open, swinging North America away from Europe and pushing the southwestern part of the continent over the Farallon Plate. Prior to that the plate had been descending under the continent more slowly and steeply as its surface load of islands and sediment was swept against the coast. Now the rate of descent increased, as did pressure on the coast. The magnetic record of plate motions imprinted on the sea floor south of Alaska indicates that north of the Farallon Plate another section of sea floor, the Kula Plate, was moving north, dragging with it terranes that slid along the West Coast, some of them becoming embedded in Alaska. But now eastward motion of the Farallon Plate, combined with westward drive of the continent, produced particularly rapid descent, or subduction, of that plate under the continent. This altered the western landscape from Canada to Mexico, producing volcanic eruptions in the Sierra Nevada and initiating early uplift of the Sierras and Rockies. As the land rose, periodic invasions of the sea that had long covered the West with flat-bedded formations came to an end, but the Rockies were eroded almost as fast as they grew. It was not until much later that the entire region as far east as the High Plains was raised a mile or more to its present elevation.

As the Farallon Plate burrowed under the continent, enormous pressure from the west disrupted most of the landscape around the Colorado Plateau. Sections of southern Arizona were thrust sixty miles northeast. Other great slabs, the Sevier Thrusts, were shoved across Nevada and Utah as far as the Sevier Desert south of

Great Salt Lake. Yet the plateau itself was spared. In a few places brittle bedrock under the high-heaped sediments broke into steplike ruptures (monoclines), like raised edges of sidewalk sections. The overlying sediments did not break but are draped over these steps in long rolls reaching for dozens of miles across the plateau. Their erosion has produced cliffs and, where several upturned layers are exposed, multiple parallel ridges that are likely to perplex air travelers. Striking examples include the Waterpocket Monocline running northwest from Glen Canyon, Comb Ridge west of Bluff, Utah, and the Echo Cliffs Monocline, almost one hundred miles long, paralleling U.S. 89 across the Painted Desert south of Page, Arizona.

Geologists have long debated why the plateau was raised basically intact while all around it the landscape was being radically deformed. No less than fourteen explanations were discussed when sixty geologists from government and academic institutions met in 1978 at a conference hosted by the U.S. Geological Survey in Flagstaff, Arizona. The conference report noted wryly that the only cause not advanced was "the large subterranean frog of classic Chinese and Japanese literature whose burping was believed to be responsible for earthquakes and volcanic eruptions." Some maintained that uplift of the mountain states was somehow related to descent of the Farallon Plate. As the mid-ocean ridge along which the Farallon Plate had been manufactured drew nearer to the coast, the portion of the plate descending under the continent was of more recent manufacture. It was therefore hotter and more buoyant. Such material may have been too buoyant to plunge deep into the earth and instead pushed eastward under the crust far enough to heat and raise terrain more than 1,000 miles inland. Others believe continuing activity under the mountain states indicates presence there of the zone of spreading sea floor, overridden by the continent after the entire Farallon Plate had gone down—a zone that survives farther south as the East Pacific Rise.

The fact that the crust of the earth beneath the Colorado Plateau is much thicker than that under surrounding areas may explain why it resisted folding. The traditional view has been that the plateau was raised chiefly during the last few million years, whereupon the Colorado River cut its Grand Canyon, Glen Canyon, and the Canyonlands farther upstream in Utah, while on the plateau's fringes water gnawed out such wonders as Bryce Canyon in Utah and the Black Canyon of the Gunnison River in Colorado. A new school of thought, however, proposes that the entire region was first raised by the Laramide Revolution, and that subsidence of land to the southwest of the plateau, rather than raising of the plateau itself, tilted the plateau slightly and set the stage for erosion of the canyons and other features.

There is no question that the low-lying area south of the plateau now occupied, for example, by Phoenix was once on a level with the plateau and drained across it to the northeast. Gravel deposited between fifty-four million and twenty-eight million years ago along the crest of the Mogollon Rim that marks the southeast edge of the plateau shows abundant evidence of having been laid down by rivers flowing to the northeast, draining what is now the low region to the southwest. The plateau itself drained eastward, presumably to the Gulf of Mexico. Either the plateau was lower or the region to the south was higher. Only after the plateau tilted westward did the drainage direction reverse, whereupon erosion produced the Mogollon Rim and the herculean

task of cutting the canyons began. Whether the plateau was first raised before subsidence of the Basin and Range Province or afterward, the canyons have been carved only in the last five to ten million years, almost certainly aided by further rising of the plateau.

Such "redesigning" of the Southwest began some thirty million years ago when there was a reversal of forces at work on the western landscape. Until then enormous pressure from the descending Farallon Plate and, presumably, its burrowing under the continent had crumpled mountain ranges into existence from California to the Rockies. Volcanoes had been erupting in Baja California, the state of California, and western Nevada. Farther east new mountains were built including the Sierra Madre Occidental of western Mexico—the southern extension of the Rocky Mountains. Large bodies of intrusive rock were emplaced in Mexico, west Texas (between the Pecos River and the Rio Grande), New Mexico, and Arizona, forming the cores of such mountains as the one south of Tucson capped by domes of the Kitt Peak National Observatory. Circulation of superheated water in and near some of the intrusions deposited ores destined to make Arizona the nation's chief source of copper. In Nevada the fabulous silver deposits of the Comstock Lode were emplaced near Virginia City, seventeen miles northeast of Lake Tahoe. By the late 1870's the lode, discovered in 1859, was producing $36 million worth of silver each year, and a federal mint was established in nearby Carson City to convert the silver into coins.

Left: The Comb Ridge monocline. This spectacular structure, west of U.S. 191 in southeast Utah, can be thought of in terms of many sheets, blankets, quilts, and bedspreads draped over the edge of a bed. The "bed" is to the left and the layers have been exposed by erosion. The most prominent ridge, to the right of the meandering stream, is a layer formed of particularly resistant sandstone. (John S. Shelton)

Right: Bryce Canyon. (National Park Service)

This period of widespread geological activity came to an end, according to a proposal by a young graduate student at the University of California in San Diego, because a fundamental change had occurred. In a 1970 paper that explained so much it became a classic, Tanya Atwater pointed out that about thirty million years ago the ridge along which the Farallon Plate was being manufactured must have begun hitting the coast. It touched first in Baja California, she said, and consequently in that sector, as shown on page 53, the northwest-driving Pacific Plate on the other side of the ridge came into contact with the continent. The latter, instead of being crushed from the west, began to be dragged obliquely northwest. The region started to be pulled apart and volcanism began changing from the mountain-building type over a descending oceanic plate, such as that which resulted in the Andes and Cascades, to the fluid form that erupts through rifts when the crust is stretched and floods large areas, as happened along the East Coast prior to opening of the Atlantic Ocean. The transformation, however, was spotty. Evidence of recent lava outpourings abounds in the Southwest and Mexico, notably in the spectacular Cerro del Pinacate lava fields just south of the Arizona-Mexican border, visible on flights between San Diego and southern destinations.

Eruptions largely, but not entirely, of the fluid lava that hardens into basalt began on the Colorado Plateau some ten million years ago and probably have not ended. They formed the White Mountains, rising more than 11,000 feet at the eastern end of the Mogollon Rim, and later the San Francisco Peaks that provide either a sooty-black

Left: Vulcan's Throne, a cinder cone on the north rim of the Grand Canyon. Its discharges into the canyon have repeatedly blocked the Colorado River, but each time the river has cut its channel anew. (Kenneth Hamblin, Brigham Young University)

Right: Clearly, S. P. Crater has erupted in the recent past. (U.S. Geological Survey)

or snowy backdrop for Flagstaff. Standing alone on the vast, level plateau they are an unmistakable landmark for transcontinental air travelers.

Originally those peaks were probably a single giant cone whose central area collapsed. There are also smaller cones and domes on the surrounding plain including Sunset Crater, whose eruption in 1064, two years before the Norman invasion of England, must have terrified local Indians. The year has been determined by applying to logs showing scars of the eruption a chronology of annual growth rings of trees in that area spanning many centuries. Year-to-year variations in weather cause all trees in a region to develop a unique sequence of wide or narrow growth rings. From modern trees and those dating back hundreds of years chronologies have been constructed that make it possible to identify the year in which a tree was wounded by the last Sunset Crater eruption.

The lava flows there are of the slow-moving type known from Hawaiian terminology as *aa* (pronounced *ah-ah*). Such lava cools into chaotic, clinkery formations so jagged that, in such terrain, hiking boots last only a week or two. The site is a national monument and one can walk smooth trails among the rugged flows. More striking from the air is nearby S.P. Crater, an almost perfectly symmetrical cinder cone from whose base basaltic lava has flowed four miles north, leaving a long black scar on the landscape. The crater's name is a delicate version of that given it by local cowboys: Shit Pot Crater. Although the crater looks as though it erupted yesterday, it is believed to have formed about 70,000 years ago. While further eruptions may occur in this volcanic field, there are no ominous signs at present.

In their heyday the plateau volcanoes poured out so much basalt that it swept over parts of the Mogollon Rim, burying it and providing the ramp up which Interstate 17 climbs to the plateau between Phoenix and Flagstaff. Many years ago lava from Merriam Crater on the eastern edge of the San Francisco volcanic field flowed ten miles eastward into the canyon of the Little Colorado River, forcing the river out of its canyon. The river now cascades over the canyon walls at Grand Falls—higher than Niagara, although dry much of the year. The Grand Canyon itself has repeatedly been dammed by lava from Vulcan's Throne, a cinder cone on its north rim, but each time the river has cut its channel anew. The most recent eruptions, thousands of years ago, did not reach the canyon floor. In some areas of the plateau where channels feeding a volcano pushed up through the many-layered deposits, the sedimentary rock has worn away, leaving volcanic "necks" towering above the plateau. The most famous of these is Shiprock in the northwest corner of New Mexico, a remnant of eruptions thirty-one million years ago. It is visible for miles in all directions as a jagged monument rising 1,400 feet above the flat terrain. Radiating in three directions from its base are dikes of volcanic rock forming a striking pattern from the air. Its chief rival to the west, ten miles north of Kayenta in Arizona, is Agathla (sometimes called Capitan), rising more than 1,000 feet from a base less than a mile in diameter. Many lesser volcanic necks stand there and among the Hopi Buttes north of Holbrook, Arizona.

Whereas the Colorado Plateau remained largely intact during the great pulling apart of the landscape, this was not true to the south and and west. Between ten and twenty million years ago the ridge that was parent to the Farallon Plate came in contact with more and more of the coast from California north. As the edge of the continent

Left: Shiprock in New Mexico with its radiating dikes. (John S. Shelton)

Right: This COCORP profile of features to a depth of 30 miles beneath Utah shows a major fault (A) sloping down from east to west along which the land above may first have been pushed east, then dragged west. (From "Cenozoic and Mesozoic structures of the eastern Basin and Range Province, Utah, from COCORP seismic-reflection data" by R. W. Allmendinger, J. W. Sharp, D. Von Tish, L. Serpa, L. Brown, S. Kaufman, J. E. Oliver, and R. B. Smith, in Geology, vol. 11, 1983, pp. 532-6.)

became subject to northwest drag by the newly arrived Pacific Plate, stretching of the landscape began. The consequent alteration of the Basin and Range Province now extends from Mexico north to southern Washington and Idaho, bounded on the west by the Sierras and on the east by the Rockies and Colorado Plateau. It is most prominent in Nevada and Utah, and on transcontinental flights that frequently cross those states the air traveler can count a dozen parallel, uniformly spaced north-south ranges. As many as one hundred are evident in space images of the entire region.

One of the earliest geologists to explore the area, Clarence Edward Dutton, recognized its peculiar geography, although no space photographs were at his disposal, and it had only been provisionally mapped. Dutton was an army major turned geologist who in 1875 joined John Wesley Powell in studying the Rocky Mountains and spent a decade surveying the Colorado Plateau. The Basin and Range Province, he said, looks like ''an army of caterpillars crawling northward out of Mexico.''

The ranges rise several thousand feet above the broad valleys between them that have largely been filled in by sediment. The vertical drop between formations on the plateau and their continuation under the basin sediments south of Phoenix is almost 20,000 feet. Death Valley, where the Basin and Range Province extends into southern California, displays extreme height variations. While it is surrounded by some of the highest mountains on the continent, its floor is 280 feet below sea level and the bedrock under its accumulation of sediments is almost 6,900 feet lower. At the north end of Death Valley is the Last Chance Range and to the south, appropriately named, is the Funeral Range. Flanking the valley are the Amargosa Range on the east and the Panamint Mountains on the west, whose Telescope Peak rises 11,045 feet above sea level. In fact the highest and lowest points in the conterminous United States are essentially within sight of one another. Mount Whitney in the Sierras, rising to 14,495 feet, looks eastward toward Death Valley and westward over King's Canyon National Park and Sequoia National Park—home of the world's largest trees. Death Valley itself probably comes closer to the classic concept of the inferno than any other part of the continent, for its summer temperatures reach 135 degrees Fahrenheit.

Throughout the Basin and Range Province the geologic structures stand out in stark relief because there is so little camouflaging vegetation. None of the meager rain that falls on its central area, the Great Basin, ever reaches the sea. The streams drain into

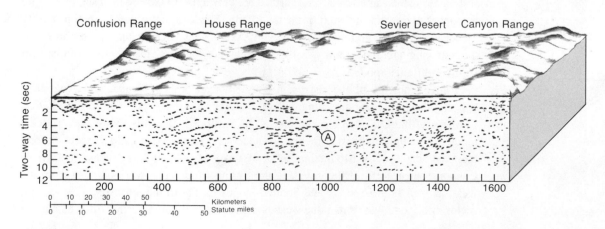

dry valleys or saline lakes. In some places, such as the Pancake Range of central Nevada, lava fields like those on the moon are a reminder that volcanoes have played a part in shaping the land.

Several explanations have been proposed for the spreading that has produced this extraordinary landscape. One theory is the presence beneath it of the spreading center that, beginning thirty million years ago, was overridden by North America. Probably the most popular explanation, however, is also used to account for the opening of the enclosed seas that lie behind such arcs of volcanic islands as Japan. This process of "back-arc spreading" is believed to have gradually carried Japan away from Asia, forming the Sea of Japan. It is proposed that lava from the plate that has pushed under the islands and beyond them rises and spreads under the crust, pulling it apart. Some believe spreading in the Basin and Range Province may have widened the distance between the Colorado Plateau and Sierras by a hundred miles or more and that, had the process continued, the earth's crust might have been torn completely open, forming a sea like that between Japan and the Asian mainland.

The classic view of the region is of alternating blocks that have stood fast or subsided as the region spread. Faults indicating such motions along the edges of the mountains dip steeply—at angles of 50 or 60 degrees. But recent seismic probing by oil companies and by academic geologists indicates that the underlying faults are relatively horizontal, indicative of sliding motions. A COCORP seismic survey, like those that revealed massive overthrusts in the Appalachians, has been conducted along a 105-mile line from the Snake Valley on the Nevada-Utah border eastward across the Sevier Desert to the Canyon Range near the eastern edge of the Great Basin. By allowing more time than in oil prospecting for the vibrations to reflect off very deep layers, the survey was able to chart structures thirty miles down. It traversed the zone where a great slab—the Sevier Overthrust—had previously been pushed eastward and revealed a series of reflecting surfaces sloping down gently from near the surface in the east for about seventy-five miles to the west, reaching depths of ten or twelve miles. There are no signs of those surfaces being broken by vertical motions. Instead it seems the reflecting surfaces mark where layers of the crust have slipped thirty miles westward. Thus thrusts that were earlier pushed scores of miles eastward appear to have been drawn back to the west by the spreading—possibly sliding along the same faults. The surface features appear no more than shallow-depth responses to this pulling apart of the landscape. The idea that it was formed primarily by vertical motions no longer seems valid. As the COCORP group reported in 1983, the "striking lateral continuity" of the deep layers "forces a reevaluation of classical Basin and Range models."

From alignments of the ranges in southern California, Nevada, and Arizona it appears that the first stretching pulled that region southwest. Gordon P. Eaton, formerly of the U.S. Geological Survey, has proposed that this may have "rafted" mountains in the southeast corner of Nevada away from the Colorado Plateau. Among them are the Muddy Mountains between Lake Mead and Las Vegas, the Arrow Canyon Range north of the city, and the Spring Mountains overlooking it from the west, as well as the Specter and Spotted ranges farther to the northwest. The central sector in Nevada was drawn due west as the process migrated northward. The current

Aniakchak Caldera in Alaska's Aleutian Range contains several craters and could hold virtually all of New York's borough of the Bronx. (M. Woodbridge Williams, National Park Service)

tension in northern Nevada appears toward the northwest, the direction of drag by the Pacific Plate.

Land-shaping processes around the edge of the Basin and Range Province still seem to be at work. Along the base of the Wasatch Mountains looking down on Salt Lake City, Ogden, and Provo, Utah, hundreds of earthquakes occur every year (most, but not all, of them small). This zone of seismicity extends north as far as Montana. The largest quakes sometimes raise the Wasatch Mountains and their popular ski areas a little higher, as is evident when looking down from the air at the base of the range. A twenty-foot-wide ribbon of fresh, unweathered rock marks the last uplift. The quake is unrecorded so it must have occurred before Brigham Young led his Mormon pioneers into the valley in 1847.

There is activity, too, on the opposite side of the Basin and Range Province, where uplift in the last few million years made the Sierras one of the grandest ranges on earth and tilted them westward, forming a mighty, east-facing wall 430 miles long. A battle continues to be waged along that front, intermittently producing great eruptions and earthquakes. Yet the combatants are poorly understood. One of the greatest volcanic explosions of the last million years left a huge caldera, or volcanic basin, along the east side of the Sierras. It is in California's Long Valley, east of Yosemite and south of Mono Lake—itself rounded like a crater. The caldera, 20 miles long and 10 miles wide, was formed 700,000 years ago by an explosive eruption estimated to have thrown 140 cubic miles of ash into the sky—600 times more than the 1980 eruption of Mount Saint Helens. After the chamber feeding the eruption had emptied, what remained of the volcano collapsed to form the caldera. The latter now helps provide water for Los Angeles. Inside it is Crowley Reservoir, which drains down Owens Valley into an aqueduct completed in 1913 to carry water 233 miles around the southern curve of the Sierras and across the Mojave Desert to Los Angeles.

The volcano underneath the giant caldera is not dead. A series of earthquakes that began there in 1978 led to a swarm of tremors in May 1980 that culminated in four severe earthquakes within a forty-eight-hour period. There were indications that molten rock, or magma, was moving into a chamber five miles under the caldera. By 1983 surveys showed that a dome produced in the caldera floor by earlier magma intrusions had risen ten inches. Fumaroles ejecting vapors near former eruption sites—including a steaming tree stump—became more active and nearby Hot Creek got hotter.

The geologic record shows there have been a dozen volcanic eruptions in that area during the past 2,000 years, including explosive ones less than 400 years ago, although none in a class with the one that produced the caldera. The most obvious indicator of such past activity to transcontinental air travelers to and from San Francisco is a twenty-mile chain of young craters, lava domes, and flows rising starkly above the forested landscape along a line from Mono Lake, whose islands are lava domes, south to Mammoth Lakes. A highway, U.S. 395, crosses the midpoint of this volcanic chain before continuing south along Owens Valley. The earthquakes were centered near a point under Mammoth Lakes, and press accounts of fears for an eruption there caused consternation among local residents and commercial interests in that ski resort.

There are other indicators that all is not quiet along the front between the Sierras and the Basin and Range Province. That front lies along Owens Valley, which, on March 26, 1872, was struck by what may have been the most severe earthquake to hit

The Mono and Inyo craters with Mono Lake and Route 120 in the foreground and the Sierra Nevada beyond. (U.S. Geological Survey)

Layers typical of the Colorado Plateau have been steeply tilted in Frenchman Mountain, ten miles east of Las Vegas. On the left a counterpart of the Supai formation overlies Redwall limestone. (John S. Shelton)

California since it was settled. Unlike earthquakes associated with the San Andreas Fault and its sister faults on the western side of California, this one was near the Nevada border and its cause is uncertain. At that time the valley was sparsely inhabited, but of fifty-nine houses in Lone Pine, most of them adobe, all but three were destroyed. Displacements of the land, both horizontally and vertically, exceeded twenty feet, as revealed by broken fence lines. A repetition today would be a major disaster.

Farther down the valley, just south of Owens Lake, is the Coso caldera and its volcanic field where increasingly energetic earthquake swarms were recorded in 1981–82, indicating possible movements in a reservoir of molten rock under that area. The fifty-two domes, lava flows, and other volcanic centers there have been produced by eruptions that began more than four million years ago and occurred as recently as 40,000 years before the present. Other volcanic scars are evident on the nearby Mojave Desert.

The chief focus of attention, however, has been on the Long Valley caldera. Four volcano specialists of the U.S. Geological Survey analyzed the situation in 1982, two of whom—Dwight R. Crandall and Donal R. Mullineaux—had published a timely but little heeded warning well in advance of the Mount Saint Helens eruption. The group reported that in the eruption 700,000 years ago massive clouds of hot gas and pumice (pyroclastic flows) swept at speeds well in excess of one hundred miles per

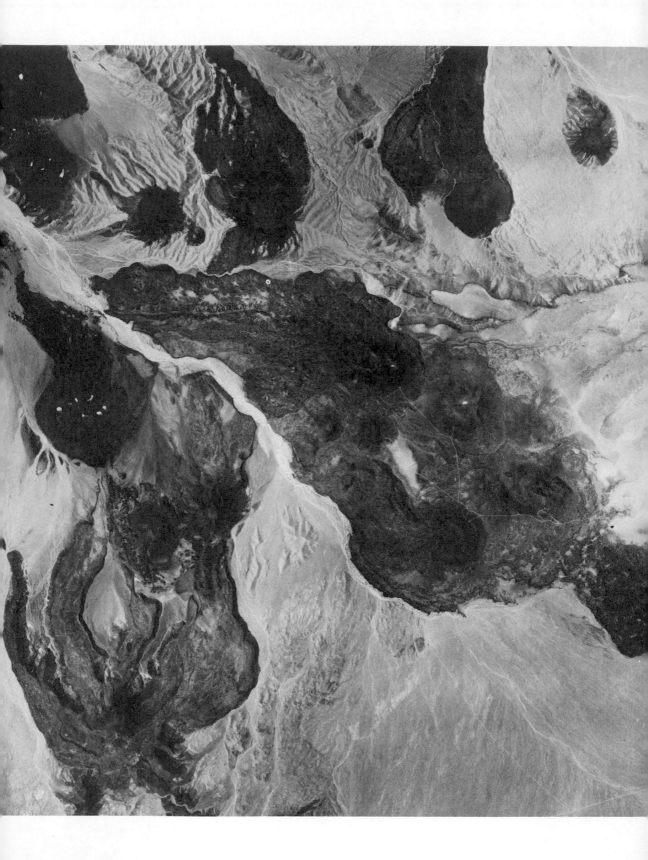

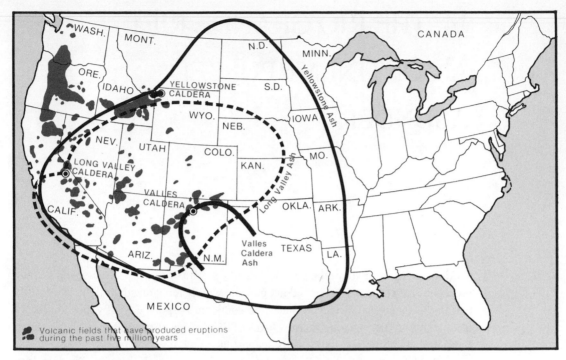

Map labels: WASH. MONT. N.D. MINN. CANADA ORE. IDAHO YELLOWSTONE CALDERA S.D. Yellowstone Ash WYO. NEB. IOWA NEV. UTAH COLO. MO. LONG VALLEY CALDERA KAN. Long Valley Ash CALIF. VALLES CALDERA OKLA. ARK. Valles Caldera Ash TEXAS LA. ARIZ. N.M. MEXICO

Volcanic fields that have produced eruptions during the past five million years

Left: Cinder cones from eruptions near Rainbow Wells, in the Mojave Desert west of Cima, California. (U.S. Geological Survey)

Above: Ash falls from three major calderas. (From "Giant Volcanic Calderas" by Peter Francis, in Scientific American, *June 1983, p. 64. Copyright ©1983 by Scientific American, Inc. All rights reserved.)*

hour over ridges thousands of feet high. One raced at least forty miles down Owens Valley, presumably killing all in its path. Local accumulations of pumice reached depths of 1,000 feet or more. Remains of the ash, known as the Bishop Tuff, can be identified across Arizona, Utah, Colorado, and parts of New Mexico, Wyoming, Missouri, and Kansas. It probably covered most of the United States. Such ash consists largely of microscopic glassy fragments, or shards, and those produced by a particular eruption—or even stage of that eruption—have certain identifiable characteristics, such as the refractive index and composition of the glass. In this way volcanologists have been able to trace, even in deep-sea sediments, the spread of ash from specific eruptions, such as the one on the Aegean island of Santorini in 1450 B.C. that may have given birth to the Atlantis legend and, some believe, caused the downfall of the Minoan civilization.

The volcanologists found no signs of an imminent eruption and concluded that if one occurs it is far more likely to be comparable with the 1980 Mount Saint Helens event than that which produced the Long Valley caldera. They pointed out, however, that the likelihood of so colossal an eruption "cannot be calculated with the data now available." Furthermore, they said, "A catastrophic eruption of a volcano like that of 700,000 years ago has occurred nowhere in the world during historic time, so the kinds and timing of precursory events and the full range of possible consequences cannot be anticipated."

14 THE RIO GRANDE RIFT—
A CONTINENT PULLED
ASUNDER

Although Warren Hamilton and W. Bradley Myers of the U.S. Geological Survey proposed it as early as 1966, it did not become widely recognized until the late 1970's that in the southwestern United States the continent is split by a rift valley similar to the one that cradles the long, narrow lakes of East Africa or the 500-mile cleft holding Lake Baikal in Siberia—the world's deepest lake with one fifth of all the fresh water on earth. All three rifts, as well as the lower Rhine Valley in Europe, are lines of deep cleavage where forces within the earth apparently have tried—unsuccessfully—to tear a continent apart. The scars of another such abortive cleavage may lie beneath sediments of the Middle West, where a sharply defined zone of abnormally intense gravity, the Mid-Continent Gravity High, runs from Minnesota to Oklahoma. The African, Baikal, and Rio Grande rifts have in common a number of characteristics: abnormally frequent earthquakes, high flow of heat through their floors, evidence of recent crustal movements, volcanic activity, and high electrical conductivity of the zone beneath them, suggesting the presence of molten or semimolten rock.

The waters of the Rio Grande originate in Colorado, following the rift south across New Mexico to El Paso, where the river becomes the boundary between Mexico and Texas. Some of the rift's features continue on into Mexico. It began opening in the south thirty-two million years ago and within five million years was splitting the landscape as far north as the Colorado mining town of Leadville in the Rockies. From there the rift now runs south through the upper valley of the Arkansas River and into New Mexico via the San Luis Valley between the San Juan Mountains on the west and the wall of the Sangre de Cristo Mountains, a 220-mile arc of glistening snowy peaks "curved like a bejeweled cutlass." Father Valverde, a Spanish priest, on first seeing the mountains, allegedly exclaimed *"Sangre de Cristo!"* ("Christ's Blood!"). The west front of the range was sharply outlined when the rift west of it subsided radically. Beneath its sediments the floor is close to five miles below sea level.

The northern part of the Rio Grande rift, lined with picturesque pueblos such as those near Taos, Santa Fe, and Albuquerque, has been a favorite human habitat for thousands of years. Its stark beauty inspired the painter Georgia O'Keeffe to make her home there in the village of Abiquiu. While the upper Rio Grande Valley evokes memories of Spanish conquest and Indian massacres, its southern end spreads into broad, parallel plains with more contemporary links. On remote flats near Alamogordo the world's first atomic bomb was detonated on July 16, 1945. Less than a year later, at nearby White Sands Missile Range, the exploration of space began with a series of attempts to launch captured German V-2 rockets. After five failures one of them made the first observations from above the atmosphere. As recently as April 1981, a crowd of engineers, medical men, and media representatives gathered before sunrise on the edge of an extra-long runway leveled on the hard-packed gypsum sands of the missile range to await a possible emergency landing of the space shuttle *Columbia,* then on its first flight. We witnessed a desert dawn in which the far-reaching sands and, beyond them in the west, the long line of the San Andres Mountains turned from purple-black under the dome of stars to pink and then red, the sands finally becoming dazzling white under full sunlight. The shuttle, however, landed as scheduled at Edwards Air Force Base in California.

From Socorro, eighty miles south of Albuquerque, one branch of the rift extends southwest to become the Plains of San Augustin. That broad, flat area, ringed by distant mountains, was chosen, because of its remoteness from human activity, for the world's largest and most powerful array of radio telescopes—the Very Large Array, or VLA, with twenty-seven dishes, each eighty-two feet in diameter, mounted along a Y-shaped rail system each of whose three arms is twelve or thirteen miles long.

It seems likely that the Rio Grande rift, flanking the Colorado Plateau on the east, was opened by the same forces that pulled apart the Basin and Range Province to the west of that plateau. The plateau itself, having resisted crumpling, also refused to be pulled apart. As with the other rift valleys, the history of this one has been a tale of repeated and often colossal volcanic eruptions. They began pouring forth lava about the time that the Mogollon Rim was being inundated more than one hundred miles to the west. Once the Rio Grande, as a newborn river, made its way to the Gulf of Mexico, its flow was sometimes blocked temporarily by such eruptions. Driving along Interstate 25 between Santa Fe and Albuquerque, one may not be overly impressed by the long, level horizons to the west, broken only here and there by volcanic cones, until one realizes those are vast lava flows.

Evidence of eruptions is visible the full length of the valley, but nowhere more dramatically than beyond its western rim in the Valles Caldera, a giant basin in the Jemez Mountains 35 miles northwest of Los Alamos. With an area of 180 square miles it is one of the largest calderas on earth—even larger than the Long Valley caldera far to the west. A series of tremendous eruptions, many of them explosive, began in those mountains twelve million years ago and reached a climax in a series of paroxysmal eruptions, little more than a million years ago, that produced a volcano perhaps 12,000 feet high. Then, after the deep-seated magma chamber under it had emptied, the entire structure collapsed, leaving the caldera. From heat flowing up through its floor and other measurements it is assumed that a residue of partially molten rock with a radius of a dozen miles lies under it. Unlike the situation at the Long Valley caldera, however, there are no hints of restiveness. The surface of the basin shows little evidence of its wild past. It is now one vast, peaceful ranch—a

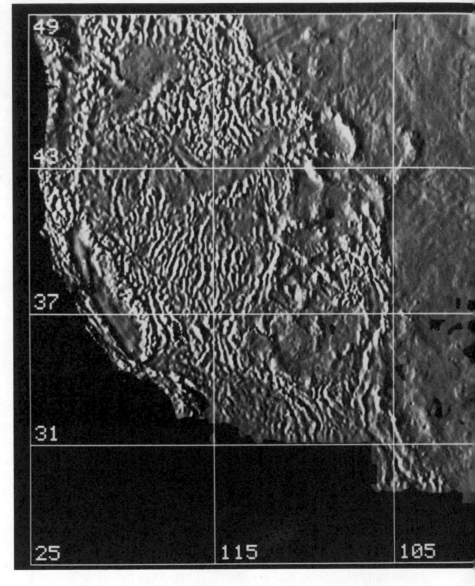

grassland bowl intruded by a number of cinder cones or plugs of volcanic rock. The immense size of this caldera is brought home when, from the overlook on a highway skirting its rim, one observes how tiny the cattle seem grazing its floor. Attempts have been made to derive geothermal energy from its edges by drilling in search of steam. The nearby Los Alamos National Laboratory has also experimented with a technique in which two holes are drilled into the hot formation and water pressure is used to crack rock between the holes. Water sent down one hole then percolates through the cracks and emerges from the other hole as steam. Initial tests were successful, but whether this will become an economic source of energy remains uncertain.

The eruptions of this volcano blanketed the Southwest, filling much of the rift in

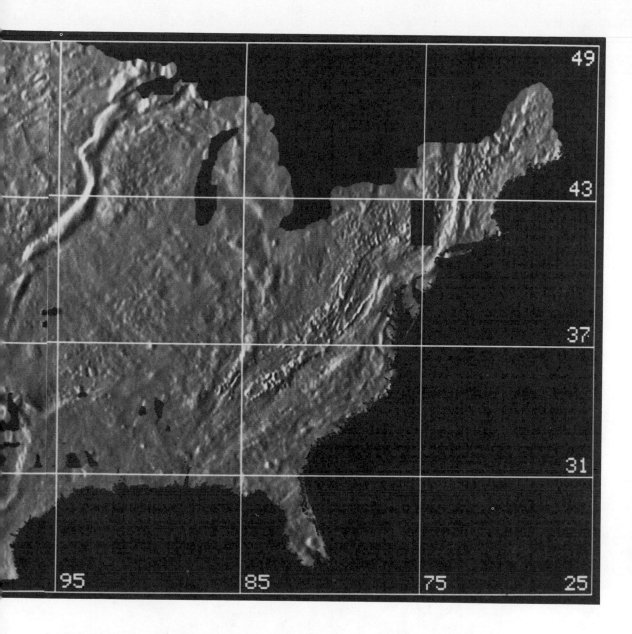

the Los Alamos region. En route up from the Rio Grande Valley to that research community where the first atomic bomb was developed, the highway climbs through layer upon layer of solidified ash—the Bandelier tuff—deeply incised by canyons in whose cliffs prehistoric Indians carved the dwellings of Bandelier National Monument. Measurements of radioactive decay in these layers have shown they were laid down between 1.1 and 1.4 million years ago. Cinder cones within the caldera, however, were formed as recently as 40,000 years ago.

There are many other focal regions of volcanic activity along the rift, as on the Taos Plateau and farther north in the Questa area on the western flank of the Sangre de Cristo Mountains. The latter, themselves lifted to their present height during the past twenty million years, include New Mexico's highest summit, Wheeler Peak, looking down on Taos from 13,151 feet. The highest summit of that range, farther north in Colorado, is Blanca Peak, a 14,317-foot giant.

The volcanic fields near Taos and Questa were active as early as twenty-six million years ago. More recent lava flows stand out dramatically when seen from the air, especially farther south where they crawl across the otherwise featureless plains. The Malpais lava beds that pass five miles west of Carrizozo, New Mexico, are described in a tourist brochure, with some justification, as "one of the most forbidding places nature ever built." The flow, forty-four miles long and as much as five miles wide, can be viewed by motorists at Valley of Fires State Park, where it is crossed by U.S. Highway 380. Indian legend has it that this was once a "valley of fires," implying that early Indians may have witnessed the eruption.

Volcanic activity along the rift has occurred as far south as Los Muertos Basin in the Mexican state of Chihuahua, forty miles south of Columbus, New Mexico. Such activity in the rift may not have ended. One of the most remarkable discoveries to come out of COCORP probing and other seismic soundings has been detection of what appears a great body of molten rock at least seventeen miles long and twelve miles wide lying a dozen miles beneath the rift between Socorro and Belen, fifty miles to the north. It is believed to be no more than a half-mile thick—a modern analogue of horizontal lava intrusions that in the past have hardened into sills of basalt like the one whose edge forms the Hudson River Palisades. The molten rock beneath the Rio Grande rift appears to be leaking upward into reservoirs from which it may some day erupt. However, recent surveys across the rift have shown no signs of marked spreading, and the tremors that usually precede an eruption have not been observed.

15 FROM INCONSEQUENCE TO MAGNIFICENCE–THE SOUTHERN ROCKY MOUNTAINS

Scenery on so grand a scale as that of the Colorado Rockies had to be formed by processes heroic in their dimensions. The rocks do, indeed, record epic periods of mountain-building, volcanic eruptions on a scale unknown today, and counterattacks by ice, wind, water, and time. For most of the past few hundred million years there were no mountains in the present area of the southern Rockies. Once the Ancestral Rockies had eroded into insignificance, as noted earlier, the region was largely covered by shallow seas. Yet, by the time pioneers first sighted the Front Range, compression followed by uplift had produced some of the grandest mountains on earth.

Their initial formation—the so-called Laramide Revolution—began some eighty million years ago as the Farallon Plate, burrowing under the West Coast, created inexorable pressure against the continent. This, it is now widely believed, drove the Colorado Plateau northeast, compressing the land beyond. Then, in the last few million years, the entire region was lifted a mile or more, converting mountains of modest elevation to the magnificent ones of today.

That uplift must have been in some way an aftermath of the continent's overriding of Pacific floor. Initially volcanic eruptions in the southern Rocky Mountain region were of the type that occurs over a descending oceanic plate, as in the Andes or Cascades. When the scenario changed and such subduction tapered off, giving way to northwest wrenching by the Pacific Plate, many of the eruptions shifted to the fluid kind that floods large areas with basalt.

This still does not account for the tremendous uplift of the High Plains and mountain states in the past few million years. Some of the Rockies were raised until they eroded down to what had been their deep cores of granite and gneiss, as in the 1,200-square-mile block near the south end of the Front Range whose summit, Pikes Peak, overlooks Colorado Springs and the Air Force Academy. Neither that mountain nor Mount Evans, part of a similar granitic block farther up the range opposite Denver, is very steep-sided, and highways reach both summits, the road to the 14,264-foot top of Mount Evans being the highest in the United States. Analysis of the massive granite bodies, or batholiths, in the Front Range has shown that they solidified deep in the earth more than a billion years ago. So high have they been lifted that in most areas all the formations above them have worn away.

Along their eastern front their rise has bent sedimentary layers of the adjacent plains upward until they protrude as vertical walls. Between Denver and the mountains such hogbacks run parallel to the range for miles, their jagged edges rising like the backs of dinosaurs in grand procession. They also appear in the Garden of the Gods farther south, near Colorado Springs. Hogbacks poke out of the flat plains along the Rampart Range and Wet Mountains—southward extensions of the Front Range—and along its northward continuation into Wyoming, where it splits into the Medicine Bow Mountains on the west and the Laramie Range looking down on the city of that name and Interstate 80. Before the days of high-flying jets, westbound planes taking off from Denver first flew north to make an end run around those ranges, since Medicine Bow Peak rises above 12,000 feet.

Straddling the northern part of the Front Range west of Estes Park is Rocky Mountain National Park—395 square miles of high mountains, including 14,256-foot Long's Peak and fourteen summits over 13,000 feet. Among the most wonder-filled drives in America is Trail Ridge Road, which for 11 miles remains above the 11,000-foot timber line, surrounded by snowy mountains. The park as a whole, with 300 miles of hiking trails, is a paradise of mountain lakes, cascading streams, and alpine meadows. On its west edge the Never Summer Mountains form the continental divide, water from one side draining to the Gulf of Mexico and from the other down the Colorado River to the Gulf of California.

For the motorist who has spent long days crossing the Great Plains westbound a first sight of the Front Range, spanning the western horizon like a mighty rampart, is an exhilarating experience. For 600 miles beyond the Missouri River the terrain has largely been flat—although imperceptibly uphill—climbing almost 5,000 feet so gradually that the driver is unlikely to notice it. This great ramp, leading to the

The Front Range of the Rockies seen from the east between Denver and Colorado Springs. (U.S. Geological Survey)

mountains, was raised by the same puzzling process that in the past few million years has lifted the entire Rocky Mountain region, initiating erosion that cut some mountains down to their root and carved river valleys into some of the most dramatic canyons on the continent.

Unlike other parts of the Rocky Mountain system, the ranges in Colorado are packed closely together. Instead of broad basins between them there are what John Wesley Powell referred to as "parks"—bottomlands hemmed in by forested slopes that cling to rocky heights. Between the Front Range and the next rank of mountains to the west, for example, are North Park, Middle Park, and South Park. Such abrupt up-and-down landscapes are a delight to mountain lovers but a challenge to builders of highways and railroads.

There are no easy routes across the Front Range. Interstate 70, heading west from Denver, must cross Loveland Pass, although the Eisenhower Memorial Tunnel avoids the 12,000-foot summit. Between the Rampart Range and Wet Mountains the Arkansas River has cut Royal Gorge (also known as the Grand Canyon of the Arkansas), which is spanned by a toll bridge suspended more than 1,000 feet above the river. The towering walls of pink granite hug the river so closely that the tracks of the Denver and Rio Grande Western Railroad have had to be built out over the rushing water. In the heyday of railroading the trip through Royal Gorge was one of the treats of transcontinental travel.

In the second line of mountains, paralleling the Front Range to the west, the Park Range reaches north into Wyoming. U.S. 40 crosses it southeast of Steamboat Springs at Rabbit Ears Pass, made memorable for my family when an overheated engine blew off the hose of its cooling system high above any source of replacement water. Interstate 70 crosses the southern extension of these mountains, known there as the Gore Range, over 11,000-foot Vail Pass near the ski resort of that name.

The mountains continue south as the Sawatch Range, whose Mount Elbert, at 14,431 feet, is highest in the United States Rockies, and there are a dozen other peaks over 14,000 feet including those named Columbia, Princeton, Harvard, and Yale. The last two were christened in 1869 when graduates of the Harvard Mining School visited the area, the other Ivy League names being added later.

The Sawatch Range is the central remnant of an enormous, elongated dome raised by the Laramide Revolution. When the eastern flank of the dome was split open by the Rio Grande rift to form what became the valley of the upper Arkansas River, part of this great structure was cut off from the main body and survives to the east as the Mosquito Range. Its rock layers slope down to the the east—testimony to their former link with the giant Sawatch dome. A highway beginning in the Arkansas Valley near Leadville climbs over the Sawatch via 12,000-foot Independence Pass and drops down into Aspen amidst mountains that in part are eroded remnants of that same structure.

Aspen was founded in 1878 as a silver and lead mining center. Its population reached 15,000, then plummeted when the mines gave out. Now, as gateway to a number of recreation areas, it is frequented by large numbers of skiers and other vacationers. Like nearby Snowmass, it is also a popular setting for executive conferences.

Hebgen Lake

ABSAROKA
RANGE

BIG HORN MOUNTAINS

Yellowstone Lake

Craters
of the Moon

Jackson Lake

WIND RIVER
RANGE

LARAMIE MOUNTAINS

Snake River Plain

WYOMING
RANGE

Bear Lake

Green River
Basin

MEDICINE BOW MOUNTAIN

NORTH PARK

Great Salt Lake

Flaming Gorge
Reservoir

PARK RANGE

UINTA MTS.

Denver

WASATCH RANGE

Green River

Pikes Peak

ELK
MOUNTAINS

Grand Junction

SAN JUAN MOUNTAINS

RANGE

Colorado River

San Luis Valley

Glen Canyon

Durango

Favorite trails for pack trips and backpackers thread through the mountains behind Aspen and, beyond, through the Crested Butte resort area. The summits include Snowmass Peak, named for the great sheet of snow trapped between its twin summits, the Maroon Bells, massive Castle Peak, and Pyramid Peak. Some of these mountains have been lifted with their horizontal bedding intact, like tall slices of rocky layer cake, but as with many of the Rockies, glaciers have clawed and whittled their sides until some have been carved into horns almost as sharp as the Tetons or the Matterhorn—the classic example of such ice action.

This region was radically transformed by volcanic eruptions during and subsequent to the Laramide period. A huge volcano formed on top of Mount Princeton. Basalt now caps many of the later uplifted mountains. The Grizzly Peak caldera near Independence Pass is the remnant of a volcano that must have blanketed a large part of the area. Along the Roaring Fork River, between Aspen and Glenwood Springs, eruptions from a 1,400-foot volcanic dome repeatedly filled the valley. The town there is appropriately named Basalt, as is the town of Marble, on the other side of the Elk Mountains, whose quarries provided the stone for the Lincoln Memorial in Washington.

The last identified eruption in this area occurred 4,000 years ago at the junction of the Colorado and Eagle rivers on Interstate 70 between Eagle and Glenwood Springs. Hot springs throughout the region indicated residual ferment below. North of the Colorado River's Glenwood Canyon layer upon layer of basalt covers the Flat Tops area. Grand Mesa south of the river, claimed as the largest flat-topped mountain in the United States, is the eroded remnant of a structure formed in much the same way.

East of the Sangre de Cristo Mountains, in the coal-rich Raton Basin, another volcanic center has left twin 13,000-foot structures that, standing in relative isolation, form a striking landmark from the air. They are known today as the Spanish Peaks, although to the Indians they were *Huajatolla*—"Breasts of the Earth." Their eruption cracked open the crust along lines radiating in all directions so that the peaks stand at the convergence of numerous basalt dikes, formed as lava congealed in the cracks. As

Left: The central and southern Rocky Mountains as seen from space. (Landsat mosaic by Agricultural Stabilization and Conservation Service, U.S. Department of Agriculture)

Right: Castle Peak in the Elk Mountains. (W. H. Jackson, U.S. Geological Survey)

The Maroon Bells in Colorado's Elk Mountains. (Ansel Adams in Portfolio VI, *New York: Parasc Press, 1974.)*

it cooled the lava baked adjacent coal deposits into coke. Erosion has left some dikes standing as high walls. One, because of its odd formation, is known as the Devil's Staircase. Another has been tunneled for passage of a local highway. The Crazy Mountains, a similarly isolated feature north of the Yellowstone River in southwest Montana, are also formed of material from a single gigantic volcano that erupted, intermittently, for several million years early in the Laramide Revolution. There, too, dikes radiate many miles in all directions, crossing a broad plain buried in the volcano's own debris. The youngest volcano in the Raton Basin is Capulin Mountain, a national monument, which erupted as recently as 2,000 years ago.

Roughly one quarter of Colorado is underlain by coal, much of it too deep to be currently tempting, but the basin east of the Spanish Peaks has been intensively mined. Its coal was shipped on the Atchison, Topeka and Santa Fe to industries in the East, and it also provided fuel for that railroad's locomotives, just as coal from the Hanna Basin, along the line of the Union Pacific in southeast Wyoming, powered that railroad's trains over the continental divide.

The Spanish Peaks looked down on what some consider to have been the fiercest fighting in the history of American unionism, and fortifications built by the coal companies can still be seen along roads there. The climax came in 1914 after a four-year strike by the United Mine Workers in which a number of lives had been lost on both sides. The strikers, evicted from company housing, had built a tent city at Ludlow, and during a running battle between militiamen and strikers the tents were set afire. Thirteen women and children who had sought refuge in pits under the tents were suffocated in what came to be known as the Ludlow Massacre.

Volcanically speaking, Colorado's big show was in the southwest, leaving as its monuments the San Juan Mountains. To my mind they are the most "Alpine" of the southern Rockies. Early in the Laramide Revolution a highland was formed there and some eruptions occurred, but it was after the onset of widespread eruptions in the Southwest, between twenty-six and thirty-five million years ago, that huge volcanoes formed, pouring out lava and an estimated 1,000 cubic miles of ash. The result was a plateau of basalt and consolidated ash (tuff) at least a mile thick that has now been eroded into the San Juan Mountains. Such erosion to the east has exposed the Needle Mountains, older features that had been engulfed by the volcanic outpourings. Ouray, squeezed into a narrow valley through the San Juan Mountains, is, with its thermal baths, like a small Alpine health resort. South of there, beyond Red Mountain Pass, is Silverton, linked with Durango, still farther south, by a narrow gauge railroad. The latter's antiquated cars take visitors on a forty-five-mile ride along the gorge of the Animas River. On the west side of the mountains the mining town of Telluride stands in the shadow of Mount Sneffels, whose horizontal bedding shows how high the lava deposits have been raised. Although Telluride and Ouray lie on opposite sides of a great mountain mass, they are linked by a network of tunnels cut by the Idarado Mining Company.

These towns all prospered when gold and silver from Colorado's mineral belt were making a few prospectors and many investors rich. That belt, which long played a dominant role in the state's history, runs diagonally northeast from the San Juan Mountains to the Front Range, cutting all the ranges "against the grain." It passes through such mining centers as Leadville, Central City, Georgetown, and Idaho Springs, as well as the picturesque town of Gold Hill, which, although now more a suburb of Boulder than a mining town, has retained its log houses and pioneer atmosphere. Except near Leadville the mineral belt is no more than a few miles wide. Why it cuts across the Rocky Mountain system in this manner is not clear. As the precious metals gave out, the emphasis changed to mining copper and lead. For a time the mine at Climax, near the summit of Fremont Pass across the Park Range, produced 90 percent of the world's molybdenum, helping make the American Metal Climax Company (AMAX) one of the nation's most prosperous. The only important metal mines outside the mineral belt were at Cripple Creek near the Pikes Peak batholith and were for a time the world's richest source of gold. In 1894 and again from 1903 to 1904 Cripple Creek was also a scene of labor-management violence and loss of life.

16 IN SEARCH OF
FUEL AND FOSSILS—
THE WYOMING BASINS

Between the southern Rockies and the northward continuation of those mountains lies a region of high plains and basins, most of which are in Wyoming. When crossing that state by car there can be long stretches when mountains are barely visible on the horizon. It was the ideal route for pioneers as well as for the first transcontinental railroad (the Union Pacific) and for Interstate 80. Not until those traveling west on the Oregon Trail had crossed South Pass at the southern end of Wyoming's Wind River Range and reached the mountains at the western end of the state did they have to do much climbing.

The Green River Basin, largest of them all, occupies most of the southwest quadrant of Wyoming and neighboring areas of Colorado and Utah. After the seas had retreated and raising of the landscape cut drainage routes, a number of large lakes formed. The floor of the Green River Basin, as well as other basins to the north and south, accumulated some of the world's major deposits of oil-bearing shale. These many-layered formations have been bent upward around the rims of the basins, forming structures whose linearity seems quite extraordinary from the air, particularly when the land is snow-covered and a low sun has cast them in bold relief. It is as though a stack of huge pancakes had been dropped into a pan too small for them, whereupon their upturned edges around the rim were trimmed to roughly the same height. The lowest layers will protrude vertically around the edge of the pan, forming a succession of hogbacks. The topmost layers will be less sharply upturned, their edges standing as little cliffs. Such structures, with a cliff on one side but only a gentle slope on the other, are known as cuestas. Both hogbacks and cuestas abound in the Wyoming basins. The aerial observer is likely to be even more puzzled by the patterns produced by strip mines and their spoil. About 40 percent of the state is underlain by coal and a number of strip mines are in operation.

Deposits in this region provide one of the world's most complete records of animal evolution from the dinosaur era to the present, and this has helped fuel the debate concerning dinosaur extinctions. Rocky Mountain deposits from the Cretaceous (Chalky) Period, when water covered much of the world, show those seas to have been inhabited by giant swimming reptiles such as the ichthyosaur and plesiosaur. In

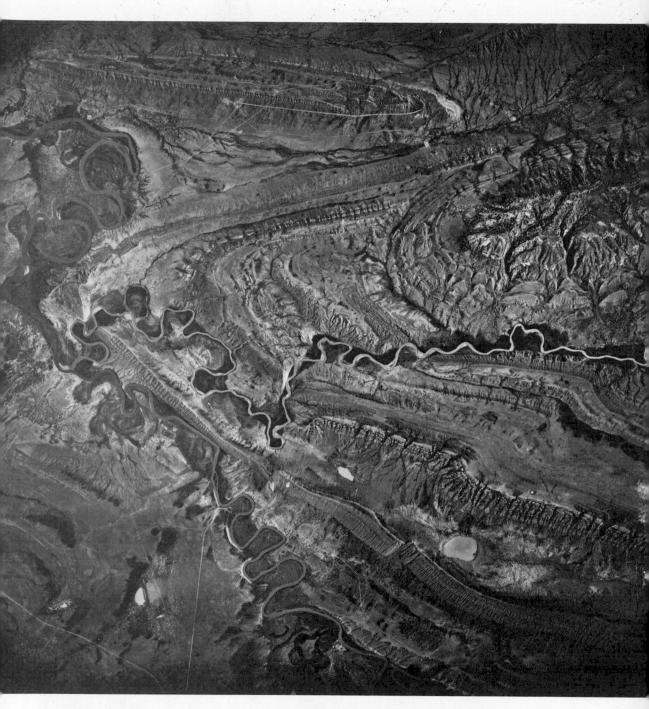

Two great anticlines, or upward folds, dominate this region north of the Medicine Bow Mountains in Wyoming. The long, narrow Oil Springs Anticline at the top of this aerial photo has been producing oil since 1918. White lines are roads leading to the wells. Below is the Flat Top Anticline whose forested summit, right center, is Pine Butte. The Little Medicine Bow River snakes across it to join the Medicine Bow River on the left. Sandstone layers exposed along flanks of this anticline are cut by numerous gullies resembling gaps between teeth of a comb. (U.S. Geological Survey)

the air were a variety of flying reptiles. The land was dominated by such formidable-looking (though plant-eating) dinosaurs as triceratops, a massive animal with a small horn on its nose, two long horns above its eyes, and a bony frill around its neck. Yet deposits almost immediately above those containing these remains show mammals and more modern plants. It would seem that the dinosaurs vanished "overnight," geologically speaking. The discovery in various parts of the world of high levels of iridium in thin deposits marking the end of the Cretaceous Period has led to the proposition that an asteroid hit the earth some sixty-five million years ago, causing a catastrophic explosion that filled the stratosphere with dust, cutting off sunlight long enough to wipe out the dinosaurs and many other species. Iridium is far more common in meteorites—and presumably asteroids—than in surface rocks of the earth. Some geologists, however, still believe the extinctions were more gradual and unrelated to an impact.

Evolution of the mammals that followed disappearance of the dinosaurs is well documented in the Rockies. At the time that a great lake occupied the Green River Basin there were palm trees growing along Puget Sound and in southern Alaska. Through humid forests in the region southwest of the Wyoming basins, now occupied by the Uinta Mountains, roamed grotesque plant-eaters—giant saber-toothed animals

Right: The layers of Sinclair Dome, six miles east of Rawlins, Wyoming, have been exposed like those in an onion whose top has been cut off. (John S. Shelton)

Left: Layers arched to produce Wyoming's Sheep Mountain stand exposed. (John S. Shelton)

with six horns, called uintatheriums by modern paleontologists. There were fleet-footed rhinoceroses (*hyrachyus*), early forms of the elephant-sized titanothere, catlike predators (*patriofelis*), several early rodents, and a lemur-type primate (*smilodectes*—closest to the human line of evolution). Particularly notable was little *eohippus,* the "dawn horse." It had four toes and was no larger than a dog, but in that region it evolved through a succession of three-toed species to the single-toed form that is the modern horse. When mountains rising to the west cut off rain clouds, the region became arid and leafy vegetation grew scarce. Large browsing mammals became extinct, but not the little horses that could crop dry grasses and survive cold winters. They may have roamed the prairies until the first human hunters crossed the Bering Land Bridge from Asia. None, however, remained when the first Europeans arrived. Nor did the camels, tigers, mastodons, mammoths, giant sloths, and other huge animals that still inhabited America when human beings entered the continent. Their disappearance with arrival of human hunters may have been more than coincidental.

The completeness of evolutionary history in this region is due in part to repeated depositions of volcanic ash, each of which buried and preserved a snapshot of life as it existed then. Some deposits covered more than half the Rocky Mountain area. Because the layers can be dated, they serve as numbered pages of life's history. Nowhere is this more dramatically illustrated than in the petrified forests of Yellowstone Park. The better known Petrified Forest of Arizona is not, strictly speaking, a forest. It is the product of ancient floods that carried logs downstream and buried them. In Yellowstone the remains stand where they grew, preserved as forests of

stony stumps. Furthermore, at least twenty-seven layers have been preserved, one atop the other, representing a record of about 20,000 years of growth, burial, and regrowth. The succession of forests, a layer cake 1,200 feet thick, has been exposed by water action near the Lamar River in northeast Yellowstone Park. Each layer of volcanic ash down the steep slope has been eroded away enough to reveal a few stumps of the forest that it buried. This has exposed a succession of terraces with the fossilized stumps of trees that grew there some 50 million years ago. Each forest was buried by about 15 feet of ash, and from modern analogues it is thought about two centuries passed before a new forest began growing atop that ash layer. From annual growth rings in the stumps it appears the forests often grew for 500 years before the next volcanic deluge.

When William Henry Holmes, an artist with a government survey expedition, discovered and sketched the forests in the 1870's, he reported that the bleached trunks "stand out on the ledges like the columns of a ruined temple." Erling Dorf of Princeton University spent the summers of 1954 through 1963 studying the deposits and at one point was kind enough to lead my family to the area on horseback. Even the youngest member of our tribe was impressed by the sight of twenty-seven ancient

Left: Little Dome is in the Wind River Indian Reservation east of the Wind River Range. (U.S. Geological Survey)

Right: At least twenty-seven fossil forests atop one another have been identified in Yellowstone Park. (From "The Petrified Forests in Yellowstone National Park" by Erling Dorf, in Scientific American, *April 1964, p. 110. Copyright © 1964 by Scientific American, Inc. All rights reserved.)*

forests, stacked one atop the other. Dorf and his students have been able to identify more than one hundred different species of fossil plant and thus develop a remarkably complete picture of the forests through which little *eohippus* wandered. They were typical of a warmer, moister climate than that of today, with fig trees, tropical breadfruit, magnolias, and the like, as well as the oaks, maples, redwoods, syca-mores, and various evergreens of temperate latitudes. He found that dissolving away the quartz that had filled the cellular structure of the petrified wood produced a residue that could be sliced and prepared for study in the same manner as modern wood.

While many of the coal deposits are in the basins, the search for oil is in the region where shoving from the west produced great overthrusts, analogous to those that led to revived oil prospecting in the southern Appalachians. During and before the Laramide Revolution, great sheets of shallow-water coastal formations were shoved east across portions of Utah, Wyoming, Idaho, Montana, and western Canada. Just how far they were transported is not yet certain, but in some areas geologists are talking of 150 miles or more.

The thrusting and folding has left a succession of north-south ranges and thrust fronts from Alberta to Utah that are currently the focus of intense searches for oil. Along the Utah-Wyoming border fifteen new oil fields were discovered in the late 1970's. Alberta has become so oil-rich that it is tilting the Canadian economy westward. The resources of the entire region can help defer a major energy crisis.

17 THE CENTRAL ROCKIES–
DIAMONDS AND MOUNTAINS
ON THE MAKE

Wrapped around the Wyoming basins on the west and north are some of North America's grandest ranges, here defined as the Central Rockies. In the west are the Uinta (pronounced *You-in-tuh*) Mountains, one of the few east-west ranges in the conterminous United States, running from northwest Colorado into Utah along the southern boundary of Wyoming. They began forming some seventy million years ago, early in the Laramide Revolution, probably as the Colorado Plateau, pressing from the south, caused humping and overthrusting of sandstones and other sedimentary rocks. The rock layers are vividly evident in the walls of such massive mountains as 12,825-foot Red Castle.

The mountains are divided into two parts with the Green River flowing between them. The western half is highest, with forty-three miles of its crest forming a ridge almost entirely above timberline.

One of the first to explore the mountains was Samuel Franklin Emmons, who accompanied the Geological Survey of the 40th Parallel, an expedition led by Clarence King, who later became first director of the U.S. Geological Survey. In the late 1860's and early 1870's the expedition assessed mineral resources within a zone one hundred miles wide from eastern Colorado to the California border along the route of the Union Pacific Railroad, then nearing completion. ''The scenery of this elevated region,'' Emmons wrote of the Uintas, ''is singularly wild and picturesque, both in form and coloring. In the higher portions of the range, where the forest growth is extremely scanty, the effect is that of desolate grandeur; but in the lower basinlike valleys, which support a heavy growth of coniferous trees, the view of one of these mountain lakes, with its deep-green water and fringe of meadowland, set in a sombre frame of pine forests, the whole enclosed by high walls of reddish-purple rock, whose horizontal bedding gives almost the appearance of a pile of Cyclopean masonry, forms a picture of rare beauty.''

Among the most impressive features of the Uintas are the canyons that cross them. As the Colorado Plateau and nearby Rockies rose to their present elevation, in the last few million years, their rivers cut more than two dozen gorges, including some of the most scenic canyons on earth. Among them, in addition to the Grand Canyon, are the

Royal Gorge of the Arkansas and the Black Canyon of the Gunnison River—both very different from the Grand Canyon, being narrow and steep-walled, cut into granites and other resistant materials. From its rim the Black Canyon of the Gunnison seems almost bottomless—somber yet strangely beautiful.

Less well known, but comparably dramatic, are canyons carved through the Uintas by the Yampa and Green rivers. The first expedition into them by boat was that of Powell, who, in 1869, set out downstream from Green River Station in Wyoming Territory, on the newly completed Union Pacific. Powell was deeply impressed by the scene ahead of his little group. ''Away to the south,'' he wrote in his diary, ''the Uinta Mountains stretch in a long line; high peaks thrust into the sky, and snow-fields glittering like lakes of molten silver; and pine forests in somber green; and rosy clouds playing around the borders of huge, black masses; and heights and clouds, and mountains and snow-fields, and forests and rocklands, are blended into one grand view.''

As they came nearer they saw a brilliant red gorge—Navaho sandstone on top of the Chinle and Moenkopi formations in numerous shades of red, ocher, and orange.

Right: Red Castle Peak in the Uinta Mountains is formed of uniformly flat-lying beds. (W. R. Hansen, U.S. Geological Survey)

Left: The Styglan depths of the Black Canyon of the Gunnison River. (National Park Service)

"This," wrote Powell, "is where the river enters the mountain range—the head of the first canyon we are to explore, or, rather, an introductory canyon to a series made by the river through the range. We have named it 'Flaming Gorge.' " The canyon is now shallower by one third, having been flooded by waters backed up from the Flaming Gorge Dam.

Powell traversed seven magnificent canyons on his journey through the Uintas and gave most of them the names they bear today. Red Canyon, immediately below Flaming Gorge Dam, is cut deeply into very ancient sandstones. This thirty-mile stretch was the expedition's first encounter with rapids, which tend to occur where flash floods on side streams have swept rocks into the river. Powell called this "Canyon of the Rapids." It opens into a broad, mountain-walled valley known as Browns Park, where, at the turn of the century, Butch Cassidy and his "Wild Bunch" are said to have hidden between raids into nearby areas of Wyoming, Utah, and Colorado.

Farther downstream Ladore Canyon is entered via a magnificent portal known as the Gates of Ladore. The sun was setting as Powell gazed toward that entrance from their camp. "The vermilion gleams and rosy hues, the green and gray tints are changing to sombre brown above and black shadows below," he wrote. "Now 'tis a black portal to a region of gloom. And that is the gateway through which we enter our voyage of exploration tomorrow—and what shall we find?"

What they found was near disaster. Usually, when the rapids became dangerous, Powell ordered the boats to land and scouted ahead on foot, but this time one of the following boats did not see the warning signal. "I turned just to see the boat strike a rock and throw the men and cargo out," Powell recorded. "Still they clung to her sides and clambered in again and saved part of the oars, but she was full of water, and they could not manage her. Still down the river they went, two or three hundred yards, to another rocky rapid just as bad, and the boat struck again amidships, and was dashed to pieces. The men were thrown into the river and carried beyond my sight." They were saved, but rations, instruments, and clothing were lost. They named this section "Disaster Falls" and another stretch of the canyon "Hell's Half Mile."

With its rim 2,000 to 3,000 feet above the river, Ladore is the deepest of the Uinta canyons. The Yampa River, which drains northwest Colorado and has cut its own canyon into the Uintas, joins the Green River below Ladore Canyon in an area of complex gorges that Powell named Echo Park. Then comes Whirlpool Canyon, cut 2,500 feet into many-layered formations, and finally Split Mountain Canyon, the most unusual of them all. It is evident, particularly from the air, that a great elongated hump, or anticline, has been sliced open down its centerline, as though the river had itself acted like a giant scalpel. The river, after its 118-mile passage through the mountains, finally emerges in Dinosaur National Monument. Its canyons, however, constitute such impediments to cross-country travel that it is virtually impossible to reach the part of Colorado that is west of the canyons except via a detour through Utah.

Near the eastern end of the range is Diamond Peak, which gained its name in a rather bizarre manner. In the fall of 1871, according to published accounts, two weather-beaten prospectors appeared at the Bank of California in San Francisco with a leather pouch of gems, which, they said, should be kept in the vault until further notice. The two men subtly aroused the curiosity of the bank official who peeked inside the pouch and saw what appeared to be a large number of diamonds, rubies, and other gems. He called in a jeweler, who confirmed their authenticity. Rumors that a rich diamond mine had been discovered swept the city. The prospectors led a party, including would-be investors, to a sandstone mesa in the Uintas where diamonds, sapphires, "rubies," and other stones lay scattered over the surface. A few were buried in anthills (although a careful observer might have noticed the disturbance left by a finger that had poked into the hill). When the expedition returned, excitement spread through the entire diamond-dealing world. In South Africa there were fears that market prices would collapse. Samples were brought to New York and shown to Charles L. Tiffany, the jewelry dealer, whose experts confirmed their genuineness. Tiffany and Rothschild money was reportedly invested in the enterprise.

The first to suspect a hoax seem to have been members of Clarence King's 40th

Ladore Canyon and the Green River in the Uinta Mountains. (U.S. Geological Survey)

Parallel Expedition. Some of them had been trained in mineralogy at Harvard and Yale, and from what they had learned the Uintas did not seem a likely source of diamonds. Furthermore diamonds and rubies do not normally occur together. Diamonds are erupted through "pipes" leading up from depths of one hundred miles or more within the earth, where temperature and pressure are sufficient to convert carbon into diamond—that element's most compact form. Although the eruption of a diamond pipe has never been witnessed, it is believed to occur when water pressure at great depth begins to push upward, turning to steam as it reaches levels of lower pressure. This then drives a supersonic eruption that breaks the surface with the sound of a thousand jets. The "diatreme" that remains appears on the surface as a circular area, often only a few dozen yards wide, filled with stones rounded by their wild

Echo Park, where the Yampa and Green rivers join. (U.S. Geological Survey)

upward journey, then later cemented together into what is known as kimberlite, since it is typical of the diamond fields at Kimberley, South Africa.

It is known that diamond pipes exist in North America, although the only one of any consequence—now mined out—is at Murfreesboro, Arkansas. Individual diamonds, however, have been found at scattered locations, most of them between Ohio and Wisconsin in heaps of material left by the last ice sheets. As early as 1670 Jesuit fathers told of diamonds on islands at the entrance to Green Bay in what is now Wisconsin, and one found later weighed a fabulous 15¼ carats. They were carried south by the moving ice, and the pipes from which they came presumably lie hidden somewhere in Canada. Geology students have long searched for them in vain. There are diatremes—potential diamond pipes—in various parts of the continent, notably at Moses Rock Dike in southeast Utah and near the Laramie Range in northern Colorado and southern Wyoming, where a tiny diamond has, in fact, been found.

By chance two members of King's 40th Parallel Expedition—Emmons and James T. Gardner—rode the train to San Francisco with what proved to be the returning party of diamond investors and prospectors. Although the latter were very secretive, they gave away enough to enable King and his associates to piece together an estimated location of the find in the Uintas—not in Arizona, as outsiders had been misled into believing. They returned to Wyoming, picked up horses at Fort Bridger, and headed for the Uintas. Footprints helped lead them to the site. They found "four distinct types of diamonds, a few oriental rubies, garnets, spinels, sapphires, emeralds, and amethysts—an association of minerals of impossible occurrence in nature." Furthermore, when they ventured beyond the footprints, no gems were to be found.

Meanwhile, on August 30, 1872, the leadoff item on the front page of *The New York Times* began as follows:

London, August 29—Messrs. Rittar, Leverson & Co., London diamond brokers, in a communication to the city editor of *The Times,* states that a few months ago an American came to this city and bought a large number of diamonds in the rough, paying no attention whatever to the weight or quality of the stones. These they intimate were used by the alleged discoverers of the diamond mines in Arizona to sanction their assertion.

It was not until November 10, however, that King reached San Francisco with proof of the fraud.

A century later Lowell S. Hilpert of the U.S. Geological Survey office in Salt Lake City found the site on a mesa near Diamond Peak and discovered that some of the "seeded" diamonds were still there. Ironically he also found "rubies" that were actually garnets of a type produced only at depths in the earth where diamonds originate. They may have come from Moses Rock Dike, but such a garnet-diamond association was not known in the last century, so this one plausible combination of gems was accidental. Like the original hoaxers, Hilpert has remained secretive about the site, not to protect his own interests but to avoid inundation of the region by diamond hunters.

North of the Wyoming basins are some of the most imposing mountains of the Rockies—the magnificent Wind River Range, a 120-mile chain of snow-clad peaks, ten of which are over 13,000 feet, including Gannett Peak, Wyoming's loftiest. This roadless, lake-strewn region on the continental divide may be, for the lovers of scenic wilderness, the most ideal refuge in the forty-eight states. Farther east the Bighorn Mountains form a great north-south arc that spans the northern half of central Wyoming. They are not as lofty as the Wind River Range, but like those mountains, their craggy heights have been hewn from once deep-seated rock.

Vibrational probing of the region by COCORP teams has shown that the Wind Rivers were raised when the floor of the Wind River Basin, to the west, was thrust under them. The same appears to have been true of the Big Horns. Yet the mountains farther north, such as the Gros Ventre Range, were formed in a very different manner. It can be likened to compression of a broad concrete floor covered with many layers of wood and vinyl flooring. The squeeze breaks it into sections, each of which pushes a considerable distance over its closest neighbor. The highest part of each overriding section is then worn down to the underlying concrete, leaving an odd situation in which the concrete (the ancient bedrock) lies over layers of wood and vinyl (more recent sediments).

While thrusting and erosion have produced some of the continent's most awesome mountains, from Wyoming to the Canadian Rockies, those processes are very different from the ones responsible for Wyoming's chief attraction—the Grand Tetons, whose pinnacled peaks are among the most precipitous in the West. French explorers called them Les Trois Tetons (The Three Breasts), and the range facing them from the southeast—the Gros Ventre—takes its name from the French designation for local Indian tribes—the Gros Ventres or Big Bellies. Between them lies the deep valley of Jackson Hole and, within it, Jackson Lake, beyond which the Tetons rise with majestic abruptness. While there are comparable peaks in the Canadian Rockies, they

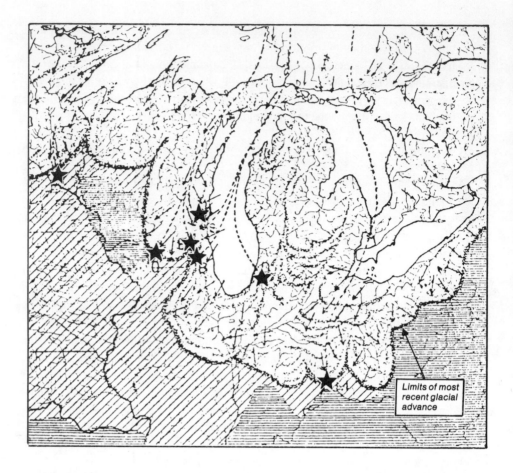

Limits of most
recent glacial
advance

are not so intimate a part of the American vacationing scene. The Grand Tetons, immediately south of Yellowstone Park, are seen by more than a million visitors yearly. The view of them, reflected in the sparkling waters of Jackson Lake, is one of the most photographed scenes in America. Yet, like the Grand Canyon, the view is grand enough to survive any amount of overexposure.

In contrast to the other nearby ranges, the Tetons are very young—less than ten million years—still growing, and apparently produced entirely by vertical uplift. They have been tilted to the west, creating an almost vertical eastern face. While they rise 7,000 feet above Jackson Hole, the latter is filled with so much sediment that the Teton summits stand 24,000 feet above the valley's bedrock. As the mountains rise, the valley floor sinks even lower—a process typical of such "block faulting." The subsidence has been about 150 feet in the past 15,000 years.

The other mountain ranges of the area are remnants of slabs that were thrust eastward tens of miles or more. Their tilted or humped structure is clearly visible in layering of the Gros Ventre peaks. That the Tetons pushed up through these slabs is evident in the Alaska Basin, east of the southern end of the Tetons, where upward tilting of the sandstone, limestone, and shale that once covered the region lies exposed.

Above left: Stars mark diamond finds in Great Lakes glacial deposits. Broken lines indicate assumed routes of transport. (From Earth Features and Their Meaning, *by W. H. Hobbs, New York: Macmillan Co., 1931.)*

Above: Split Mountain, traversed by the Green River. (U.S. Geological Survey)

Like the Blackhawk slide in California, a great landslide produced this formation west of the Pahsimeroi River and eight miles northeast of Doublespring Pass in south-central Idaho. (John S. Shelton)

Ongoing alterations of this landscape may be gradual on a geologic time scale, but in terms of human experience they can be very abrupt. In a matter of seconds a mountain may rise ten feet or more, accompanied by a violent earthquake. The scars of such events can be seen along the bases of some mountains, as in the band of fresh rock along the western base of the Wasatch Mountains in Utah (themselves an example of block faulting). Other evidence of sudden violence is visible at a number of sites in the zone running north from there along the Wyoming-Idaho border into Montana, as though it were a continuation of the process at work along the Wasatch front. In 1925, for example, a quake centered east of Helena did extensive damage within a 600-square-mile area. When one struck Hebgen Lake west of Yellowstone on August 17, 1959, taking twenty-eight lives, an eighty-million-ton section of mountainside, possibly lubricated by a cushion of air, slid into the Madison River with such velocity that its front edge climbed 400 feet up the opposite canyon wall. With the river newly dammed, treetops in the valley were submerged within two days as Earthquake Lake came into being. During the quake, water in Hebgen Lake sloshed back and forth, sweeping over the dam at one end and threatening to demolish it. The entire lake was tilted and moved north. Docks along its north shore were submerged; those on its south side were left high and dry—no longer on the lake.

As the mountains rise, they may become unstable, particularly where soft, lubricating rock lies between harder layers on a steep slope. On June 23, 1925, a large slab slipped into the valley where the Gros Ventre River emerges into Jackson Hole, its front edge climbing 350 feet up the opposite slope. A huge scar remained on the mountainside and the slide formed a dam behind which waters of the swift-flowing river began to accumulate. Within three weeks the new lake was 200 feet deep, but the dam was leaky and not until the spring floods of 1927 was it overflowed. Within a few hours the water cut 100 feet into the dam. A wall of water raced down the valley, destroying all in its path and taking the lives of several residents. When the Hebgen Lake earthquake similarly blocked the Madison River thirty-four years later, army engineers hastened to build an erosion-resistant spillway to prevent another such disaster.

That massive landslides can swiftly alter the landscape is well known to many Californians. Most, following heavy rains, are mudslides that can wreck homes built on steep slopes, but sometimes a large section of mountainside slips down onto a valley floor, a dramatic example being the prehistoric Blackhawk slide, whose end can be seen from California highway 247 east of Lucerne Valley. It slid from the north side of the San Bernardino Mountains onto the Mojave Desert, leaving an apron five miles wide that from the air looks like a giant bear's paw.

18 MARCHING AND SOARING LANDSCAPES– THE NORTHERN ROCKIES

The northern Rocky Mountains, whose ranges are more closely spaced than to the south, were chiefly formed by thrusting associated with arrival of the "terranes" that became the coastline to the west. As sea floor descended under the continental shelf it pushed these terranes against the continent, and at the same time subduction of the oceanic plate generated volcanic eruptions and compression farther inland.

The timetable of deformation indicates that the first rank of composite terranes hit the edge of the continent some 170 million years ago in the region immediately west of the Canadian Rockies. Rocks that now form the Columbia Mountains were compressed and deformed while still in the outer part of the continental shelf. About 115 million years later they were shoved east as far as the present location of the Rocky Mountain Trench, which now separates them from the Northern Rockies. Seen from space that trench, running northwest for 900 miles from west of Glacier Park in the United States, the length of British Columbia almost to the Yukon Territory, is one of the most striking features of the North American landscape. Yet its origin remains uncertain. Some Canadian geologists believe it marks a zone of lateral slippage, everything west of it having shifted several hundred miles northwest as terranes were being hauled toward the Alaskan "catcher's mitt" by the drag of the north-moving Pacific floor. Evidence has been offered that 600 miles of offset has occurred during the past 100 million years in formations that once crossed the northern part of the trench, but in the south structures formed earlier cross the trench with no evident lateral offset.

About 100 million years ago a second amalgam of terranes was swept against the continent where the Coast Mountains of Canada now stand; and compression much farther inland began thrusting vast surface layers over the stable underlying crust, building the magnificent mountains of Glacier National Park and the Canadian Rockies. Raymond A. Price, director of the Geological Survey of Canada, has estimated a 200-kilometer (124-mile) telescoping in that region. A broad section of landscape—the famous Lewis Thrust—was shoved eastward over terrain along the border between Montana and Alberta, its existence recognized from geologic mapping long before deep seismic probing revealed how widespread such thrusting has

The Rocky Mountain Trench in British Columbia viewed by Landsat. The main range of the Rockies flanks it to the northeast, and the Columbia Mountains do so on the southwest (lower left). Snow-capped Mount Robson and mountains of Jasper National Park in Alberta are to the right of center. Below them the Fraser River flows from Moose Lake through the mountains into the trench, which it follows northwest. North of Prince George, beyond the picture, it doubles back and reaches the sea near Vancouver. Waters from McNaughton Lake, cradled in the lower right segment of the trench, drain in the opposite direction into the Columbia River and flow past Portland. Rivers in the upper right part of the picture drain into the Arctic Ocean. (EROS Data Center, U.S. Geological Survey)

been. From the Lewis Thrust in the Glacier Park area have been carved the Lewis, Clark, and Livingston ranges (the first two named for leaders of the Lewis and Clark Expedition to the Northwest). The Lewis Range is capped by rock as ancient as that in the Inner Gorge of the Grand Canyon; some of it, according to Price, appears to have formed from material "supplied by a very large river system of the size and character of the modern Mississippi. . . ." These deposits built outward from the margin of the continent after another landmass had split off and drifted away more than 500 million years ago, much as Africa and Europe later separated from North America. Under those ancient sedimentary rocks on the east side of the Lewis Range far younger rocks are visible. Likewise, north of the border in Alberta, deep valleys have cut through the thrust, exposing the same, younger deposits. The discovery that oil was seeping from them led to the drilling of wells that further confirmed the regional extent of the Lewis Thrust. It is known to have overridden the younger deposits at least 60 miles and perhaps as much as 100. Its easternmost extension has largely been eroded away, but one remnant of it—pyramid-shaped Chief Mountain—stands all alone at the eastern edge of Glacier Park.

One of the more spectacular sights along Going-to-the-Sun Highway in Glacier Park is the Garden Wall, a long escarpment of the Lewis Range whose flat bedding shows that the formation rode east with little crumpling. The Chinese Wall along the continental divide in the million-acre Bob Marshall Wilderness south of the park is a similar battlement. Indeed, many of these mountains, including some of the sharpest and most perilous spires of the Canadian Rockies, show such horizontal layering, since they were not formed by upthrust or folding but by horizontal sliding, slab upon

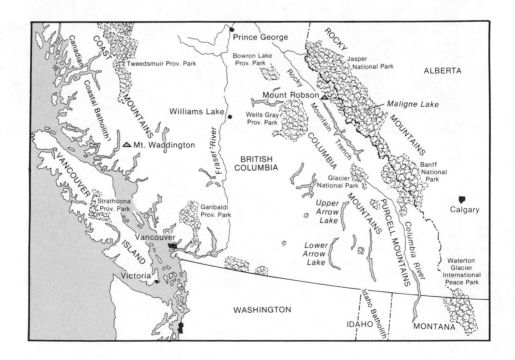

slab, followed by radical erosion. Often the layers tilt gently down toward the west, as would be expected from the piling up of thrusts from that direction.

Along the spine of the mountains from Glacier National Park to the northwest are the grandest of the Canadian Rockies—certainly some of the most beautiful mountains on earth—lying within a succession of national parks (including Canada's own Glacier National Park, which is in British Columbia, to the west of Banff). Like the mountains on the American side of the border, many are flat-bedded monuments, such as 12,972-foot Mount Robson, highest of the Canadian Rockies, and Castle Mountain (Mount Eisenhower) looming over the Trans-Canada Highway between Banff and Lake Louise. That lake, set like a gem among snowy giants of the same type, is probably the most photographed landscape in Canada. A less well-known rival is Maligne Lake, a ribbon of water walled in by the mountains of Jasper National Park to the northwest. In some cases the continuity of gently sloping layers can be traced from mountain to mountain across an entire panorama. While this is a special feature of the Canadian Rockies, among them are also mountains whose structures have been sharply tilted, such as those whose ski slopes overlook Banff. To the west of the central Rockies, where the crunch was far more severe, some formations are tightly folded. A steep-walled ridge near the Sullivan River in southeast British Columbia is formed from top to bottom of gigantic accordion folds.

The Garden Wall. (Glacier National Park)

Right: The Chinese Wall in Montana's Bob Marshall Wilderness. (C. R. Mudge, U.S. Geological Survey)

Below: Mt. Robson. (Geological Survey of Canada)

*Mt. Victoria near Banff.
(Associated Press)*

Northwest of Lake Louise, on the highway to Jasper National Park, the road passes the Columbia Ice Field and Athabasca Glacier, flowing off Mount Columbia. These are reminders that this region is far enough north and close enough to moist air off the Pacific to endure heavy snowfalls. The particularly rugged nature of the Canadian Rockies can in part be attributed to the intensity with which they have been clawed by glacial action during temperate as well as glacial epochs.

In addition to thrusting, two processes on a heroic scale have helped shape the mountainous landscape of western Canada and the northwestern United States: the intrusion of monumental granite batholiths and great volcanic eruptions, such as those that built the Absaroka (pronounced *Ab-SORE-key*) Mountains east of Yellowstone. Some of the world's largest masses of granite are exposed along the coast of British Columbia, in Idaho and in the Sierra Nevada, either from volcanic activity where sea

floor descended under the continent and was partially melted or from the mountain-building effects of terrane collisions.

The batholiths along Canada's West Coast may be the roots of what were enormous mountains. Canadian and American geologists have calculated that these granites formed under conditions existing at least fifteen miles underground. An enormous amount of uplift and erosion must have occurred. Yet there is no sign of the eroded material along the Canadian coast or east of the mountains. It may have been washed

Left: Accordion folds near the Sullivan River in southeast British Columbia. (Geological Survey of Canada)

Right: Evolution of the rotated and overturned structures where the Trans-Canada Highway crosses Kicking Horse Pass between Lake Louise, Alberta, and Golden, British Columbia. (H. R. Balkwill, Geological Survey of Canada)

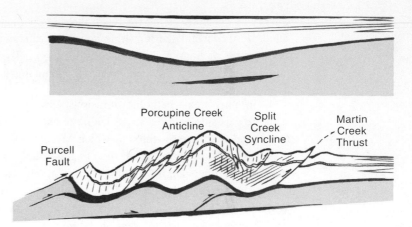

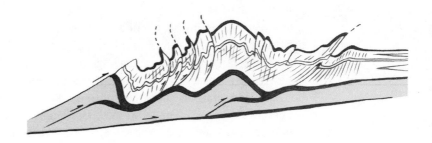

down rivers on the east and, in the west, may have ridden northward-moving sea floor to be scraped off in southern Alaska as the Chugach Mountains.

The Idaho Batholith is about 250 miles long and 100 miles across at its widest. Rivers have cut valleys as deep as 5,000 feet through this rock, producing mountains whose crests tend to be of uniform height, notably the Clearwater and Salmon River mountains that dominate central Idaho. The snowcapped Bitterroot Range, forming the Idaho-Montana border along the east side of the batholith, rises about 1,000 feet higher.

There is no general agreement on what produced the tremendous overthrusting and the massive batholiths in the northern Rockies. The granite bodies along Canada's west coast seem to have formed as sea floor was descending under the continent's rim, whereas those inland formed much later. Just as explaining the relatively recent uplift of the southern Rockies is a challenge, so is it difficult to account for timing of the overthrusts and batholith formations to the north. While it is possible that the thrusts were produced by pressure on the western edge of the continent that was transmitted far inland, some geologists prefer to think that during this period the squeeze came from the east as the continent was drifting away from Europe and Africa. They envision the rim of the original North American landmass diving under the newly acquired structures to the west, producing great compression along what became the northern Rockies. In this regard James W. H. Monger of the Geological

Survey of Canada sees the westward-moving continent "ploughing into the accumulated, semi-consolidated 'mush' to the west (which may have been travelling south to north across its bow)." There is considerable evidence that the edge of the previous continental basement now lies under the mountains just west of the Rocky Mountain Trench.

As in other areas, batholith intrusions sometimes—but not often—are associated with ore deposits. Cutting across the north end of the Idaho Batholith is a break—the Lewis and Clark Line—through which Meriwether Lewis and William Clark made their way west in 1805 to win the Oregon country for the United States. It is now traversed by Interstate 90, linking Missoula, Montana, with Spokane, Washington. Along this break is the Coeur d'Alene mining district whose place names—Burke, Wallace, and Kellogg—call to mind once prospering lead, silver, and zinc mines as well as turbulent efforts to organize the miners. The district continues along the Pend Oreille Valley of northeast Washington and across the Canadian border to the Sullivan Mine, which has produced 93 percent of British Columbia's lead and 85 percent of its zinc.

Another great intrusion, the Boulder Batholith, formed in Montana between Helena and Butte. Almost one third of all copper extracted in the United States has come from Butte, as well as zinc, lead, gold, and silver. The origin of these ores is controversial. Presumably the agent was superheated water that percolated through hot rock, extracting its metal constituents, then deposited them as veins when the water reached cracks in the formation cool enough to permit each metal to drop out of solution. Some geologists believe this occurred beneath an ancient ocean in the manner now being observed where metal-rich geysers—"black smokers"—are erupting through newly formed sea floor along the Pacific Ocean's East Pacific Rise. Others relate the process more closely to formation of the batholiths themselves.

Along the southern border of Montana, immediately north of Yellowstone, a great mass of granite forms the lofty plateau of the Beartooth Mountains. The rock is far older than that of the batholiths, its radioactive residues indicating an age of 3.1 billion years. It is traversed, between Red Lodge, Montana, and Yellowstone, by a seventy-mile, wonderfully scenic highway that climbs to 10,942 feet at Beartooth Pass.

Red Lodge is at the edge of a major coal field and much of Montana east of the mountains is underlain by coal. Strip mines in some areas have cut deep scars in the landscape, as at Colstrip in the southeast part of the state, where the extensive Fort Union coal deposit has been mined. Some of this coal was ignited in the distant past, perhaps by lightning, and the smoldering fires baked overlying deposits of shale and sandstone into various shades of red. These bands of "scoria" now decorate some of the otherwise drab hillsides with brilliant red ribbons.

To the southeast, on the western edge of South Dakota, a great compressive dome survives as the Black Hills. From it nature has eroded the soaring spires of the Needles, and on Mount Rushmore the sculptor Gutzon Borglum carved the faces of four former presidents. More gold has been extracted from the Homestake Mine at Lead, in the Black Hills, than from any other source on the continent.

19 ORDEAL BY ERUPTION AND EXPLOSION—EVOLUTION OF THE CASCADES AND COAST RANGES

Until May 18, 1980, when a jet of incandescent ash and volcanic debris from the side of Mount Saint Helens killed everything and everyone in its path, few Americans were aware of the extent to which eruptions have built the landscape of the Pacific Northwest. Furthermore, until recently, it was a basic principle of geologists that the world has been shaped entirely by processes we now see taking place around us, although operating over extremely long periods. Mountains rise in increments of inches or a few feet, then are worn down, even more gradually, by rain, wind, and frost action. Canyons are cut at almost imperceptible rates. The principle is called uniformitarianism and was the nineteenth-century response to the earlier belief that there have been global catastrophes such as the biblical flood.

But uniformitarianism has had to be modified. The Northwest has a tale to tell of lava floods inundating thousands of square miles in a few hours or building new land by filling the sea with 100,000 cubic miles of molten rock. There have been explosions whose effects are difficult to imagine, for none on so vast a scale has been witnessed in modern times. And, during the more recent ice ages, the Northwest was subjected to floods of almost biblical magnitude.

Although volcanism was active on both coasts when oceanic plates were descending under the continent, it is in the Northwest and in Mexico that the effects are overwhelmingly evident. The most obvious monuments in the Northwest are the Cascade volcanoes, forming a chain of cones and domes—some of them beautifully symmetrical and perpetually snow-clad—rising above a carpet of evergreens from Mount Garibaldi, forty miles north of Vancouver, British Columbia, past Mount Rainier south of Seattle to Mount Lassen in northern California. Not only is their spacing strikingly uniform, but so is their distance from the coast—roughly one hundred miles. Obviously they stand where the sea floor descending from the west (the Juan de Fuca Plate) reaches sufficient depth for some of it to melt and produce lava.

Their counterparts in Mexico—a chain of such mighty volcanoes as Orizaba, Popocatépetl, and Ixtacihuatl—run east-and-west south of Mexico City. They are children of a northeast-plunging section of Pacific floor known as the Cocos Plate, as

Left: The Northwest as viewed from Landsat. (Mosaic by Agricultural Stabilization and Conservation Service, U.S. Department of Agriculture)

Right: The northern Cascades, relatively rugged and granitic, are the oldest part of the range. (M. Woodbridge Williams, National Park Service)

are the many active volcanoes of Central America. Mexico's volcanic zone lies at the convergence of that country's two great mountain systems: the Sierra Madre Oriental paralleling the Gulf of Mexico coast and, along the opposite coast, the Sierra Madre Occidental.

The Cascade volcanoes are relatively young. Some may be only a few hundred thousand years old. They stand, however, on a ridge averaging 5,000 feet above sea level—the backbone of the Cascades—built over forty million years as part of the grand orogeny that produced mountains along the entire western side of the continent. In fact the range north of the latitude of Seattle is even older and, unlike the rest, is not primarily volcanic.

Like the other western ranges, the Cascades received their share of granite intrusions. So did their northern extension in the Coast Mountains of British Columbia, a magnificent range that runs 1,000 miles north from the Fraser River, past southeast Alaska and almost to the Yukon Territory—much of it little known because of its remoteness. Its highest summit, 13,177-foot Mount Waddington, rises almost directly from the sea in Knight Inlet, one of the fjords that snake far inland among these jagged, heavily glaciated mountains (as shown in the map on page 134).

The Cascade Range, thirty to eighty miles wide, presents a formidable barrier between the hinterland and the coast. Only one river—the Columbia—cuts across it between the Fraser River in British Columbia and the Klamath River in southern Oregon. Interstate 90, to reach Seattle, must climb over Snoqualmie Pass. Interstate 80-N reaches Portland through the Columbia River Gorge and The Dalles (which

rhymes with "pals"). When French voyageurs first reached there they were struck by the flagstone appearance of basalt layers through which the river had cut its way and they named it Les Dalles (the Flagstones). It became the western terminus of the Oregon Trail and is now a port for oceangoing ships. The river, in its life-or-death struggle with the rising land, has been able to maintain its route as the Cascades lifted across its path.

The main uplift began about sixteen million years ago, as great floods of relatively fluid lava were burying most of the coastal hinterland in Washington and Oregon. Within a few million years, folding, thrusting, volcanic eruptions, and granite intrusions had raised the Cascades several thousand feet. The uplift is dramatically evident in the tilt of basalt flows, which obviously were flat when deposited. Near Bonneville Dam, where the Columbia River has cut through the lowest part of the range, basalt layers climb several thousand feet to the crest of the mountains. In the Wenatchee Mountains, on the inland side of the range in Washington, flows tilt upward 8 degrees to a height of 7,000 feet. In some areas the flows have been severely folded, indicating local compression.

The Cascade volcanoes that have grown on top of this great hump are of the steep-sloped variety typical of the "ring of fire" encircling the Pacific. Their slopes are at an angle of about 30 degrees, as opposed to mid-ocean "shield" volcanoes, whose lava is so fluid that it flows rapidly away from the summit crater, producing a structure whose slopes are very gentle, like those of a shield. Volcanoes of the Pacific rim were formed by alternate eruptions of lava and of "pyroclastics"—ash, pumice, cinders, and even shattered fragments of the mountain itself. Explosions like those of Saint Helens can blow out the plug of lava that had solidified inside the crater after the previous eruption. Of critical importance in determining whether such a volcano will explode is the composition, and therefore the fluidity, of its lava. If it does not flow easily, it is apt to plug the volcano's vents until gases accumulating inside develop enormous pressure. The plug may then fly out like a champagne cork—or the entire mountain may explode. Much of the accumulated gas is probably steam, derived in part from water that soaked into the oceanic plate when it was sea floor, then was carried under the continent and brought up dissolved within the molten rock. Volcanic explosions are usually aimed upward, but this is not always the case and unfortunately Saint Helens was one of the exceptions.

Early in 1980 it became evident that the volcano was preparing for an eruption. Additional seismographs installed around it recorded "harmonic tremor," assumed to mean that magma was forcing its way upward from below. Precision surveys showed the volcano to be swelling and a huge bulge developed on its north side, expanding about five feet a day. Pyroclastic eruptions sent clouds of ash high into the sky. Despite these and other warning signs, what followed was totally unexpected.

On the morning of May 18, David A. Johnston, a thirty-year-old volcanologist of the U.S. Geological Survey, was monitoring the volcano from a ridge five miles away. Below him, on the edge of Spirit Lake, Harry Truman, aged eighty-four, was at his lodge with his sixteen cats, having ignored all warnings to leave. A popular travel-poster view was of snow-white Saint Helens rising behind the glistening blue waters of Spirit Lake and framed by the deep green of densely forested shores. That was not the scene on May 18, 1980.

Left: Mount Shishaldin on Unimak Island in the Aleutians is a classic volcano of the steep-sloped type. (U.S. Geological Survey)

Right: St. Helens in eruption. (Robert Krimmel, U.S. Geological Survey)

MAY 18 '80

Geologists are not sure which came first—the earthquake or the great landslide. Presumably one caused the other. But the few witnesses who happened to be watching the mountain saw the great bulge on its north slope begin sliding down. Overhead two geologists, Keith and Dorothy Stoffel, were circling in a small plane, and Keith (as recounted by Charles Rosenfeld and Robert Cooke in their book on the eruption) saw the slide begin. "The nature of the movement," he said later, "was eerie, like nothing we had ever seen before. The entire mass began to ripple and churn up, without moving laterally. Then the entire north side of the mountain began sliding to the north along a deep-seated slide plane."

Like a great sliding door the landslide opened the side of the mountain, allowing a jet of searingly hot gas and pyroclastics to shoot north like a mammoth blowtorch. Johnston, at his post in the path of the jet, called to Geological Survey headquarters in nearby Vancouver, Washington: "Vancouver! Vancouver! This is it!" He was never heard from again. The scorching jet probably moved at close to one hundred miles an hour. Thirteen miles to the north it melted plastic parts on a truck. When I visited Johnston's ridge later I found its trees completely gone, leaving only a few splintered stubs, all bending north. Below no sign of Harry Truman's lodge remained. The lake shore was deeply buried under volcanic debris, and the lake itself was blanketed with seared logs stripped of bark and branches. They also covered the hillsides in all directions. Never, even in wartime, had I seen such utter devastation. As we flew by helicopter over the blasted terrain the pilot pointed out the trace of a road along one log-strewn slope. Protruding from the deep blanket of ash at one point on the road was the top of a van. At another spot we could see the scorched wreck of a car. No one in either vehicle apparently survived. Most of the fifty-seven people assumed to have died were never found.

The timber was leveled over about 150 square miles, much of it belonging to the

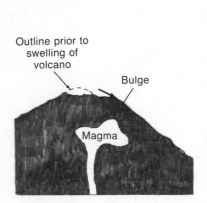

1. May 18: Newly formed bulge slides down mountain

2. Volcano expels incandescent debris at several hundred miles per hour.

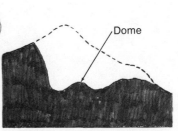

3. Dome repeatedly forms in crater, then is blasted off.

Weyerhauser Company. Ash and melting snow on the volcano's previously pristine slopes had combined to form mud flows that raced down the Toutle River and on to the Columbia River. Logs were driven against the Toutle River bridges like battering rams until the spans collapsed. Logs and debris blocked 20 miles of the Columbia River seaway.

Although the jet was largely horizontal, the eruption also sent ash 70,000 feet aloft in a boiling, churning cloud frequently illuminated by lightning strokes. Prevailing westerlies carried the ash eastward, and in Yakima noon was like nighttime. The ash fall in Spokane, 245 miles to the northeast, was so heavy that traffic virtually came to a halt. The ash felt fluffy, but under a microscope one could see that it contained countless tiny bits of volcanic rocks and minerals. Once the ash had spread through the stratosphere and its heavier particles had fallen out, there was not enough to have an appreciable effect on climate, but that was far from the case with earlier North American eruptions, and such events are likely to be repeated.

A striking preview of the manner in which Saint Helens blew out its side occurred with the 1956 eruption of Bezymianny in Kamchatka. It sent floods of mud fifty miles down neighboring valleys and left the volcano with a large gap in its side, much like that of Saint Helens. And, as with the Cascade volcano, its explosion was followed by several years of smaller eruptions that repeatedly built lava domes inside the crater, then blew them off.

Five years before the Saint Helens explosion three scientists of the U.S. Geological Survey who had reconstructed its eruptive history warned that of all the Cascade volcanoes, it was the one to watch most closely. Over the last few thousand years, they said, it had been "more active and more violent" than any other American volcano outside of Hawaii and Alaska. In about 1900 B.C., for example, it spread an estimated one cubic mile of ash over the Northwest—more than that from the A.D. 72 eruption of Vesuvius that buried Pompeii and Herculaneum. Saint Helens had been dormant since 1857, they said, but rarely had remained so more than 100 to 150 years. They urged that the likelihood of further eruptions be taken into account in development of this sparsely inhabited region. Saint Helens, said the authors (Dwight R. Crandall, Donal R. Mullineaux, and Meyer Rubin), was sure to erupt again, "perhaps before the end of this century."

The most recent previous Cascade eruption had been that of Lassen Peak, which in 1915 blew a jet of hot gas from its side after lesser eruptions that had begun the year before. The explosion was not as devastating as that of Saint Helens, in part because that part of northern California was sparsely inhabited. Nevertheless massive trees were torn away and mud flows swept down Hat Creek and Lost Creek valleys. The Cascade eruptions have left their mark on much of northern California east of Interstate 5, even as far south as Sutter Buttes in the Sacramento Valley near Yuba City. Their pushing up of the valley floor sediments produced traps for natural gas that are now being exploited. Outpourings from Lassen Peak are encompassed within a national park and travelers on Interstate 5 pass close to the eternally snow-covered cone of Mount Shasta. To the northeast, between Shasta and Lava Beds National Monument (almost on the Oregon line), rivers of obsidian that flowed off Glass Mountain in about A.D. 900 look from the air like black glaciers, but they are

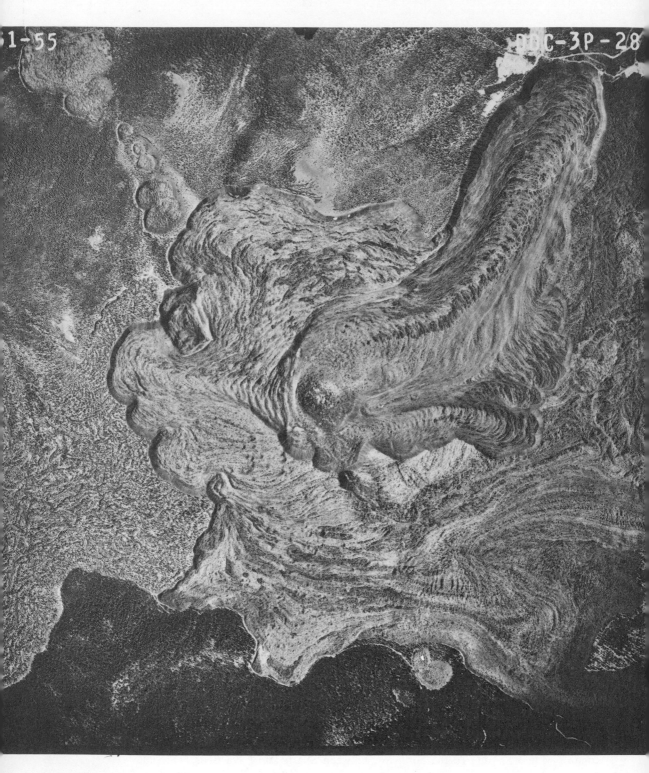

Glass Mountain, near the Oregon line in northern California, is formed of volcanic glass (obsidian) erupted 900 years ago. (U.S. Department of Agriculture)

solidified volcanic glass, some of it so flawless it has been used to make telescope mirrors. Primitive peoples often chipped obsidian into arrowheads or other sharp implements.

In the years before Saint Helens erupted the focus was on Mount Baker, one of the northern Cascades. It rises 10,750 feet amidst a chaotic array of steep-sided, glacier-draped mountains east of Bellingham, Washington. In 1975 snow and glacier ice began melting from parts of its crater. Plumes of steam rose from new vents. But there were no ominous tremors.

There has also been concern regarding Mount Rainier, grandest of the Cascades. Although its summit is often shrouded in steam, its snows feed twenty-six glaciers—candidates for rapid melting. Some 5,000 years ago an eruption sent mud flows racing down two glacial valleys north of the mountain. Downstream they joined to form a massive flow that spread across the lowland near Puget Sound, burying under as much as seventy feet the present sites of such communities as Enumclaw, Buckley, Kent, Auburn, Sumner, and Puyallup. A special reason for concern is that like Mount Erebus in Antarctica, the volcanoes at the north end of the Cascades probably contain interbedded layers of ice that when the volcano heats could melt and mix with ash, producing an unstable interior.

The greatest Cascade eruption for which any information is available left as its remnant one of the gems of the American landscape—Crater Lake in southern Oregon, filling what would otherwise be a gap in the roughly uniform spacing of volcanoes in that chain. Measurements of carbon 14 in charred logs buried by pumice from the eruption have shown that it occurred some 6,700 years ago and must therefore have been witnessed by early Indian inhabitants.

Geologists call the former volcano Mount Mazama. Crater Lake partially fills the caldera, 5 to 6 miles wide, which was left after the volcano exploded and collapsed into its subterranean reservoir. The lake, plumbed at almost 2,000 feet, is the deepest in North America. Within it a subsequent eruption has produced Wizard Island, a small volcano with a crater in its summit. Mapping what remains of the mountain in sloping formations around the edge of the lake indicates that the volcano was a multiple structure, formed by a long series of eruptions whose domes were not always centered on one another. The summit was probably several thousand feet higher than the surviving rim. The eruption that destroyed the mountain was of mammoth dimensions. All told an estimated 30 cubic miles of material was erupted, most of it spread over 350,000 square miles of the West from Nevada to British Columbia. From pollen grains in successive ash layers, it has been deduced that the first eruption was in the spring and that ash falls continued intermittently for three years.

Another large caldera, known as Newberry Crater, lies east of the Cascades and twenty-five miles south of Bend, Oregon. It is filled by twin lakes (Paulina Lake and East Lake) separated by cinder cones that erupted from the caldera floor. What resembles a black glacier flowing toward the south shore of Paulina Lake is an extensive flow of obsidian. Twenty miles farther south is Hole-in-the-Ground, a crater that from the air looks so much like those at the Nevada test site one would assume it was the product of an atomic explosion. It is perfectly circular, several thousand feet wide, and largely devoid of vegetation, its rim raised several hundred

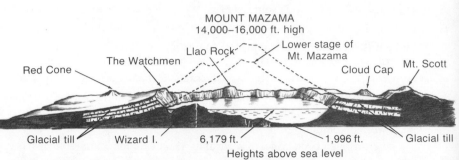

*Right: Mount Mazama.
(From* The Physiographic
Provinces of North
America, *copyright © 1940
by Wallace W. Atwood.
Ginn and Company [Xerox
Corporation],* Lexington,
Mass., *p. 456. Reprinted by
permission.)*

MOUNT MAZAMA
14,000–16,000 ft. high

Red Cone   The Watchmen   Llao Rock   Lower stage of Mt. Mazama   Cloud Cap   Mt. Scott

Glacial till   Wizard I.   6,179 ft.   1,996 ft.   Glacial till

Heights above sea level

feet above the surrounding terrain, like those of craters produced by explosive impacts such as the one that formed Meteor Crater in Arizona. This one, however, is thought to have been the result of a "phreatic," or gaseous, volcanic explosion with no associated lava outpouring.

While fruits of the volcanic activity that helped build the Coast Range along the shoreline of Washington and Oregon are less obvious than in the Cascades, they are displayed along the rugged coastlines of both states—particularly on the magnificent Olympic Peninsula. Much of the Olympic Peninsula is underlain by a deposit of basalt that locally is about ten miles thick. Tracing the details of its extent is difficult because lower levels of the mountains are covered with a dense growth of Douglas fir, Sitka spruce, hemlock, red cedar, and black cottonwood, whereas the heights are heavily glaciated. If all the snow that falls on the Olympic Mountains in a year were converted to water it would be fifteen to twenty feet deep. On the ocean side, where rains are heaviest, the result is a classic "rain forest," which visitors to Olympic National Park can penetrate along a road following the Hoh River in from the coast. At the end one can wander humid trails through a wonderland of lush green undergrowth and towering trees.

Highway 101, on the north side of Olympic National Park, skirts Crescent Lake, hemmed in by massive walls of basalt. This is the Crescent Formation that under various other names is found on Vancouver Island to the north and along the Coast Range into Oregon to the south. Its total volume, erupted forty to fifty million years ago, has been estimated at more than 100,000 cubic miles—5,000 times the volume of Mount Rainier and more than was spread over Washington and Oregon by the great lava floods of more recent times. The lava first began accumulating under water, possibly some distance off shore, but it built up until above the sea. Then, perhaps, the formation was swept against the coast during assembly of the coastal terranes. Finally, as with so many of the western mountains, it has been the raising and tilting of these massive deposits in the last few million years that have made them into the mountains of today. This same basalt stands out in some of the most prominent capes and headlands along the Oregon coast.

Left: Hole-in-the-Ground, site of a volcanic gas explosion twenty miles south of Paulina Lake, Oregon. (Delano Photographics)

20 LAVA FLOODS, ANIMAL STAMPEDES, AND THE YELLOWSTONE "PLUME"

The most spectacular outpourings of lava for which we have detailed evidence have been those that blanketed the interior of Washington and Oregon, chiefly between 13 and 17 million years ago, as tension pulling the earth's crust apart reached that region. The highly fluid lava repeatedly poured out of multiple fissures, some of them miles long, and formed advancing lava fronts as much as 100 miles in width. The fissures were primarily in southeast Washington and northeast Oregon, near the Idaho border, and virtually all were oriented west-of-north to east-of-south. The lava, prevented from flowing east by the Idaho mountains, raced westward, filling valleys and burying hilltops of what had been an intensely folded landscape. The result was a vast basalt plateau, on the average more than a half-mile thick, covering all of southeast Washington, almost all of northern Oregon, and parts of western Idaho. A single eruption spread fresh lava over as much as a third of this vast region within a few days. The resulting deposits ranged in thickness from a few feet to 400 feet, but most were 50 to 100 feet, leading to a total accumulation of 77,000 cubic miles. Between the periods of eruption there was time for grasslands to reestablish themselves and again become inhabited by horses, camels, rhinoceroses, mastodons, and other creatures. According to a reconstruction of this history, published in 1982 by Peter R. Hooper of Washington State University, during the peak period of eruptions, between 14.5 and 16.5 million years ago, more than sixty outpourings produced the Grande Ronde Basalt (85 percent of the total accumulation). They were spaced about 10,000 years apart, whereas in other periods they tended to be more widely separated. Many flows can be traced across the entire extent of the plateau through the special properties of each outpouring, much as volcanologists can trace the ash from a specific eruption.

One of the most thoroughly studied is the Roza Flow, which, in two pulses within a few hundred years of one another, covered 15,000 square miles with an estimated 680 cubic miles of basalt. While the eruption of such highly fluid lava does not build volcanoes, fiery fountains along fissures from which the lava is pouring leave cones of cinders, pumice, and glassy fragments. Although some of these traces were buried by later eruptions or have eroded away, others are still evident, such as Big Butte in

The canyon walls at Palouse Falls expose many of the Columbia Plateau lava flows. (Josef Scaylea)

the southeast corner of Washington, or they have been exposed by construction work. It appears that the Roza Flow erupted from closely spaced fissures in a zone 3 miles wide and 125 miles long running from the northeast corner of Oregon to a point about 30 miles southwest of Spokane. By then the entire plateau had been tilted gently westward and the lava flowed rapidly in that direction. When it reached lakes near Pasco, more than 100 miles away, it was still so hot that lava entering the water turned to almost pure glass, indicating that almost no cooling had taken place. Its average speed of advance, according to the Hooper analysis, must have been about 3 miles per hour. A few days later, after traveling 200 miles to the Columbia River Gorge and The Dalles, it was still hot enough to flow.

"The enormity of this event," wrote Hooper in the journal *Science*, "is hard to visualize." A smoking, steaming, flaming lava front sixty miles wide was marching across the landscape, its 2,000-degree (Fahrenheit) temperature incinerating everything in its path before burying all under one hundred feet of basalt. It has been proposed that some flows moved considerably faster. In any case the effect must have been an animal drive of incredible dimensions. Imagine such a front sweeping across a region larger than the combined areas of Connecticut, Massachusetts, and Rhode Island, driving before it all creatures that could run or fly. Fleeing before it must have been hordes of three-toed horses, long-necked camels, lumbering rhinoceroses, a Noah's-Ark mélange of smaller mammals, ancestral lions, tigers, and other predators running among their normal prey in a democracy born of mutual panic. And overhead the sky must have been darkened by birds, continuously alighting, then rising again to flee farther.

Direct evidence for the fate of the animals is meager, since the lava was so hot it disintegrated all with which it came into contact. The most dramatic find has been the cast of a small rhinoceros that was trapped by the advancing basalt near Dry Falls in the lower part of Grand Coulee. Nothing of the animal itself remains—not even a few bones—but the imprint in the rock is unmistakably that of a rhinoceros. Logs and other remains were apt to survive if buried under protective soil. Remnants of a forest were preserved at Ginkgo Petrified Forest near where Interstate 90 crosses the Columbia River at Vantage in central Washington. Several hundred species of tree and plant have been identified, including the ginkgo, a tree native to China with characteristically fan-shaped leaves.

The Pomona Flow, a subsequent outpouring that originated in Idaho twelve million years ago, crossed the entire width of Washington and Oregon to the Pacific Ocean. Its telltale basalt has been identified on the coast west of Portland, 340 miles from its source. Such long-distance travel may have been aided by channeling between walls of the ancient Snake and Columbia river canyons, which became heated and so insulated the lava stream from further cooling.

The final result of these eruptions, the Columbia River Plateau, must have been even larger than today, some of its edges having eroded away. Another 300,000 square miles of basalt are thought to have flooded the interior of British Columbia during this period, although not from the same fissures.

Wherever water action has cut through the plateau it has exposed massive sequences of basalt layers, as in Grand Coulee, in Moses Coulee (twenty miles east of Wenatchee), at Palouse Falls and in the canyon of the Grand Ronde in southeast Washington, along the Imnaha River in northeast Oregon, and many stretches of the Snake and Columbia rivers. Some highway cuts have laid bare cliffs of columnar basalt reminiscent of such formations as the Hudson River Palisades, the Devil's Postpile southeast of Yosemite, and Devils Tower in northeast Wyoming. The last is a massive cylindrical structure that rises in lonely splendor 1,300 feet above the surrounding grasslands. In 1906 it became the country's first national monument. One passes more modest columnar formations, for example, en route to the Spokane airport. Columns in the lower part of a flow tend to be about 2 feet wide whereas near the top, where they cooled faster, they are narrower and less regular.

Because of the arid climate and sparse vegetation, the role of volcanic activity in shaping eastern Oregon and Washington is very evident from the air. The region north of the Blue Mountains, where Oregon, Washington, and Idaho come together, appears underlain by oceanic rock. This is where exotic terranes docked against the

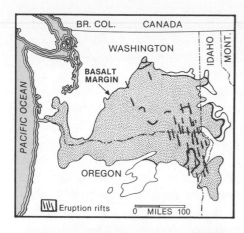

Left: The Grand Ronde
eruptions covered much of
Washington and Oregon in
a single day.

Below: During the great
outpourings, lava froze into
place as it cascaded down
the cliffs of Picture Gorge
on the John Day River in
eastern Oregon. (Delano
Photographics)

original edge of the continent, and Hooper pointed out, it may be more than a coincidence that when tension pulled the crust apart it was there that fissures opened and began flooding the landscape with lava. Farther south, in southeastern Oregon, the landscape has the stamp of the Basin and Range Province.

More recent than the eruptions that formed the Columbia River Plateau have been those responsible for Yellowstone and the largest explosions for which we have any evidence in North America. Except from the perspective of space, the multiple calderas that they produced are not very obvious. They form an irregular basin from twenty-eight to forty-seven miles in diameter occupying a large fraction of Yellowstone National Park and encompassing Yellowstone, Lewis, and Shoshone lakes. The terrain north of both Yellowstone and Shoshone lakes (the latter close to Old Faithful Geyser) has been humped by a succession of molten rock intrusions since the last great eruption 600,000 years ago. Beginning in the 1960's the area has been intensively studied, providing evidence that a large reservoir of magma, or molten rock, lies under the northeast edge of the caldera.

The suspected presence of such a reservoir, its roots possibly extending to a depth of 150 miles, was confirmed from the effect it has on seismic waves from artificial explosions and natural earthquakes traversing the region at various depths. For example, in 1978, shock waves were monitored from three nuclear tests in Nevada, from quarry blasts, and from experimental detonations each involving four tons of explosives. The recordings were made with 220 seismographs, most of them portable, placed at about 1,000 locations. Measurements have also been made of regional magnetism, gravity, electrical conductivity, and the flow of heat from beneath the ground. All the results point toward the existence of molten or partially molten rock beneath the caldera, accounting for the geysers, boiling mud pots, fumaroles, and hot springs that attract more than two million visitors to the park each year.

An early indication that something extremely violent had taken place in the Yellowstone area was recognition that some of the volcanic rocks there were similar to those produced in Alaska's 1912 Katmai eruption by a blast of ash, hot gas, and rock fragments that flowed across the area with hurricane force. The recent investigations have defined two great periods of volcanic activity in the area. The first, about

Cross-section of the Yellowstone area. (From Explosive Volcanism: Inception, Evolution, and Hazards *by R. B. Smith and L. W. Braile. Washington, D.C.: National Academy Press, 1984.)*

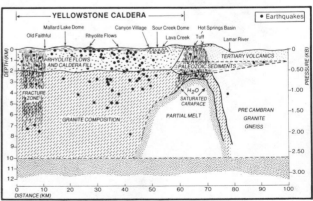

forty million years ago, built the many-layered Absaroka Mountains stretching north and south for 150 miles to the east of the park, their highest summit being 13,140-foot Francs Peak. At least thirteen major vent complexes contributed to their construction. Where the road running east from Jackson Hole climbs over the southern end of that range at Togwotee Pass, 1,100-foot cliffs to the north display a towering sequence of volcanic layers, many set off by thin intervening beds of white tuff.

Yellowstone was also influenced by these eruptions, but there followed a hiatus of almost forty million years before onset of the explosive cycles that still may not be ended. Each explosive phase has been preceded and followed by long periods of intermittent lava eruption, some of which partially filled the caldera produced after

The Menan Buttes are two cones of glassy volcanic debris on the Snake River twenty miles north of Idaho Falls. (U.S. Geological Survey)

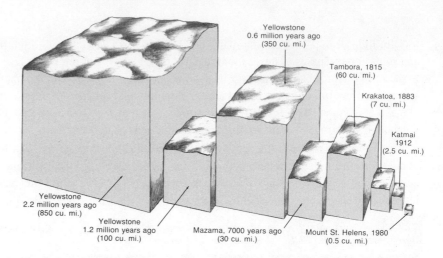

The three great Yellowstone eruptions dwarfed more recent ones in volume of ejected material. (From Explosive Volcanism: Inception, Evolution, and Hazards *by R. B. Smith and L. W. Braile. Washington, D.C.: National Academy Press, 1984, and other sources.)*

Yellowstone 0.6 million years ago (350 cu. mi.)

Tambora, 1815 (60 cu. mi.)

Krakatoa, 1883 (7 cu. mi.)

Katmai 1912 (2.5 cu. mi.)

Yellowstone 2.2 million years ago (850 cu. mi.)

Yellowstone 1.2 million years ago (100 cu. mi.)

Mazama, 7000 years ago (30 cu. mi.)

Mount St. Helens, 1980 (0.5 cu. mi.)

the last explosion. Tiny crystals and glass shards thrown into the sky by these explosions are found as far away as Mississippi, California, and Saskatchewan in Canada.

The first and most voluminous episode, 2.2 million years ago, culminated in one or more explosions that spread some 850 cubic miles of material over North America, as shown in the map on page 101. The magma chamber under the volcano must have been huge to have produced so much material in a single eruption. The next episode, 1.2 million years ago, was on a somewhat smaller scale, with an estimated output of more than 100 cubic miles. Following that, according to an analysis by Robert L. Christiansen of the U.S. Geological Survey, a series of lava eruptions penetrated the crust to form a ring of weakness. He and Robert E. Smith of the University of Utah believe it was this that permitted release of the most recent explosive eruption, 600,000 years ago. The volume of ash-flow sheets spread across the land as volcanic tuff was more than 350 cubic miles. Lava eruptions continued intermittently until 50,000 years ago and may not be ended.

The Yellowstone caldera lies at the end of a long trail of volcanic activity that in the past fifteen million years has marched 350 miles northeast across the full width of southern Idaho into Wyoming. Between Twin Falls and Idaho Falls its path is followed by Interstates 86 and 15. Most of the trail has subsided, forming the Snake River Plain with such relics of past eruptions as Craters of the Moon National Monument (on U.S. 26/93), Big Southern Butte, and the Devil's Orchard. They were recent enough for the fruits of volcanic activity to remain fresh looking—relatively smooth-topped flows of the fast-moving type known by the Hawaiian term *pahoehoe* (*pa-hoy-hoy*), flows whose creeping pace produced the tortured, impassably rough type called *aa* (*ah-ah*), as well as tubes formed where a stream of lava continued to flow through hardened lava, then drained away. Within the national monument there are nearly ten miles of flows, as well as 800-foot cinder cones and steep-sided shatter cones left by fountains of fiery lava. So like the lunar surface is the terrain that it was used to acclimatize Apollo astronauts before their great journeys across space. For those of us who cannot follow in their footsteps, a walk through the Craters of the Moon is probably as close as we can ever come to such an experience.

One of the first pioneers to see this area was Captain Benjamin Bonneville, who, as recounted in Washington Irving's *Adventures of Captain Bonneville,* headed west in 1832 with 110 men, twenty-eight mule-drawn wagons laden with provisions and ammunition, as well as horses and oxen. Bonneville described the Craters of the Moon as "a desolate and awful waste, where no grass grows or water runs."

The thesis of Smith, Christiansen, and others is that the Snake River Plain marks the path along which the volcanic activity now at Yellowstone has migrated at a rate of one or two inches per year. In 1983 Smith and Lawrence Braile of Purdue University proposed that it is still moving toward Montana. Probably the most popular explanation is that of a hot spot or plume rooted in the depths of the earth beneath the moving North American Plate. When Jason Morgan of Princeton proposed the plume concept in 1972 he cited Yellowstone and the Snake River Plain as a prime example of such a phenomenon. Yellowstone's eastward migration seems roughly the reverse of North America's drift to the west. Not all geologists are persuaded by Morgan's hypothesis that beneath Yellowstone a plume of partially molten rock is rising more than a thousand miles from the zone where the mantle, or rigid interior of the earth, surrounds the liquid core. The origin of the eruptions, they say, could be a shallower phenomenon, such as existence beneath the moving crust of a stationary concentration of radioactive rock sufficient to produce melting.

Smith and Christiansen noted the "Hawaiian" nature of the lava that has erupted along the trail—such as the pahoehoe and aa. Basalts that erupted at Yellowstone and onto the Snake River Plain, they said, "are much like magmas that form beneath oceanic islands" and migration of the volcanic activity is strikingly similar to that which has produced the Hawaiian chain. At a 1979 symposium on Yellowstone, Harmon Craig of the University of California at San Diego noted that the abundance of helium 3 in rock erupted there indicated a very deep origin. On or near the earth's surface the other form of helium (helium 4) is constantly replenished by radioactive processes, diluting the trace amounts of helium 3, but this is not true deep inside the earth, and material from such depths therefore has higher relative amounts of helium 3. Because of the high helium 3 to helium 4 ratio at Yellowstone, said Craig, that area may sit atop "a pipeline straight down into the mantle."

What is the likelihood of further eruptions at Yellowstone or along the path of its migration? Surveying of the caldera in recent years has shown that the two domes within it are rising at least a half inch per year, "about the growth rate of a human fingernail," according to Smith and Christiansen. This, they said, was "extraordinarily high." The rate is comparable, they added, "to those sometimes measured on the active volcanoes of Hawaii and Iceland" and could mean either that magma is moving up beneath the domes, or that gas is being released from a deeper magma body. Yellowstone is also an area of periodic earthquake swarms. Not one of the magnetic, seismic, gravity, electric, heat flow, or survey observations "unambiguously proves that any magma still occupies Yellowstone's shallow chamber," wrote the two geologists, "but all are consistent with such an inference," suggesting "a reasonable possibility of further volcanism." There is a small chance that it could be of the most violent kind, they said, but probably any renewal of volcanism "would be signaled by precursory phenomena, such as intense localized earthquake activity, increased gas emissions, etc."

21 MARS IN WASHINGTON–
THE ICE AGE FLOODS

The story of the floods that deluged the Northwest at the end of the last Ice Age is one of accumulating evidence for events so cataclysmic that geologists long found them incredible. It is a tale, as well, of personal ridicule, followed by ultimate vindication. And it has culminated in realization that something akin to what happened in the Pacific Northwest some 13,000 years ago may explain the extraordinary scouring of the Martian surface, as revealed in photographs sent to Earth by *Viking* spacecraft in orbit around that planet.

The hero of the story is J Harlen Bretz, for more than thirty years a member of the geology faculty of the University of Chicago. In the early 1920's he took students on summer field trips into the Columbia Gorge between Washington and Oregon and then into the so-called scablands, southwest of Spokane in eastern Washington. There a maze of interwoven channels has been carved out of the rolling Palouse country, the fertility of whose soil (a wind-deposited loess) has made its wheat fields among the nation's most productive. Even the underlying basalt of the Columbia Plateau has been deeply scoured. Between these channels are islands of undisturbed land, each tapering in the upslope direction as though carved by swift water.

While the extraordinary—and Mars-like—pattern of the scablands can be truly appreciated only in photographs from space or very high altitude, Bretz recognized their significance from extensive ground observations and in 1923 proposed that as the last Ice Age ended, the land was swept by a flood of almost unbelievable magnitude. In a series of papers during the 1920's he described the scablands thus:

"Like great scars marring the otherwise fair face of the plateau are these elongated tracts of bare, or nearly bare, black rock carved into mazes of buttes and canyons. Everybody on the plateau knows scabland. It interrupts the wheat lands, parceling them out into hill tracts less than 40 acres to more than 40 square miles in extent. One can neither reach them nor depart from them without crossing some part of the ramifying scabland. Aside from affording a scanty pasturage, scabland is almost without value. The popular name is an expressive metaphor. The scablands are wounds only partially healed—great wounds in the epidermis of soil with which Nature protects the underlying rock. . . . The region is unique: let the observer take

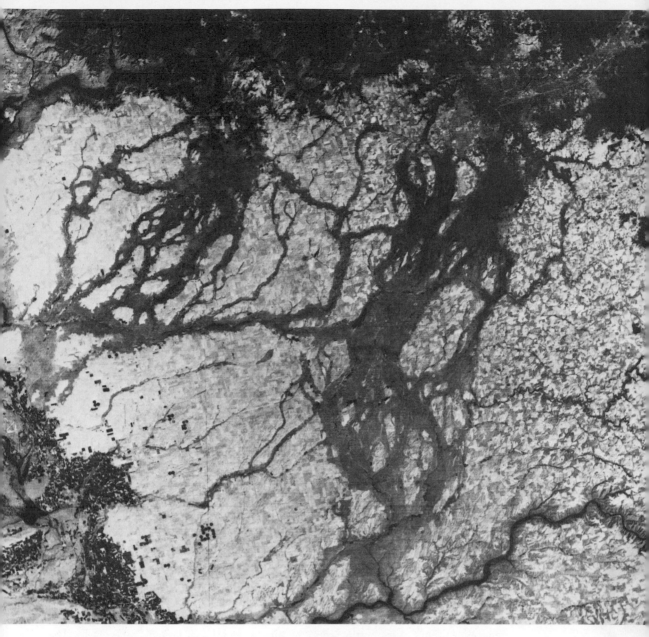

Scablands scouring shows in this Landsat image. Spokane is upper right. The Columbia River is impounded at Coulee Dam, upper left. The Snake River is lower right. (NASA)

the wings of morning to the uttermost parts of the earth: he will nowhere find its likeness.''

Interstate 90 follows the scablands southwest from Spokane, passing some of the ''islands'' and traversing some of the gouges, or coulees, cut by the flood before reaching Moses Lake in Quincy Basin. The latter is an arid region south of Grand Coulee that, Bretz proposed, was deeply flooded during his hypothetical debacle. He pointed out that the whole plateau, covering most of eastern Washington, is tilted, forming a slope that drops off southwestward at about 20 feet per mile. It was down this slope, he said, that the flood raced, carving out such heroic features as Grand Coulee, racing through the Columbia Gorge, past Portland, and on to the sea,

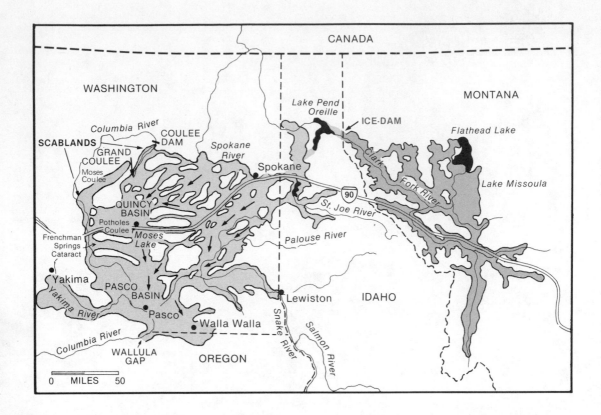

depositing a broad delta at the mouth of the Columbia and Willamette rivers. All the soil, 100 to 150 feet thick, was swept away from an area of 2,800 square miles, and the racing water cut deeply into the lava fields of underlying basalt. Downstream, Bretz said, another 900 square miles were buried under the eroded material.

The Columbia River at that time was diverted by ice into a temporary channel that was now buried in a torrent of racing water. A giant cataract more than 800 feet high and like nothing to be seen on earth today formed at what is now Coulee City. The lip of the cataract was eroded under the boiling rapids at a seemingly incredible rate, retreating twenty miles northward to the present vicinity of Grand Coulee Dam. The process was unlike that of waterfalls, such as Niagara, where plunging water undermines the cliff. Here the entire canyon was submerged beneath a torrent of swift-flowing water whose turbulence continuously undermined the cataract's rim. In its wake this erosion left what is now the upper Grand Coulee, whose walls of stacked basaltic lava flows rise vertically more than 800 feet. At its southern end is the remnant of another great cataract, the famous Dry Falls, nearly four miles wide and 400 feet high. Below that the lower Grand Coulee, another canyon with walls several hundred feet high, extends seven miles to Soap Lake, where it opens into Quincy Basin. What particularly confounded the contemporaries of Bretz was his proposal that so much water poured into Quincy Basin that its overflow into the Columbia River trough simultaneously produced four mighty cataracts. Two of them, at Frenchman Springs and the Potholes, were eroded into canyons strikingly like such features

Left: Repeated collapses of an ice dam allowed waters from Lake Missoula, right, to scour out the scablands, left, along routes shown by arrows. An aerial view of Moses Coulee appears on pages 166 and 167.

Right: Dry Falls cataract with Coulee City in the distance. Banks Lake, formed by flooding of the Upper Grand Coulee, is near the horizon on the left. Dry Falls Lake is under the cliffs. Basalt above the Dry Falls was scoured by left-to-right flow of the torrent. (John S. Shelton)

on Mars. In response to the contention of others that these were formed sequentially, one at a time, Bretz pointed out that all had clearly been cut by overflow from a lake of uniform height—an unlikely coincidence if they were formed at separate times.

As evidence of the colossal rate of flow he referred to the manner in which the surviving islands of soil, or loess, had been shaped. A striking feature, he said, is the way they taper at their northern ends, forming "great prows, pointing up the scabland's gradient.... It is impossible to study these prow-pointed loessial hills, surrounded by the scarred and channeled basalt scablands, without seeing in them the result of a powerful eroding agent.... The magnitude of the erosive changes wrought by these glacial streams is nothing short of amazing." The gouging of the Columbia Plateau and the valleys of the Snake and Columbia rivers, he wrote, "cannot be interpreted in terms of ordinary river action and ordinary valley development.... Enormous volume, existing for a very short time, alone will account for their existence." From the indicated depth of impoundment above the Wallula Gap, where the Columbia River cuts through the Horseheaven Hills before turning west, he calculated that the flood daily discharged forty-two cubic miles of water. For a day or two, above the gap, it buried the area of Pasco, Washington, under more than 1,000 feet of water.

His theory was greeted with dismay, if not horror, by a geological community conditioned by James Hutton's "uniformitarianism" to abhor any suggestions of catastrophe. Late in the eighteenth century Hutton, a Scottish geologist, had promulgated the principle that the present is key to the past. When Bretz was invited in 1927 to make a presentation before the Geological Society of Washington, D.C., it was, according to Victor R. Baker of the University of Arizona (himself a student of the scablands), "a purposeful invitation: a veritable phalanx of doubters had been assembled to debate the flood hypothesis." After Bretz had finished, according to his own recollection, "six elders spoke their prepared rebuttals. They demanded, in effect, a return to sanity and uniformitarianism." His theory was greeted, he added, as "a retreat to catastrophism, to the dark ages of geology."

In fairness to the skeptics it should be noted that Bretz still did not have a plausible explanation for the flood. He considered a sudden climate warming, but could it really have melted forty-two cubic miles of ice a day? Another hypothesis was what Icelanders call a *jökulhlaup,* where the underside of an ice cap on a previously dormant volcano is melted by volcanic heat, allowing the entire cap to slide off and wreak havoc in its path. There was no evidence of any such volcano upstream of the flood. The situation of Bretz was like that of Alfred Wegener, who was then arguing, in the face of great indignation, that the continents are drifting about, plowing through the ocean floors like great ships. His theory lacked the completeness that has now made its revision, as "plate tectonics," acceptable.

In the case of Bretz the explanation was not long in coming. By 1928 he realized that during the advances and retreats of the last Ice Age, a lobe of the great northern ice sheet had filled the narrow valley where the Clark Fork River, a tributary of the Columbia in Montana, enters northern Idaho and Pend Oreille Lake. The ice cut off drainage from a large region of Montana east of the Rocky Mountains, forming what geologists now call Lake Missoula. As the climate warmed ice melted, and the lake became steadily deeper and larger. Its successive beach lines can be seen on the slope behind Missoula, the highest being 950 feet above the University of Montana stadium. The lake finally covered 3,000 square miles and in places was 2,000 feet deep. Not only was ice melting to the north, but so was the ice "cork" of the Clark Fork River. Finally the dam broke—the cork popped—and 500 cubic miles of water raced past Spokane at an estimated rate of 1 cubic mile every seven minutes—ten times the present combined flow of all the world's rivers. It carried with it giant fragments of the collapsed ice dam, including icebergs in which large boulders were embedded. Blocks of basalt more than 30 feet broad were captives of the torrent, crashing into one another to produce "percussion marks" visible on them today. The torrent swept over some of the ridges that stood in its way, leaving clues to the maximum height of flooding. It carved out not only Grand Coulee but other such coulees, or dry valleys: Moses Coulee, Rocky Coulee, Bowers Coulee, Lind Coulee, Washtucna Coulee, and Old Maid Coulee.

It was at Staircase Rapids, two miles north of Washtucna, that Richard Foster Flint, a noted ice age specialist at Yale University, made a discovery that he thought would help debunk the flood hypothesis. He found what he took to be gravel terraces produced by ordinary river action. A few years later, however, his discovery was seized upon as overwhelming evidence for the rapid passage of enormous volumes of water. The "terraces" were identified as ripple marks on an almost unbelievable scale. Flint had accurately described them as undulations 20 to 100 feet long, up to 10 feet high, running transverse to the Snake River. It was hard to imagine they were ripples like those no more than a few inches high that are produced in sand under flowing water. Thanks in large measure to aerial photography, more than one hundred rippled areas have been found along the path of the flood in Washington and Montana, notably where Crab Creek passes Odessa, sixty-five miles southwest of Spokane on Highway 28, at Wilson Creek farther down that stream, at sites such as Malaga on the Columbia River, along the Snake River, and on what was the bottom of Lake Missoula. They were not readily spotted from the ground, often being

Left: "Islands" of fertile loess in the otherwise barren scablands. (U.S. Geological Survey)

Right: Former beach lines, representing various stands of Lake Missoula, are visible on the slope up to 950 feet above Missoula, Montana. (U.S. Geological Survey)

Overleaf: Scabland cataracts in Moses Coulee seen from the air. North is to the right. (U.S. Department of Agriculture)

masked by sagebrush. Some, however, are highlighted by linear patterns of vegetation, as near Spirit Lake in northwest Idaho. Those in Quincy Basin were not discovered until the U.S. Bureau of Reclamation surveyed the area from the air in preparation for the Grand Coulee irrigation project. The ripples, composed of coarse gravel rather than sand, had also been difficult to recognize because of their improbable size—many so large that someone standing between them cannot see over their tops. Among the largest were those formed in Montana as Lake Missoula drained like an unplugged bathtub. They are 20 to 30 feet high, some of them two miles long and spaced 200 feet apart. They can be seen from the air covering a large area where

waters of the fast-subsiding lake poured over Markle Pass, midway between Great Falls and Spokane and thirty-five miles southeast of Flathead Lake.

It is now believed that the scablands are not the work of a single flood. Rather the Clark Fork ice dam is thought to have formed and collapsed a number of times. Richard B. Waitt, Jr., of the U.S. Geological Survey, believes he has documented about forty floods, most of them during the last Ice Age, but some of which may have occurred in the previous one. Few of the floods, if any, were as tremendous as the most recent. It has been dated at 13,000 years ago because its deposits include ash from an eruption of Mount Saint Helens, whose age has been well established.

The repeated flooding has been indicated by "rhythmic bedding" of sediments laid down in areas where flood waters, over and over, backed up and laid down successive layers of sediment. The bedding is rhythmic in the uniform spacing of its stacked layers, each twenty to forty inches thick and changing from sand on the bottom of the layer (laid down at the start of the flood) to fine silt on the top. They are exposed at numerous sites along the Yakima and Walla Walla rivers in the Pasco Basin, which was repeatedly flooded as water backed up from the Wallula Gap. In Montana, where Interstate 90 follows the Clark Fork River across what had been the floor of Lake Missoula, rhythmic bedding can be seen in a cut near Ninemile Creek. Between the flood deposits are lake sediments in which Waitt has counted from twenty to fifty-five annual layers, indicating that the floods were spaced twenty to sixty years apart.

There is, of course, no historic record of these floods, but it is remotely possible that the last was witnessed and, perhaps, cost human lives. Some 13,000 years ago—if not earlier—Asians were moving down the corridor between the shrinking ice sheet centered on Hudson Bay in the east and ice covering the Rocky Mountains to the west.

Left: These giant ripples alongside the Columbia River below Trinidad, Washington, were formed by the Spokane deluge. (John S. Shelton)

Right: These many evenly spaced flood deposits, exposed near Walla Walla, indicate that there may have been as many as forty floods. (R. B. Waitt, Jr., U.S. Geological Survey)

When the *Viking* cameras began recording detailed images of areas on Mars that looked strikingly like the scablands, geologists wondered whether, in scars left by the Spokane floods, they might find the answer to the Martian puzzle. Today it never rains on Mars. Its air is thin, with very little moisture. Yet it may not always have been so. Water vapor, when exposed to sunlight high in Earth's atmosphere, breaks up into hydrogen and oxygen. The gravity of Earth is not strong enough to keep the hydrogen from flying off into space, but it does hold on to the oxygen, and that is why Earth's atmosphere has lost its hydrogen. The gravity of Mars cannot long hold onto either oxygen or hydrogen, but in its infancy, before such loss became significant, the planet may have been relatively wet. There are sinuous, meandering streambeds and drainage patterns on Mars like those produced on Earth by flowing water, as well as areas of deep scour that could be the result of catastrophic floods. All are on a grander scale, even, than the scablands. Because Mars is so dry, some geologists have suggested glaciers, lava, mud flows, or even wind as the erosive agent.

In 1978 the National Aeronautics and Space Administration sponsored a conference to consider what was known about the Spokane floods and their relevance to the Martian puzzle. The conference proceedings, dedicated to Bretz, then aged ninety-five, documented efforts to understand how the scablands and Grand Coulee were formed—an undertaking made particularly difficult because nowhere on earth today can such large-scale water action be observed. Victor Baker (then at the University of

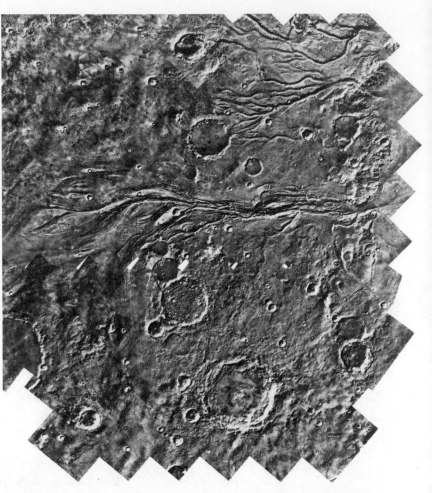

Catastrophic flooding akin to that of the scablands gouged out these scars on Mars. (Mosaic of Viking orbiter images/NASA)

Texas) proposed that the water flowing through such channels as Grand Coulee reached thirty meters per second (sixty-seven miles per hour). Great swirls—underwater tornadoes—were generated and, combined with high pressure at the bottom, tore huge chunks of rock from the underlying basalt. Being of the columnar type, whole pillars of basalt were carried off and deposited many miles downstream.

One of Flint's arguments against the flood hypothesis was similarity of the scablands to scoured formations in Idaho at Red Rock Pass and where the Snake River flows past Twin Falls. These features, in fact, are now thought to have been produced about 14,000 years ago by another flood of monumental dimensions when Lake Bonneville—an enlarged version of Great Salt Lake that extended from Utah into Idaho—spilled over Red Rock Pass, sweeping away its soft sediment like a breached dike to produce a channel that drained the lake and sent a torrent down the Snake River and through Hells Canyon. In a matter of hours the pass was cut down to bedrock, lowering it by 344 feet. Then, as the years passed, overflow continued to lower it another 13 feet.

Lesser scars across the Great Plains on both sides of the Canadian-American border were produced where the ice blocked normal drainage northward toward Hudson

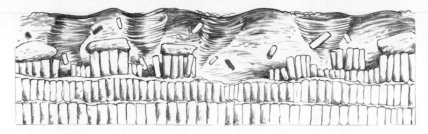

How "hydraulic tornadoes" tore loose entire columns of basalt, rapidly eroding Grand Coulee, as envisioned by Victor R. Baker.

This canyon on the Snake River below Twin Falls, Idaho, was carved by the deluge from Lake Bonneville. (Victor R. Baker)

Bay, impounding large quantities of meltwater that then cut through glacial deposits toward the south. As the ice front retreated, lower escape routes were exposed and new channels cut. As pointed out by the Canadian geologist Victor K. Prest, these water-carved gorges seem incongruous, cutting across what is now an arid landscape. In his book *Canada's Heritage of Glacial Features* he cites ten of them within a small area near Lethbridge, Alberta. Alan E. Kehew of the University of North Dakota believes that a "domino effect" may have occurred when a lake near Regina, Saskatchewan, discharged a mass of water into North Dakota, causing additional glacial lakes to break loose, scouring the landscape east of Minot. Canadian geologists have identified two canyons formed by torrents, laden with erosive sand and gravel, that periodically broke out of Lake Agassiz—for thousands of years the largest lake in North America (see map on page 258). Overtooth Canyon delivered water from that lake into what is now Lake Nipigon, north of Lake Superior. Ouimet Canyon then carried it south into Lake Superior itself. None of these floods, however, was in a class with those that produced the scablands of Washington.

Lake Bonneville and Lake Lahontan, another huge body of water covering much of Nevada to the west, were not formed primarily by meltwater—as in the case of Lake

Missoula—but during what geologists call a "pluvial" period of heavy rainfall presumably associated with the ice ages. Prolonged, torrential rains may not have been necessary. If the air of that region—now extremely dry—were humid, as would have been the case when ice to the north was melting, lakes would have formed, even if rainfall were not extremely heavy, because evaporation was reduced, due both to high humidity and low temperature. Melting to the north may also have made the climate rainier.

Lake Bonneville covered almost 20,000 square miles, and for a time its surface was more than 1,000 feet above the present level of Great Salt Lake (and Utah's major cities), as is evident in beach lines high on surrounding mountain slopes. Lake Lahontan and its sister lakes extended into California and Oregon. Fragments of the lake remain, such as Pyramid Lake (named for the sharp rock promontory in its midst) and Walker Lake near the western boundary of Nevada, but much of the lake bed is now the Black Rock Desert. Similarly a large part of the old floor of Lake Bonneville is the Great Salt Lake Desert, southwest of the present lake (Salt Lake City being to its southeast). In that desert are the Bonneville Salt Flats, where many world records for fast driving were set.

Through much of the successive ice ages Lake Bonneville seems to have waxed and waned, as indicated by the steplike succession of its beach lines. Material extracted from a hole drilled more than 1,000 feet into the south shore of Great Salt Lake indicates more than a score of such cycles in the past 800,000 years. Apparently only once, however, did the lake burst through Red Rock Pass to rival the repeated Spokane floods.

Fossil finds tell us that the shores of the lake were inhabited by such giant ice age animals as the Columbian mammoth, the giant short-faced bear, the American lion, and extinct species of camel, horse, bison, and musk-ox. Freshwater fish abounded in the lake itself.

Typical landscape in Badlands National Monument, South Dakota. (National Park Service)

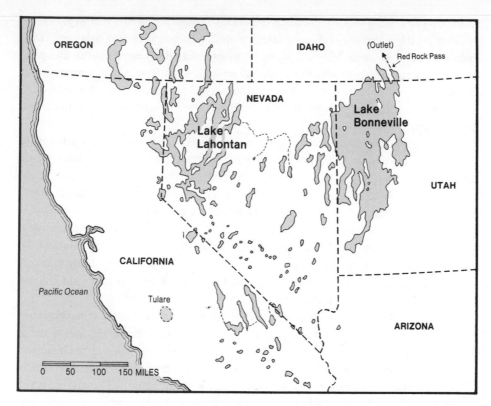

The great western ice age lakes. (Adapted from "Map of the Pleistocene Lakes of the Basin-and-Range Province and Its Significance" by O. E. Meinzer, in Geological Society of America Bulletin, vol. 33, 1922, p. 543.)

Its shrunken remnant, Great Salt Lake, is still the largest body of water west of the Mississippi and is populated by millions of waterfowl and migratory birds, particularly in the marshes of the Bear River delta in its northeast corner. When John C. Freemont's expedition reached the lake in 1843, he described the scene in his journal: "The whole morass was animated with multitudes of water fowl, which appeared to be very wild—rising for the space of a mile at the sound of a gun, with a noise like distant thunder. Several of the people waded out into the marshes, and we had to-night a delicious supper of ducks, geese, and plover."

The lake has been cut into three parts by causeways built to carry the Southern Pacific Railroad, and each part has its own water quality and wildlife. The first causeway, built from 1902 to 1903, isolated the large bay in the northeast corner into which the Bear River discharges. As a result the bay became far less saline than the rest of the lake. Freshwater marsh vegetation spread along its shores and became a favorite place for ducks, geese, herons, swans, pelicans, and ibis to pause in their migrations or to nest.

Large fluctuations in lake levels allowed the salinity to return periodically and this, plus commercial hunting, greatly reduced the flocks. In 1928 Congress established the 65,000-acre Bear River Migratory Bird Refuge, and once basins around the river delta were diked to keep the water fresh, birds in transit rose to as many as two million a year. A high lookout tower now permits visitors to gaze far across the delta.

After World War II the rest of the lake was divided when the trestle that carried the railroad over the main body of water was replaced by a causeway. As readily observed from the air, the water of the southern half is now fresher and bluer than that of the northwestern part. In spring and summer its islands provide nesting sites, safe from predators, for five species of colonial nesters: herons, cormorants, gulls, terns, and pelicans.

The pluvial period that produced the vanished lakes of the West is also believed to have created the savage, deeply eroded badlands of the Dakotas and elsewhere. Of all campsites occupied by my family on transcontinental trips none was more dramatic than one in the Dakota badlands. It was like a visit to a strange, pinnacled, multicolored world or a return to the era before plants and animals colonized the land. Pluvial period erosion, some believe, also carved such canyons as that of the Canadian River, which has cut a gorge almost 1,500 feet deep across the Las Vegas Plain, east of the Rockies in New Mexico, and that of the Cimarron River to the north. The rainfall of the present era seems grossly inadequate to have produced those features. In fact the Cimarron River is dry most of the year.

The bright, almost white patches of lowland seen by air travelers in the arid region between the Rocky Mountains and the Sierra Nevada serve as reminders that at times in the not-too-distant past the climate there was very different. Most of these former lake beds are dry, although occasional rains—even flash floods—send torrents sweeping down from the surrounding mountains, spreading alluvial fans (symmetrical, fan-shaped deposits) where the water spreads sediment onto the plain, and carving braided streambeds that as seen from the air sometimes cover all slopes feeding a single lake bed. Even along the sides of Death Valley, where one might think it never rains, there are magnificent alluvial fans (as shown on page 202).

Salts that have accumulated in dry lake beds after repeated cycles of rain and evaporation have made them unsuited for virtually all forms of plant life. When the Spanish pioneers first saw these circular, near-white patches of salt and sand they called them *playas* from the Spanish for "beach." Like the larger lake beds of the Great Salt Lake Desert and the Black Rock Desert, as well as the scablands of Washington, they stand as reminders that periods of the American past were very different from the present.

22 THE HAWAIIAN ISLANDS—
CHILDREN OF THE GREAT
PACIFIC HOT SPOT

Hawaiian landscapes are particularly wonderful not only because of their extraordinary beauty but also for their uniqueness. Nothing on the North American continent even closely resembles them. They are a product of forces peculiar to the central Pacific: the outpourings of highly fluid lava that produced them, constant pounding by waves driven from the northeast by the trade winds, and "one-sided" erosion by rains persistently dumped onto their windward slopes by these moisture-laden winds. Armies of waterfalls fed by those rains have carved magnificent, accordion-shaped cliffs clothed in vegetation, such as the ones that face the wind along the entire northeast side of Oahu. Waterfalls have likewise dug valleys so deep and steep-walled that they seem to have been cut by a giant knife.

Despite the marvelous diversity of the islands they have all been made in much the same way. They differ chiefly because of their respective ages. Probably all were originally much like the island of Hawaii—the Big Island—with its enormous shield volcanoes that slope gently down to the sea and then continue that slope beneath the water to the deep floor of the Pacific. Mauna Kea rises 13,796 feet above the sea and about 29,000 feet above the ocean floor, making it the largest such protuberance on earth (rivaled only by such giants as Olympus Mons, the volcano that dominates the landscape of Mars). The combined undersea base of Mauna Kea and its sister volcano, Mauna Loa, is more than 100 miles wide, and their volume is 10,000 cubic miles.

As noted earlier, the islands have been created by volcanic eruptions from a source that has remained fixed within the earth as the Pacific Plate drifted over it toward the northwest. If one follows the chain in that direction, each island becomes older and more eroded. The oldest have sunk until nothing remains above water except coral reefs that have built layer upon layer atop their now deeply submerged volcanic cores, as at Kure and Midway. At French Frigate Shoals only a lava pinnacle remains within its fringing reef. Beyond Kure the islands are completely submerged as seamounts. The line continues northwest until suddenly it bends almost due north, becoming the Emperor Seamount chain. This elbow in the line—like a bend in the contrail left by an airliner—marks where motion of the Pacific Plate changed direction millions of years ago. Drilling into the Emperor Seamount summits has confirmed that they, too, were an island chain. Since the other islands probably once resembled the island of Hawaii, the story of how they evolved must begin with that of the Big Island.

HAWAII

Eruptions began forming the island of Hawaii some 800,000 years ago ("yesterday," geologically speaking) and since then it has moved steadily northwest. Its volcanic activity, fed by the deep-seated hot spot, has therefore migrated in the opposite direction, from Mauna Kea, the dome dominating the island's northern half, to Mauna Loa and its neighbor Kilauea. Actually the island consists of five overlapping volcanic structures. Of the two major volcanoes—Mauna Kea and Mauna Loa—the former is slightly higher. Most of the year its summit is a desolation of black cinder cones tinted sulfurous yellow and pink. In winter, however, it is white with

Major historic lava flows on Hawaii, and the island's few rivers. (Adapted from Volcanoes in the Sea, *by G. A. Macdonald, A. T. Abbott, and F. L. Peterson. Honolulu: University of Hawaii Press, 2nd edition, 1983.)*

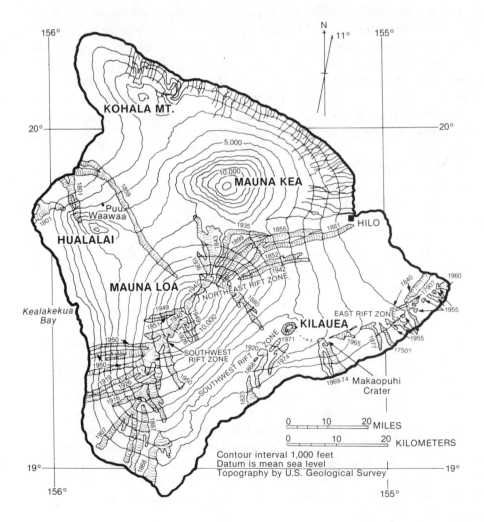

snow, and skiers schuss down its slopes within long-range view of beaches where surfers are riding the waves. Astronomers from Britain, Canada, France, and the United States have assumed that Mauna Kea is a dead volcano, and because of its high elevation, low latitude, and accessibility by road, the greatest concentration of observatories in the world has been assembled there. Its nearness to the equator means that unlike most observatory sites, it can scan most of the celestial sphere. At low elevations on the island moist trade winds often cover the coast with cloud banks that at night aid the astronomers by cutting off light from the coastal towns. On the other hand, the air above Mauna Kea is extremely dry—ideal for celestial observations (particularly at infrared wavelengths). The atmosphere is also so thin, however, that some astronomers find concentration difficult. The observers live at a station several thousand feet below the 13,800-foot summit.

A geophysical observatory near the top of Mauna Loa, the sister volcano to the south, is also reached by road, but it is not at the summit. Mauna Loa is definitely not dead. My first visit to that observatory, in the 1960's, was in an army truck rugged enough to manage the road that then led across a long succession of lava flows. The driver maintained constant radio contact with the observatory in case of an eruption, since, he explained, pahoehoe lava—the fast-flowing kind—might cross the road. Knowing which route it was following could be "useful." When lava flows down the mountain, the central part of the stream may reach thirty-five miles per hour. It tends, however, to feed a broad front that advances more slowly. It was observations by the Mauna Loa Observatory, beginning in 1958, that first documented the steady increase in atmospheric carbon dioxide, due to the worldwide growth in fuel burning.

Mid-ocean volcanoes such as those of the Hawaiian chain and Iceland tend to erupt along rift zones that sometimes almost completely traverse the mountain. On Mauna Loa rifts extend from the summit both northeast, toward the port city of Hilo, and in the opposite direction toward the southwest coast. The southwestern rifts have erupted at least ten times since 1851, sending flows across the coastal road at a number of places. Some of these rivers of black, chaotic lava, although decades old, look as though they arrived yesterday. Where a flow plunged into the sea, the lava, quenched by rapid cooling, formed a black, glassy substance that has been ground by the surf into a black sand beach like the one at Kalapana. One of the older flows formed an ideal landing site on the otherwise steep coast of Kealakekua Bay where, in 1779, Captain James Cook, European discoverer of the islands, went ashore and was soon killed by the Hawaiians.

In 1950 a two-week eruption from the southwestern rifts buried thirty-five square miles of the island. It began near the top of the rift zone and within fifteen minutes more than two miles of fissures began ejecting fiery-red lava. Added fissures opened farther down the mountain and soon an eight-mile line of lava fountains was spurting molten rock 1,000 feet into the air. As the main river of lava crossed the coastal highway it destroyed a restaurant and other buildings. The police struggled with traffic jams and sought to control reckless sightseers among the thousands who came to watch. Ice cream and soft-drink vendors had a field day.

Kilauea, Mauna Loa's less lofty neighbor, erupts more frequently, and since Hawaiian volcanoes tend to be predictable and well behaved, it is a favorite tourist attraction. The summits of both Mauna Loa and Kilauea are included in Hawaii Volcanoes National Park. Kilauea (which in Hawaiian means "rising smoke cloud") has one of the world's most awesome calderas, eight miles in circumference and 500 feet deep. Perched on its rim is the Volcano Observatory of the U.S. Geological Survey, from which one can look down into the deep pit on Kilauea's floor known as Halemaumau ("house of the everlasting fire"). The floor of this crater-within-a-crater is a ninety-five-acre lava lake whose surface rises and falls at the whim of the volcano. Several times, from 1919 to 1921, it overflowed onto the floor of the caldera and, at one point, undermined the caldera edge. Chunks dislodged from the wall floated in the lava like black icebergs in a fiery sea. Sometimes hardened lava covering the lake in Halemaumau breaks into cracks through which the red-hot lava can be seen. At night it is hard to imagine a more theatrical sight. "Here," wrote Mark Twain, when he first saw Kilauea in 1866, "was a yawning pit upon whose floor the armies of Russia could camp, and have room to spare." He likened the intricate pattern of fiery cracks on the lava lake to "a colossal railroad map of the state of Massachusetts done in chain lightning on a midnight sky."

At Kilauea most of the activity in recent years has been along its two rift zones. One runs from the caldera southeast past Kilauea-iki and a chain of similar craters—frequently in eruption—toward the town of Kalapana on the coast (itself threatened by a flow in 1977). The rift curves eastward past a subdivision, where a dozen homes were engulfed in 1983, and on to the coast past the village of Kapoho, which was buried in 1960. An eruption at the east end of this rift produced the strange black columns of Lava Tree State Monument, formed where lava swept through a forest, coating each tree. Only lava in contact with the wood cooled enough to solidify, leaving "lava trees" that remained although the charred wood disintegrated.

The most noteworthy eruption along the other, southwest rift zone of Kilauea was that of 1790, in which poisonous gas killed every man, woman, and child of a small Hawaiian army on the march. Today Kilauea eruptions and their lava fountains periodically feature on television newscasts, especially if the river of molten rock reaches the sea, producing spectacular steam clouds.

Mauna Loa and Kilauea are destined for extinction and a successor is already growing under the sea thirty miles to the southeast. Known today as Loihi Seamount, it still has a long way to go, since its summit is 3,200 feet below the ocean surface, but it is already a formidable mountain on the sea floor. Seismic recordings indicate that it is being fed through its own volcanic ducts, rather than by branches of those feeding Kilauea and Mauna Loa.

So permeable to rainwater is the younger part of the Big Island that it has virtually no rivers. None reaches the coast from Hilo, on the east, around the entire southern and western shores of that giant island. Instead rainwater percolates down through the volcanic deposits and accumulates on top of seawater that has infiltrated from the sides at sea level. Water supplies in the islands depend heavily on wells that tap such layers of fresh water but do not reach the brackish water underneath. Since there are no rivers and streams at this early stage in the island's evolution, its slopes remain remarkably smooth and symmetrical, uncut by erosion. This preserves the volcano's classic profile of a flat-lying shield. Once eruptions have ended, however, and new

Halemaumau Crater in the floor of Kilauea Caldera. (Agatin T. Abbott)

lava layers no longer coat the surface, chemical weathering of the rock begins to create soils that cement the holes and cracks, making the formation less permeable. Consequently valley erosion begins—initiation of the long process that has produced the most spectacular Hawaiian scenery.

Along the northeast coast of Hawaii, where the slopes of Kohala Mountain face squarely into the trade winds and are frequently deluged with rain, four deep valleys (Waipio, Waimanu, Honokane, and Pololu) have been eroded. In contrast to valleys in other parts of the world formed by horizontally flowing water, these have largely been cut by waterfalls. The volcanic terrain is a multilayered series of basalts alternating with more easily eroded volcanic rubble. The plunge pool at the bottom of each waterfall works on one of the weaker layers, undermining the entire structure above it. While the basalt is more resistant, it tends to cleave into columns that come tumbling down, helping to form a vertical cliff—the same process that enabled catastrophic floods rapidly to carve Washington's Grand Coulee. The waterfall, perhaps only a few feet high when it sets to work at the coast, eats its way inland and

up-slope, growing more than 1,000 feet high and producing a valley that can be incredibly steep-walled and narrow. The gorge of Koula Stream, a branch of the Hanapepe River on the island of Kauai, is so narrow that it is said sunlight can reach its floor for only one hour a day.

Numerous waterfalls may form along a coast and march inland, side by side. Where they merge, narrow, isolated walls remain between them. As pointed out by Gordon A. Macdonald and Agatin T. Abbott of the University of Hawaii in their book, *Volcanoes in the Sea,* a climber on one of those knife-edges "can almost believe he feels the ridge swaying under him in the wind."

One action of the heavy rains has been to remove other constituents from the volcanic deposits, leaving a concentration of aluminum in the form of bauxite. There are an estimated 112 million tons of bauxite on the northeast coast of Hawaii. Other deposits have been found in the rainier parts of Maui and Kauai, but the bauxite contains too much iron to be tempting in terms of present refining methods. Otherwise the islands are generally poor in commercial minerals.

Left: These three waterfalls at the head of Haiku Valley are carving "vertical valleys" into the Koolau Range on Oahu. (Agatin T. Abbott)

Right: The wind-driven sea has cut these cliffs into lava flows on the northeast side of Kohala volcano on Hawaii. (Agatin T. Abbott)

MAUI

Maui, the next island up the chain, was formed primarily between 400,000 and 1.3 million years ago, and the volcano at its northwest end has been extinct long enough for erosion to begin, particularly along its northeast slopes, which receive the second heaviest rainfall in the islands. There the gently sloping volcanic landscape has been eroded into the extraordinarily precipitous Iao Valley, which penetrates the heart of the volcano's ancient caldera. Although the caldera, after formation, was filled to the brim with numerous lava layers, they were then weakened by volcanic gases percolating up from below, making them more vulnerable to erosion than the caldera walls. The Iao Valley has carved an amphitheater within this inner sanctum of the caldera but has left the oft-photographed Iao Needle as a remnant of the original, many-layered accumulation.

West Maui's scenery would be far less dramatic, were it not for its height, culminating in the 5,788-foot elevation of its summit, Puu Kukui. Islands in the Hawaiian chain with no tall volcanoes to intercept the trade winds, such as Maui's neighbors Lanai and Kahoolawe, do not produce enough rain to erode deep valleys.

Maui is shaped into a lopsided dumbbell by its two volcanoes: West Maui on the northwest and Haleakala on the southeast. Haleakala, 10,023 feet high, is younger and far more massive. Its crater, seven miles long, two miles wide, and a half-mile deep, is sometimes described as the world's largest, although it is smaller than a number of calderas. Its large size derives in part from erosion of a mountain that was probably as monumental as Mauna Loa. Two deep valleys were cut into the rim of the crater on the north and south, then were partially filled by lava flows one of which, passing through the Kaupo Valley gap on the south, spread into the sea as a fan-shaped apron clearly visible from the air. Wisps of steam rising within the crater are reminders that a small eruption occurred there as recently as two centuries ago. There

are few fears for a renewal, however, and horseback riders roam freely across its strange landscape in search of the remarkable silversword that clings to a fragile existence there. This plant, offering a delicately rounded burst of silver spikes to the sky, almost became extinct until goats were denied access to its habitat. It looks more suited to a tropical rain forest than the sterile, windswept, and often frigid environment of the crater floor. Yet, almost alone, it thrives on the cinder cones, decorating their black slopes with patches of silver.

MOLOKAI

Molokai, northwest of Maui, was born between 1.3 and 1.8 million years ago and, like Maui and Oahu, along with Hawaii, is the child of twin volcanoes. Its north coast, particularly in the east, consists of cliffs rising nearly 4,000 feet from the sea. They face the constant onslaught of waves driven across the open ocean by the trade winds and are classic examples of the sea cliffs produced by wave erosion along many

Left: Haleakala Crater on Maui has been breached in two areas. Kaupo Gap is lower left and Koolau Gap is to the right. (Agatin T. Abbott)

Right: Sea cliffs on the windward side of Molokai. (Agatin T. Abbott)

Hawaiian coasts. They tend to be straight, rather than pleated like those formed by waterfalls, or in some cases have been carved into crescent-shaped embayments.

The slopes of Molokai's shield volcanoes originally reached the sea, but waves worked on them like an army of mice nibbling at a gently sloping mountain of cheese on a flat floor. If the mice remained at floor level, just as the waves stay at sea level, they would produce a cliff that became higher and higher as they ate their way into the heap.

Long after the sea cliffs of this coast were eroded a small shield volcano erupted on their seaward side, forming Kalaupapa Peninsula, site of an airfield and famous for Father Damien's ministrations to a leper colony there. A crater at the volcano's summit extends below sea level, and from the air one can see a long crack running downslope from the crater rim—a collapsed lava tube.

Father Damien, a Belgian-born missionary, came to the islands in 1863 and learned of the misery of some 600 lepers sent to Molokai with no provisions for their livelihood. In 1873 he moved in with the lepers, did what he could for them, and within eleven years had contracted the disease himself. Today leprosy is usually treatable, and while at last report a few lepers were still living out their lives on Molokai, the colony that became a federal leprosarium has been closed.

On reefs along the more sheltered south shore of the island the ancient Hawaiians built more than fifty fish ponds, some of them as large as 500 acres. The ponds, in which they raised mullet, are partially silted up and overgrown with mangroves. At the west end of that shore sand dunes, some of them sixty feet high, form a belt a half-mile wide that almost crosses the island—similar to a belt of dunes across the isthmus linking the two halves of Maui.

OAHU

The first of the two great volcanoes forming Oahu began rising from the sea more than three million years ago and its survivor is the Waianae Range along the island's west coast. It was followed by formation of the volcano whose remnant is the Koolau Range running the full length of the island's opposite coast from behind Waikiki and Honolulu to its northwest end. (As with most Hawaiian names the double vowels are pronounced separately—*Ko-oh-lau.*) Both ranges are elongated along the path of the island's motion over the hot spot that formed them. The Waianae Range is now relatively arid, being cut off from the rain-bearing trades by the Koolau Range, but it seems to have been heavily eroded before the Koolau volcano rose high enough to perform such a role. A relatively uneroded, lofty remnant of the original Waianae shield has survived in the flat summit of Mount Kaala, 4,025 feet above sea level and the highest point on Oahu. There a mile-wide swamp filled with stunted trees resembles a natural bonsai garden.

The outpourings of the Koolau volcano formed the broad slope between the two ranges that is now covered with sugarcane and pineapple plantations as well as military reservations. Although the Koolau volcano is younger, most of its northeast half has eroded away. Nevertheless a multitude of dikes—vertical walls of basalt left by lava intrusions—delineate the roots of its rift zone. The dikes, ranging in width from a few inches to a dozen feet, are exposed in road cuts where the Pali Highway descends toward Kailua and elsewhere in the hills that, from Kaneohe to Kahana, lie between the sea and the towering cliffs of the Koolau Range. As many as 600 per mile have been charted.

The volcano apparently collapsed into a caldera whose long axis extended eight miles in a northwest-southeast direction and was about four miles wide. One side of it lay close to the present line of the Pali—the magnificent series of precipices that face the trade winds on the northeast side of the Koolau Range. The caldera's opposite rim, along the coastline past Kaneohe, has been totally annihilated by wind and water. The buried heart of the caldera may account for unusually intense gravity recorded in the zone of old plantations and new condominiums between the Koolau Range and Kaneohe Bay. It seems to emanate from a deep-seated lump of dense minerals that settled out of the old erupting lavas.

This caldera, like others in the Hawaiian Islands, was filled by successive outpourings of lava, but as in the older of Maui's two volcanoes, volcanic gases eventually made these lava beds more easily eroded. Most of those that once filled the caldera have vanished, apart from the ones below sea level. Some, however, survive in Olomana Peak, whose 1,643-foot spire between Waimanalo and Kailua indicates their original thickness.

The accordion-pleated cliffs, or "vertical valleys," that for thirty miles form the windward walls of the Koolau Range are masterpieces of waterfall erosion. Until geologists guessed their origin they wondered how, if the Koolau volcano once resembled the gentle slopes of Mauna Loa, such magnificent battlements could have evolved from such low-pitched beginnings. They proposed wave action or lifting of the cliffs by radical fault movements.

The Hawaiian word for cliff is *pali* and the awesome Nuuanu Pali is the most famous of the Koolau precipices. It is reached by a road that climbs from Honolulu up the gently sloping Nuuanu Valley to its brink (if one bypasses the tunnel near the top). The cliffs drop sheer from the summit to the coastal plain far below. Although almost vertical, they are coated with greenery constantly agitated by the northeast trades sweeping up their faces. Rarely can one look along the range and not see rain showers feeding the curtains of waterfalls that have carved each pleat of the accordion. Originally some waterfalls may have cut through lava within the ancient caldera faster than their neighbors, creating a deeply indented mountain front. Their advance slowed, however, when they reached the stronger rock of the caldera wall, allowing the other waterfalls to catch up and form what is now a single great battlement of volcanic rock. Some of the cliffs closest to the sea, however, were probably cut by

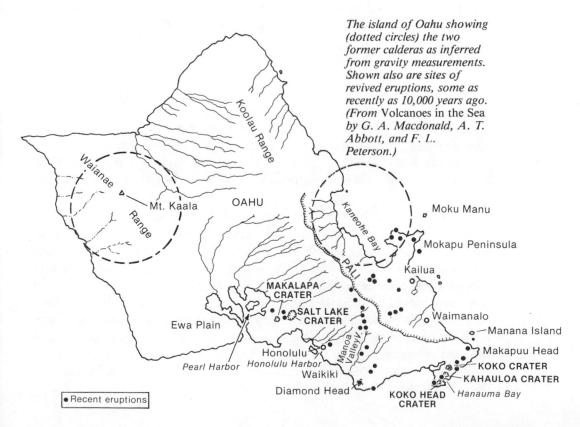

The island of Oahu showing (dotted circles) the two former calderas as inferred from gravity measurements. Shown also are sites of revived eruptions, some as recently as 10,000 years ago. (From Volcanoes in the Sea *by G. A. Macdonald, A. T. Abbott, and F. L. Peterson.)*

waves. Above Waimanalo Bay they are so lofty that hang gliders leap from the top, sail far out over the ocean, and glide down to the shoreline.

Elsewhere along the Koolau Range waterfalls have produced amphitheater-headed valleys that to some extent resemble cirques formed in colder regions by the clawing action of glaciers. Sometimes this process uncovers horizontal layers that trap water percolating down through the rock. Where such a formation emerges from the face of the cliff the water, now liberated, gushes forth as a "perched spring" and tumbles down.

If the Koolau and Waianae volcanoes were originally as high as Mauna Loa, their height above sea level has now been halved, partly by erosion and partly by sinking of the entire island, some of whose stream-eroded valleys are now 1,000 feet below the sea surface. Once one of the islands has moved past the hot spot that made it, the crust beneath it cools and shrinks. Consequently the island sinks, destined ultimately to become a seamount.

Sea level itself has also varied, building coral reefs both higher and lower than those of today. Pearl Harbor, with its several inlets or "lochs," was cut into coral by converging streams when sea levels were lower—probably during the last Ice Age. The harbor has been formed by flooding of these valleys. The Ewa Plain, covered with sugarcane plantations west of Pearl Harbor, rests on coral formed when the sea was higher, as between ice ages.

Whereas the rainy windward side of Oahu has been shaped by running water, its leeward side owes its landscape in part to the paucity of rain there. By the time the trade winds have crossed both the Koolau and Waianae ranges they have been drained of moisture, and the southwest shore of Oahu, beyond the Waianaes, is a cactus-studded desert.

Rain often falls on the side of the Koolaus forming a backdrop for Honolulu and Waikiki, although the scenery is no match for the great cliffs on the opposite side. The rain feeds streams that have cut deep valleys through the Honolulu area. Yet the city itself does not receive much of the rain and therefore, between those valleys, are terraces that have been little eroded. They have preserved the original slope of the ancient volcano. Such terraces rising behind Honolulu and Waikiki include St. Louis Heights and Wilhelmina Rise. They are covered with housing and at night form islands of sparkling lights that greet those gliding down toward Honolulu International Airport.

After the prolonged eruptions that produced the Koolau volcano there was a two-million-year pause during which wind, wave, and rain cut valleys 2,000 feet deep, and carved out the great Nuuanu Pali and other features dominating the island's modern landscape. Then, over a period of several hundred thousand years, more than thirty eruptions occurred in eastern Oahu. Why is not clear, for by then the island had presumably moved well past the hot spot that gave it birth. Although these eruptions were on a modest scale they produced features, such as Diamond Head, prominent in Hawaiian travel posters. The last eruption may have occurred less than 10,000 years ago, and according to Macdonald and Abbott, since some intervals between the eruptions were longer than that, "we cannot say that the Honolulu volcanic activity has ended forever."

Above: The downwind side of Diamond Head Crater is highest. (Agatin T. Abbott)

Right: Pali Cliffs on the windward side of Oahu. Waimanalo is the town on the beach; the cliffs at bottom are a favorite of hang gliders. (Agatin T. Abbott)

The eruptions occurred primarily in a cluster of sites east of Pearl Harbor as well as in two linear zones: One is a chain of a dozen cones and craters running from Diamond Head through Round Top, Sugarloaf, and Tantalus, overlooking Honolulu to the crest of the Koolau Range. At least two lava flows descended the Nuuanu Valley from vents in this chain and parts of them can be seen as the highway climbs toward the Pali. A short distance south of its junction with the Old Pali Road the highway cuts through the Makuku cinder cone, source of one flow. At the Pali overlook the bank of red cinders on the southeast side of the parking lot came from an eruption on the crest. Beyond there craters are scattered across the coastal plain as far northeast as Mokapu Peninsula and Moku Manu Island.

The other chain follows the eastern shore from Koko Head through Hanauma Bay (twin craters sheltering a favorite snorkeling reef), Koko Crater, and behind Makapuu Point to Manana (Rabbit) Island. The coast highway, Route 74, follows this line of vents and craters, crossing two of their lava flows, the most obvious of which emanated from the Kalama cinder cone and reaches the sea east of Sandy Beach as a chaotic nightmare of jumbled aa lava. The other flow is crossed by the highway at Sea Life Park and Makapuu Beach.

The eruptions that occurred along the coast became explosive on contact with water, throwing debris far enough on all sides to form broad cones with a central, shallow crater. The ejected material accumulated chiefly on the downwind side, and therefore the southwest rim of Diamond Head is by far the highest, forming the famous profile seen from Waikiki. The debris solidified into a tuff that at Diamond Head contains fragments of coral reef blown out by the eruption. The tuff is cemented by calcite, and the crater gained its name because calcite crystals that British sailors found there were taken to be diamonds.

Eruptions farther from the sea ejected their material more vertically, forming smaller, steeper cones. It is a combination of three such cones—Round Top, Sugar-loaf, and Tantalus—that rises 2,000 feet behind Honolulu. Round Top Drive circles part of the summit area and offers sweeping views of the city and southern coast. Near these craters, in addition to volcanic cinders and other typical ejecta, one can find round lava balls up to four inches in diameter. Black, glassy ash from their eruptions is uncovered in almost every excavation for a new building in the booming, down-town area of Honolulu.

In one of the last Oahu eruptions, about 14,000 years ago, Sugarloaf sent a river of lava plunging into the Manoa Valley, part of it passing beyond the present-day Lunalilo Freeway—chief artery on the south side of the island. The lava filled part of Manoa Valley, forming the terrace on which the main campus of the University of Hawaii has been built.

The cluster of young craters east of Pearl Harbor includes Aliamanu Crater (now a military reservation), Makalapa, on whose slopes overlooking the naval base Admiral Chester W. Nimitz had his headquarters as Pacific Fleet commander during World War II, and Salt Lake, now filled in as the golf course of the Honolulu International Country Club. Punchbowl, another crater formed in this period, rises above the heart of Honolulu and cradles the National Memorial Cemetery of the Pacific.

KAUAI

Kauai lies farthest to the northwest of the larger islands and was formed earliest—chiefly between 3.8 and 5.6 million years ago. It is dominated by a single massive volcano. Mount Waialeale (pronounced *Wye-ah-lee-ah-lee*) on the caldera edge rises 5,170 feet into the trade winds, making Kauai's interior the wettest region of the islands and perhaps on earth. An accumulation of 624 inches (52 feet) of rainfall was recorded in a single twelve-month period from 1947 to 1948.

On the dry, southwest side the original slope of the great shield has remained relatively intact, as can be seen from the air. The caldera of Waialeale, ten to twelve miles wide, is the largest in the islands and it, too, was later filled with lava to form a high plateau. Part of the latter has been severely eroded by runoff from the constant rains, forming Waimea Canyon. The latter runs ten miles inland from the point on the coast where, in 1778, Captain Cook made his first landing in what he called the Sandwich Islands. The canyon walls are reminiscent of the Grand Canyon, although the layers in its reddish walls are far more numerous and uniform, representing a prolonged series of eruptions rather than sediment accumulations. The canyon also differs from the one in Arizona in having far more greenery. It is only half as deep,

That Kauai originated as the dome of a great shield volcano is evident in this aerial view. (Agatin T. Abbott)

Left: The countless lava flows that built Kauai are exposed in the walls of Waimea Canyon. (Agatin T. Abbott)

Right: Honopu Valley on the Napali coast of Kauai. (Agatin T. Abbott)

but a highway along its western side provides spectacular views into its depths. The highway continues beyond the upper end of the canyon to where one can look down into the Kalalau Valley, facing the sea in a giant amphitheater surrounded by the towering Napali cliffs. The view into that isolated valley, filled with native vegetation and thus far unspoiled because it cannot be reached on wheels, is unforgettable.

As on Oahu, Kauai experienced an unexplained revival of volcanic activity after long quiescence. The interlude lasted from 1.5 to 3.0 million years ago, whereupon activity continued until about 600,000 years ago. Some forty volcanic vents and craters from that period have been found. Their flows covered about half of the eastern part of the island and created some of the level coastal areas that are now heavily cultivated.

Macdonald and Abbott, citing the past renewals of volcanism on Oahu, Kauai, and nearby Niihau, have warned of "a distinct possibility that more eruptions may take place on these islands, or, indeed, on any of the other islands."

23 INSTANT METAMORPHISM–
ASTEROID IMPACTS AS
SHAPERS OF THE LAND

Close-up photographs of the moon, Mars, and Mercury obtained from spacecraft in recent years have shown the surfaces of those bodies to be largely covered by craters of all sizes presumably produced by impacts of meteorites, asteroids, and comets. To what extent is this true of the North American landscape? Obviously it does not look like the moon. Our planet has an atmosphere, as the moon does not, and this means that wind, water, rupture by freezing, and scouring by ice are constantly altering the scenery. So do the forces from within the earth that build mountains and flood the land with lava.

Impact craters, therefore, cannot remain visible on this planet very long, geologically speaking, and until after World War II geologists paid little heed to the possibility that they have played a role in shaping the land. The most obvious candidate was Meteor Crater, a giant scoop blasted out of the flat, generally treeless Arizona plateau six miles south of Interstate 40. It is three miles in circumference and almost deep enough to hide the Washington Monument. "At least twenty football games could be played simultaneously on the crater floor," visitors are told. "Two million spectators could be accommodated on its sloping sides." The crater was originally thought to be volcanic, but toward the end of the last century A. E. Foote, a Philadelphia chemist and mineralogist, collected more than a hundred iron meteorites at the site, then known as Coon Butte, and he found microscopic diamonds in some of them. Following his report to the American Association for the Advancement of Science, Grove Karl Gilbert, chief geologist of the U.S. Geological Survey, visited the crater and because, contrary to his contemporaries, he believed similar structures on the moon had been produced by impacts rather than volcanic eruption, he suspected that the crater marked where an object had plunged into the earth and lay buried. It must have been enormous, he reasoned, to produce so large a crater, yet magnetic measurements showed no signs of so huge an iron body. Gilbert reluctantly concluded that a volcanic explosion had been the cause, and this view prevailed for many years.

Nevertheless, when in 1902 Daniel Moreau Barringer, a Philadelphia lawyer and mining engineer, heard of the crater and the meteorites around it, he speculated that a huge hunk of meteoritic nickel-iron was, in fact, buried there and began a long, costly effort to mine it. In response to his application for mining rights President Theodore Roosevelt signed a federal patent granting such permission and by 1909 twenty-eight exploratory holes and several mining shafts had been sunk into the crater floor. The first 550 feet of drilling penetrated "breccia"—a mixture of highly fragmented rock that included some meteoritic material. Below that was undisturbed Supai sandstone—the formation exposed deep within the Grand Canyon. This seemed to confirm that whatever blasted out the crater came from above—not from below—but it also cast doubt on Barringer's hope that a huge body of iron had plunged deeper. Barringer noted, however, that even when a bullet is fired into mud obliquely, it still leaves a round hole. He proposed that the meteorite had penetrated at an angle and lay under the crater's southeast rim. Drilling there reached 1,376 feet, but after being repeatedly halted, apparently by meteoritic material, it jammed and the cable broke. The stock market crash of 1929 frustrated all efforts to raise money for continuation

Meteor Crater. (Center for Meteorite Studies, Arizona State University)

of the project, and later that year Barringer died after having spent almost three decades and a large part of his fortune on the enterprise.

Detailed studies of the crater have been made by Eugene M. Shoemaker of the Geological Survey, documenting, for example, how flaps of the layers that form the Colorado Plateau, such as the Moenkopi Formation and the Grand Canyon's Coconino sandstone, were blasted up and folded outward, "somewhat like the petals of a flower blossoming." From his and other studies it is estimated that the crater was produced some 25,000 years ago when an object roughly 140 feet in diameter—far smaller than Gilbert's assumption— hit the earth at about 45,000 miles per hour. The energy of its impact caused an explosion thought to have been comparable with that of fifteen million tons of TNT—the yield of a very large hydrogen bomb. Most of the meteorite, Shoemaker believes, was melted and much of it may still be present in the crater as microscopic spheres embedded in glass, particularly in the lower part of the fractured rock under the crater floor.

After World War II candidates for other impact sites began to proliferate. In 1947 Robert S. Dietz of the U.S. Navy Electronics Laboratory in San Diego proposed that remarkable-looking rock structures known as shatter cones, found at a circular, supposedly volcanic feature at Kentland, Indiana, indicated an impact origin. Shatter cones are produced in rock by passage of a supersonic shock wave (one moving faster than the speed of sound in that material). Their apexes point toward the source of the shock wave and those at Kentland, said Dietz, designated a source above—not below—the formation. He therefore proposed that it was a deeply eroded impact crater, or astrobleme.

Meanwhile C. S. Beals of the Dominion Observatory in Ottawa and his colleagues were finding a number of suspicious scars, particularly in areas of the Canadian Shield where there is little soil or vegetation to camouflage them. In 1953 the Royal Canadian Air Force completed a photo survey covering much of Canada, and more than two million photographs were studied by the geologists. By the 1980's some forty "probable" and "possible" astroblemes had been identified in the United States and Canada. Probably the most impressive one is the Manicouagan structure 150 miles north of the Saint Lawrence River in Quebec. This strikingly circular feature, almost sixty miles in diameter, looks like a gigantic bull's-eye, for it holds a circular lake, Manicouagan Reservoir, surrounding a large island. It is thought to be the eroded remnant of an impact about 210 million years ago. A number of such probable impact structures are found in the Mississippi drainage region, some of them with a central peak similar to those produced by rebound in impact craters on the moon. In Ohio such a rebound lifted the center of the Serpent Mound cryptoexplosion structure 950 feet and has left a ring of forested hills clearly visible from the air. The famous Serpent Mound, built by prehistoric Indians, is on the structure's southwest side. At Manson in Iowa and Desplaines near Chicago's O'Hare Airport the existence of impact structures has been deduced from wells sunk to bedrock. Two strikingly circular features show up on geologic maps of Tennessee at Wells Creek and Flynn Creek, but they are partially masked by vegetation. One of the most impressive is the Sierra Madera structure, six miles in diameter with a mountain in its center, on a cattle ranch south of Fort Stockton in West Texas.

This crater, 1,280 feet wide and 320 feet deep, was produced in Nevada by a 100-kiloton nuclear explosion, code named Sedan, detonated 635 feet underground in 1962. The smaller craters are from other tests. (Department of Energy)

Such very large, circular features as the Gulf of Mexico, the southeast part of Hudson Bay, and the sediment-filled basin under the Michigan Peninsula have been proposed as impact scars, but for none of them is there any supportive evidence. A more likely candidate is Sudbury Basin in Ontario, forty miles north of Georgian Bay on the Trans-Canada Highway. It is an irregular oval, with an average diameter of eighty-five miles, formed some 1.84 billion years ago by an explosion of almost unimaginable power—estimated by nuclear-weapons specialists as equal to 50,000 billion tons of TNT. Around the rim of the basin are mines from which more than half of the world's nickel has been extracted, as well as gold, silver, platinum, lead, zinc, copper, and cobalt.

There are several tests of an explosive origin that can be applied to such features, including the presence of shatter cones and of minerals produced by extreme shock, such as diamonds (like those from Meteor Crater), coesite, or stishovite (two very dense forms of quartz named for those who first produced them in laboratory tests). Some of these clues are found at Sudbury and it is argued that the basin was originally circular, then later distorted by stresses within the earth. The ore, according to this hypothesis, was deposited by processes set in motion by shattering the earth to great depth. An opposing view is that the explosion was volcanic, on a scale far greater than any more recent eruptions, such as those at Yellowstone.

Obviously, major impacts are rare, but even those producing much smaller craters

Suspected and confirmed impact sites. (Adapted from Astronomy, *April 1981, p. 19, and from "Buried impact craters in the Williston Basin and adjacent area" by H. B. Sawatzky, in* Impact and Explosion Cratering—Planetary and Terrestrial Implications, *D. J. Roddy et al., eds. New York: Pergamon Press, 1977.)*

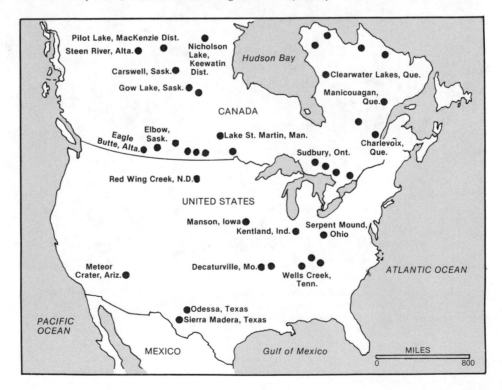

could have a devastating effect on earth's inhabitants. In October 1981, astronomers, geologists, explosion experts, paleontologists, and other specialists met at Snowbird, Utah, to consider "geological implications of impacts of large asteroids and comets on the earth." A map on the front cover of the conference proceedings shows ejection rays that might have radiated from the Manicouagan crater had it been formed by an asteroid several miles in diameter. The rays reach as far as Britain and Mexico as well as across Canada almost to Alaska. On the back cover is the same diagram, but with the continents assembled as they probably were at the time of the impact, 210 million years ago.

The meeting, sponsored by such agencies as the National Academy of Sciences, National Science Foundation, Office of Naval Research, and National Aeronautics and Space Administration, was called largely in response to the proposition of Luis and Walter Alvarez at the University of California in Berkeley and others that such an impact sixty-five million years ago blackened the sky long enough to cause mass extinctions at sea and on land, wiping out the dinosaurs. Because, as noted earlier, abnormally abundant iridium had been discovered in thin layers of sediment laid down at various widespread locations at about the time of these extinctions, it was widely assumed that it had come from an asteroid.

One of the questions facing the conferees was whether the five or six great extinctions identifiable in the fossil record were all caused by asteroid falls. As noted by Leon T. Silver of the California Institute of Technology, chief organizer of the meeting, in some of those extinctions as many as 80 to 90 percent of all species living in the sea were wiped out, although how suddenly that occurred is uncertain. Whether any impact, apart from the one that may have spelled doom for the dinosaurs, was associated with an extinction is not clear. It is certain, however, that some cataclysms have spread glassy debris—so-called tektites—over as much as 20 percent of the earth's surface. These objects appear to be droplets of molten rock shaped by flight through the atmosphere. The last such event, scattering tektites from the Philippines across Southeast Asia to Australia and almost across the Indian Ocean to Africa, occurred 700,000 years ago at a time when there do not appear to have been major extinctions.

At the Snowbird meeting Eugene Shoemaker and George W. Wetherill of the Carnegie Institution of Washington proposed that asteroids six miles in diameter probably hit the earth, on the average, every 40 million years. Of an estimated 1,000 asteroids that are a half mile or more in diameter and in orbits crossing that of the earth, about three hit per million years, whereas those half that size—capable of producing craters six miles wide—hit once every 100,000 years. There are far more small asteroids (in effect, large meteorites), and so their falls are more frequent.

Shoemaker has calculated that projectiles big enough to form half-mile craters fall victim to the earth's gravity once per 1,000 years, but most disintegrate in the atmosphere or land in oceans. Only iron meteorites of this size are dense and strong enough, he believes, to penetrate the atmosphere and only about 5 percent of meteorites are irons. Hence continental impacts such as the one that produced Meteor Crater should average out to one per 25,000 years.

Asteroidal or cometary fragments weighing 500 tons or less plunge into the

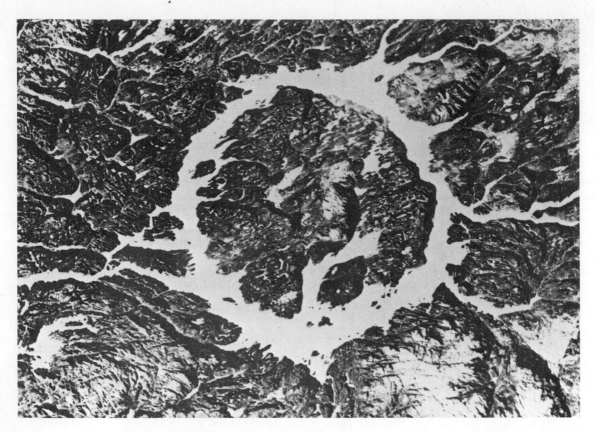

The Manicouagan impact structure in Quebec, as seen from Landsat. It is almost sixty miles wide. (NASA)

atmosphere roughly once a year, but most are not rigid enough to withstand the shock of entry and disintegrate—sometimes explosively—before reaching the ground. A particularly fearsome example would be the oft-discussed explosion that in 1908 leveled a large region of forest in the Tunguska area of Siberia. Smaller rocky or iron meteorites are sufficiently cohesive to penetrate, probably doing so daily. While most land in the sea or remote areas, Antarctica has proved a wonderfully efficient collector of such objects. They fall onto the ice in the interior of the continent, become buried (and perfectly preserved) as snow piles on them and turns into ice. Then the flow of ice carries them to the coast where, in some areas, the flow is stalled by mountains, the ice is eroded away, and the meteorites emerge. The world's inventory of meteorites has been more than doubled by the discovery of such assemblages.

Shoemaker and Wetherill told the Snowbird meeting that, contrary to widespread belief, the threat of asteroid, comet, and meteorite impacts is just as great now as a billion years ago. Asteroids and comets swept up by collision with the earth are steadily replaced by new ones escaping from the belt of asteroids between the orbits of Mars and Jupiter and from the cloud of comets far beyond the outermost planets. Impact rates, now and in the past, have been estimated from relative ages of the resulting scars, large and small, on the earth, moon, and other bodies. As would be expected, impacts during the first billion years after the solar system was formed, 4.6 billion years ago, were far more common, since the moon and planets were still sweeping up material left over from the formation stage, but since then the rate does not seem to have changed much.

While devastating impacts, although rare, seem inevitable, nevertheless they are becoming more predictable, particularly where the approaching body is large enough to be identified well in advance. Eleanor Helin of the California Institute of Technology has made a specialty of scanning the heavens for asteroids whose orbits come near enough that of the earth to present a long-term threat of impact. She discovered ten of the more than fifty identified by 1983. That, probably, is only a small fraction of the total. A highly automated system, such as the Spacewatch camera being developed by Tom Gehrels at the University of Arizona, should find many more and make it possible to monitor their orbits.

A meeting held at Snowmass, Colorado, and (like the subsequent one in Snowbird, Utah) sponsored by NASA, explored the possibility of diverting objects headed for a collision with the earth. Calculations showed that the energy needed to divert an asteroid a half mile in diameter was equivalent to the explosion of 10,000 tons of TNT—half the yield of the atomic bomb dropped on Hiroshima. The energy (explosive or otherwise) would be used to blast off some of the asteroid's own material in such a manner as to retard or accelerate its orbital motion, changing the shape of its orbit enough to miss the earth. For maximum effectiveness, it was found, the shove should be applied when the asteroid was nearest the sun (at perihelion). One participant said later that with the aid of the Space Shuttle, launching such a diversionary mission should be possible by 1995, assuming there was international agreement on making an exception to the ban on nuclear explosions in space.

In his introduction to the Snowbird conference proceedings, Silver warned that the study of large impacts and their possible role in the history of life is a relatively new field and he urged his colleagues not to become prematurely committed to one view. He cited the willingness of "so skilled and careful an observer as Gilbert," when he first examined Coon Butte (Meteor Crater), to set aside his impact hypothesis, pending availability of "fresh tools and new insights." A full assessment of the role of large-body impacts in terrestrial evolution, said Silver, "will no doubt require new minds and fresh handles on the many problems. Patience, friends, they are coming."

9 · 48

ALASKA–2

24 MEANDERS–MASTERPIECES OF FLOWING WATER

Almost all of the American landscape has been shaped to some extent by water. Rare but violent flash floods have carved arroyos or gorges in arid western lands. Fans of sediment have been spread over valley floors where streams emerge from the mountains. Noble canyons have been cut deep in areas where a river has fought to maintain its route as the land under it gradually rose, most spectacularly in the Grand Canyon of the Colorado River. Water draining from a plateau cuts not only a central valley but also tributaries that feed into it, forming a tree-branch pattern.

No water-formed feature, however, is more remarkable than the meanders, visible on almost any flight across America, as they snake back and forth across a flat valley floor in strikingly uniform loops. The term comes to us from the winding river in Phrygia (now part of Turkey) once known as the Maiandros (and today called the Menderes). From it the ancient Greeks derived their word for winding.

Meanders occur in all sizes, from the mighty loops of the Mississippi to tiny streams whose snaking path across a snow-covered field stands out in bold relief. They are not confined to Earth. Spacecraft orbiting the moon and Mars have photographed meandering streambeds produced in the distant past by water, lava, or some other flowing fluid.

Although meanders on earth normally migrate back and forth across a flood plain, if the land begins to rise, their wandering ceases and they begin to carve a deep channel whose curves nevertheless remain intact. Perhaps the most spectacular such "entrenched meanders" are the so-called goosenecks of the San Juan River before it joins the Colorado River in southeast Utah. So circuitous are the curves of this mighty canyon that the river takes twenty-two miles to advance one mile westward. Forty miles north of Pittsburgh, where Route 68 crosses the Allegheny River at Bradys Bend, the river forms a six-mile loop, returning to within a half mile of its course. There are entrenched meanders along the Ohio River as well as where the Susquehanna cuts across the plateau region of northeast Pennsylvania, in the Letchworth gorges

Snow cover highlights meanders on the Kogosukruk River, tributary of the Colville River on the North Slope of Alaska. (U.S. Navy)

Above: Occasional rains have produced alluvial fans where streams discharge onto the Death Valley floor. (Fairchild Aerial Photography Collection, Whittier College)

Facing page, above: Meanders of the North Fork of the Shenandoah near Woodstock, Virginia, have become entrenched in the valley floor. (U.S. Geological Survey) Below: As the Colorado Plateau rose, the San Juan River deeply entrenched these gooseneck curves in southeast Utah. (E. C. La Rue, U.S. Geological Survey)

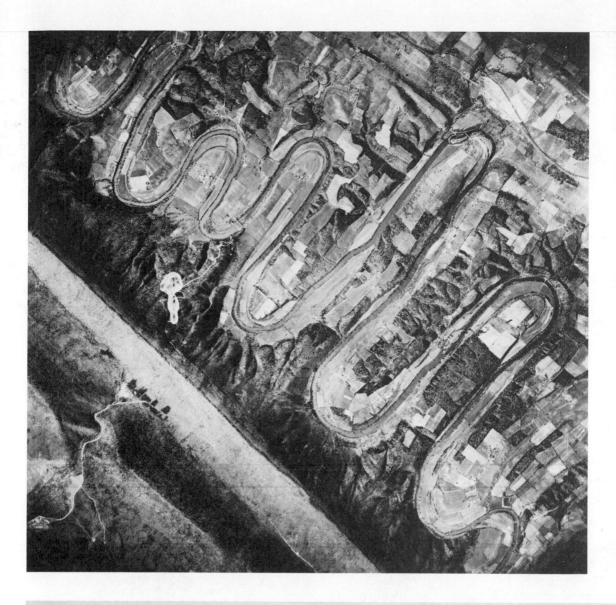

of the Genesee River in western New York State, and on the North Fork of the Shenandoah River in Virginia.

How meanders originally form, why their loops are so uniform, and why a meandering riverbed constantly migrates back and forth across its valley floor are questions long pondered by scientists and river pilots—notably on the Mississippi. Efforts to understand the peculiarities of a meandering river go back to the days in the 1850's when a young cub pilot named Samuel L. Clemens was learning to avoid shoals and other transient hazards on that great river. Because he depended on the leadsman's cries, giving depths in fathoms: "Half twain! . . . Quarter twain! . . . M-a-r-k twain!" he took that last cry, which meant clear sailing, as his pen name.

It was obvious in Mark Twain's day that the river, pushed outward on the curves by centrifugal force, eats away the outer bank there. On the curves the water is deepest and the current strong. Yet the river gets no wider for all this eating away. The point on the inside of each curve grows as fast as the opposite "cut bank" is eroded. The way in which this happens has been clarified by experiments such as those conducted by the United States Waterways Experiment Station at Vicksburg, Mississippi, using scale models of the river and batches of colored sand. The material eroded from the cut bank on each curve tends to be deposited at the "point" on the inside of the next curve downstream.

Just as the river is swiftest on the outside of the curve, it flows slowest around the opposite point. Pilots working upstream try to pass as close as possible to the point without grounding. Describing his apprenticeship Twain tells how his pilot master coached him up the river, warning that there was a shallow bar off each point. "You are well up on the bar now," the pilot told him. "There is a bar under every point, because the water that comes down around it forms an eddy and allows the sediment to sink. Do you see those fine lines on the face of the water that branch out like the ribs of a fan? Well, those are little reefs; you want to just miss the ends of them, but run them pretty close."

During periods of low water flow sediment is picked up in the straight stretches and

How meanders evolve: Earlier stages are shown in dashed lines. Arrows indicate the main current.

deposited off the point in the slower-flowing bends, forming shoals that gradually extend the point. During flood periods the river seeks to flow a straighter path and may cut a shallow channel, or chute, across such a point. On many meandering rivers, as well as the Mississippi, the air traveler can trace past migrations of the riverbed in the curving, successive chutes that it has left behind. Although some may be centuries old, their traces seen from aloft remain in curved swamps, fields, or lines of trees. Someone on the ground may live out his life unaware that his field's long, narrow, curving shape records past migrations of a distant river.

Between each curve there is a "reach" where the current that carved the cut bank of the upstream bend must cross over to carve the cut bank where the river curves in the opposite direction. Here, at what river pilots call a "crossing," the river widens, the current slows, and sediment sinks to form ever-changing shoals and sandbars. On the lower Mississippi in Twain's day the loops became so extreme that those on the same side of the river finally came close enough for the river to break through. This shortened the river, increased its slope, and formed a swift-flowing cutoff that quickly widened.

"When the river is rising fast," wrote Twain in *Life on the Mississippi*, "some scoundrel whose plantation is back in the country, and therefore of inferior value, has only to watch his chance, cut a little gutter across the narrow neck of land some dark night, and turn the water into it, and in a wonderfully short time a miracle has happened: to wit, the whole Mississippi has taken possession of that little ditch, and placed the countryman's plantation on its bank (quadrupling its value), and that other party's formerly valuable plantation finds itself way out yonder on a big island; the old watercourse around it will soon shoal up, boats cannot approach within ten miles of it, and down goes its value to a fourth of its former worth. Watches are kept on those narrow necks, at needful times, and if a man happens to be caught cutting a ditch across them, the chances are all against his ever having another opportunity to cut a ditch."

When the river starts to cut such a new channel "it is time for the people thereabouts to move," Twain wrote. "The water cleaves the banks away like a knife. By the time the ditch has become twelve or fifteen feet wide, the calamity is as good as accomplished, for no power on earth can stop it now. . . . I was on board the first boat that tried to go through the cutoff at American Bend, but we did not get through. It was toward midnight, and a wild night it was—thunder, lightning, and torrents of rain. It was estimated the current in the cutoff was making about fifteen or twenty miles an hour; twelve or thirteen was the best our boat could do." The pilot took advantage of a swift upstream eddy, but every time the steamer hit the main current in the pass, it was spun around and swept downstream. "Under the lightning flashes one could see the plantation cabins and the goodly acres tumble into the river; and the crash they made was not a bad effort at thunder. Once, when we spun around, we only missed a house about twenty feet, that had a light burning in the window; and in the same instant that house went overboard. . . . A day or two later the cutoff was three-quarters of a mile wide, and boats passed up through it without much difficulty, and so saved ten miles."

After another such breakthrough a boat reportedly tried to follow the old, looping

Left: Alaska's Muddy River is a classic braided stream. (Bradford Washburn)

Right: Braided-stream patterns are common on arid slopes, as here on the northwest side of the Sacaton Mountains in Pinal County, Arizona. (U.S. Geological Survey Professional Paper 590)

route, its pilots unaware of the new channel. "It was a grisly, hideous night, and all shapes were vague and distorted," Twain wrote. "The old bend had already begun to fill up, and the boat got to running away from mysterious reefs, and occasionally hitting one. The perplexed pilots fell to swearing, and finally uttered the entirely unnecessary wish that they might never get out of that place. As always happens in such cases, that particular prayer was answered, and the others neglected."

Another gamble of the river pilots at high water, especially in the heat of a steamboat race, was trying to run a chute—one of the shallow cutoffs across a point. Part of Twain's apprenticeship was learning to anticipate how much water would be in a distance-saving chute ahead by examining key stumps and other water-level indicators along the route.

Excavated channels are being used by the Army Corps of Engineers to shorten the channels. Near Greenville, Mississippi, a cut 4,530 feet long shortened the river by thirteen miles. The slope through the cutoff was fifteen times steeper than around the bend. On the Red River between Shreveport, Louisiana, and the Mississippi the bends are so sharp that tug pilots with long lines of barges have difficulty negotiating them. The army has been excavating "pilot channels" between loops, then allowing the river itself to finish the job.

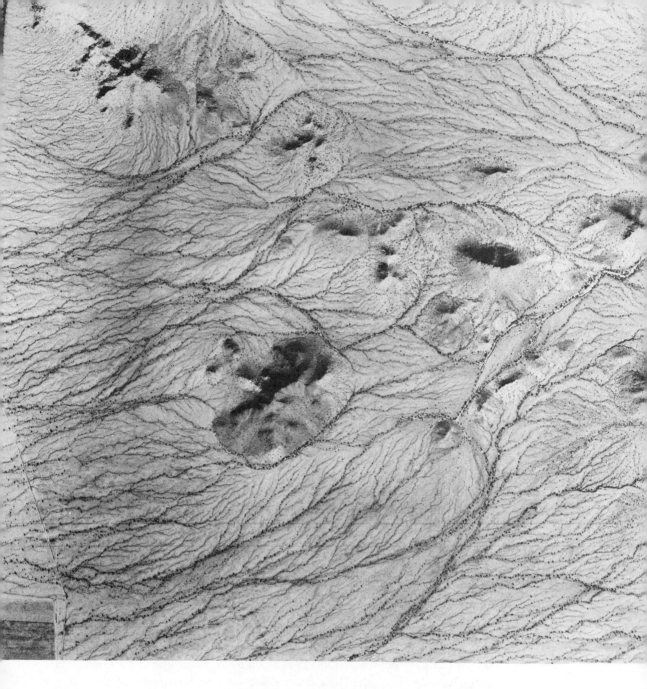

When a loop is cut off it may survive as an arc-shaped lake, or oxbow. In the delta region at the southern end of the Mississippi the slow-flowing loops are known as bayous. Large lakes are also a typical by-product of the delta-forming process, Lake Ponchartrain alongside New Orleans being an example. A peculiarity affecting flow of the Mississippi in northeast Louisiana is a very gradual rise of the landscape known as the Monroe Uplift. According to an analysis of repeated surveys reported in 1983 it is rising five millimeters (one fifth of an inch) per year, but since the river's slope is only one hundred millimeters per mile, the slope of the riverbed in that sector is reduced by 5 percent yearly. For a four-mile stretch near Lake Providence the river actually runs uphill.

If the slope of the riverbed is sufficient for the water to flow fairly fast and it carries a substantial load of sand and gravel, a "braided" stream may form with many channels weaving in and out of one another. This can be seen in a number of rivers on the coastal plain of northern Alaska. Such patterns were typical of rivers carrying meltwater from the great ice sheet. Early in this century branches of the Platte River in Nebraska formed braided networks of ever-changing channels, but flood control has so much reduced their load of sand that in places their width has narrowed from a mile to a few hundred feet.

For a series of meanders to be uniform in their wavelength—the spacing between loops—as well as in the dimensions and shapes of the loops, the factors controlling those dimensions must remain constant along the valley. These include the downhill slope of the valley, the rate and volume of water flow, its burden of sediment, and the properties of the soil forming its banks. The combination of these factors in a particular valley determines the rhythm of the meanders much as—in a very different environment—uniform factors produce the even spacing of bumps in the "washboard" that forms on dirt roads. The suspension systems of cars—springs and shock absorbers—respond to unevenness in the surface in a fairly uniform manner. On a rough road the wheel assemblies begin to bounce up and down in a characteristic rhythm. Each car that passes is guided into the same rhythm and—assuming the properties of the road itself are fairly uniform—the washboard becomes established. If car suspensions were less uniform, this would not occur. Controlling factors, so far as meanders are concerned, differ from place to place and so the patterns vary but can remain uniform for long stretches.

The flood plain across which a meandering river flows is itself a product of the river's action over centuries. The plain is not formed primarily by floods, although they may spread silt over the valley from time to time, but rather by the slow migration of the meanders back and forth between the valley walls.

When the lower Mississippi, in its natural, uncontrolled state, overflowed its banks, the flow of its overbank water was slower, and sediment settled just outside the channel to form natural levees. At New Orleans these are twenty feet high and may be more than a mile wide, in contrast to the narrow, man-made levees of the Army Corps of Engineers. As a result water level in the river at times may be higher than that of the neighboring flood plain. The natural levees are evident from the air because roads and houses tend to be placed on them, rather than in the swampy land farther from the river. The Great River Road, sometimes described as "the longest parkway in the world," runs along some of these levees. The Great River Road is not a single highway but a series of roads running 5,600 miles from the northernmost part of the Mississippi Basin, in Canada, to the Gulf of Mexico, following as much as possible the route of that great river. It is marked along the way and on road maps by a ship's wheel symbol.

Looking down on a meandering river one sees what in reality is a snapshot of a

The ever-changing meanders of the Ohio River have carved this pattern as it passes Henderson, Kentucky. (U.S. Geological Survey)

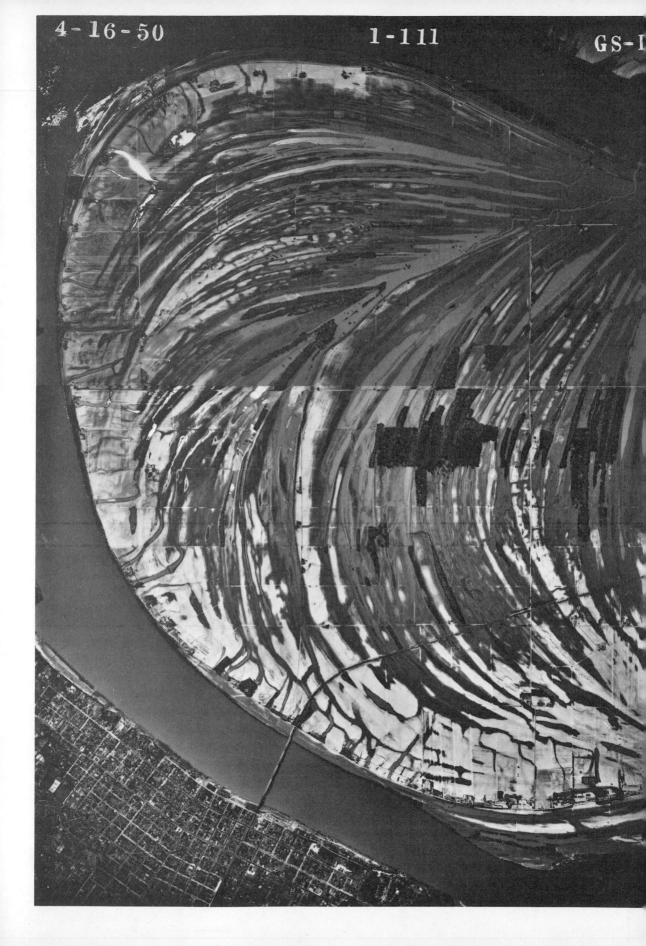

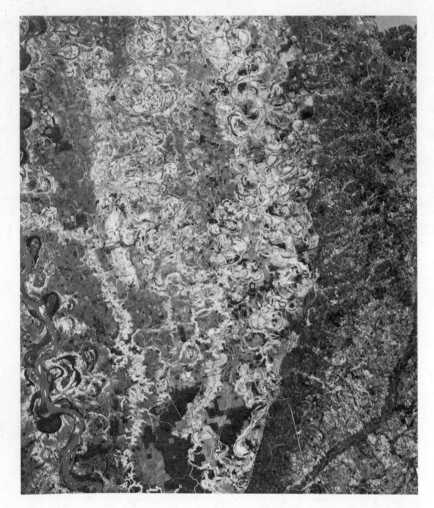

Left: Over thousands of years the Mississippi River, wandering back and forth across its broad valley in the state of Mississippi, has left a "worm's nest" of countless meanders and oxbows, far more evident from space than on the ground. The river is on the left, and Granada Lake is in the upper right corner. The loess-covered Bluff Hills form the eastern margin of the valley. (Landsat/NASA)

scene in constant flux. It is not easy to comprehend that the river is slowly moving back and forth across its flood plain. Along some stretches of the lower Mississippi, however, oxbows and other traces of its past migrations lie so far from the present channel that it is hard to believe they are children of a river now more than sixty miles distant.

In Mark Twain's day about half of the lower Mississippi abandoned its old bed every decade and carved a new one. Such a change, he pointed out, "plays havoc with boundary lines and jurisdictions: for instance, a man is living in the State of Mississippi today, a cutoff occurs tonight, and tomorrow the man finds himself and his land over on the other side of the river, within the boundaries and subject to the laws of the State of Louisiana! Such a thing, happening in the upper river in the old times, could have transferred a slave from Missouri to Illinois and made a free man of him." He cites the strange fate of Hard Times, a town in what is now Mississippi but which was in Louisiana until the river moved two miles west. "Nearly the whole of that one thousand three hundred miles of old Mississippi River which La Salle floated

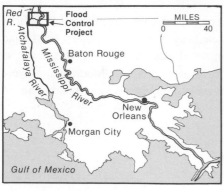

Above: In this view from space, sediment can be seen spreading into the Gulf of Mexico from the Mississippi delta. (Landsat/NASA)

Left: Some fear the Atchafalaya will capture the present flow of the Mississippi.

down in his canoes, two hundred years ago,'' wrote Twain in the 1870's, ''is good solid dry ground now.''

Because of cutoffs and other course changes, he said, the river was shorter by 242 miles than it had been 176 years earlier. That was a shortening of one and a third miles per year. Satirizing scientific practice of extrapolation—guessing the truth far beyond the reach of observations—he argued that ''just a million years ago next November, the Lower Mississippi was upwards of one million three hundred thousand miles long, and stuck out over the Gulf of Mexico like a fishing rod. And by the same token any person can see that seven hundred and forty-two years from now the Lower Mississippi will be only a mile and three quarters long. . . . There is something fascinating about science. One gets such wholesale returns of conjecture out of such a trifling investment of fact.''

Since Mark Twain's day the Army Engineers have built more than 2,000 miles of control structures along the river and its tributaries including 1,608 miles of levees along the lower part of the river. By 1941, to provide for swift discharge of flood waters and shorter navigation, sixteen cutoffs had been excavated across meander loops, shortening the distance between Memphis and Baton Rouge by another 170 miles. Articulated concrete mats are mass-produced at more than a half-dozen sites along the river and are hauled by barge to reinforce the banks. All of this has ''tamed'' the river, but it constantly seeks to rebel and resume its old wanderings.

The area where a revolt is most feared—one that could have catastrophic consequences—is where the Red River discharges part of its water into the Mississippi seventy-five miles north of Baton Rouge. The Red River rises on the Llano Estacado of eastern New Mexico and western Texas, then flows along the Texas-Oklahoma border before crossing Louisiana to meet the Mississippi and Atchafalaya rivers. The Atchafalaya flows to the sea through a maze of swamps and bayous, carrying the Red River outflow as well as up to 30 percent of the flow of the Mississippi. When the latter is in flood, part of its flow crosses over and races down the Atchafalaya, enlarging that stream and threatening to abandon its old channel past Baton Rouge and New Orleans. If it did so, the greatly increased flow down the Atchafalaya would sweep away entire towns, such as Morgan City. The lower part of the Mississippi would become a saltwater estuary, depriving New Orleans and extensive industries along the lower river of their water supply. As stated in a booklet by the Mississippi River Commission and Army Corps of Engineers, this would be ''a disaster of catastrophic proportions.''

In 1954 Congress authorized an extensive engineering effort to control flow from the Mississippi through this link to the Atchafalaya, including dams, locks, and levees. The first test of the project came in the floods of 1973. Turbulent waters scoured and undermined some of the structures, which collapsed. Modifications were undertaken to reduce the turbulence, but some hydrologists believe that sooner or later the great river will ''win.''

25 HARNESSED RIVERS

From time immemorial rivers have shaped North America, but more recently man has shaped the rivers. When European settlers first colonized the East Coast one of their earliest efforts was seeking out sources of water power. Apart from clearing of the forests for farming, impoundment of the rivers was one of the first ways in which human intervention substantially altered the landscape, culminating in such herculean enterprises as harnessing of the Colorado, Columbia, Missouri, and Tennessee rivers as well as construction of the Saint Lawrence Seaway. As noted earlier, cities like Philadelphia, Baltimore, and Richmond sprang up on the fall line, where rivers tumble from the Piedmont onto the Coastal Plain. Canada has a fall line of its own, where rivers tumble from the plateau of the Canadian Shield into the Saint Lawrence River lowlands, and these have been dammed at many sites along the Ottawa, Bersimis, St. Maurice, and Saguenay rivers, in the last case providing power for a major aluminum-refining industry.

As early as 1634 water began turning a grinding mill in Milton, Massachusetts, and most sites of New England cities and towns were chosen because such power was available. Louis C. Hunter, in his history of American industrial power, points out that in many communities gristmills and sawmills were built before schools, churches, stores, and wagon roads. In 1793 there were 262 mills in a single county of Massachusetts—one for each 250 inhabitants. While water was gradually replaced by steam power during the latter half of the nineteenth century, a federal census in 1919 found that there were still 21,135 flour mills and gristmills in operation.

During 1813 and 1814 Francis Cabot Lowell, one of the variously talented members of Boston's Lowell family, built the world's first factory capable of processing raw cotton through all manufacturing stages to finished cloth. It set the stage for an industrial revolution that affected all of New England. A canal had been built to carry boats around Pawtucket Falls at a wide bend in the Merrimack River. The drop in water level from one end of the canal to the other was thirty-two feet—a tempting power source—and by 1823 a side canal had been built to carry water from above the canal lock to mills being built on the river's edge at East Chelmsford, a little farming community within the bend in the river. The village was renamed for Lowell and, according to Hunter, became America's "first wholly industrialized city."

It did so in large part because of the ten canals and an elaborate system of control gates, penstocks, and millraces built to deliver controlled amounts of water to each of eleven mills that sprang up there. Upstream a dam across the Merrimack impounded a large millpond in which water accumulated during night hours, when the mills were idle and the canal gates were shut. This doubled the amount of water that could be delivered the next day. To impound more water the dam was fitted with flashboards that made it higher but were designed to collapse during flood periods instead of diverting flood waters into Lowell.

In developing a utility that delivered power to many consumers, none of whom alone could have maintained so elaborate a system, the Lowell enterprise anticipated the great hydroelectric utilities that were to follow. In Hunter's words it was "a pioneering engineering and managerial achievement of the first order." Mill towns that sprang up along the Connecticut, Merrimack, and other New England rivers copied the Lowell system, and the long brick facades of their mills—most of them converted or abandoned—still line the riverbanks in such cities as Manchester, New Hampshire.

The agency controlling water delivery to the mills in Manchester, Lowell, Lawrence, and other towns along the Merrimack was known as the Proprietors of Locks and Canals on the Merrimack River. By 1846 increased demands for power and periodic water shortages during droughts or winter freeze-ups led that agency to acquire control of the outlet of Lake Winnipesaukee, New Hampshire's largest body of water, as well as those of Squam Lake, Newfound Lake, and other lakes feeding the river in central New Hampshire. Although these reservoirs helped control the flow during periods of drought or flood, there were times when almost no water reached Haverhill, the last town before the river's mouth at Newburyport, and this exposed its populace to the stench of a bare, muddy riverbed. Upstream, in New Hampshire, inhabitants protested that industries in the "foreign" state downstream were ruining their enjoyment of the lakeshores by periodically draining the lakes.

As coal and then cheap oil became abundantly available, industry along the eastern rivers turned away from water, which has less energy potential and dependability. The millraces and turbines fell into disrepair. But in the 1970's, after the sharp rise in oil prices, there were widespread efforts to reactivate some of those dams for electric generation. In 1980 the Army Corps of Engineers reported that among 12,000 possible locations in the Northeast, it had identified 656 suitable for new or upgraded hydroelectric projects. In New York State a study ordered by the governor pointed to 1,672 sites that, if fully developed, could produce 10 percent of the state's needs, although at considerable capital cost.

Although there has been a surge of interest in small-scale hydroelectric power, there has also been concern for the safety of the older dams that might be used. In 1976 the Teton Dam near Newdale, Idaho, failed, and this was followed the next year by the collapse of Kelley Barnes Dam at Toccoa Falls, Georgia, killing thirty-nine people. President Carter ordered the Corps of Engineers to inspect nonfederal dams throughout the country. Of 8,818 dams inspected, 2,925 were found unsafe, chiefly because of inadequate spillway capacity. In 1982, before there was much corrective action, 6 dams collapsed in Connecticut after torrential rains and 14 others were breached, causing widespread flooding.

More closely monitored have been the big federal dams and in the United States it is they, and those of the Tennessee Valley Authority, that have impounded the waterways most noticeable to air travelers. A prolonged drought in the 1890's that dried up irrigation systems in Nebraska and Wyoming led Congress in 1902 to pass an act, creating what became the Reclamation Service (and later the Bureau of Reclamation). One of its first achievements was construction of Pathfinder Dam, completed in 1909 on the North Platte River in Wyoming. Another project, the Roosevelt Dam, one of the first great dams in the Southwest (and named for Theodore), was built under the auspices of the Reclamation Act to impound the Salt River in Arizona, irrigating a quarter of a million arid acres and generating electric power. Souvenirs of this region's volcanic history linger in the rock and when workmen sought to excavate a 500-foot tunnel that would carry water to the power plant they encountered so many hot springs that temperatures in the tunnel hovered at 130 degrees, forcing the men to work almost naked and come out periodically for fresh air.

When this dam, 280 feet high and 1,125 feet long, was completed in 1911 it was considered an engineering milestone, but within five years the Bureau of Reclamation was building Arrowrock Dam on the Boise River in Idaho, 350 feet high and, for a time, the loftiest in the world. Today there are many dams throughout the world more than twice its height. One—Rogun Dam on the Vakhsh River in the Tadzhik Soviet Socialist Republic—is more than three times higher.

The real milestone was Hoover Dam, the first across the Colorado River. That stream had run unimpeded to the sea, so laden with silt that it was said to be "too thick to drink, too thin to plough." In 1901 water from the river, near where it enters Mexico, had been diverted into the newly completed Imperial Canal to irrigate arid Imperial Valley, hemmed in by sand dunes and barren mountains in southernmost California.

The irrigation scheme was a disaster. During droughts the river was a trickle and crops withered. During spring floods the river surged down the canal, buried the farms in muck, and silted up the canal. Attempts to control the flow with dikes and levees only made things worse. In 1904, with the river in full flood, water surged into the Imperial Valley and filled its lowest region, known as the Salton Sink. The result was the Salton Sea of today.

The only solution seemed building a monumental dam that would hold back the river during floods and release water during droughts. By a strange turn of history Arthur Powell Davis, the man who picked the site for this great dam and did its preliminary design, was the nephew of John Wesley Powell, who led the first expedition down that river. Davis became one of the world's leading specialists in grandiose engineering and irrigation schemes. He participated in the Panama Canal Project, advised the Imperial Government of Russia on irrigation of the Kara Kum Desert, and after the revolution played the same role regarding Turkestan and Transcaucasia. In China he conducted surveys for the Huai River Conservancy Project.

It was, however, in the 1890's, as topographer and hydrographer for the U.S.

Geological Survey in the Southwest, that he developed his expertise. In 1903 he became a supervising engineer with the newly formed U.S. Reclamation Service that was then struggling to cope with the Imperial Valley floods, and in 1914 he was named its director, supervising construction of Buffalo Bill Dam on the Shoshone River in Wyoming and Arrowrock Dam in Idaho—each for a time the world's tallest. Arrowrock, with its gracefully curving wall of concrete, anticipated some of the more esthetically pleasing dams to follow, including those that would use the principle of the arch, rather than merely their enormous weight, to withstand the water pressure.

The Davis plan for the Colorado was for a dam more than twice as high as any in existence that would impound the world's largest man-made body of water (later called Lake Mead)—so large it would take the river two years to fill its 115-mile basin. The huge power plant beneath the dam would illuminate southern California, provide drinking water to thirteen cities, and stabilize flow below the dam, allowing dependable irrigation of the Imperial Valley. Opponents questioned its safety, arguing that an earthquake like the one that had hit San Francisco a few years earlier, in 1906, could crack the dam and create havoc downstream. Furthermore, states drained by the upper part of the river feared that all the benefit would go to California, whereas California worried that the upstream states might divert enough water to choke off flow to the lower river.

President Harding appointed Herbert Hoover, himself an engineer and then Secretary of Commerce, to head a commission whose membership included representatives from the seven states involved. The result in 1922 was a landmark compromise, still in effect, specifying how much each region can take from the river. Quotas were defined in terms of flow past Lee's Ferry, Arizona, with a treaty commitment that Mexico should receive 10 percent of it. The allocations, however, were based on the river's performance during unusually wet years and are now considered to have been "overbooked" by about 110 percent.

In 1928 Congress voted $165 million for construction of the dam and of the All American Canal that, farther downstream, would carry water from the river eighty miles along the Mexican border into the Imperial Valley. In 1923, however, Davis had lost his job as director of the Reclamation Service, apparently under pressure from landowners who resented being required to pay some of the irrigation costs. Secretary of the Interior Hubert Work said the agency should be run by a businessman, not an engineer, and the post held by Davis was abolished.

Originally the dam was to be called Boulder Dam, but by the time construction began in 1930, Mr. Hoover was president and its name was changed to Hoover Dam. This did not last long. When Franklin D. Roosevelt became president in 1933, Secretary of the Interior Harold Ickes had it changed back to Boulder Dam. Finally, in 1946, a Republican-sponsored bill changed the name for a third time—to Hoover Dam—and so it has remained.

Building this mammoth structure on a scale never attempted since construction of the Pyramids captured the imagination of the American public. Newspaper and magazine pictures portrayed every stage in its growth. Following its completion in 1936, a succession of other dams were thrown across the Colorado, including three downstream of Hoover Dam. In the opposite direction Parker Dam impounds Havasu

Lake, a long, narrow ribbon of water along the Arizona-California border that serves as a landmark on transcontinental flights to and from Los Angeles. The lake also acts as a settling basin for silt before the water is passed on to California communities. Farther upstream Davis Dam forms Lake Mohave along the Arizona-Nevada border. In Utah, above the Grand Canyon, Glen Canyon Dam impounds huge Lake Powell.

Before the completion of Hoover Dam, Franklin D. Roosevelt, in his effort to boost the country out of the depression, initiated three more projects on an equally grand scale. One was to dam the Columbia River at Grand Coulee. Another was to harness the Missouri River with a four-mile dam at Fort Peck, Montana, creating a reservoir two thirds the size of Lake Mead. The third was to tame the Tennessee

Hoover Dam. (Union Pacific Railroad)

River. By 1936 almost twenty large dams were under construction.

Even before work began on Grand Coulee, Bonneville Dam was being built where the Columbia River cuts through the Cascades. Today its power output is carried by a heavy capacity, direct current tie as far as Los Angeles. Long before the 1930's local citizens had urged that the Columbia also be harnessed at Grand Coulee and its waters used to irrigate the arid region of central Washington in the "rain shadow" of the Cascades. Grand Coulee, as noted earlier, had been cut through the Columbia Plateau by the great Ice Age floods, presumably when ice diverted the Columbia River from its normal path. When the ice retreated, the river resumed its original route, leaving an empty canyon of awesome dimensions. The world's most massive concrete dam was built across the Columbia with a power plant whose output still ranks first in the world. Some of its electricity is used to pump water from the river into the Grand Coulee, which was dammed to form a reservoir in which to store the water before distributing it through 500 miles of irrigation canals. Subsequently additional dams were built, including the Chief Joseph, Dalles, John Day, and McNary dams below Grand Coulee, plus others upstream. In all there are some twenty large dams in the Columbia Basin, including privately owned dams in Hells Canyon and Hungry Horse Dam on the Flathead River, a tributary of the Columbia, in Montana.

Dams on the Missouri form a procession of long lakes, from Fort Peck Reservoir in Montana, to Lake Sakakawea spanning the western half of North Dakota (impounded by Garrison Dam) and the 200-mile-long Oahe Reservoir that runs from Bismarck, North Dakota, across half of South Dakota to Oahe Dam. The river pauses again at Fort Randall and Gavins Point dams before leaving the Dakotas. Because this is not mountainous country, these dams, apart from their spillways, are all long, low ramparts of earth. The Fort Peck dam, whose crest is 21,026 feet long, is listed in almanacs as the second most massive on the continent. The one ranked first in the world is New Cornelia Tailings Dam in the copper-mining region near Ajo, Arizona. There are a number of these "tailings" dams in the West and in Appalachia, their role being to impound water from mine washings that is too laden with heavy metals to discharge into streams.

The Tennessee Valley Authority, as described in Roosevelt's message to Congress, was to be "a corporation clothed with the power of government but possessed of the flexibility and initiative of a private enterprise." It was to plan for "the proper use, conservation, and development of the natural resources of the Tennessee River drainage basin and its adjoining territory for the general social and economic welfare of the nation." Opponents called it socialism, as they had said of the other public power projects. Public utilities saw the government usurping their role. But for the area affected it was to bring about revolutionary changes, with electrification, industrial development, stabilization of the land, reforestation of eroded slopes, and freedom from floods.

The scope of the scheme was enormous. None of the dams is comparable with Grand Coulee or Hoover, but it has been calculated that their combined mass is twelve times that of the Pyramids. The Tennessee River itself begins just east of Knoxville, between the Cumberland and Great Smoky mountains, at the confluence

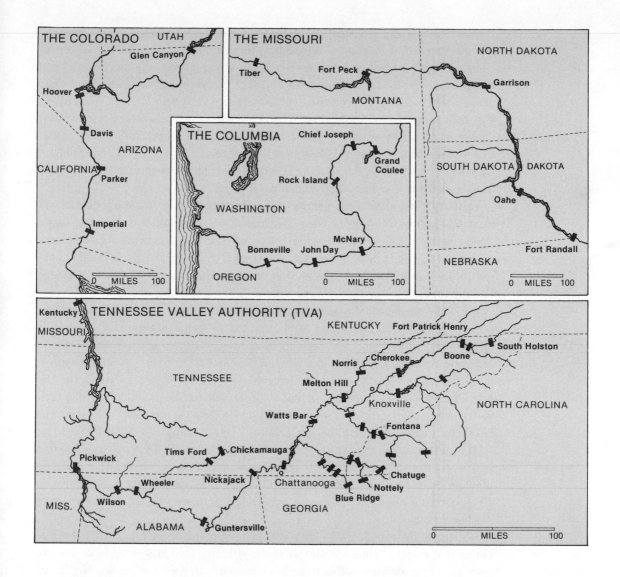

THE COLORADO

UTAH

Glen Canyon

Hoover

Davis

ARIZONA

CALIFORNIA

Parker

Imperial

0   MILES   100

THE MISSOURI

Tiber   Fort Peck

MONTANA

NORTH DAKOTA

Garrison

SOUTH DAKOTA   DAKOTA

Oahe

Fort Randall

NEBRASKA

0   MILES   100

THE COLUMBIA

Chief Joseph

Grand
Coulee

Rock Island

WASHINGTON

McNary

Bonneville   John Day

OREGON

0   MILES   100

Kentucky   TENNESSEE VALLEY AUTHORITY (TVA)

MISSOURI

KENTUCKY   Fort Patrick Henry

South Holston

Boone

Cherokee

Norris

Melton Hill

Knoxville

NORTH CAROLINA

TENNESSEE

Watts Bar

Fontana

Tims Ford   Chickamauga

Pickwick

Chatuge

Wheeler   Nickajack   Chattanooga   Nottely

MISS.   Wilson   Blue Ridge

GEORGIA

ALABAMA   Guntersville

0   MILES   100

of the Holston and French Broad rivers. From there it runs 650 miles in a great U to where it joins the Ohio at Paducah, Kentucky, after draining parts of seven states. To control flooding as well as provide irrigation and electricity to a severely underdeveloped part of the country, some four-dozen dams were built on the river and its tributaries.

In a crash program initiated during World War I the Tennessee had been dammed at Muscle Shoals, in the northwest corner of Alabama, to produce electricity for the manufacture of nitrates needed for explosives. The first of three dams projected for the complex was not completed until 1925, and the nitrate plants proved hopelessly inefficient. Henry Ford offered to buy and operate the plants, but Senator George W. Norris, Republican from Nebraska, opposed transfer of the plants to private hands.

One problem was that Wilson Dam, at Muscle Shoals, could not produce much power during dry seasons. Additional dams that were to have controlled the flow had not been built. Norris repeatedly sponsored bills for building such dams and developing the valley, but they were vetoed by Presidents Coolidge and Hoover. In his campaign against Hoover, however, Roosevelt urged revival of Muscle Shoals and construction of a Saint Lawrence seaway. In 1933, almost as soon as Roosevelt had taken office, the TVA was launched and the first dam to be built, on the Clinch River, was named for Norris. In the 1940's, under the pressure of wartime demands for energy, some dams were built to standard designs and at remarkably high speed. Construction of four dams was begun on the same day (July 17, 1941) and Douglas Dam was completed in a record thirteen and a half months. Fontana Dam on the Little Tennessee River was the highest east of the Rockies.

Forty-eight dams had been completed by the 1960's, nine of them with locks to permit the passage of shipping. Since initiation of the project there had been no major flood damage. With most tributaries of the Tennessee dammed it is sometimes possible, when other parts of the Ohio-Mississippi drainage area are in flood but not the Tennessee, to "turn off" rivers of the Tennessee Basin, limiting their discharge into the Ohio.

In view of the abundant coal resources of the region it seemed more economical, in postwar years, to build coal-fired plants, and the TVA now has some of the world's largest plants of that type. The building of additional dams, such as Tellico Dam on the Little Tennessee and Columbia Dam on the Duck River, met with strong opposition from conservationists and those being driven from homes or rich farmlands. The Little Tennessee was thought for a time to be the sole habitat of a little fish, the snail darter, which proponents of Tellico described as a "useless minnow." The dam was built, but in early 1984 the Columbia Dam was still in limbo.

The great power-producing capacities of Grand Coulee and TVA played a key role in development of the first atomic bombs. The abundant energy needed to separate the uranium 238 needed for a bomb was provided to the Oak Ridge plant in Tennessee by TVA. Grand Coulee fed power to the nearby Hanford Works, whose reactors produced plutonium.

Because of dams built by TVA as well as other projects, the folds of the Appalachians from eastern Tennessee southwest into Alabama hold many long lakes that can provide a dazzling view for air travelers between New Orleans and the Northeast. When the sun glistens off their waters, high-speed pleasure boats churn the lakes into interweaving, ever-changing wave patterns.

Other river systems have been extensively dammed, such as the Arkansas in eastern Oklahoma and the Sabine River, forming Toledo Bend Reservoir along the Louisiana-Texas border. In California's Sacramento Valley, Shasta Dam, Oroville Dam on the Feather River (the country's highest), and Trinity Dam (one of the highest earth dams) help feed the irrigation systems of that region. Friant Dam near Fresno and other dams along the San Joaquin Valley play similar roles. To accommodate the lake above Shasta Dam thirty-one miles of railway had to be relocated.

Construction of the Saint Lawrence Seaway as a joint Canadian-American effort followed a long period of international negotiation and internal debate. The discovery of high-grade iron ore along the Quebec-Labrador border offered a new source of supply to industrial centers on the Great Lakes, such as Cleveland, Gary, and Chicago, which were facing depletion of the iron mines closer by, and in 1951 the Parliament in Ottawa decided Canada should start building the seaway on its own. The United States had to act or be left out and in 1954 Congress accepted the plan for joint construction of the great chain of locks, canals, and dams. Islands in the river were linked to divert water through the Moses-Saunders Power Dam, whose electric production is in a class with Grand Coulee. In July 1958, ships began using the new seaway, which presents a scene that would hardly be recognizable to Jacques Cartier, who first sailed up the river in 1534 and 1535, or to the French colonists who followed.

Canada, with its hydroelectric potential, avoided the massive shift to dependence on coal and oil that took place in the United States. In the late nineteenth century hydroelectric plants were built at Montmorency Falls in Quebec and at Niagara Falls in Ontario. Later, at Beauharnois, northwest of Montreal, water flowing through a canal that bypassed rapids on the Saint Lawrence was tapped for energy as were rivers flowing south from the interior of Quebec into the lower Saint Lawrence Valley, such as the Outardes and the one draining the reservoir in the huge Manicouagan impact structure. Dams were built across the Abitibi that flows north toward Saint James Bay as well as at several sites on the Winnipeg River flowing into Lake Winnipeg. The Saskatchewan River, which also empties into that lake, has been exploited as well as the Nelson River, flowing from the Lake to Hudson Bay, and the Churchill River reaching Hudson Bay farther north. In some cases lengthy power lines were needed to bring the energy to consumer areas. British Columbia has enormous hydroelectric potential since its mountains receive more rain than anywhere else in Canada. Fears for harming the salmon runs have inhibited development of such major resources as the Fraser River, although the Nechako, a tributary of the Fraser, has been dammed to provide power for a large aluminum refinery at Kitimat.

As a result of such efforts four of Canada's provinces—Newfoundland, Quebec, Manitoba, and British Columbia—derive almost all their electricity from water power and Canada has continued to expand exploitation of this potential, as at Churchill Falls in Newfoundland, almost twice the height of Niagara. The output of its underground hydroelectric plant is second only, on this continent, to that of Grand Coulee.

The dams and hydroelectric plants of North America have helped transform the landscape in another way. By the 1930's more of Canada's rural areas had been electrified than those of the United States. As part of his New Deal Roosevelt then created the Rural Electrification Administration, which sped the process through loans to farmers and utilities. When airliners first began crossing the continent most of the countryside was dark, but now it sparkles with lights from ocean to ocean. In daytime much of the landscape is crisscrossed by high-tension power lines. Where their towers are difficult to see from high-flying aircraft, their paths are easily identified, cutting broad trails through forests, marching straight across mountains along routes no engineer would choose for a road.

26 WHAT PAINTED
THE LAND RED?

Much of the most dramatic scenery in western North America is red, or some variant of that color—maroon, pink, magenta, or copper. Erosion of these "redbeds" has produced such features as Bryce Canyon and Zion Canyon in Utah, the Painted Desert of Arizona, the Garden of the Gods in Colorado, the Sierra Diablo near the western tip of Texas, the monumental red layers in the Grand Canyon, and the Chugwater Formation that decorates much of U.S. 26 from Casper, Wyoming, through Dubois and over Togwotee Pass. Erosion of redbeds along the eastern seaboard has reddened soils in Nova Scotia, along the Connecticut Valley, south across central New Jersey, eastern Pennsylvania, central Virginia, and North Carolina, evident in countless excavations and plowed farmland.

How the redbeds acquired their brilliant color has tantalized generations of geologists, forcing them, in search of explanations, to gaze far back along the vistas of the continent's history—its wanderings as world geography changed, its radical variations of climate, its early period before animal life emerged from the sea, and its epoch of intense geologic upheaval when the continents split apart and dinosaurs roamed the land.

Some have argued that the redbeds were produced in deserts that then lay near the equator. Others saw a major source in laterites—bricklike soil that forms in the moist tropics. In 1968 A. V. Sochave of the Soviet Union proposed that the redbeds were formed during a period when the earth's atmosphere was highly enriched in oxygen. In contrast, coal beds, he suggested, were laid down when the earth's air was rich in carbon dioxide (as during a period of intense volcanic activity).

It was early agreed that redbeds derive their color from ferric oxide, a compound in which two atoms of iron are mated with three of oxygen. In its purest form it is known as hematite, a substance used by primitive peoples as a red dye. Its variants occur in such pigments as Venetian red, iron red, and red ocher.

The puzzle has been: Why are some landscapes tinted and not others, even though they are equally abundant in iron compounds? An early clue was that older formations are usually redder than younger ones, suggesting that, at least in some cases, time was a factor. Often, as well, they occur in sandstones, like those of the Colorado Plateau, formed under desert conditions, suggesting that prolonged exposure to a dry climate was involved. In sediments ferric oxide readily picks up water molecules to form a variety of drab-colored minerals. It appears that only when the water molecules, over long periods of time, are released from such material can it become red hematite.

Recent studies in Baja California and the Sonora Desert, straddling the border between Mexico and Arizona, have shown that material freshly eroded out of mountains is drab, but as it begins its slow conversion into desert sand, its redness increases. Apparently water chemically bound to ferric oxide in the sand is gradually removed in the hot, dry environment, the iron compounds gradually turning from gray-brown to red in a process that continues after the sand has been buried. This trend in shading is seen in some dunes of Australia, Africa, and southeast California. The oldest part of each dune is reddest. The same effect typically occurs when bricks are fired in a kiln. Iron rust (a mixture of iron oxides bound to water molecules) reddens if you bake it. In the desert, where temperatures are less extreme than in an oven, the process moves more slowly. It can be reversed where reddish soil is washed into a streambed, again becoming hydrated and brown.

But not all redbeds are formed of desert material. They include such products of water action as alluvial fans and flood-plain deposits, as well as mudstones laid down on tidal flats. The redbeds of the Connecticut Valley were clearly moist when dinosaurs left their footprints in the valley's swampy floor. Shales remaining from the rift valleys that formed along the East Coast as the Atlantic Ocean began opening contain the remains of freshwater fish. Yet sandstones from these areas are now reddish-brown.

Geologists continue to debate how such formations underwent the reddening process. Some argue that it took place during a prolonged period when the formation was buried but exposed to sufficient oxygen to convert the brown oxide to the red form. Lacking enough oxygen it turns into ferrous oxide—one atom of oxygen joined with one of iron—and the rock becomes drab. Other geologists blame the laterite process of rainy, subtropical environments that now occurs to some extent in the southeastern United States, but far more intensely in Brazil and Southeast Asia, where the natural cover provided by rain forests has been cleared for agriculture. Rain leaches soluble components from the bare soil, leaving iron and aluminum oxides that are baked by the sun into a reddish, bricklike crust. The resulting laterite is sometimes so hard it can be used for building material, as in construction of the fabled temples at Angkor Wat in Cambodia. This process of "laterization," however, ruins the land for farming.

When red sandstone or shale is examined under high magnification, it can be seen that in many cases ferric oxide merely coats the grains of quartz, feldspar, or other material. In other formations it is associated with particles of clay that fill pores between the grains. The amount of iron in such deposits is usually no more than 4 or 5 percent, but it acts as a powerful dye, much as tiny amounts of copper can make a mineral brilliantly green. In a few places, such as Minnesota's Mesabi Range, the ferric oxide has been far more strongly concentrated, possibly by some form of sea-floor process that billions of years ago produced a rich source of iron ore. In the more widespread redbeds a relatively modest level of concentration has occurred through weathering that removed other, more soluble constituents of the material (such as silicates and carbonates), leaving ferric and aluminum oxides. Many of the redbeds, however, are not significantly richer in iron than other sedimentary deposits. They are red because the iron has been transformed into its reddish form.

The slow reddening that can now be seen taking place in parts of North America, Africa, Australia, and elsewhere has occurred, under suitable conditions, for 2 billion years, including periods when the areas were in low latitudes—less than 30 degrees north or south of the equator. Some 350 million years ago the region where the Catskill Mountains now rise in New York was coastal, and rivers laid down extensive deltas that today are exposed as redbeds there and south into Pennsylvania. Also deposited when North America was farther south than today were the more recently formed redbeds of Canada, Connecticut, and Massachusetts, as well as those of the Chinle, Moenkopi, and other formations that brilliantly color much of the magnificent scenery of the Southwest. The sandstones, shales, and mudstones forming those monuments were laid down during the Triassic Period, some 200 million years ago, then solidified and reddened over long periods of geologic time before being eroded into such landscapes as Monument Valley, the Painted Desert, and the Canyonlands.

The Jurassic Period, or Age of Dinosaurs, 150 million years ago, produced the red-streaked "Navaho sandstone" exposed in the canyons and badlands of Colorado, Utah, and Arizona. As noted earlier, it was laid down when a great sand sea comparable with the Sahara covered the West. Thanks in part to oil prospecting its remains have been traced from Arizona to northern Wyoming. The long period in which its sand dunes formed, moved on, and reformed is evident, notably in Zion National Park, in the way in which numerous layers, tilted in many directions to form cross-bedded patterns, are heaped, one upon the other.

One of the beauties of the reddening process is its lack of uniformity. The formations that it colors range through shades as diverse as the conditions under which they were formed. The resulting landscapes, therefore, are never uniform, never monotonous, all thanks to light-scattering properties of the tiny molecules we call ferric oxide.

27 THE EVER-CHANGING BARRIERS

From New Hampshire down the eastern seaboard to Florida and around the Gulf Coast to Mexico a succession of long, narrow islands, sandspits, and baymouth bars stand as barriers to the onslaught of ocean waves. They constitute the most continuous and extensive chain of barrier islands in the world. Waves have spread their sands to form numerous islands and 2,700 miles of beaches, some of which are straight as far as the eye can see, or almost imperceptibly curving.

From aloft it is easier than from the ground to appreciate the inconstancy of these features. Beneath the water one can see sandbars that swirl with extraordinary grace as tidal currents, "overwashes," and other water actions constantly reshape the land. Nowhere is such sculpturing of the sea floor more beautifully evident than off Cape Cod and Nantucket Island (on flight paths from New York to Europe). The submarine bars form concentric, curving patterns whose complexity is difficult to understand, but which demonstrate some of the ways that currents constantly change the landscape, above and below water.

Only through research conducted chiefly since the early 1970's has the migratory nature of the barrier islands become clear. They have a remarkable tale to tell of inexorable movement—a tale that many geologists rejected until the evidence became overwhelming. It is now argued that since the sea began rising after the last Ice Age, some of the islands have migrated fifty miles or more westward as the coastline retreated.

Barrier islands line almost the full length of Long Island: Fire Island, Jones Beach, Long Beach, Rockaway Beach, and Coney Island. They front the ocean in New Jersey and along the Delmarva Peninsula (whose name is a composite of the three states to which it belongs: Delaware, Maryland, and Virginia). Such islands arch far out into the ocean as the Outer Banks, including Cape Hatteras and Kitty Hawk, whose strong, stable winds aided the first airplane flight. Along the Florida coast the islands and spits bear such well-known names as Daytona Beach, Cape Canaveral, Palm Beach, and Miami Beach. One of the longest in the world is Padre Island flanking the coast of southwest Texas for 140 miles.

Typically between barrier islands and the mainland are long, narrow sounds, like

Great South Bay off Long Island or Indian River between Cape Canaveral (site of the Kennedy Space Center) and the mainland. Much of Florida's fruit is grown near the shores of that "river."

Lagoons and marshes behind the islands serve as nurseries for large numbers of fish that are later caught at sea as well as countless birds. The region between Padre Island and the Texas shore, for example, supports at least 500 species of waterfowl and other birds as well as providing the winter feeding ground of the whooping crane, a towering species with a seven-foot wingspread that has been rescued from the brink of extinction.

Although the barrier islands, spits, and bars are in constant flux, several cities are perilously perched on them, including Atlantic City, Miami Beach, and Galveston.

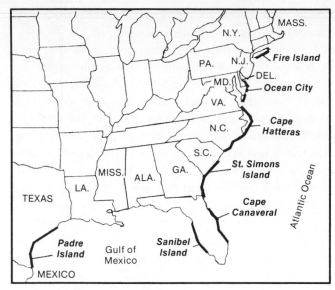

The major barrier islands.

Early colonizers knew better than to build directly on the beach. They placed their cottages behind protective dunes and their long, narrow lots extended across much, if not all, of the island. Thus, as the sea advanced, they could move the cottage back. Some were moved as many as three times. Land was cheap—in Atlantic City it sold at four cents an acre (in 1690). Today shore property values are so high that elongated lots have become prohibitively expensive.

The rate of home-building on the islands has been phenomenal. In 1950 the total area developed was 90,000 acres. By 1980 it had reached 280,000 and there was increasing concern that hurricanes could become disastrous. For example, Seabrook, Kiawah, and Hilton Head islands near Charleston are now fashionable resorts, but in 1893 a hurricane flooded all three, and although they were sparsely inhabited, 2,000 lives were lost. In 1900 such a storm hit Galveston with a loss of 6,000 lives—the worst natural disaster in American history—and that city was again hard hit in 1983. When the great hurricane of 1938 hit Hampton Beach on Long Island, 153 of the 179 homes there were lost, yet 900 new homes had been built there by 1980. When Hurricane Hazel swept over Long Beach Island, south of Wilmington, North Carolina, in 1954, it wiped out all but 5 of the 357 houses there, but the population of homes soon grew to 2,000. By the 1980's, following rapid development of the Florida keys, the inhabitants of that 150-mile string of islands had grown to 70,000, yet their only land route of escape from a threatening hurricane is a two-lane highway with fifty bridges.

Such developments are not surprising, for the barrier islands provide some of the nation's most delightful summer resorts. Furthermore, with the help of a few canals, the islands have made possible the Intracoastal Waterway that furnishes smooth sailing between Massachusetts, Key West, and Brownsville, Texas. A canal carries the waterway across Cape Cod. Another, linking Delaware Bay and the north end of Chesapeake Bay, is often visible on flights from Washington, D.C., to New York. A third, the Dismal Swamp Canal, runs between Norfolk, Virginia, and Elizabeth City, North Carolina, linking Chesapeake Bay with Albemarle Sound.

At first glance the manner in which the barrier islands formed seems simple enough, although, as in much of nature, on closer examination simplicity gives way to complexity. For millions of years the eastern seaboard, unlike the West Coast, has been free of geologic upheaval. Sand grain by sand grain, waves have sculpted the coastline without their work being wiped out by radical changes in the landscape.

Waves are an extremely efficient vehicle for transporting the solar energy transferred to them by winds. The waves accumulate their energy across the vast reaches of an ocean, such as the Atlantic, approaching the shore in usually innocuous-appearing swells. But when they reach shoaling water they rise up, topple, and pound the beach, grinding rocks into sand and transporting the sand along the coast.

Rarely do waves roll in exactly head-on. They come in at an angle. A wave breaks with a crashing roar, sending an apron of foaming, sand-laden water scudding up the beach. As the water retreats the sand is carried seaward, but the next wave throws it

Above and right: In the
New York Bight, average
sand transport along both
the New Jersey and the
Long Island coasts is
toward New York harbor,
producing the spits—Sandy
Hook and Rockaway
Beach—that flank the
harbor entrance.
(Landsat/NASA)

Left: The Ash Wednesday
storm of March 7, 1962,
created havoc on New
York's Fire Island. (UPI
photo)

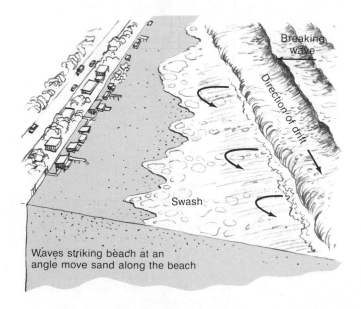

Waves striking beach at an
angle move sand along the beach

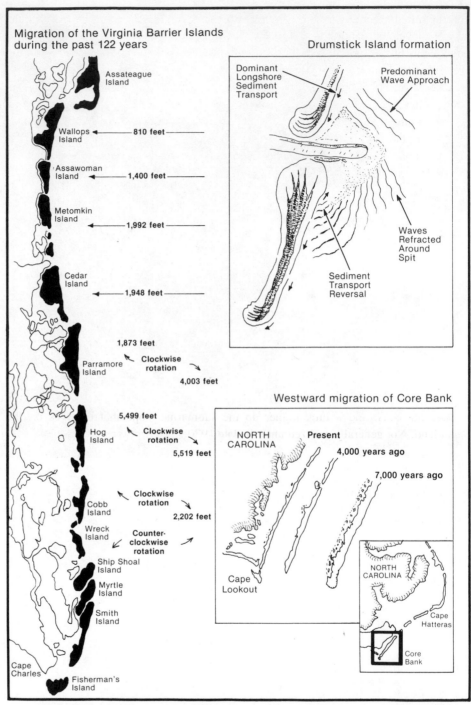

Migration of the Virginia Barrier Islands during the past 122 years

Assateague Island

Wallops Island ← 810 feet

Assawoman Island ← 1,400 feet

Metomkin Island ← 1,992 feet

Cedar Island ← 1,948 feet

1,873 feet

Parramore Island ← Clockwise rotation →

4,003 feet

5,499 feet

Hog Island ← Clockwise rotation →

5,519 feet

Cobb Island ← Clockwise rotation →

2,202 feet

Wreck Island ← Counter-clockwise rotation →

Ship Shoal Island

Myrtle Island

Smith Island

Cape Charles

Fisherman's Island

Drumstick Island formation

Dominant Longshore Sediment Transport

Predominant Wave Approach

Waves Refracted Around Spit

Sediment Transport Reversal

Westward migration of Core Bank

NORTH CAROLINA   Present

4,000 years ago

7,000 years ago

Cape Lookout

NORTH CAROLINA

Cape Hatteras

Core Bank

(Left: From "Virginia barrier island configuration: a reappraisal" by S. P. Leatherman, T. E. Rice, and V. Goldsmith in Science, vol. 215, 1982, p. 286. Copyright © 1982 by the American Association for the Advancement of Science. Right: From figure 12A on page 17 of "Barrier Island Morphology as a Function of Tidal and Wave Region" by M. O. Hayes and figure 16 on page 232 of "Quaternary Evolution of Core Banks, North Carolina: Cape Lookout to New Drum Inlet" by T. F. Moslow and S. D. Heron, Jr., in Barrier Islands from the Gulf of St. Lawrence to the Gulf of Mexico, S. P. Leatherman, ed.)

back a little farther down the beach than its point of origin. The result in the surf zone is net movement parallel to the beach known as the longshore current. In storms it may be as fast as a brisk walk but is usually less. Swimmers experience it when, on returning to shore, they find they are no longer opposite their beach towels.

The waves are at work, day in and day out, year after year, century after century. Some days they move the sand in one direction. Then, when the waves arrive at a different angle, the drift may be reversed, but there is usually a prevailing direction. On much, but not all, of the East Coast it is typically from the northeast. The barrier islands along the coast of Long Island, forming the northeast side of the New York Bight, are migrating southwest and each tends to overlap its neighbor. Fire Island's western end has grown five miles since 1825. Jones Beach, at the west end of the next barrier island to the west, is likewise a product of recent growth.

Sand produced by the pounding of surf on a rocky promontory is spread by longshore currents to either side of that point, forming long spits. Material from various sources—glacial deposits, deltas produced by rivers or tidal flow, and shoals formed by wave action—is similarly spread into barrier islands. Where the growth of an island is stopped by tidal currents, as at a harbor entrance, the sand, instead of migrating farther, forms a hook, like Coney Island and Sandy Hook, which flank the entrance to New York Harbor.

As many who live on barrier islands know all too well, the latter are subject to rapid change, particularly during winter storms and hurricanes. The battering surf of a stormy winter can halve the width of an island. During the next summer gentler waves may bring the sand back. If an island is entirely destroyed it can be reborn, but a little nearer the coast and a little higher up the submarine slope that emerges on the mainland. Not generally realized until the late 1970's was that most of the islands are migrating inexorably toward the mainland, whose rim is itself very slowly being submerged by the advancing sea. The oceans are rising, and in some areas the land is sinking.

When the most recent ice sheets began melting, between 12,000 and 18,000 years ago, sea levels were so low that much of the now-submerged continental shelf was dry. The melting at first was rapid and so were the sea-level rise and the westward retreat of the coastline. When the rise of the sea was rapid, the barrier islands that grew were very thin. They did not remain in one place long enough to become wider until about 5,000 years ago.

The traces of these island migrations lie embedded in the ocean floor far out to sea. Offshore samples of sediment obtained by oceanographers or oil prospectors by coring (driving or drilling tubes into the bottom) contain oyster shells like those now laid down behind barrier islands in lagoons such as Long Island's Great South Bay. The cores contain, as well, sand deposits typical of those formed by tidal flow between islands.

On scores of today's barrier islands oyster shells found along beaches facing the ocean were laid down in salt marshes behind the island when it was farther out to sea. Peat remaining from such marshes is found by clam diggers beneath the sand on Cape Cod's Nauset Spit. The Cape itself is not a typical barrier island and Robert N. Oldale, discussing its future in a U.S. Geological Survey guide, offers a gloomy prognosis. Eventually, he says—although not for many generations—"Cape Cod will be nothing more than a few low sandy islands surrounded by shoals."

Barrier islands off the Carolinas are also in retreat. Tree stumps exposed at low tide on their seaward side have been dated by their content of radioactive carbon (carbon 14) showing that less than 200 years ago they grew on the sheltered, inner side of the banks. Evidence indicates that Core Bank extending 40 miles northeast from Cape Lookout has migrated 4.2 miles landward in the past 7,000 years. All told the Outer Banks may have moved 40 or 50 miles since sea level began to rise. It has been proposed that the Sea Islands of Georgia have traveled 80 miles and that some islands in the Gulf of Mexico have moved more than 100 miles.

At least one island community, Broadwater, Virginia, has been left behind by such movement. Its remains lie submerged several hundred yards off the Delmarva Peninsula's Hog Island. Brigantine Island, adjoining Atlantic City, appears to have retreated 4,500 feet in the past 6,000 years, which does not augur well for the long-term future of the casino city next door.

Hatteras Light, historic landmark at the apex of the Outer Banks, stood 1,500 feet from the surf in 1872, but by 1983 it had come within 150 feet. The National Park Service, responsible for the lighthouse as part of the Cape Hatteras National Seashore, had spent $2 million restoring beaches near the lighthouse and was faced with the possibility that continued efforts would simply leave it isolated on an islet of resistance to inevitable retreat. As Orrin H. Pilkey, specialist in barrier island dynamics at Duke University, has put it, "the Outer Banks are not disappearing but they are moving landward right out from under man's various accoutrements such as lighthouses, motels and highways."

That parts of the East Coast have been more than moderately submerged is evident from its deeply indented coastline (compared, for example, with that of the West Coast). Chesapeake Bay is the flooded lower valley of the Susquehanna River. That river and its former tributaries that now empty into the bay, such as the Potomac and Rappahanock, formed the "dendritic" pattern of a typical river system, like a tree trunk and its branches.

Delaware Bay is also a drowned river valley. Probing the sediment under its floor has revealed a channel 230 feet below present sea level through which the Delaware River flowed to the ocean when seas were lower (and, perhaps, the land was higher). Narragansett Bay also has the look of a drowned river valley as, to some extent, do Mobile Bay and the Back Bay of Biloxi on the Gulf Coast.

The earlier sea-level rise was almost entirely due to ice melting. Today the accumulations of frozen water in the polar regions and high mountains are more stable, but some glaciologists believe the massive ice sheet covering west Antarctica—that part of the South Polar continent south of the Pacific Ocean—is discharging icebergs faster than replacement of the ice by hinterland snowfall. Changes in sea level are being monitored by the Shorelines Commission of the International Quaternary Association, and some estimates put the current rise along the East Coast at from one foot to a foot and a half per century. Melting of ice is thought to account for about half of this rise, with most of the remainder attributed to warming and consequent thermal swelling of the upper part of the world oceans. A small amount may result

These stumps on Caswell Beach on the southernmost coast of North Carolina are the remains of a forest that grew on the inland side of the island. The island has moved and the stumps are on the ocean side. (James Page, Duke University)

from subsidence of the continental shelf under the added weight of seawater as oceans rise.

There is some evidence that the climate is warming, probably in response to the increased amount of carbon dioxide in the atmosphere. As previously noted, that gas is produced by all forms of combustion, and since the industrial revolution initiated a rapid rise in fuel burning, it is estimated that atmospheric carbon dioxide has increased 17 percent. Carbon dioxide acts much like the glass of a greenhouse in preventing the radiation of heat back into space.

In 1983 members of the Strategic Studies Staff of the U.S. Environmental Protection Agency sought to assess the effects on sea level of global climate warming caused by the carbon dioxide "greenhouse effect." One possibility considered was far more rapid discharge of west Antarctic ice into the sea, although it was thought that this would still be spread over several centuries. A series of proposed scenarios envisioned rises ranging from 1.59 to 12.1 feet by the year 2100. A 10-foot rise would, for example, flood large areas of the Gulf Coast, Florida, and coastal New Jersey, and more modest rises would greatly increase the vulnerability of those regions to invasions by the sea during storms.

Part of the apparent rise now being recorded is actually caused by land subsidence, for which there are several possible explanations. Along the Gulf Coast extensive withdrawals of oil, gas, and water are deflating the land. In the Houston area Texas City and Baytown have both sunk more than five feet in twenty-five years, chiefly because of water extraction now partially curtailed. Some of those living along the lower San Jacinto River have had to move into their second stories and Houston's Hobby Airport has sunk four or five feet.

In the delta region of Louisiana and Mississippi rapid loss of land to the sea is attributed in large measure to the building of levees to prevent flooding by the Mississippi. Normally such floods spread sediment over the delta region, replacing land lost to erosion, subsidence, and wave action. A study by the U.S. Fish and

Wildlife Service found that in 1955 the delta had 892,500 acres of swamps and marshes, but by 1978 this had declined to 405,000 acres. According to a 1981 survey for the Louisiana state legislature the state was losing forty-seven square miles of land to the sea each year.

"Over time, and increasing in geometric proportion," said the report, "coastal Louisiana is disintegrating as protective barrier islands and the shoreline of the state erode away and subside, as fragile and productive wetlands deteriorate and shrink back through the intrusion of salt water into delicately balanced ecosystems."

A more universal, but very gradual, cause of subsidence may be cooling and shrinking of the earth's interior beneath the continent's eastern rim. The splitting of North America away from Europe and Africa, 100 to 150 million years ago, was accompanied by deep-seated volcanic activity along the line of rupture. As the continents have moved apart, the interior of the earth beneath what had been the zone of cleavage has cooled and shrunk. So has the region beneath sea floor, moving away from the Mid-Atlantic Ridge where it was volcanically formed. Consequently the basin of the Atlantic Ocean is deepest at large distances from the Mid-Atlantic Ridge, and if the floor of the ocean has been sinking, so, probably, has the adjacent coast.

In any case, as noted earlier, sea level along the East Coast is rising from one foot to a foot and a half per century, the rate in New England being less rapid, possibly because the sea-level rise is being countered by rebound following departure of the region's heavy ice load. A rise of 1 foot in sea level can mean a retreat of 500 to 1,000 feet in the gently sloping coastline. In some areas, such as North Carolina, the mainland coast has retreated faster than the islands. As a consequence Cape Hatteras and the Outer Banks lie far offshore, separated from the mainland by the broad waters of Albemarle and Pamlico sounds. In northern New Jersey, from Sandy Hook south past Asbury Park to Point Pleasant, the islands have overtaken the coast and are plastered against it. At Miami Beach the broad apron of sand that once spread between the hotels and the sea is so shrunken that, were it not for heroic efforts, waves might already be rolling into hotel lobbies. $65 million was spent in 1979 and 1980 on beach restoration with little prospect that it would be long-lasting.

The rate of island migration is highly variable. In the Gulf of Mexico the Chandeleur Islands, forming a beautifully uniform, north-south arc east of the Mississippi delta, are moving west at sixty-five feet a year (more than a mile per century). On the average the East Coast barriers are retreating at from three to five feet yearly.

This does not necessarily mean they are diminishing. An essential element of the island-migrating process is that as the seaward side erodes, new material is added to the landward side. The process has been likened to the motion of a tractor tread. Sand is swept across from the front to the rear by storm waves—washovers—as well as by tidal currents flowing through inlets and, to some extent, by onshore winds acting on sand dunes.

Washovers, past and recent, are easily identified from the air. The sand that was swept up by storm waves as they crossed at a vulnerable point forms a fan-shaped deposit in the lagoon behind the island. Washovers tend to occur during storm surges—times when several factors conspire to make the raging seas abnormally high. Low air pressure on the sea surface, associated with the storm, allows the ocean to rise. Strong winds drive the water even higher against the shoreline. And if there is an unusually high tide, as at full or new moon, the effect is even more severe.

Wholesale movements of material occur during so-called northeasters that strike the East Coast chiefly in winter. These are storms whose wind systems, in the manner of the Northern Hemisphere, circulate counterclockwise around a center of low pressure. This motion, as the storm moves up the coast, produces violent winds and pounding waves from the northeast. The winds of a hurricane circulate in the same manner but even more violently.

While most of the barrier islands are subtly on the move, some seem to be anchored to an underlying rock formation, as is the case with the so-called Sea Islands of Georgia, some of them famed as exclusive resorts. They are stubby and the lagoons behind them have become filled in with salt marshes. Jekyll Island, once an exclusive club, is now a state park. Cumberland Island, southernmost of Georgia's Sea Islands, has been designated a national seashore. Like other islands along this coast it has numerous middens—huge heaps of oyster shells left by the Timucuan Indians who lived there for more than 3,000 years. Early settlers mined these middens to produce "tabby," a building material formed of burned oyster shells (as a source of lime), sand, and water. Structures made of tabby still remain on the island.

The studies of recent years have focused on factors that determine where barrier islands will be stubby, where long and skinny, where cut up into segments shaped like drumsticks, and where nonexistent. Rarely do they form when the range between high and low tide exceeds a dozen feet. This presumably explains why there are none along the coasts of Maine and Nova Scotia. With so large a tidal range an island that begins forming at low tide is swept away at high tide. Instead, intertidal mud flats, shoals, and tidal-current ridges are produced. Barrier islands do occur farther north along the south side of the Gulf of Saint Lawrence, off New Brunswick, Prince Edward Island, and the Isles de la Madeleine, where tides are less extreme.

Where tidal range is minimal—less than six feet—long, thin islands form. Their dunes are low enough to permit frequent washovers, but tidal currents are too weak to keep open large numbers of inlets across the barriers. Such islands line the Gulf Coast and eastern Florida and form the Outer Banks of North Carolina. Tides of intermediate range—from six to thirteen feet—are typical of southern New England, South Carolina, and Georgia, producing shorter islands such as the drumsticks along the South Carolina coast. A typical drumstick is Sullivans Island at the entrance to Charleston harbor.

Flood tides flowing inland between such islands deposit deltas inside the lagoons. Ebb tides flowing outward do likewise on the ocean side, although waves and longshore currents may partially disperse these deltas. Waves rolling past the ebb-tide deltas are swung around (refracted) and deposit sand at the upwind end of each island, forming the fattened head of the drumstick. From the air one can see how the ends of the islands have been built up, layer by layer, like tree rings or growth ridges on a clamshell.

The key role of vegetation in preserving barrier islands is evident along the ten miles of trails laid out for Cumberland Island visitors. Where wild and domestic horses, as well as swine and cows, have denuded the tall "back dunes," their sand

Waves passing this sandspit on Fire Island are bent or "refracted" around the corner. (William Geissler, Columbia University)

has been blown into the forest on the inland side of the island, burying live oak trees to their tops. Sea oats send roots deep into the sand, making them ideal for stabilizing dunes and the plant is protected under Georgia law. Near the beach "pioneer" plants, such as panic grass, sea croton, and marsh elder, establish themselves in clumps after a storm and little dunes form downwind of them.

Variations in the flora are believed to explain, in part, why the southern islands are so different from those in the northeast, such as at Cape Cod. The dominant growth on the Cape shore is American beach grass, which tends to cover and protect the dunes, enabling them to form a relatively continuous barrier against overwashes. Behind the dunes is a form of salt meadow cordgrass that cannot survive overwash burial—or crushing by wheeled vehicles, such as beach buggies. Farther south, on the other hand, sea oats and a more upright, stiff-stemmed cordgrass dominate. Since the sea oats grow in clumps, promoting the growth of separate dunes rather than a continuous dune line, islands in the South are less resistant to overwash. The cordgrass, however, survives overwash burial and, within a year after being covered with a foot or two of sand, will have grown back to the surface.

Overwashes are a way of life—more properly, a guarantor of immortality—for these islands. They heap up sand on the back side of the island, preparing a new front line for the inevitable rise in sea level, and over the centuries they enable the migrating island gradually to climb the gentle slope of the coastline. From aerial photographs taken between 1935 and 1977 it has been deduced that 85 percent of the Outer Banks were swept by overwashes during that period. It is also evident that in the past century or so, the banks have repeatedly been cut by inlets that then closed up.

These two processes account for the irregular lagoon shorelines of the islands in contrast to the extreme linearity of their frontal beaches—as uniform as a superhighway across the Great Plains. When an inlet is plugged, the delta formed in the lagoon by tides flowing through that passage remains. From the air many of these extinct deltas, with their salt marshes and snaking channels, are still visible.

Florida's barrier islands continue past Miami Beach and out to sea as a gentle curve shaped by the northward flow of the Gulf Stream between Florida and the Bahama Banks. This is the 150-mile chain of the Florida keys, terminating in Key West. The manner in which the keys were formed, however, has been quite different from that of islands to the north. Florida's dominant—though subtle—feature is a ridge a few miles wide that runs virtually the entire length of the state's east coast. Even at its highest point in Coconut Grove, south of Miami, it is no more than twenty feet above sea level, but it is higher than much of the peninsula's interior and a large percentage of Floridians live on it. The ridge is composed of a limestone (oolite) formed of tiny limestone spheres known as ooides because they resemble fish eggs. They were deposited some 100,000 years ago, between the last two ice ages, when global sea levels were about twenty-five feet higher than now, presumably because more Antarctic ice had melted than today and a large part of Florida was flooded. The so-called Pamlico Shoreline of that period is evident in wave-cut bluffs, seashell accumulations, and other telltale remnants in the interior of the peninsula. When the sea receded and the deposits were exposed to air and leaching by rain, they became cemented into the oolite limestone that is widely used for local construction and is also exported. Many Florida ponds featured in real-estate developments are water-filled oolite quarries.

During the period of high sea level, coral reefs grew along the keys from Miami southward, but with onset of the subsequent Ice Age the sea subsided and the coral polyps that built the reefs, being dependent on seawater, died. Coral reefs on the islands immediately south of Miami Beach—Virginia Key and Key Biscayne—therefore stand well above sea level. The coral, known as Key Largo limestone, has, however, anchored sand carried south along the coast by longshore currents. Quartz grains in this sand must have been carried a long distance down the coast, since there are no local quartz deposits. All of the islands as far down the line as Big Pine Key are built of the ancient Key Largo limestone and many are still flanked by living coral.

These islands are elongated along the graceful curve of the chain. Beyond Big Pine Key, however, their character changes. They are oriented at right angles to the curve of the chain, separated from one another by narrow channels that necessitated the building of numerous bridges for the long Overseas Highway to Key West. They differ from the northern part of the chain because they are made of the oolite limestone that underlies Miami, and they were cut by numerous tidal channels during their formation.

Enclosed by the northern part of the chain is Florida Bay—850 square miles of shallows and islands. A few thousand years ago, before the oceans reached their present level, the bay was filled by a southern extension of the Everglades that, combined with Big Cypress Swamp to the west, cover the heartland of southern Florida. Nowhere is the bay deeper than eight or nine feet. At Flamingo, southernmost community on the mainland, one can rent a canoe and paddle along the mangrove-covered shoreline, observing an occasional alligator, trees laden with numerous species of heron, roseate spoonbills, storks, ibis, pelicans, sandpipers, man-o'-war birds, and other species. One must be watchful of the ebbing tide, which can strand the unwary on an expanse of mud.

The Everglades themselves are the chief wonder of the Florida landscape. They are, in effect, a grass-covered river seventy miles wide, carrying water from Lake Okeechobee (inland from Palm Beach) to Florida Bay. While dotted here and there with clumps of cypress, slash pine, and other trees, much of the central part of Everglades National Park is an open grassland flooded by water of remarkable clarity, only a few inches deep, and flowing imperceptibly southward. Rarely, except in parts of the Great Plains, does one see so large an expanse unbroken by man or nature. The waving "saw grass," reaching from horizon to horizon, seems to be holding up the sky. Here and there the underlying limestone, dissolved into grotesque shapes, protrudes above the water.

Elsewhere in the park the "hammocks," or islands of clustered trees on slightly higher land, are more numerous, and boardwalks enable visitors to penetrate these sanctuaries. The Florida panther and other creatures take refuge in the hammocks but keep well out of sight. In more open areas one can see the remarkable anhinga bird perched on a branch with its large wings spread to the sun for drying. The anhinga spears fish on its sharp, slender beak, then alights in a tree, throws the fish up, and catches it. Unlike most fishing birds, however, its feathers are not waterproofed by oil and it must dry them in the sun.

Fire, sweeping across the grasslands in the dry season, has always been a necessary part of vegetation cycles in the Everglades. Today canals prevent widespread fires and parts of the park are subjected to controlled burning. Stability of the Everglades also depends on a steady flow of water from the north. Extensive areas in the northern Everglades have been drained for agriculture and levees have been built around Lake Okeechobee to prevent flooding of those lands during wet periods. Among lakes entirely within the United States, Okeechobee is second in size only to Lake Michi-

Tidal flow through Hatteras Inlet into Pamlico Sound formed a tidal delta there. (U.S. Coast and Geodetic Survey)

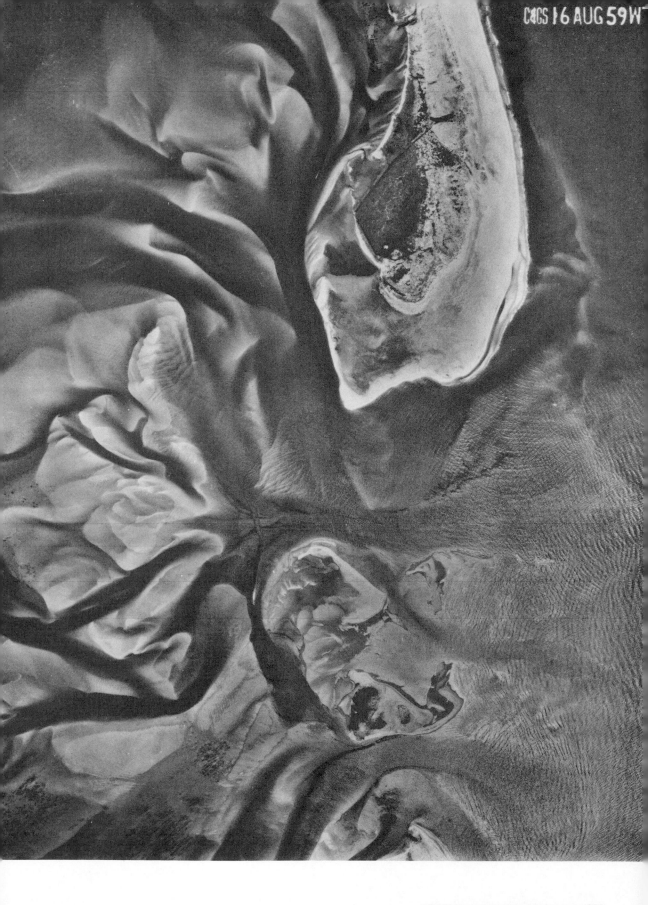

CGS 16 AUG 59 W

gan. An elaborate canal system controls the flow and drainage of water in the region north of—and into—Everglades National Park.

Between the park and the Gulf lies Big Cypress Swamp, an area of 2,400 square miles that includes a variety of landscapes—sandy islands, wet prairies, dry prairies, and mangrove swamps. About one third of it is covered with small cypress trees of the dwarf pond variety. Most of the giant cypresses from which the area takes its name have been made into coffins, pickle barrels, stadium seats, gutters, P T boat hulls, and other artifacts. Some of them, several centuries old, remain, however, their bulbous lower trunks emerging from the protected waters of what has become Big Cypress National Preserve. In 1968 it was proposed to build a large jetport on the eastern edge of the swamp to relieve pressure on Miami International Airport. After a great outcry from those who feared irreparable damage to both the swamp and the Everglades, the plan was shelved.

Concentric beach ridges on this island off the Florida panhandle southwest of Tallahassee bear witness to constant alteration of its shoreline. (U.S. Geological Survey)

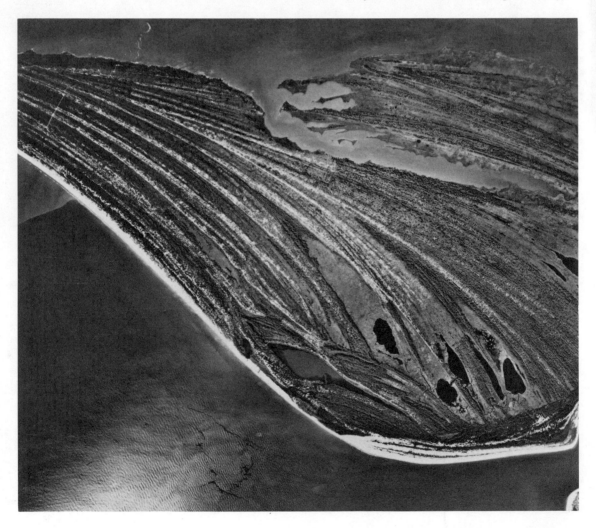

Beyond Big Cypress, along the Gulf Coast, is one of the largest coastal swamps known. Its 200 square miles are reminiscent of the heavily vegetated swamps that produced the world's coal beds. Along its coastal fringes oysters and mangroves have labored to produce the Ten Thousand Islands. The first step toward giving birth to a new island there is formation of a sandbar by longshore currents. If favorably located it is then colonized by oysters that thrive as long as the current brings them nutrients. Once the bank of oyster shells has grown enough to be exposed at low tide, mangroves take over. They readily establish themselves in shallows exposed at low tide and eventually trap and deposit enough material to form dry land.

Mangroves dominate the landscape on both sides of the keys as well as along Florida's west coast, providing spawning grounds for many forms of marine life. Farther north the coast continues to be covered with swamps, especially at the mouth of the Suwannee River, which drains Georgia's Okefenokee Swamp, with its monumental, moss-draped cypress trees. There are similar swamps along the Louisiana coast between the Mississippi Delta and Texas, but barrier islands rarely form along such shorelines.

It has been predicted that by the end of this century three out of four Americans will be living within fifty miles of the sea, and the pressure on oceanfront recreation facilities will be even greater than now. Some barrier islands are already saturated with developments. Some are paved over with four-lane highways and parking lots that leave little room for the tens of thousands who come there on summer weekends. From end to end of the barrier islands there are confrontations between those with long-term motivations and people with more immediate concerns—preservation of a summer home, development of new enterprises, or protection of old ones.

Specialists in barrier-island dynamics argue that most efforts to control the natural cycle of erosion and replacement only prevent the latter from occurring. They question the value of trying to stem beach erosion by building groins to block the prevailing longshore current. Some beaches are lined for miles with closely spaced groins. Sand accumulates on their upstream side but erodes on their downstream side. Fresh sand cannot flow in, and soon very little beach is left, as can be seen along parts of the Jersey shore where waves lap sea walls built to prevent further erosion along the now-vanished beaches.

Facilities such as New York's Jones Beach are well planned, providing much needed recreation for nearby city dwellers. But some citizens object to spending extensive public funds for projects that benefit only a few and are unlikely to do so for long. A typical case was the proposed use of $38 million in federal funds to rebuild a bridge connecting Dauphin Island, near the entrance to Mobile Bay, with the Alabama mainland. The previous, relatively insubstantial link had been destroyed by Hurricane Frederic in 1979. Winds estimated as high as 120 miles an hour destroyed all but six houses in a colony of one hundred. The Sierra Club and the Natural Resources Defense Council both brought suit in federal court to block rebuilding of the bridge, but the case was lost.

For centuries Dauphin Island, like others of that chain, has been migrating westward, parallel to the Gulf Coast rather than toward it. At times it has linked up with its neighbor to the west, Petit Bois Island (once called Massacre Island). Between 1848 and 1974 Petit Bois crossed the border from Alabama into Mississippi. Storms and hurricanes have repeatedly changed the local geography. According to one early account, half of Dauphin Island, then twenty miles long, was washed away in a 1740 hurricane.

Another type of confrontation pits fishermen and yachtsmen against those who would let nature take its course, as in the $114-million proposal of the Army Corps of Engineers to build two jetties into the sea on either side of Oregon Inlet, the only entrance to northern Pamlico Sound from the open sea. Like most barrier inlets, this one is constantly on the move, and the engineers argued that the jetties would keep it in place and prevent the continuous shifting of sands that forms new shoals and sometimes brings boats to grief. Opponents, including the National Park Service, argued that the jetties would result in severe beach erosion for miles to both sides of the inlet. As of early 1984 the issue was still unresolved.

While about a third of the barrier islands, spits, and baymouth bars have been developed to varying degrees, the coastal states and the National Park Service, which supervises a dozen national seashores and recreation areas, now control more than half the coastal barriers, marshes, and lagoons. In the mid-1970's the National Park Service abandoned further efforts to stabilize shorefronts along most of the seashores under its control. Private groups have also moved in. In the 1970's the Santee Club, a group of South Carolina sportsmen, gave to the Nature Conservancy more than 23,000 acres of barrier island and coastal marsh at the outlets of the Santee River northeast of Charleston, although their market value was put at $20 million. The Conservancy spent close to $5 million to acquire most of the islands along the southernmost seventy-five miles of the Delmarva Peninsula. Farther up that coast all of Assateague Island is either a national seashore or a wildlife preserve in which the wild Chincoteague ponies are free to roam. On the Gulf Coast of Florida a deal was made whereby the Delton Corporation, a developer, turned over to the state 15,000 acres of wetland on Marco Island, including extensive mangrove swamps, in return for 160 acres of prime industrial property near Miami International Airport. The Army Corps of Engineers had refused to allow the developer to fill in marshland on Marco Island by nearby dredging. The trade left the developer free to sell the industrial property and use the proceeds for a less environmentally sensitive project.

Several states have enacted strict controls over further seashore development. In 1982 Congress passed a law forbidding further use of federal funds for building bridges, roads, boat landings, sewers, and other facilities on barrier islands. It had been estimated that for every acre developed on those islands, at least $25,000 had been spent in federal support. Also terminated was federal underwriting of flood insurance for new developments there, although existing insurance was continued and property owners could also seek commercial coverage.

Prospects for preservation of the barrier islands have also been greatly improved by recognition of the factors governing their life cycles. Despite the pounding of countless winter storms and hurricanes, they have survived thousands of years and will continue to do so if treated reasonably well.

28 ICE–THE MONUMENTAL SCULPTOR

To a degree few inhabitants of the northern states and Canada realize, the land that is their home has been shaped by flowing ice and by water released as it melted. The fruits of these glacial engineering feats are remarkable in their diversity: the meltwater inland seas that became the Great Lakes, narrow ridges called eskers that snake across the land like walls built by some forgotten civilization, terminal moraines marking the farthest advances of the ice sheets such as those now comprising Cape Cod and Long Island along the East Coast, and such strangely shaped hills as drumlins and kames. Debris carried by the ice has buried river valleys comparable with that of the Mississippi and has created new ones. Meltwater torrents have carved magnificent gorges at numerous points near the southern fringe of the ice sheets.

These events are not of the remote past. They occurred only yesterday, geologically speaking, and some were witnessed by the ancestors of America's true natives. For their descendants, as for the rest of us, it is difficult to imagine that ice-covered world. Yet only by doing so can we understand the landscape of today. A visit to Greenland or Antarctica would help, but those lands are almost entirely covered with ice, whereas in North America the ice reached only as far south as New Jersey, Pennsylvania, and (broadly speaking) the valleys of the Ohio and Missouri rivers. South of the ice the land was inhabited by a wondrous fauna of giant animals—lions, bearlike sloths that could pull down the topmost tree branches to forage, camels with necks long enough to compete for such foliage, huge beavers, as well as woolly rhinos, zebralike horses, rodents as large as ponies, great herds of hulking super-bison, and the ice age elephants.

The latter included mastodons that stood almost ten feet high at the shoulder and munched twigs in the spruce forests that had retreated far south. There were mammoths with domed heads that stood even taller than the mastodons and whose tusks curved back toward their eyes. Their immense molars were adapted to grinding up tundra grasses. The remains of more than 150 mastodons and 50 mammoths have been found in Ohio alone. Whether early hunters or some other decimator, such as a sudden climate change, caused their extinction remains uncertain.

According to traditional accounts there were four great ice ages during the past

Left: Farthest advances of the ice sheets covered almost all of Canada—probably including Hudson Bay. Separate lobes flowing south through Minnesota and the Lake Michigan valley never fully joined, leaving an unglaciated area in Wisconsin. (Illustration by Jerome Connolly from page 11 of Face of North America: The Natural History of a Continent *by Peter Farb. New York: Harper & Row, 1963. Reprinted by permission.)*

Right: As the land east of Hudson Bay, relieved of its ice load, rose, a broad staircase of parallel beaches, bars, and spits was formed. (Department of Energy, Mines and Resources, Canada)

million years, designated in American terminology consecutively as the Nebraskan, Kansan, Illinoian, and Wisconsin ice ages for the states where their effects are most obvious. Recent studies of clues in sea-floor sediments and elsewhere suggest that over the past three million years there actually may have been as many as thirty ice advances and retreats, with the advances—some of which did not advance very far south—spaced at intervals of roughly 100,000 years.

An explanation that has gained wide support is that the ice ages began when the northern continents moved into positions where they almost enclosed the Arctic Ocean, largely isolating it from the tempering influence of warm currents such as the Gulf Stream. The Arctic became colder, ice formation there being controlled by cyclic changes in the earth's orbit around the sun and in the tilt of the earth's spin axis (the greater the tilt, the more extreme are the differences between winter and summer at high latitudes).

The last ice maximum—the Wisconsin Ice Age—reached its peak some 20,000 years ago when cave dwellers in southern Europe, Africa, and Asia were executing remarkably bold paintings of the animals they saw. Not until about 4000 B.C. had the ice sheets fully retreated from Canada and Scandinavia. By then the giant animals that shared the landscape with the cave dwellers had vanished.

The Antarctic glaciation of today is awesome. In places its ice is more than three miles thick and part of it buries an archipelago in a would-be sea. Much of North America was probably under a comparable thickness of ice. More than 95 percent of Canada was buried and now constitutes the world's largest area of formerly glaciated terrain. The weight of so much ice caused the land to subside, particularly under the central, thickest part of the ice cap around Hudson Bay. After the ice melted and before the land there could rise again, it was flooded by the sea, and now that the land has partially rebounded, beaches formed at the time are as much as 1,000 feet above sea level. The area around Hudson Bay is still rising about 3 feet a century. The Maine–New Hampshire coast was sufficiently depressed for the sea to penetrate inland as far as Dover, Augusta, and Bangor. The north shore of Lake Michigan has risen 850 feet relative to its south end. The bones of seals and whales who swam in the vicinity of Lake Champlain are now found in deposits several hundred feet above present sea levels.

As the ice flowed south, its enormous weight also ground the landscape below, rounding the summits of the Adirondacks, the White Mountains of New Hampshire, and other mountain ranges. Glaciers flowing down from mountain summits carved theater-shaped cirques out of the mountainsides and shaped the valleys into U's (as opposed to the V-shaped cross sections of water-worn valleys). Yosemite in California is a typical glacial valley. The head walls of cirques are often almost vertical, fine examples being Tuckerman's Ravine in the White Mountains, those in the Adirondacks that have shaped Whiteface Mountain into a sharp peak, and numerous ones in the Sierras, Rocky Mountains, and other ranges of northwest Canada and Alaska.

New Yorkers can see evidence of the grinding power of the ice in their own Central Park, where ledges (such as those east of the Heckscher Playground at the south end of the park) have been "machined" by boulders embedded in the ice's underbelly, forming smoothly polished grooves that run from northwest to southwest. Among the largest in the world were those three to fifteen feet deep and hundreds of feet long cut into limestone on the north shore of Kelleys Island in Lake Erie (north of Sandusky, Ohio), although most have been quarried away.

As long as the ice to the north was accumulating generous amounts of snow and not losing much of it in summer, the ice fronts in the south continued to advance. Considering the plastic properties of ice it has been calculated that for the ice over Cleveland to be massive enough to squeeze out the ice front that advanced southward across Ohio as far as Chillicothe or Hamilton, it had to be a mile thick over the present site of the city. Its front, however, was only 50 to 200 feet high. It has been calculated that it flowed down the Scioto Valley south of Columbus at speeds that may have reached 6 feet daily.

Left: Ice advances left these concentric moraines and kettle-hole ponds near Alkaline Lake in south-central North Dakota. (Army Map Service)

Right: Glaciers in the Uinta Mountains have carved a series of steep, theater-headed valleys, or cirques. (John S. Shelton)

The advance halted when melting along the southern front balanced the rate at which snow accumulation to the north replenished the loss. Thus its front remained relatively stationary for centuries. The ice, however, was not immobile. It continued to flow south all that time, picking up rocks and other material along the way. Where it melted along its southern front it deposited its load, forming the ridges and hills that survive as moraines. The ice acted like an extremely broad conveyor belt constantly delivering rock, sand, gravel, and silt at its southern end. For 3,000 to 4,000 years after its last major advance across Ohio the ice remained within fifty miles of its farthest limit, but, as elsewhere along its long front, repeatedly shifted back and forth, leaving a complex pattern of moraines, most of whose larger boulders were derived

from formations in Ontario, having been transported from north of the Great Lakes. Once the ice began to retreat in earnest, it still paused from time to time, forming a series of ''recessional moraines'' roughly parallel to one another.

Today terminal moraines produced at the extremity of the ice advance by a combination of bulldozing and the conveyor-belt process are visible from New York and New England to the Pacific Northwest. A series of those left by the last advance extend, as an almost continuous feature, from New York City to Cape Cod in Massachusetts. One of them forms the entire North Shore of Long Island, although for its inhabitants it may seem astonishing that none of the hills there have cores of bedrock. They are simply great heaps of glacial debris. This line of moraines continues from Orient Point under Long Island Sound, emerging as Plum Island and Fishers Island, then runs past Charlestown on the Rhode Island coast and along the Queen Elizabeth Islands to Cape Cod, where it forms the eastern shore of Buzzards Bay. There it makes a sharp turn to the east along U.S. 6, forming a ridge almost 300 feet high known on the Cape as the Sandwich Moraine.

Prior to formation of this line of moraines the ice pushed farther to seaward, leaving a moraine that follows the Long Island Expressway much of its route down the centerline of that island and forms Montauk Point. Beyond that it dips under the sea to emerge as Block Island, the little island of No Mans Land, and the islands off Cape Cod—Martha's Vineyard and Nantucket. Only parts of the islands are terminal moraines. As the ice melted, water flowing away from the ice front spread sand and gravel over broad, flat regions known as outwash plains. The level South Shore of Long Island is such a plain as are the flat parts of the Vineyard and Nantucket. The outer hook of Cape Cod is also formed of outwash material deposited by the melting of a lobe of ice on its seaward side. As is particularly evident in the Great Lakes, the southernmost extensions of the great ice sheet were not along a straight front but in a series of lobes—glaciers that had followed the route of least resistance (usually down old river valleys). In Massachusetts one lobe filled what is now Cape Cod Bay, then melted to produce a large lake that drained south along the present route of the Cape Cod Canal. Another seaward lobe deposited its meltwater into that lake, producing some of the deposits on the outer Cape.

It appears that the ice, at its maximum, extended far off the present coast. With so much water stored in ice sheets, worldwide sea levels were some 300 feet lower and the shallow continental shelves were exposed far beyond present coastlines. Off the East Coast the shelf offered rich pastures for grazing mastodons, perhaps pursued by Stone Age hunters. Fishing trawlers scoop up mastodon teeth as much as 125 miles off New York City. The ice pushed a considerable distance out across the shelf off Massachusetts, probably covering much (if not all) of Georges Bank. In samples extracted from beneath the sea floor 50 and 110 miles southeast of Nantucket scientists with the U.S. Geological Survey reported in 1980 that they had found sediment compacted as though by a heavy load of ice, and similar evidence has been found by the Geological Survey of Canada off Nova Scotia.

Across the hills and mountains of northern New Jersey (through Morristown and Dover), and across Pennsylvania and northeast Ohio, the moraines are hard to follow. They are more easily seen in the plains states from Ohio to the Dakotas. Among

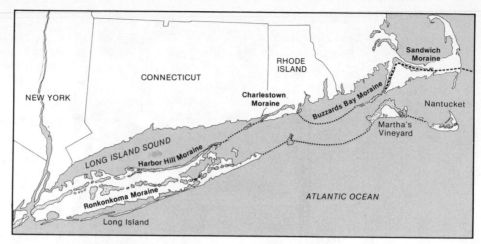

Parallel moraine systems, from Cape Cod to New York, mark the farthest advances of the last ice age.

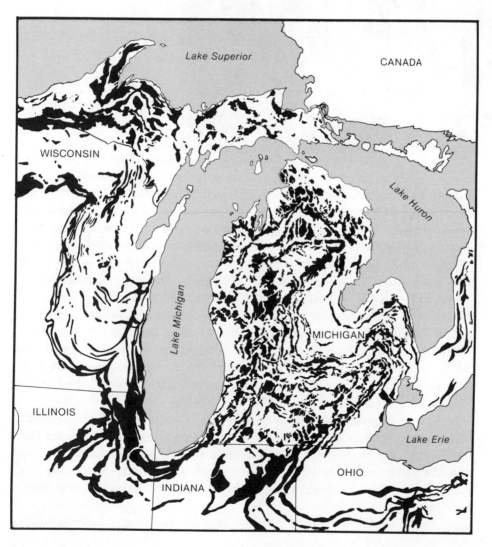

Moraines in the Great Lakes area. (Michigan Department of Natural Resources, Geological Survey Division, 1975)

Left: Kettle-hole ponds within the great checkerboard of northeast North Dakota. The squares are one mile on a side. (U.S. Department of Agriculture)

Right: Rivers that once flowed under the ice sheet deposited these eskers that now snake across the barren landscape east of Boyd Lake, Northwest Territories, midway between Great Slave Lake and Hudson Bay. (Department of Energy, Mines and Resources, Canada)

features left by the ice before its retreat is the Valparaiso Moraine, which skirts the shore of Lake Michigan for several hundred miles from southern Wisconsin through the outskirts of Chicago and northern Indiana to west-central Michigan. Because of intensive urban development, little of it can be seen in the Chicago area, but it seems to mark the farthest advance of an ice lobe that filled and overflowed the Lake Michigan basin. The Kalamazoo Moraine lies north of Interstate 94 in western Washtenaw and eastern Jackson counties in Michigan. Although moraines along the ice fronts from Ohio to Minnesota and beyond are too numerous to catalogue, a succession of prominent ones was left by ice advances across Wisconsin, Minnesota, and the Dakotas, culminating in those deposited by an ice lobe that 14,000 years ago reached Des Moines, Iowa. Its eastern edge buried the present site of Minneapolis, which had previously been covered by lobes that flowed southwest from Lake Superior and left the Saint Croix Moraine which winds 450 miles across central Wisconsin and Minnesota.

From an aerial perspective some of the most spectacular moraines are those in parts of Canada where they are not masked by heavy vegetation, such as the De Geer moraines in northern Quebec that cover terrain east of Hudson Bay like a succession of uniform water waves. However, they are remote from most air routes. There are numerous moraines, as well, in the provinces between Ontario and the Rocky Mountains.

As the ice withdrew it often left behind large blocks of ice and sediment-laden

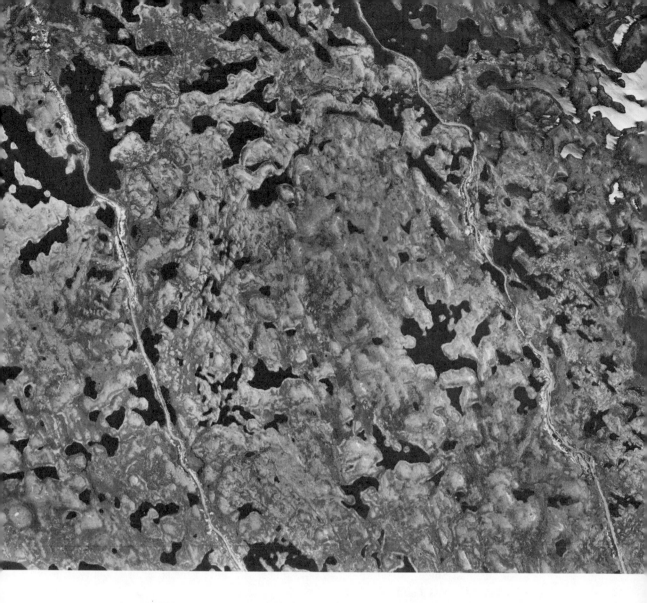

water from the retreating ice surrounded them with "drift" that was to become rich farmland. When the blocks finally melted they left small ponds—"kettleholes"— such as those that dot the landscape in northeast counties of North Dakota. In Massachusetts there are numerous examples south of Route 6 on Cape Cod.

Perhaps the most striking features, when clearly visible from the air, are the eskers—narrow, snaking ridges superimposed on the landscape. Few features of the American scene were more puzzling until their origin was guessed. They were left by streams that flowed in tunnels under or, sometimes, on the ice. Running water normally deposits its sediment in a valley of its own cutting, but here it built walls that in some cases can be traced more than 300 miles across the landscape. The meltwater deposited sediment on the floor of an ice tunnel and when all the ice was gone, this former streambed was left as a "wall." Some eskers are more than a hundred feet high and may be from a few dozen feet to a mile or more in width. Many have been exploited for their sand and gravel and, in the marshier parts of Maine, have been used since Colonial times as roadbeds for highways and railroads. There are estimated to be more than 1,400 miles of eskers in that state alone. The Kennebec eskers are 230 miles in length. Along Route 16 near Eustis, Coplin, and Wyman, northeast of the Rangeley Lakes, there is a sharp-crested esker up to 100 feet high dug into by many gravel pits and crossed by the Appalachian Trail.

In New Hampshire Richard P. Goldthwait of Ohio State University has studied a network of eskers produced in the eastern lowlands from Conway south to Lake Winnipesaukee during the melting of a dirty ice cover several hundred feet thick. The eskers converge south of Ossipee Lake to form a five-mile ridge seventy to one hundred feet high along the east side of Route 16. While the esker is clearly visible from the air, to those on the highway it is little more than a steep, densely wooded bank until, just south of Ossipee, one passes a giant pit where sand and gravel are being mined from the esker and shipped to Boston by the trainload. The clean-washed material is ideal for making concrete.

There are several eskers in northwest Pennsylvania, such as the one in West Liberty, east of Interstate 79 and fourteen miles south of its intersection with Interstate 80. The remarkably straight segments of this esker may have been formed by water flowing along a giant crevasse in the ice sheet. The verdant setting of that ridge today is a far cry from the great crevassed ice sheet that gave it birth. In southern Michigan the Blue Ridge Esker lies along U.S. 127 south of Jackson and there is another near Mason, south of Lansing. In Ohio an esker parallels U.S. 23 from Circleville northward toward Columbus, the highway crossing it before reaching South Bloomfield. Farther south, at Chillicothe, the same highway follows the Scioto River through a major terminal moraine.

As the ice withered over eastern Minnesota meltwater carved a series of roughly parallel tunnels under the ice from Saint Cloud to the northeast, leaving shallow valleys with eskers along their centerlines. Probably the most dramatic eskers, when seen from the air, however, are those that wander across the more barren parts of the Canadian Shield, standing out in bold relief with little vegetation or human disturbance to mask them.

Equally strange among ice age relics are the hills of glacial material called kames. They look as though sand had been dribbled from a narrow source, as sand in an

This esker, near Ossipee, New Hampshire, is mined for sand and gravel that are shipped by train to Boston. (Photo by the author)

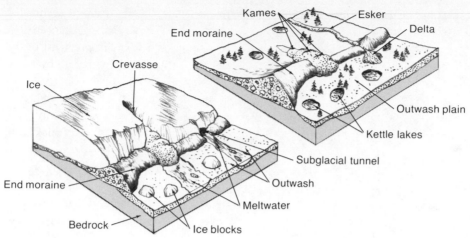

How kames and eskers were formed.

hourglass, to produce an almost perfect cone. They were apparently formed by silt-laden meltwater plunging down holes in the ice. Kames dot the Ohio landscape along a three-mile stretch of U.S. 23 south of its intersection with U.S. 270, the highest (just north of the Scioto Downs racetrack) known as Spangler Hill.

Three of the terms applied to ice age relicts are Irish or Scottish, presumably because they were first recognized there. Esker is of Gaelic origin, kame is Scottish, and drumlin is from the Irish for "little hill." Although drumlins are widespread in regions once covered by the ice, how they were formed is still uncertain. They are elongated hills, typically shaped like partly buried eggs or (as they are often called) whalebacks. They occur in groups of tens to thousands, their long axes parallel to the former direction of ice flow. Often the ends that faced the oncoming ice are blunt whereas the trailing ends are tapered. The upper part seems to have been formed under the ice by layer-on-layer accretion during the final, withering stages of the last Ice Age.

In south-central Wisconsin they are strikingly evident from the air because farmers have aligned their fields with the drumlins, disregarding property divisions that conform to the checkerboard of the National Survey. Hundreds can be seen when flying between Madison and Milwaukee late in the day, when the sun is low in the sky. In Canada a similar effect occurs near Peterborough, north of Lake Ontario, where the landscape is fluted by drumlins cutting diagonally across the checkerboard of property lines. In central Minnesota there are swarms of them near Brainerd and Pierz as well as snaking eskers and hundreds of kames near Lake Johanna, east of Glacial Lakes State Park (sixty-five miles west of Saint Cloud). North of Duluth the Toimi drumlin field lies parallel to the Lake Superior shoreline. Drumlins can be seen, as well, in the northeast part of Michigan's lower peninsula and in the Connecticut Valley around Gill, east of Interstate 91 and six miles south of the Vermont border. In some areas, as in northeast Pennsylvania, along Venango Township's Macedonia Road, highways crossing a succession of drumlins swoop and dip in roller-coaster fashion.

Drumlins aligned with the ice flow across south-central Wisconsin have forced farmers to lay out their fields in the same direction, ignoring north-south, east-west property lines. (U.S. Department of Agriculture)

In New York State some 10,000 of them lie between the Finger Lakes and Lake Ontario. Most of the hills between Rochester and Syracuse are drumlins, and from the air one can see where they have been cut through by rail lines, the New York State Barge Canal (formerly the Erie Canal), and the New York State Thruway. For motorists it is evident in the Thruway cuts that these hills have no rocky cores. The most famous is Mormon Hill (known to the Mormons as Hill Cumorah), two miles north of Exit 43 on the Thruway and twenty miles southeast of Rochester. It was in a crypt on that hill, Mormons believe, that Joseph Smith, under divine guidance, found and transcribed from gold tablets what became the Mormon scriptures.

Scores of drumlins occur around Boston, the most famous being Bunker Hill overlooking the harbor. In 1775 the Revolutionary leaders decided to fortify Bunker Hill during the night lest British artillery use it to dominate Boston. Apparently in the darkness its less lofty twin, Breed's Hill, was mistakenly occupied, but the heavily fought engagement that followed is known as the Battle of Bunker Hill. Although British ships were anchored less than a half mile away, their crews apparently did not hear the sound of digging as 800 colonials threw up earthworks six feet high on the drumlin crest. Hence after dawn the British were surprised to discover that the hill had been fortified. Clifford A. Kaye of the U.S. Geological Survey believes the digging was not observed because the Americans penetrated only the top few feet of silt. Had they dug deeper, into the glacial mixture of pebbles and rocks, the din would have been heard.

Other drumlins in the area include Parker, Meeting House, and Monterey hills in Boston proper and many of the islands one sees approaching or leaving Boston's Logan International Airport, including Spectacle, Bumpkin, Georges, and Peddocks islands (the last being formed of five drumlins). Kaye has likened most drumlin assemblages to "a school of fish with their noses to the current." Those around Boston, however, are more, he says, like fish "frightened by a pebble falling into the water." The reason, he believes, is that ice movements there were not uniform in direction.

The mixture of sand, silt, gravel, clay, and boulders left strewn rather uniformly across the land after the ice departed is known as drift because, in early days, it was thought to have been carried there during the biblical flood. Actually, by the time the flowing ice had traveled as far south as the northern tier of states, its underbelly was packed with material picked up en route and it was all deposited wherever the ice melted. The southern region, subject to repeated advances, retreats, and melting of the ice, gained most of the deposition. In much of Ohio it is more than fifty feet deep, whereas in northern Ontario a great deal of the bedrock is bare and those glacial deposits that occur are only a few feet deep.

Air travelers across the Great Plains can usually tell whether the land below is covered by drift or lay south of the farthest ice advance. If, as in northern Iowa, the region was glaciated, it is relatively level or gently rolling. In southern Iowa, beyond the reach of the last ice, the land is eroded into valley systems that resemble a tree and its branches. Farther north such landscapes were leveled by the ice and filled in with drift. The drainage systems were destroyed, leaving terrain that was often marshy when settlers arrived, as in southern Minnesota, northern Iowa, parts of Illinois and Ohio. Today drains often cut diagonally across the fields, and the land, like that of central Indiana, looks mottled from the air because of uneven drainage.

In Ontario, northern Wisconsin, and Minnesota the ice ages have left a multitude of swamps and lakes, such as those of the Boundary Waters Canoe Area—ideal for recreation but more suited to forestry than mechanized farming. The ice bypassed southwest Wisconsin and the terrain there remains deeply carved into valleys. To the east, nearer Lake Michigan, terminal moraines, wet lowlands, and scattered lakes have made the land difficult to cultivate and ideal for pasture. This is the region that has made Wisconsin famous for its cheeses and other dairy products.

Glacial drift buried one of the great river systems of pre-Ice-Age America. A clue to its existence—not immediately recognized—came in the early 1880's when a newly organized coal-mining company sank an exploratory shaft on the north side of Urbana, Illinois. At a depth of 125 feet water began pouring into the excavation, and so the coal company decided to become the Union Water Supply Corporation. In 1983 wells supplying two dozen public and industrial water systems in the area were producing fifty million gallons a day with no sign of serious depletion. The water is being drawn from what is now known to be the valley of a great river filled to depths as great as 300 feet with glacier-deposited material.

Some early explorers of the Ohio River drainage basin realized there was something odd about its landscape. In 1838 S. P. Hildreth, in the first annual report of the Geological Survey of Ohio, said: "Great changes have, evidently, been made in the direction of all our water courses before they found their present levels."

In 1886 Gerard Fowke began wondering how the deep gorge west of Chillicothe, Ohio, could have been formed by the present-day trickles of Paint Creek. He embarked on a prolonged campaign to win acceptance of the view that this was part of a great river system most of which lies buried under glacial deposits. As with Harlen Bretz's catastrophic explanation for the scablands, Fowke's views had only begun to win acceptance when he died in 1933.

One of his allies had been William G. Tight of Denison University in Granville, Ohio, who had puzzled over the origin of the valley cut deeply into West Virginia between Charleston and the Ohio River at Huntington. Beyond Saint Albans, where the Kanawha River turns sharply north, no river of any significance flows through the valley, although it was chosen as the ideal route for the Chesapeake and Ohio Railroad.

Tight proposed that this carried a mighty river that drained the present basin of the Ohio River, but followed a more northerly route across Ohio and Indiana. He called it the Teays (rhymes with "pays") River for a little known locality in West Virginia.

Today its headwaters have been traced into the Appalachian highlands of Kentucky, Virginia, West Virginia, and North Carolina, all of which lay south of the area affected by ice action. Farther north, from tens of thousands of well-drilling records in the region covered by glacial drift, geologists have reconstructed the river's route northwest across Ohio in a trench hundreds of feet deep that, many now believe, drained most of that state, Indiana, and Illinois before emptying into the ancestral Mississippi south of Peoria. The stretch crossing Illinois is called the Mahomet Valley for the village where it is most deeply buried. There is some uncertainty as to whether this was the lower part of the Teays or a separate river. In any case, as Goldthwait has put it, if the overlying drift were removed, the valley of the Teays River "would be one of the most scenic features of the eastern landscape."

Today most of Ohio drains south to the Ohio River, which formed just south of the ice lobes, but before the ice ages much of the drainage was northward. The Teays, for example, flowed up what is now the valley of Ohio's south-flowing Scioto River. That river, as it passes Columbus and Chillicothe, rides on a deep bed of glacial deposits, but beneath them is the bed of the ancient Teays, tilted in the opposite direction.

A number of rivers that have survived the ice ages have reversed direction. It was such changes in drainage that helped create the Great Lakes. Before the ice ages most of the Great Lake region drained down the Mississippi, but the ice helped scoop out lake basins and built moraines, cutting off southern drainage routes. Today the Great

Lakes account for about one third of the world's freshwater surface. Lake Michigan, Lake Huron, and Saginaw Bay (which extends from Lake Huron deep into the Michigan Peninsula) are the shadows of three great ice lobes that pushed south (probably along old river valleys), then retreated, their meltwater forming inland seas considerably larger than the present lakes. Lake Chicago spread beyond southern Lake Michigan, covering the present city of Chicago, and drained down the Mississippi. The glacial seas that evolved into the eastern Great Lakes drained for a time down the Mohawk Valley into the Hudson along what became the path of the Barge Canal. This route, past the present site of Buffalo, had to surmount a broad accumulation of glacial drift and therefore, once the ice had retreated farther north, shifted northeast to pass through Lake Champlain and into the Hudson. This persisted until the Saint Lawrence Valley opened all the way to the sea.

With departure of the ice, rivers that once drained toward the Gulf of Mexico began flowing into Lake Erie and ultimately down the Saint Lawrence. The Saint Joseph runs southwest, as it used to, until at Fort Wayne, Indiana, its waters enter the opposite-flowing Maumee River, which travels northeast to Lake Erie at Toledo.

Rivers on the east side of the Rockies that formerly drained northeast into Hudson Bay now feed the Misssouri system. The Missouri itself has been rerouted. In

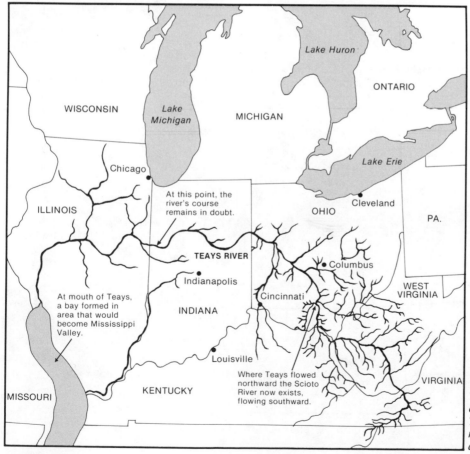

At this point, the river's course remains in doubt.

TEAYS RIVER

At mouth of Teays, a bay formed in area that would become Mississippi Valley.

Where Teays flowed northward the Scioto River now exists, flowing southward.

The probable course of the Teays River two million years ago.

Right: Parallel beach ridges, formed along the shore of former Lake Agassiz, cut diagonally across the farmland of North Dakota west of the Red River. (U.S. Department of Agriculture)

Below: Glacial Lake Agassiz (in lighter shading) and existing lakes. (From Life, Land and Water *by J. A. Elson, Winnipeg: University of Manitoba Press, 1967.)*

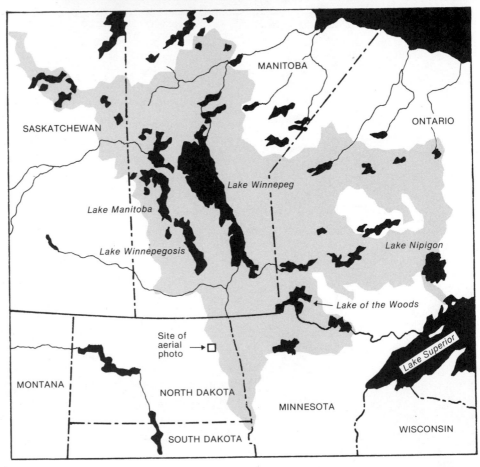

Montana it originally flowed northeast from Great Falls through Big Sandy and down the present valley of the Milk River, joining the Missouri of today just below the Fort Peck Dam. After being redirected by ice into a more southern path, the river never returned to its former course, but its old route is followed by the Great Northern Railroad.

Western New York State gained hundreds of magnificent gorges and cataracts as a result of changes wrought by the ice. When the Genesee River came back to life after the ice retreat, its former route was blocked midway between its headwaters in Pennsylvania and its exit into Lake Ontario at the present site of Rochester. It cut a new channel through the flat-lying sedimentary rocks laid down much earlier, when that region was covered by a shallow sea, producing a succession of impressive gorges in Letchworth State Park.

The gorges, cataracts, and waterfalls of the Finger Lakes have a different tale to tell. The Iroquois are said to have believed that the five largest lakes were formed by the imprint of the Great Spirit's hand. It appears, however, that each of the lakes—eleven in all—is a fjord that was cut by a tongue of advancing ice. Crowding into existing river valleys, the tongues gouged them until the valley floors were lowered some 600 feet, two of them, under Lakes Cayuga and Seneca, being well below sea level. Tributary streams that had serenely flowed into the valleys from the sides now plunge down waterfalls and cataracts into the deep lake troughs. In Ithaca such a stream has cut a chasm across the campus of Cornell University, high above Cayuga's waters. Before the ice ages the floor of the valley in which that lake is cradled is thought to have been on a level with the university campus.

On the west side of the lake Taughannock Falls, highest in the northeastern states, drops 215 feet into a deep gorge. The torrents of meltwater also produced some of the world's most spectacular plunge pools and potholes, such as those at Watkins Glen, long a famous tourist attraction at the south end of Lake Seneca. Potholes are gouged by water swirling with sufficient energy to batter the walls with stones and drill a deep shaft. Six miles south of Scranton, Pennsylvania, along Route 6 there is a formidable pothole 38 feet deep and 42 feet wide. In Whirlpool Canyon, a third of a mile west of Pennsylvania Route 115, near Exit 47 on Interstate 81, a succession of seven potholes is known as The Tubs. There are also exceptionally large potholes in Interstate Park on the Minnesota-Wisconsin border, south of U.S. 8 and downstream from the gorges of the Saint Croix River (now a National Scenic Riverway). So well displayed are ice age features in the vicinity of Wisconsin's Kettle Moraine State Forest, southwest of Sheboygan, that the region has been designated the Ice Age National Scientific Reserve.

Meltwater also altered the landscape on a far grander scale. As noted earlier, when drainage down the Saint Lawrence Valley was blocked, water raced toward the Hudson River, first down the Mohawk Valley, then down through Lake Champlain and Lake George. The Hudson became a gargantuan torrent, carrying seaward turbid water from the Great Lakes and the melting ice sheet beyond them. This deluge cut into the continental shelf, laid bare by the lowered sea level, and where the flow continued underwater landslides of accumulated sediment periodically raced down-slope, carving a canyon that extends all the way to the shelf's outer edge. If the ocean did not hide it, this would appear as one of the great canyons of the world.

It was, however, the Mississippi, muddy and swift, that most extensively changed the landscape. The sediment that it carried built much of America's heartland. With the oceans so much lower, it cut a deep valley down the center of the continent. The slope of the riverbed was greater than today. The river flowed faster, and the density of its heavily silt-laden water was so great that it carried fist-sized stones far down the river to its mouth. Then, as ice melted and oceans rose, the river that had carved so deep a valley filled it up again. At Cairo, where the Ohio and Mississippi rivers join, the old streambed lies under 200 feet of sediment. Near the Gulf it is buried 350 feet deep.

These are effects of the most recent Ice Age, but when the earlier ones are taken into account, the amount of material spread over the lower Mississippi Valley and the Gulf Coast was thick and heavy enough to provide in its depths the heat and pressure needed for conversion of organic material within the sediment into oil and gas. The resulting fuel reservoirs of the Gulf region helped make the United States, for a long time, one of the most energy-rich countries of the world.

Between former ice ages more of the Antarctic ice apparently melted than today, for sea levels rose higher than at present, flooding the coastal plains of the eastern and southern states. The Mississippi, responding to the higher sea level, formed a flood plain as much as forty feet above the present delta region. About 15,000 square miles of this elevated flood plain remain as a plateau, including the fertile rice-growing area of Arkansas.

While the Great Lakes are a residue of the ice ages, other large lakes did not survive. Among these Lake Agassiz, the grandest, was produced when ice cut off the northward flow of the Red River of the North. That river today defines the North Dakota-Minnesota boundary, then flows into Lake Winnipeg and, finally, Hudson Bay. With its route dammed, meltwater spread into a lake far larger than today's Lake Superior. It extended from Minnesota and eastern North Dakota deep into Canada. Blocked to the north, the Red River reversed its direction, draining Lake Agassiz southward to the Minnesota and Mississippi rivers.

Parallel beach ridges along the former shores of this lake, readily visible from the air, cut diagonally across the North Dakota farmland west of the Red River (which has resumed its northward flow). The lake-bed soil on both sides of the river is dark and exceptionally rich. The beach ridges, left by fluctuating lake levels, are twenty to thirty feet high but slope gently enough for cultivation.

Lake Maumee, an extension of Lake Erie across northwest Ohio, has also left a series of parallel beach ridges whose sandy remains can be seen from aloft as pale or reddish soil bands across the fields. Early settlers found them well-drained sites for homes or roads. Perhaps the most obvious of these former lakeshores is Ridge Road, running westward from Rochester to Niagara and Canada. It parallels the south shore of Lake Ontario some eight miles inland. For much of its distance it is followed by New York's Route 104 and, in Canada, by Route 8 as far as Hamilton. The ridge was used as a trail by the Indians, and it amazed De Witt Clinton, early in the nineteenth century, when he traveled it in search of a route for his proposed canal linking the

Alaska's Bering Glacier, the largest in the United States. (Austin Post, U.S. Geological Survey)

Great Lakes and the Hudson River. He recognized the ridge as a seventy-eight-mile segment of former lakeshore and ''a stupendous natural turnpike.'' Clinton, whose efforts finally led to building of the canal, served as a U.S. senator, as mayor of New York, and unsuccessfully campaigned for the presidency against James Madison.

Lake Passaic, which covered part of northern New Jersey when ice blocked passage of the Passaic River through a gap in the ridges at Paterson, was not in a class with Lake Agassiz, but it was large, extending from the loop of Watchung Mountain near Somerville north through what is now the Great Swamp National Wildlife Refuge to the lowlands between Boonton and Paterson.

The glacial lakes grew large, not only because ice often blocked normal drainage of the landscape but also because in a relatively short time they received meltwater

Left: Lateral moraines, formed by past glacial advances from the Sierra Nevada, flank both sides of Green Creek ten miles south of Bridgeport, California. (John S. Shelton)

Right: Moraines form a complex pattern on Malaspina Glacier, fed by the snows of Mount Saint Elias. (Austin Post, U.S. Geological Survey)

Below: Tributaries converging on Yentna Glacier in the Alaska Range have produced numerous medial moraines. Mount Foraker, 17,400 feet high, a neighbor of Mount McKinley, rises beyond. (Austin Post, U.S. Geological Survey)

derived from precipitation, which over thousands of years had fallen as snow on the region to the north and been placed in cold storage.

While few are lucky enough to see an ice age in action in Greenland or Antarctica, there are extensive ice fields and glaciers in Alaska and Canada's neighboring Yukon Territory, notably those in the St. Elias and Chugach mountains as well as the Alaska Range. Numerous glaciers also occur farther south in the Canadian Rockies, Glacier National Park, the Olympic Peninsula of Washington, and along the east side of the Sierra Nevada (whose name, in Spanish, means "snow-capped mountains"). They demonstrate how ice can carve rock, gravel, and sand from mountain walls and transport it down U-shaped valleys to be deposited in moraines.

For those in California and Nevada a drive along U.S. 395 where it skirts the eastern flank of the Sierras can become a rich tour of Ice Age features. The 200-mile stretch from Owens Lake to Reno offers views of cirques, moraines, U-shaped valleys, and other glacial artifacts. On both sides of McGee Creek, where the highway runs between Lake Crowley and the mountains, it cuts through fresh lateral moraines—the kind piled up alongside a flowing glacier. Other moraines can be seen from side roads into the mountains, and it is evident that glaciers there have advanced and retreated more than once since the last Ice Age. Forested upper slopes on the valley walls give way below, along sharply defined trim lines, to barren, recently glaciated lower zones. Because the moraines contain layers of pumice and ash attributable to well-dated eruptions of the western volcanoes, the history of glacial advances and retreats there has been rather completely reconstructed.

The most dramatic examples of moraine formation, however, are viewed from the air farther north, particularly those produced where two or more glaciers meet to form a single one. Material picked up by the edges of each glacier farther upstream ends up being carried down the middle of the combined glacier, forming a "medial" moraine. Particularly impressive for those flying over Alaska on a clear day are Barnard Glacier, northwest of Juneau, and Yentna Glacier, flowing off the Alaska Range southwest of Mount McKinley. Their many tributary glaciers have produced so many medial moraines that each resembles a multilane freeway. A few glaciers begin "galloping" when enough ice has accumulated at their upper ends to make them unstable. They then slump, or surge, in a manner that may push the lower front of the glacier several miles down its valley in a matter of months.

While the origin of kames and eskers was long a puzzle, the processes apparently responsible for their production can be witnessed along retreating glaciers in Greenland and Alaska. In Alaska's Glacier Bay one can walk along an esker to the front of the glacier that made it and into the tunnel under the ice where it is still being formed. Nevertheless, because we cannot look under the ice sheets, it is nowhere possible—not even in Antarctica—to see at firsthand the formation of those odd whalebacks, the drumlins.

29 THE AGE OF WINDS

Although dust storms have had a bad reputation as the cause in the 1930's of great suffering and farmer migrations on the High Plains of the West, it was such storms, repeatedly occurring over intervals of 10,000 years, that made much of the Midwest fertile.

During the last Ice Age the source regions of this silt were utterly different from today. South of the ice front meltwater spread over the landscape sand, gravel, and "rock flour" accumulated by the great ice sheet on its long march southward. This formed great "outwash plains," and when the melting lessened and river levels dropped, parts of the outwash plain dried and were attacked by fierce winds from the west. Winds that today blow across the Great Plains are normally (but not always) of modest intensity, painting patterns that sweep across ripening grain fields like flying shadows. During the ice ages the typical winds may have been considerably stronger. The westerlies of today are strongest in winter because that is when temperature differences between the tropics and high latitudes are greatest. The atmosphere itself attempts to equalize those temperatures, causing large-scale circulation, and during an ice age the temperature differences must have been greater and such circulation more intense. Analysis of layers laid down in the Greenland and Antarctic ice sheets during the last Ice Age indicate that the atmosphere then was one hundred times dustier than today.

The outwash plains would also have been subject to powerful "katabatic" winds of the type experienced today only by those living close to the edge of an ice sheet, such as the ones in Greenland or Antarctica. Cold air, hugging the surface of the ice sheet, flows off it and down its frontal slope in a cascading torrent. Sir Douglas Mawson, the Australian explorer of Antarctica, in his book *The Home of the Blizzard*, describes life in such a situation during the long period of winter darkness and intense winds. The expedition's hut, though firmly anchored to the rocky terrain, shook constantly. It was like living on a train roaring through the night. Gusts estimated at nearly 200 miles per hour pelted the hut with rocks. Those who ventured outside had to lean into the wind until their heads were almost at knee level, then fell on their faces when the wind suddenly dropped.

South of the ice front in North America the skies must often have been dark with great clouds of windblown dust moving eastward, and it was over the river valleys that the clouds became particularly dense. As now occurs along some Alaskan rivers, enormous quantities of meltwater wove an ever-changing, braided pattern across the valley floors, forming broad bars of gravel, sand, and silt that, particularly during dry periods, provided an abundant source of dust for eastward transport by the prevailing westerlies. As a result accumulations of one hundred feet or more formed east of the Missouri and Mississippi river valleys.

The material thus deposited is known as loess (which in common American parlance rhymes with cuss) from the German word for ''loose.'' Much of the Midwest's richest farmland is carpeted with loess, which is easily tilled—and easily eroded. The deep accumulations east of the Missouri and Mississippi rivers and closest to the loess sources are known as the Loess Hills (or Bluff Hills).

Their erosion has produced a special kind of landscape found in China and to some extent in other regions of loess accumulation such as the Soviet Union, central Europe, and Argentina. From the air the contrast between the flat, alluvial river valleys and the deeply eroded Bluff Hills is dramatic. The river valleys are intensively farmed, whereas the steep-sided hills are not, and the deep-cut valleys between them tend to be forested. It is only to the east, where the loess is thinner, that farming takes advantage of its properties.

The particles of quartz within loess are so tiny that attraction between their molecules makes them cohesive. Consequently the valley walls are steep, as are those of road cuts through the loess, an example in central Missouri being on Interstate 70 between Columbia and the bridge over the Missouri River. Periodically small sections of the valley walls slip down-slope, and the cumulative effect is to give the hillsides a

Left: "Cat steps" formed on the sides of loess hills in western Iowa. (Jean C. Prior, Iowa Geological Survey)

Right: The Sand Hills of Nebraska as viewed from space by Landsat. Crossing them, from top to bottom, are the North Loup, Middle Loup, and Dismal rivers. (NASA)

terraced appearance. These ranks of little terraces (known in some regions as catsteps) can be seen throughout the loess hills. The loess loses its cohesiveness once the original deposit is disturbed, and in wet weather slumping along road cuts can keep maintenance crews busy. Where Interstate 29 follows the Missouri River valley northward from Kansas City it passes many loess hills, particularly above Saint Joseph as well as in Squaw Creek National Wildlife Refuge near Mound City and between Rock Port and Hamburg, Iowa.

While loess hills lie along most of the Missouri Valley in eastern Iowa and downstream to Kansas City, they become less evident from there to the river's confluence with the Mississippi. They are also prominent all along the east side of the lower Mississippi Valley, the deposits being particularly thick between Vicksburg

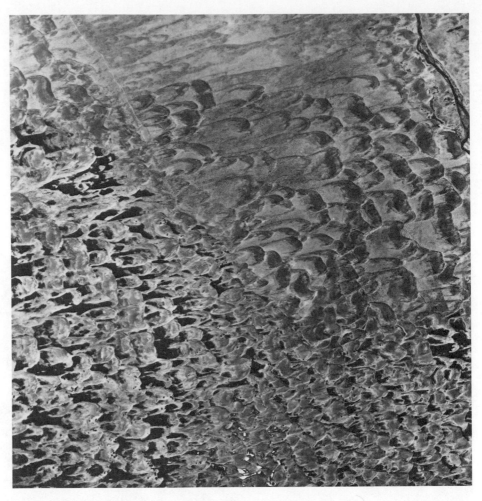

Parabolic dunes, partially stabilized by vegetation, near Moses Lake, Washington. Prevailing winds are from the left. (U.S. Geological Survey Professional Paper 590)

Right: Barchan dunes west of the Salton Sea. Their horns point east, away from the prevailing winds. (John S. Shelton)

and Natchez, where, as seen from the air, they form a sharp boundary along the edge of the level flood plain.

Because of the prevailing winds some areas of the plains were upwind of loess sources and fared poorly. In western Nebraska and the adjacent area of Wyoming most of the light, silty material has been blown away, exposing underlying "mortar beds" cemented by limestone. In central Nebraska winds produced the Sand Hills that cover a quarter of the state—18,000 square miles of it, with another 1,000 square miles to the north in South Dakota. The wind, picking up material from nearby glacial flood plains, quickly dropped the coarser part, heaping it into chaotic hills that, in the eastern part of the region, are ordered into east-west ridges more like true sand dunes, although they are now "dead dunes" stabilized by vegetation. When viewed from the air the region looks like a stormy sea whose giant waves have suddenly become

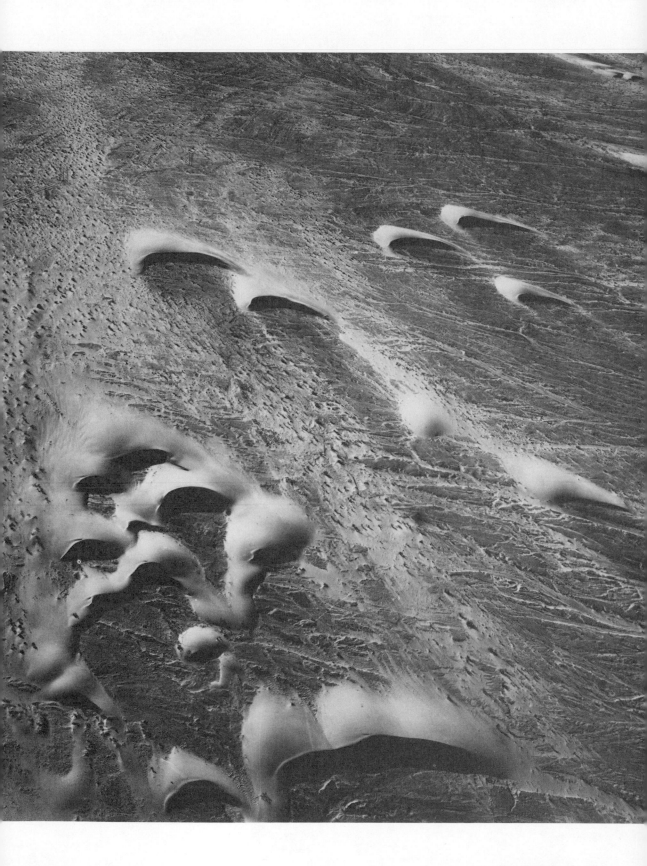

motionless. Although originally thought unsuited to farming, much of it is now watered by centerpivot irrigation.

The effectiveness of wind transport was demonstrated from 1933 to 1939 when prolonged droughts converted the High Plains of Kansas, Colorado, New Mexico, Oklahoma, and Texas into a "dust bowl." Winds carried off the fertile soil, leaving sand that was blown into drifts thirty feet high, burying roads and fences, forcing farmers to abandon their land. In a test conducted in 1935 near Lincoln in eastern Nebraska it was found that in three days winds from the west deposited 4,800 pounds of material on a single acre. Had this continued for a month it would have amounted to a tenth of an inch.

During the ice ages loess deposition occurred as far east as Ohio and also west of the Rockies in Washington, Oregon, and Idaho. Wind lifted silt from the basins of the Columbia and Snake rivers, leaving coarser material behind and depositing the silt on higher ground to the East. In the rolling Palouse Country of southeastern Washington the resulting loess, mixed with small amounts of mineral-rich volcanic ash, blown east from the Cascade volcanoes, forms a blanket commonly several tens of feet in thickness. Grain harvests there have made the Palouse farmers among the nation's most prosperous. Most of the deposit predates the last glaciation, since it was already there to be swept away when the ice dam of Lake Missoula collapsed.

As pointed out by Kenneth L. Pierce of the U.S. Geological Survey, a leading authority on loess deposits, when wind-transported silt forms a thin deposit, six to twelve inches thick, it is a "very precious commodity," constituting the rich topsoil that covers many parts of the country. It has traditionally been thought of as a natural product of in-place weathering. According to Pierce, however, it was not formed by weathering of the underlying rock, but deposited by the wind. Once gone, it can only be replaced by very slow wind accumulation, chiefly during ice ages. Although seemingly not very impressive, this thin coating deserves special protection because it blankets much less fertile soil or rock material.

In addition to depositing loess, prevailing winds have shaped sands produced by the ice age floods and by more recent erosion into dunes of extraordinary diversity. They occur, for example, throughout the scablands and as far up the Snake River as the Bruneau Dunes south of Mountain Home, Idaho. The most prominent in central Washington are near Potholes Reservoir south and west of Moses Lake. Some are parabolic dunes, crescent-shaped and partially stabilized by vegetation, their horns pointing up-wind. West of the Salton Sea in California are migrating dunes of the classic crescent type known (from the Russian-Kirghiz term) as barchans. In contrast to the parabolic dunes their long horns trail downwind from each side, marking the direction in which the dune is migrating. During the last Ice Age such dunes formed as far east as Pennsylvania (for example, east of the West Branch of the Susquehanna River opposite Lewisburg).

Ice age dunes survive alongside the Great Lakes. Waves in the glacial lakes pounded moraines and glacial drift on their shores, producing sand that was heaped into dunes, some of which survive, particularly along the edge of Lake Michigan, as at the Sleeping Bear Dunes in the northwest corner of Michigan's lower peninsula and

Dunes in Death Valley. (John S. Shelton)

at the southern end of the lake in the Indiana Dunes National Seashore between Gary and Michigan City. Migration of the Sleeping Bear is said to have buried three villages during the last century. Much of Chicago was built on the westward extension of the Indiana Dunes and early in this century some within the city still had not been leveled. It was then that a highly emotional campaign to "save the dunes" was launched, led by such figures as Jens Jensen, founder of the Prairie School of landscape architecture and designer of Chicago parks. With the dunes rapidly disappearing as industry spread along the south shore of the lake, their preservation was equated with preserving a bucolic world and gentle culture that were fast vanishing. In 1913 young ladies in flowing gowns, trailing long filmy scarfs, danced in a masque entitled "Duna, the Spirit of the Dunes." Carl Sandburg responded in verse:

> What do we see here in the sand dunes of the white moon along with our
>   thoughts, Bill,
> Alone with our dreams, Bill, soft as the women tying scarves around their
>   heads dancing...

The battle continued into the 1960's with Secretary of the Interior Stewart Udall joining in a "save the dunes" rally. Finally, in 1966, legislation created the Indiana Dunes National Seashore, encompassing a remnant of the cherished dunes. Also preserved within the Pictured Rocks National Seashore that faces Lake Superior are Michigan's Grand Sable Dunes.

In some regions winds have continued to shape and reshape dunes long after the last Ice Age, molding them into pure abstractions of exquisite grace. The most monumental dune field is that of Great Sand Dunes National Monument on the eastern side of the San Luis Valley in southern Colorado. Some of the dunes are nearly 700 feet high. Sand eroded by streams flowing from the Sangre de Cristo Mountains to the east is carried west and spread on the arid valley floor, then blown back by prevailing winds that drop it onto the lower slopes of the mountains. Sometimes, however, the wind reverses direction, reshaping the top of each dune. Amidst these monuments of sand one could imagine being in the Sahara except for the snow-covered backdrop of the Sangre de Cristo range. The migrating dunes sometimes bury a forest, then later move on, reexposing gaunt remnants of the former tree trunks.

The dunes at White Sands National Monument in southern New Mexico, near where the first atomic explosion was detonated, have formed on the east side of the valley, fed in this case by gypsum dust blown from the vast expanse of flat valley floor. Some of the dunes, buffeted by winds from the southwest, migrate northeast twenty feet or more per year, and roads in the national monument sometimes have to be rerouted. White clouds of gypsum blowing across the valley on windy days have threatened to delay space shuttle missions that might have to land on the long runway of the White Sands Missile Range.

Dunes also occur—apart from their well-known habitat along sandy coastlines—in other arid, sandy areas, such as the Coral Pink Sand Dunes southeast of Zion National Park in southern Utah, near Stovepipe Wells in Death Valley, around dry lake beds, on the Llano Estacado plateau spanning the Texas–New Mexico border, and in the Algodones Dune Field east of California's Imperial Valley. The largest active dune field in North America covers much of the Gran Desierto in the northwest corner of Sonora, Mexico, between Arizona and the Gulf of California. Barchan dunes of the classic crescent shape are marching across the landscape west of California's Salton Sea at rates as great as 130 feet per year. An extensive dune belt lies in southwestern Wyoming north of the stretch of Interstate 80 between Rock Springs and Rawlins, extending from the Bridger Basin in the west into the Red Desert to the east. By looking down at such dunes the air traveler, assuming the prevailing winds there blow from the west, can guess the flight direction.

30 KARSTS AND SUCH MYSTERIES AS THE CAROLINA BAYS AND MIMA MOUNDS

Much of the landscape of western Kentucky and southern Indiana is pitted in a manner strikingly like some areas of the lunar surface. In fact, images sent to earth by *Ranger* spacecraft in the final seconds before crashing onto the moon in 1964 and 1965 showed conical pits so like those of Indiana and Kentucky "karst lands" that geologists wondered whether the lunar features might have been formed in the same manner. It was a startling thought, for on earth karst formations depend on abundant rainfall. It became apparent, however, that the lunar features were impact craters.

The pitted landscape of a karst terrain is formed where an underlying layer of limestone or dolomite has been partially dissolved away by slightly acidic groundwater, forming networks of tunnels and caverns. The groundwater contains traces of carbonic acid from the reaction of rainwater with carbon dioxide and organic matter in the soil. Where the roofs of these cavities have been breached, the overlying land has drained into the hole, forming a pit much like that assumed by sand as it drains through the narrow aperture of an hourglass. Pits made by ant lions to trap their prey are also similar. The sides of the pits, formed of loose sand, are so steep the victim (often an ant) cannot climb out and is seized by the long jaws of the ant lion, buried in sand at the bottom. In exploring the pits, or sinks, in karst country one must be cautious, for the bottom may suddenly give way into a deep cavern.

Karst formations take their name from the region of Yugoslavia east of Trieste where they are common. Caverns in such an area can be extensive. There are more than 200 miles of explored passages in Mammoth Cave and its sister caverns in Kentucky. The world's largest such chamber, in the Carlsbad Caverns of New Mexico, is of awesome dimensions: 4,000 feet long, 625 feet wide, and 350 feet high. It is the home of millions of bats that like clockwork emerge from the cave at dusk in a dense, flapping cloud to begin their nightly hunt for insects.

In parts of western Kentucky the fields are dotted with so many sinks that cultivation is extremely difficult. Often the sinkholes are filled with brush, making them easily visible from the air. Aerial observers are apt to find that a brook suddenly disappears where it has dropped into a cavern. At least twenty-one streams flowing north onto Sinkhole Plain, traversed by Interstate 65 south of Mammoth Cave

Above: Landscape west of Sonora in Hardin County, Kentucky, is mottled by karst pits. (U.S. Department of Agriculture)

Right: The 1981 sinkhole in Winter Park, Florida. (AP photo)

National Park, vanish into such "swallow holes." Likewise a stream may seem to appear from nowhere when it emerges from subterranean flow.

To the north, in Indiana, sinkholes dot the Mitchell Plain that runs south through Bloomington to the Ohio River in Harrison County. The Ozarks of Missouri and northwest Arkansas are overlain by more than 1,000 feet of dolomite, and as a result there are more than 2,500 caves in Missouri alone. Furthermore, because of mountainous terrain and generous rainfall, the region abounds in springs, some of which boil out of the ground in sufficient volume to feed a small river. Big Spring in Missouri's Carter County is the most voluminous of all and, during spring floods, disgorges an estimated 1,300 cubic feet of water per second—more than any other American spring—into the Current River, which is part of the 140-mile Ozark National Scenic Riverways. In Oregon County the lower outlet of Greer Spring is another powerful "boil" and Roubidoux Spring, on the edge of Waynesville, boils dramatically in the spring.

Other springs, such as Blue Spring in Shannon County, emerge into a serene pool—in this case from a cave that early in the day is illuminated by sunlight, turning the pool within it into a glowing blue gem. The springs are fed through a maze of subterranean caverns and channels. Enterprising divers sometimes don scuba gear and are lowered by boatswain's chair down the Devils Well sinkhole in Shannon County to explore such water-filled caverns. In pioneer days springs that gush forth at high elevations among the sharp ridges and deep valleys of the eastern Ozarks were tapped for water power. The Buffalo River has cut through the Ozarks of Arkansas to form

what has been designated a National Scenic Riverway. Whatever lifted the Ozarks may also have produced the mineral belt, known as the Viburnum Trend, that cuts across the Ozark Plateau in southeast Missouri and has produced much of the continent's lead.

There are numerous sinkholes and caverns within the Great Valley of Virginia. Along Interstate 81 white outcrops of limestone poke through the green fields and a procession of road signs entice the motorist to visit a seemingly endless procession of caverns. They occur, as well, in West Virginia, Tennessee, Illinois, Iowa, southeast Minnesota, western Ohio, Pennsylvania, Maryland, South Carolina, Georgia, and at the Howe Caverns forty miles west of Albany, New York. Sinkholes were not known in Delaware until 1978, but since then six have collapsed in the Hockessin Valley. In the West there are karst formations in Arizona, in New Mexico, on the Edwards Plateau of Texas, and in South Dakota, whose Wind Cave is one of the most extensive of such formations in the United States. In Canada, karst areas are scattered along the continental divide. The river draining Maligne Lake in Jasper National Park vanishes underground for a distance. There are also sinkholes in parts of eastern Canada, notably upper Ottawa Valley.

Central Florida, underlain by about 1,000 feet of limestone (with some dolomite layers), is also a karst area. The circular lakes in and around Orlando are karst sinks filled with water. Before building a house in such regions it is advisable to test the ground for hidden cavities. In 1981 a sinkhole in Winter Park swallowed a house, five sports cars, a camper, and a swimming pool. After a night and day of slow subsidence the pit was larger than a football field and more than eight stories deep. During a few weeks in 1967 at least fifteen sinkholes subsided near Lakeland, one of them engulfing a section of road. Without forewarning drivers of two cars were unable to stop and plunged into the pit, but without injury. Normally the Florida caverns are filled with water, which helps support their roofs, and it is when the water table falls during a drought or after heavy withdrawal from wells that cave-ins are most likely.

Such collapses also occur elsewhere. Within a fifteen-year period at least 1,000 were recorded within a ten-square-mile area of central Alabama. One that collapsed in 1973 with a terrifying roar left a crater 400 feet wide.

Ultimately karst terrain may erode away until most of the limestone and the land that once lay above it are gone. Vestiges of the original surface remain as hills of uniform height, as in large areas of Puerto Rico, or in even more dramatic form in the improbable-looking karst towers of the Guilin region of China, so often depicted by Chinese landscape painters.

THE MYSTERIOUS BAYS

Scattered across the coastal plain from Virginia to Florida, but chiefly in the Carolinas, are thousands of uniformly oriented, oval features known locally as bays (and sometimes as pocosins). Unlike the pits in karst regions, their origin is still debated. For a time it was suspected that the East Coast had been bombarded by a shower of meteorites, each large enough to leave a crater. This would explain why they are all oriented in the same direction—southeast to northwest. They would be oval, it was argued, because the meteorites plunged at an oblique angle, although Daniel Moreau Barringer, in his long search for the origin of Meteor Crater, concluded from bullet impacts in mud that such craters would always be round. Magnetic surveys in search of meteoritic nickel-iron debris under the bays, however, have shown no evidence of such material.

The ovals range in size from a few acres to several square miles. A number are shallow lakes. Others are oval swamps or combine pond and swamp within the same oval perimeter. The shapes are remarkably symmetrical, sometimes outlined by a sandy rim described by geologists who believe they were formed under water as ''Neptune's racetracks.'' Most of the bays lie between fifty and one hundred miles in

Florida sinkhole lakes seen from space. Between previous ice ages the sea rose higher than today, invading the peninsula from east and west until the waters met in central Florida, leaving parallel beach lines visible in this image. (Landsat/NASA)

Above: Typical "bays." These, including Little Singletary Lake, are on the Bladen-Cumberland county boundary east of Jerome, North Carolina. (U.S. Department of Agriculture)

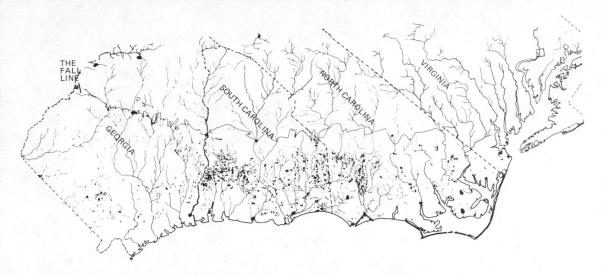

Sites of Carolina "bays." (From "Carolina Bays and Their Origin" by W. F. Prouty, in Geological Society of America Bulletin, *vol. 63, 1952, p. 170.)*

from the coastline. They seem randomly scattered, although sometimes grouped or aligned in chains. Many are concentrated in the region of North Carolina bounded by the South River and Cape Fear River, which join and empty into the sea via Wilmington and Cape Fear, and the Lumber River to the southwest. In Georgia more than 1,000 have been mapped from aerial photographs, most of them in the southeast quadrant of the state. They range in length from a few hundred feet to five miles.

Had they been farther north, the ubiquitous northwest-southeast alignment of their axes would have suggested a relationship to flowing ice. It has been proposed that they were produced by subterranean drainage in a more subtle form than that responsible for karst features. It has even been suggested that they were formed under water by the elliptical schooling of fish. Since they are aligned at right angles to the coast, some geologists attribute their origin to ocean currents or waves when the region was submerged. They are carved out of sediments laid down during a period between ice ages when the Coastal Plain from Sandy Hook, New Jersey, to the southern tip of Florida was covered by the sea. Perhaps, it has been suggested, they were formed by elliptical, wind-driven currents or tide-generated eddies in lagoons behind coastal barrier islands, as seen today in the Bering Strait area.

The swamps within many of the bays are thickets of bay trees, which may explain why they have long been called bays. The term "pocosin," derived from an Indian word that means something akin to "dismal," is more properly applied to irregular swamps that abound in the region between the Dismal Swamp on the Virginia-Carolina border south of Norfolk and the Okefenokee Swamp spanning the Georgia-Florida boundary north of Jacksonville. Somewhat similar features extend from the Delmarva Peninsula on the seaward side of Chesapeake Bay north into southern New Jersey. In Maryland, where they are known locally as "whale wallows," 1,482 of them have been identified from aerial photographs. They lack the uniformly oval

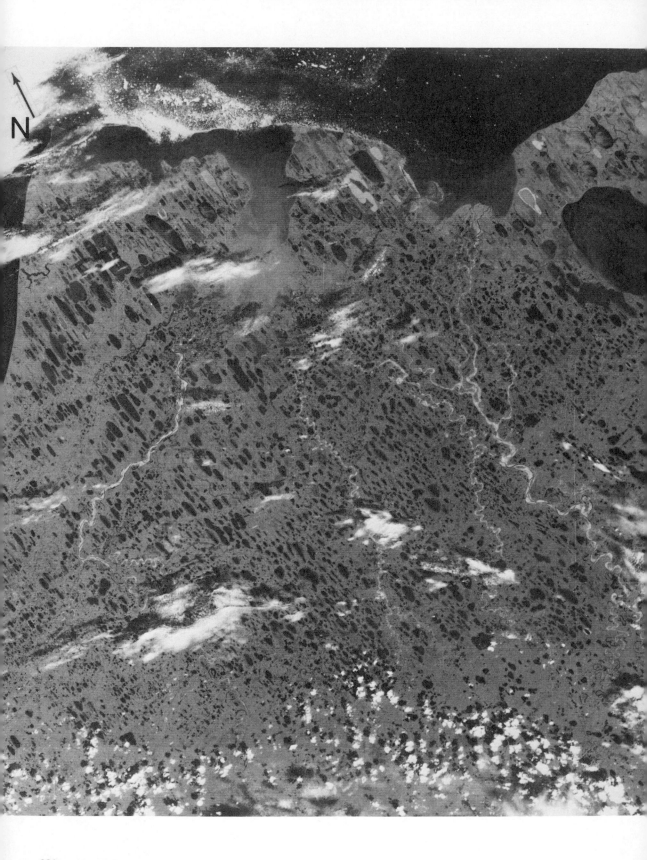

Far left: Why these lakes at the northern tip of Alaska are oriented north-south is unknown. (Landsat/NASA)

Left: Highways cross the mound-covered Mima Prairie in Washington. (Victor B. Scheffer)

configuration of true bays and they have been attributed to icebergs that grounded during a period of high sea level, although it is hard to believe bergs would have drifted so far south during what would have been a particularly warm interglacial period. Like the bays they are often encircled by sand ridges. These were used by the Indians and early settlers as trails and roads past otherwise swampy terrain and some became the sites of colonial mansions.

A multitude of uniformly oriented lakes cover the frozen ground of northernmost Alaska south of Point Barrow. They are aligned almost due north and south. While, as with the Carolina bays, their origin is hotly debated, they differ in being dynamic features, constantly drained and reformed.

Equally mysterious features of the North American landscape are the uniform mounds that cover some western grasslands like blisters on the terrain. They are widely known as Mima mounds because they cover much of the Mima Prairie south of Olympia, Washington. They occur, however, from Saskatchewan and Manitoba in Canada to Baja California and Sonoma in Mexico. They dot parts of California's San Joaquin Valley and mesas in the San Diego suburbs. They are found as well in Minnesota, Iowa, eastern Texas, and the area west of the lower Mississippi. Because such ''prairie pimples'' are usually on top of terrain too hard for deep burrowing, the mammologist Victor B. Scheffer has proposed that they have been heaped up by successive generations of pocket gophers seeking to protect their shallow burrows from predators and winter cold. Wherever they occur the spacing of the mounds is strikingly uniform, manifesting, Scheffer believes, the territorial range of each gopher. They are never more than six feet high, but each may contain more than 50 tons of soil—presumably too much for the efforts of a single gopher. No one, however, seems to have watched a gopher building its mound, and the dirt heaps are often inhabited by other animals. Other explanations include the action of wind, ants, early Indians, or giant ice age rodents. The mounds, wrote the explorer Charles Wilkes when he visited Puget Sound in 1841, ''have the marks of savage labour and care and such a labour as a whole Nation had entered into.'' As with the bays, however, the speculative field is still open for air travelers to look down and form their own conclusions.

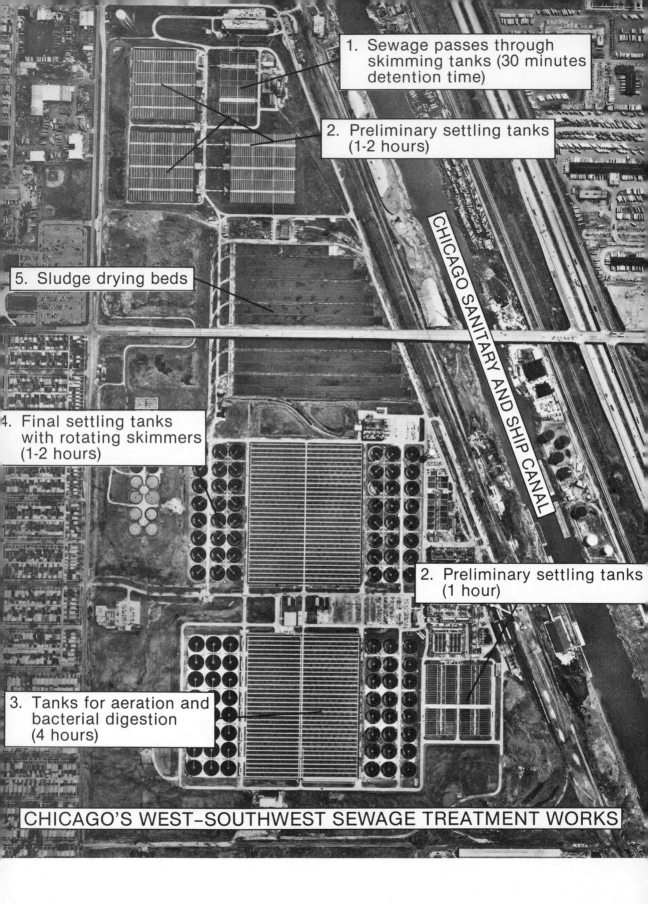

1. Sewage passes through skimming tanks (30 minutes detention time)

2. Preliminary settling tanks (1-2 hours)

5. Sludge drying beds

CHICAGO SANITARY AND SHIP CANAL

4. Final settling tanks with rotating skimmers (1-2 hours)

2. Preliminary settling tanks (1 hour)

3. Tanks for aeration and bacterial digestion (4 hours)

CHICAGO'S WEST–SOUTHWEST SEWAGE TREATMENT WORKS

31 INDUSTRIAL AMERICA

Human activity has altered the landscape in ways that when seen from the air can be awesome, esthetically fascinating, dismaying—or tantalizingly mysterious. Those whose lives have been circumscribed largely by congested urban or suburban areas, shopping centers, and cluttered highways are often surprised, once aloft, to see how much of the continent shows no evidence of human intervention. But hard on the heels of this realization may come the feeling that human transformation of the landscape from its pristine beauty to contrived ugliness is spreading like a cancer.

In any case that which can be seen from the air tells its own story of human intervention and industrial development. Some of the patterns, broadly speaking, are familiar, even though their inner workings may remain obscure—the cubist geometry of electric switchyards, the clustered towers, giant retorts, and intricate piping of an oil refinery or petrochemical plant. Equally familiar are the neatly arranged sedimentation basins, churning aeration pools, and sludge digestion tanks of a sewage disposal plant. Nuclear plants are recognizable from the containment domes built in case of an accident. Power plants with no access to abundant cooling water are identified by their cooling towers—fat cylinders that flare to even greater girth at their bottoms. One can often spot cement plants from great distances by white plumes trailing many miles downwind from their extra-tall stacks. In some cases industrial smoke, before enforcement of pollution control, blighted the surrounding landscape, leaving scars that have persisted long after the controls went into effect. They can be seen, for example, around the Sudbury, Ontario, smelters or Ducktown Basin in southeast Tennessee. In the latter case, according to Edward T. Luther, assistant state geologist in Tennessee, fumes from nineteenth-century copper smelters "killed all vegetation for miles around and poisoned the soil so thoroughly that even today [1982] much of the basin looks more like waterless Nevada desert than anything in Tennessee." The area can easily be identified in space photographs.

It is, however, the less familiar sights that are apt to excite or puzzle someone

Typical of many large sewage plants seen from the air is the West-Southwest Sewage Treatment Works, which processes Chicago sewage through a succession of stages, only some of which are indicated. (Chicago Aerial Survey)

The Kennecot Copper Corporation mine at Bingham, Utah. (Office of Surface Mining)

crossing the land by plane or car. Probably the most dramatic are the gigantic pits of some copper mines. Granddaddy of them all is the Kennecott Copper Corporation mine at Bingham, twenty miles southwest of Salt Lake City. From above, it resembles a gigantic spiral, but it is actually a series of concentric terraces where machines chew at the copper-laden walls, removing each day 108,000 tons of ore and almost 250,000 tons of waste. This gradually enlarges the pit. After more than seventy years of mining it is so deep that New York's World Trade Center or Chicago's Sears Tower, the world's tallest building, could sit on its floor and not come level with the top. Gold, silver, molybdenum, and other metals also come out of this mine.

While it is said to be the world's biggest open-pit mine, there are several other huge ones in Nevada alone, such as the Ruth Copper Pit operated by Kennecott four miles west of Ely (on Nevada 44 off U.S. 50). A few miles south of where Interstate 80 passes through Battle Mountain in northern Nevada two open-pit mines are operated by the Duval Corporation and there is a large pit of the Anaconda Company at Weed Heights, forty miles east of Lake Tahoe. These pits, seen from the air or from viewing points provided for motorists by some companies, are awesome.

One of the most famous is on the edge of Butte, Montana, some of whose homes have had to be moved as the pit grew. Probably the most amazing patterns, however, are those of the Arizona mines, five of which, clustered southwest of Tucson, produce one quarter of all American copper. One, Duval's Esperanza Mine, is

The Esperanza mine of the Duval Corporation in Arizona. (Manley Commercial Photography)

terraced like the others but in an opposite manner, for a mountain is being cut down along concentric terraces instead of a pit being dug. In southeast Arizona, on U.S. 666 near Clifton, the Morenci Mine of the Phelps Dodge Corporation has carved out of the mountains a pit whose spiral pattern looks almost identical to that of the Bingham Mine. By contrast, the terracing of the Santa Rita mine near Silver City, in southwest New Mexico, is far more irregular. Near this and other copper mines are leaching basins where bacteria aid in the extraction of low-grade ore.

Not all the great pits that one sees from on high are copper mines. Along the ranges of Minnesota, Wisconsin, and Michigan that flank western Lake Superior are pits and mines from which have come most of the iron that has made the United States an industrial nation. Particularly productive has been the Mesabi Range, parallel to the north shore of the lake's tapering west end. U.S. 169 runs along the range from Grand Rapids to Mountain Iron. Other iron-producing ranges of Minnesota are similarly aligned in southwest-northeast directions—the Cuyana, Vermilion, and Gunflint ranges, the last of which extends far into Ontario. South of the lake, in Wisconsin and Michigan, are the Gogebic, Marquette, and Menominee ranges. Although the high-grade ore is depleted, almost 90 percent of domestic iron used by the steel industry in 1978 was from these ranges. The deposits all seem to have been formed about two billion years ago, at least some of them through extraction of the metal by the circulation of superheated water through freshly erupted rock. Silica, which at the time was deposited between layers of the iron compounds, was later removed by water action, producing ore soft enough to be easily extracted.

In central-southern Wyoming uranium is mined from a gaping pit near Jeffrey City on U.S. 287. At Boron, California, near the north edge of Edwards Air Force Base, where the early Space Shuttle missions landed, is the only open-pit boron mine in the

Above: Seven open-pit mines at Hibbing in the Mesabi Iron Range. Long trains of rail cars are visible. (Durant Barclay, Jr.)

Right: In the pit at the Jim Bridger coal mine in Sweetwater County, Wyoming, a shovel loads coal into a hauler. In the background a dragline with a seventy-two-cubic-yard bucket removes overburden. (Jan Groeneboer, U.S. Bureau of Mines)

world. In southwest Utah there are open-pit beryllium and iron mines. A mine producing rare earths (elements with many high-technology applications) forms a large pit in California east of Baker on the route from Los Angeles to Las Vegas along Interstate 15. Huge molybdenum mines are visible at Climax in Freemont Pass, Colorado, and in the Sangre de Cristo Mountains northeast of Taos, New Mexico. Close to where U.S. 6 crosses into California from Nevada, east of Mono Lake, a dazzling white pit indicates the mining of diatomite, a mineral formed of tiny, flat, closely packed shells of oceanic diatoms. It is ideal for filtering wines, soft drinks, petroleum products, and other uses. There is another such mine where California 1 approaches Lompoc from the south. Lesser pits and quarries, of course, occur from coast to coast, producing marble, limestone, gypsum (for wallboard), and other industrial minerals.

Competing closely with the open-pit mines as scars on the landscape are strip mines from which coal is extracted in vast quantities. Viewing one of these operations at close hand is like a visit to Brobdingnag, the mythical land in Jonathan Swift's *Gulliver's Travels*, in which everything was absurdly large. Take, for example, Big Muskie, a mobile digger or "dragline," used to clear overburden from above a coal deposit at the Muskingham Mine, a dozen miles southwest of where Interstate 40 passes through Cambridge, Ohio. Big Muskie's bucket is suspended by cables from twin booms that reach hundreds of feet in front of the monster. When the bucket is dropped to the ground and dragged toward the digger, it scoops up 325 tons of overburden at a single pass. The digger swings, dumps the load, and swings back for another pass. In such mining there may be more than one hundred feet of overburden to be loosened by blasting and ripped off by a dragline. Giant shovels then load the underlying coal into giant trucks to be hauled away, processed, and either burned in a nearby power plant, shipped by rail, or mixed with water and sent via slurry pipeline to far distant points.

In the West this type of strip mining is being carried out on a rapidly growing scale. Western coal production increased fivefold from 1971 to 1981. Eastern states—notably Kentucky and West Virginia—are still the biggest producers, but Wyoming is close behind. A few giant mines in the Powder River Basin of northeast Wyoming and southeast Montana account for a large percentage of western production. Amax Coal Company's Bell Ayr Mine in Wyoming led the nation in 1981, extracting more than fifteen million tons. Coal from Wyoming may ultimately be shipped worldwide via slurry pipelines to docks in Houston, the Great Lakes, and Portland, Oregon.

Working mines no longer leave the odious scars of earlier days, since state laws require the land to be restored. As in earlier times a dragline removes the overburden from a strip of coal and dumps these rubbly "tailings" into the trench left by excavation of coal from the neighboring strip. If restoration is not enforced, as this process moves across the coalfield, strip by strip, it leaves a series of rocky ridges that from the air present a desolate landscape of giant, motionless waves. Under present rules the tailings must be smoothed out and the soil conditioned for pasturage or other use. Only one row of tailings may therefore be visible at any one time. A number of the earlier sites, however, have not been restored and still provide a striking view, particularly when carpeted with snow.

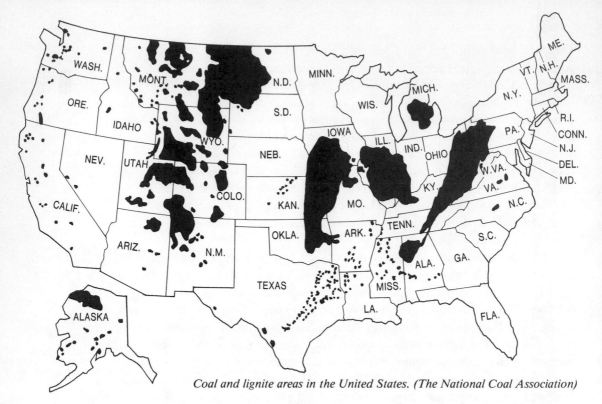

Coal and lignite areas in the United States. (The National Coal Association)

Some of the large mines in northeast Wyoming lie on both sides of Interstate 90 near Gillette. One is seven miles north of Sheridan, and there is another at the north end of the basin near Colstrip, Montana. Closer to transcontinental flight and motoring routes is the Hanna Mine north of Interstate 80 between Laramie and Rawlins. There are strip mines in western North Dakota and, to the south, at Kayenta, Arizona, and Navajo, New Mexico. On the West Coast there is at least one—at Bucoda, Washington, off Interstate 5 near Centralia.

In the Middle West, although we associate Iowa with corn, its chief product, for a time, was coal, and there is a zone of strip mining from the south-central part of that state along the Missouri-Kansas border to northeast Oklahoma. Interstate 35 in Iowa crosses a large coalfield south of Des Moines. A mine at La Cygne, Kansas, feeds 4,000 tons of coal a day to a giant power plant just across the border in Missouri, twenty-one miles south of Louisburg. Where this coalfield continues south into Oklahoma the Peabody and Garland Coal companies operate a number of strip mines, some of which predated the state's 1968 conservation law. They can be seen north and south of U.S. 60, fifteen miles west of Vinita, and along U.S. 66 between Vinita and Tulsa. A second heavily exploited coalfield lies near Eufaula Lake and Stigler, south of Interstate 40. Coal from Stigler is shipped to Germany for use as coke in metal processing.

Another strip-mining zone crosses central Illinois and southwest Indiana into Kentucky, where there are more than ninety large surface mines, a number of them visible along the Western Kentucky Parkway between its intersections with U.S. 231 and U.S. 41. South of the parkway, near Greenville on Kentucky 181, is the TVA's Paradise power plant, largest coal-fired plant in the world when built. Much of the

Strip mining near Arcadia, Kansas, before land restoration was required, left these scars in each mile-square section. (Fairchild Aerial Surveys)

coal mined in this region is used by the TVA. Farther south, in the northeast corner of Texas, a number of large strip mines have begun in recent years to dig lignite (low-grade coal) for use in nearby power plants.

The nation's chief source of coal, however, is still the Appalachian Plateau from Ohio to Alabama. In that region of deep, steep-walled valleys more of the mines are underground than in other areas, but there are also extensive "area" strip-mining operations, like those in the West, and "contour" mining that exploits coal exposed in a steep hillside. Like area mining, the contour process generates scars visible from airliner elevations. The exposed coal seam is excavated along the side of the hill, a terrace being formed by dumping the waste down the slope. If the coal seam tilts uphill, the next higher level is excavated in the same way, dumping the waste onto the lower terrace. The process is continued up the slope as long as the coal seam is reasonably accessible. The effect is to produce a barren, ribbed hillside. As with area mining, companies are now required to restore such slopes, but those mined earlier are still clearly visible.

There are about 1,400 coal mines in eastern Kentucky, 200 of which are strip mines. Many, active or abandoned, lie on both sides of U.S. 23 between Ashland and Prestonsburg. The same is true in West Virginia where U.S. 52 follows the southeast border of the state between Huntington and Bluefield, as well as in Tennessee along Interstate 75 between Lake City and Jellico.

In central Florida, south of Bartow, strip mining is used to exploit the world's richest known phosphate deposit. The phosphates, like diatomite, are derived from sea creatures that lived millions of years ago and are essential for the production of fertilizers as well as many detergents. The residue from processing the phosphates is stored in "slime ponds," which in 1980 covered some 41,000 acres of the region. At that time, of the 150,000 acres mined, only 30,000 had been restored in response to the new regulations. The slime ponds and mined areas are easily identified from the air.

A close relative of strip mining is the extraction of gold from gravel deposits by placer mining. Its traces can be seen in such gold-mining regions as central Alaska and the Placerville area of California, crossed on eastbound flights from San Francisco. In placer mining the topsoil is washed away and a pool is formed in the deposit by digging a pit in the gravel. A monster dredge, floating in the pool, then digs gravel from in front, runs it over mercury beds inside the dredge, which capture the gold, and dumps the waste gravel out the rear. In this manner the dredge eats its way through the deposit, leaving behind a pattern somewhat like that of strip-mine tailings.

It was near Placerville that gold was discovered in 1848, bringing thousands of "forty-niners" to that area the next year. In the turmoil that followed "frontier justice" was summarily enforced in Placerville, which came to be known in the West as Hangtown.

Some of the sights one sees from the air are tantalizing puzzles. The extreme northeast corner of Oklahoma—for example along U.S. 69—is dotted with conical heaps of crushed rock looking from the air like piles of sand excavated by gigantic burrowing insects. These are piles of "chat"—crushed rock discarded by zinc-ore concentrating mills. Air travelers over forested regions of the Pacific Northwest may wonder at fanlike markings on slopes that have been clear-cut of timber. These are lumbering scars. After a road has been built to a summit, logs are hauled to that loading point from all sides, producing a pattern of converging skid tracks. Far more extensive, among perplexing sights visible from the air, are designs on the land that cover much of the region midway between Phoenix and Houston. They look like the empty, arid countryside near rapidly growing cities such as Phoenix, where entire

Left: "Contour" mining for coal on a steep slope in the Appalachians. (Office of Surface Mining)

Right: Placer mining in California. (Caterpillar Tractor Company)

Strip mining in Rogers County, Oklahoma. When photographed in 1972, spoil banks in the area to the right had already been leveled and restored. (Kenneth S. Johnson, Oklahoma Geological Survey)

communities of streets have been laid out by land developers, forming grids on the land with not a single home in evidence. On a Phoenix-Houston flight similar patterns can be seen, but they go on for tens or even hundreds of miles. Furthermore, off each street are what appear to be driveways leading to house lots—but no houses. When I first saw this puzzle I finally marched to the rear of the plane to make inquiries. A passenger explained: ''That,'' he said, ''is the west Texas oil field.'' Each of those house lots was a well.

Oil fields are, of course, to be seen in many regions—even in the heart of Los Angeles and Long Beach, where offshore derricks have been disguised as decorative towers to temper local objections. In areas such as western Pennsylvania where oil fields are long established, they are often camouflaged by vegetation, but motorists can see the derricks, pumps, and even capped wells. Many of the great oil fields are crossed by interstate highways. Interstate 20 traverses one between Louisiana and Dallas. Another is crossed by Interstate 45 north of Houston, and the Kelly-Snyder field, one of the nation's largest, lies north of Interstate 20 west of Abilene. A field lies on Interstate 10 just east of Houston and north of Baytown. A number of the west Texas oil strikes were on University of Texas land and have made that university and Texas A & M among the few with no serious endowment problems.

In Oklahoma oil derricks can be seen on both sides of Interstate 40 as it goes through Oklahoma City, and there are even producing wells on the grounds of the state capitol. In the southwest corner of Kansas U.S. 56 crosses the Hugaton gas field, one of the world's largest. In Wyoming Interstate 80 traverses a field east of Rock Springs as well as the Denver-Julesberg Petroleum Basin between Ogallala, Nebraska, and Pine Bluffs, Wyoming, and farther west, the Patrick Draw Oilfield east of Rock Springs. North of Casper, Wyoming, Interstate 25 skirts the Salt Creek

Field, passing west of Teapot Dome, site of the federal petroleum reserve that in 1922 was leased by Secretary of the Interior Albert B. Fall to the oil magnate Harry F. Sinclair without competitive bidding. In the famous Teapot Dome scandal that followed Fall resigned and was convicted of accepting bribes.

Day or night, flying over the Gulf Coast is, to the uninitiated, an amazing experience. Offshore rigs seem to cover the entire sea and at night, instead of being dark, the sea is a galaxy of lights—far more illuminated than nearby land areas.

A startling sight to those descending for a landing at San Francisco is the patchwork quilt of large ponds along the east shore of the bay, each a brilliant shade of red, pink, yellow, or brown. In the fall some of the rectangles may be dazzlingly white, for the ponds constitute a ''farm'' whose harvest is salt evaporated from the bay waters. For five years each pondful of water sits in the sun as evaporation makes it saltier and saltier. Early in the process fish can tolerate the salinity, but when it nears the limit of their tolerance, the fish are sold as bait. Brine shrimp can live in saltier pools, but it is various species of salt-tolerant algae that give the ponds their many hues. When the salt concentration becomes high enough, crystals form and sink to the bottom of the two-foot-deep pools, which are then drained and the salt harvested. From the ponds, enclosed by dikes and spread over 38,000 acres, the Leslie Salt Company harvests about one million tons a year. After the salt has been refined to various grades of purity, 37 percent goes to industry, 3 percent to home use, and the rest to such applications as cattle feeding, food preservation, and highway salting.

There are salt-drying ponds elsewhere, such as at Great Salt Lake, near San Diego, and in western Oklahoma, where brine is pumped out of wells sunk into salt formations, but probably none are as colorful as those on San Francisco Bay.

32 FOOTPRINTS OF THE PIONEERS–THE GREAT AMERICAN CHECKERBOARD

No other large area of the earth's surface is so dominated by geometry as the flat-lying regions of the United States from Ohio westward. A vast uniformity was imposed as federal surveyors blocked out new lands for sale to pioneering settlers. By 1910 the resulting checkerboard (not all of it evident from the air) reached to the Pacific Ocean and the Gulf of Mexico.

Thus written upon the landscape is a history of expansion whose roots were in the bold planning of Thomas Jefferson and Hugh Williamson, Jefferson's fellow delegate to the Continental Congress. They are chiefly credited with what, after modifications, became the master plan: dividing the land into squares (''townships'') six miles on a side, which were subdivided into ''sections'' one mile square. In fertile areas these are now typically bounded by county roads, emphasizing the endless checkerboard of squares, themselves divided into patchwork quilts of fields.

The formulation of such a plan in 1784, before the young republic had even agreed on its constitution, was motivated by the demands of veterans for land as a reward for their services and by the enormous indebtedness of the government following the Revolutionary War. So great was the national debt that two thirds of federal income (derived from requisitions to the thirteen states) was needed for interest payments. (In the 1982 budget 20 percent was for debt servicing.)

On March 2, 1784, the Continental Congress, then sitting in Annapolis, Maryland, appointed a five-man committee under Jefferson ''to devise and report the most eligible means of disposing of such part of the Western lands as may be obtained of the Indians. . . .'' The previous day the government had ostensibly become land rich when it accepted Virginia's cession of the extensive territory that state claimed north of the Ohio River. The claim had been based on the success of Virginian troops in capturing from the British much of the region between the Ohio River, the Great Lakes, and the Mississippi River.

There were other more modest claims. Massachusetts had spoken for part of what is now New York State and a strip of land west to the Mississippi across the present territories of Michigan and Wisconsin. Connecticut, in a strip immediately to the south of that, also claimed as far as the Mississippi.

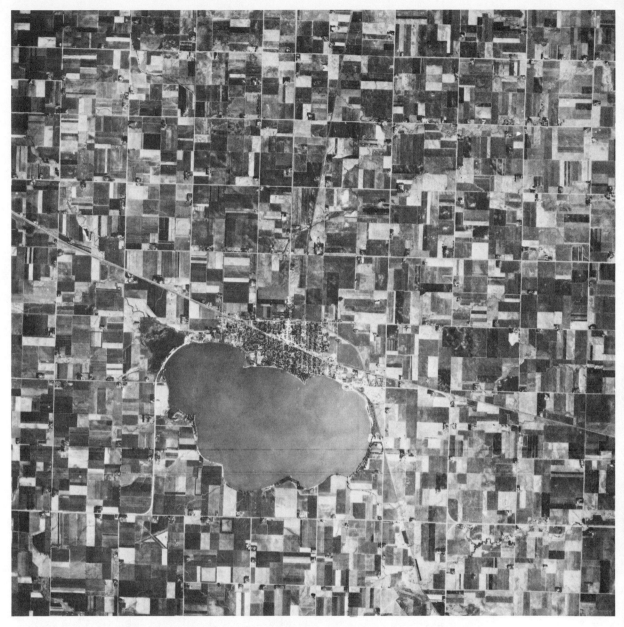

The "checkerboard" in Iowa. The town of Storm Lake is on the north shore of the lake of that name. The Chicago, Milwaukee, St. Paul and Pacific Railroad comes up from the south, rounds the lake, and continues northwest. The farmland, divided into squares one mile on a side, was covered by ice of the Des Moines lobe. (Army Map Service)

The vastness of the Virginia claim had caused neighboring Maryland, with far less territory, to refuse to ratify the Articles of Confederation. Not until 1781, when Virginia offered to cede most of the region north of the Ohio River, did Maryland agree to join the Union. In addition to several smaller tracts, Virginia withheld part of southern Ohio to redeem warrants issued to its own veterans. These ranged from 100 acres for a private with less than three years' service to 15,000 acres to a major general who had served for four years.

By 1786 Massachusetts and Connecticut had ceded their claims, apart from Connecticut's "Western Reserve" in what is now northeast Ohio, to which Connecticut clung (temporarily) in frustration after having been denied the Lehigh Valley area in the heart of Pennsylvania, occupied by settlers from Connecticut. In a compromise with New York, Massachusetts forfeited sovereignty over western New York but retained the right to sell the land there. It was later bought by Robert Morris, a signer of the Declaration of Independence. After being surveyed into rectangular townships it was acquired by the Holland Land Company on behalf of merchants in Amsterdam and sold to settlers. The Holland Land Company lots, a half mile on a side, are still evident on flights across western New York.

Within two months after appointment of the Jefferson committee its checkerboard plan was ready. In combination with a separate plan for the creation of new states to the west the proposals, written, like the Declaration of Independence, in Jefferson's own hand, have been rated landmark documents of American history. There were to be two north-south tiers of states between the original thirteen coastal states and the Mississippi. Their boundaries would be a grid of east-west latitude lines and north-south meridians of longitude. Their proposed names reflected Jefferson's classical bent as well as his desire to perpetuate Indian names. The rectangle embracing the Michigan Peninsula was to be Cherronesus (Latin for "peninsula"). Between Michi-

(Adapted from Beginnings of the American Rectangular Land Survey System, 1784-1800 *by W. D. Pattison, pp. 9 and 18, and* The Papers of Thomas Jefferson, *vol. 6, May 1781 to March 1784, Julian P. Boyd, ed. Princeton, N.J.: Princeton University Press, 1952, p. 591. Copyright renewed 1980 by Princeton University Press. Reprinted by permission.)*

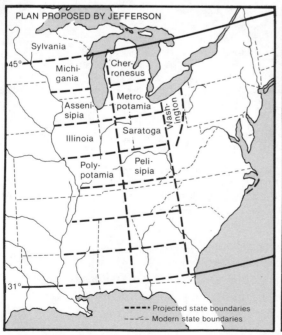

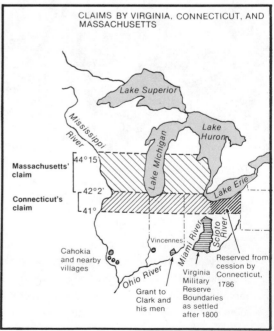

gania (west of Lake Michigan) and Illinoia, farther south, was to be Assenisipia, through which the Rock River (called Assenisipi by the Indians) flows to join the Mississippi at Davenport, Iowa. The rectangle in which the Ohio, Mississippi, and other rivers come together was to be Polypotamia (Greek for "many rivers"). Farther up the Ohio was a state to be called Pelisipi (local name for the Ohio) and, to the north, Metropotamia ("Mother of Rivers").

Fortunately for future generations only two of these names survived (as Michigan and Illinois), but the use of latitude and longitude lines as state boundaries became standard where other considerations did not prevail. In its report the committee stipulated that "there shall be neither slavery nor involuntary servitude in any of the said states, otherwise than in punishment of crimes, whereof the party shall have been duly convicted to have been personally guilty."

Jefferson hoped to impose metric-style decimal systems both on the land and on American measurement. He proposed an "American mile" (akin to the nautical mile based on minutes of latitude), which was to be divided into one hundred "chains" subdivided into one hundred "links." The checkerboard squares would measure ten of these miles on each side, forming "hundreds" of one hundred square miles. In surveying the squares true north was to be used, rather than the magnetic north preferred by surveyors since the magnetic compass was their tool.

The Continental Congress was no more enamored of a shift to new measurements than its modern counterpart. The plan that it approved, while derived from the proposals of Jefferson and his colleagues, provided for "townships" six miles on a side, rather than ten, measured in ordinary (statute) miles. Townships were to be sold alternately intact or subdivided into mile-square sections. It was hoped that the intact townships of thirty-six square miles would be bought (at one dollar or more per acre) by sectarian groups seeking to move west as units. Villages of farmers formed by such groups would be safer from Indian attack than isolated homesteads. Despite Jefferson's preference for true north, surveying was to be based on magnetic directions. Congress, however, later revised this ordinance to require the use of true north in all surveying. Almost the entire American checkerboard is therefore oriented on true north-south lines.

Jefferson's efforts to make the decimal system an integral part of American life were not entirely in vain. When he was later asked by the Congress to devise a new form of currency he proposed one based on a silver dollar divided into ten silver dimes and one hundred copper cents, which was adopted.

The determination of Jefferson and his colleagues that the land be surveyed before being sold was to avoid the chaotic conditions that had prevailed in the colonies where surveying was done after grants had been allocated. Surveyors, beholden to the settlers who paid them, often staked out tracts far larger than called for in the grants. In some cases the lands thus claimed were twice the specified area. Lots were described in terms of ambiguous "medes and bounds"—such landmarks as trees, rocks, ridge crests, and streams. This led to overlapping claims and litigation that in some areas persists to this day. Elias Boudinot, representative from New Jersey, told Congress in 1790 that "more money had been spent at law, in disputes arising from that mode of settlement, in New Jersey than would have been necessary to purchase all the land of the State.''

By surveying the land before selling it, and doing so in the simplest, cheapest way—the checkerboard—such disputes could be avoided and, it was hoped, maximum revenue obtained.

As a way of encouraging westward settlement the southern states had adopted a ''headright'' system whereby each family head was entitled to a certain amount of unclaimed land, depending on family size. After the system proved successful in the Carolinas it was adopted by most of the southern states. Georgia's first land act, passed in 1777 (the year when the state constitution was adopted), provided that:

> Every free white person, or head of a family, shall be entitled to, allotted, and granted him, two hundred acres of land, and for every other white person of the said family, fifty acres of land, and fifty acres for every negro, the property of such white person or family.

It was in the central region of eastern Ohio that the first attempt was made to prepare a wilderness for sale under the 1785 Ordinance. Since the survey was conducted before the requirement that true north be used, north-south county lines in that region to this day are tilted east of true north—that is, toward the magnetic pole. The work, carried out from 1785 to 1788 under ''gentlemen surveyors,'' was hampered by their inexperience as well as by the wild and rugged terrain. Several times surveying was halted by reports of Indians on the warpath. Some tribes had ceded land under military pressure but the Shawnee, in particular, were fighting back. It was not until 1794, after General Anthony Wayne captured several strategic points in Indian territory, including what is now Fort Wayne, Indiana, and broke Indian resistance at the Battle of Fallen Timbers near the west end of Lake Erie, that the way was cleared for the westward march of federal surveyors.

The national survey, born of the proposals of Jefferson and his colleagues and for which the Ohio survey was a dress rehearsal, then took final form in the Land Act approved by President George Washington on May 18, 1796. It launched what has probably been the greatest surveying effort in history. During the century that followed federal surveyors worked their way as far west as California, Oregon, and Washington and as far south as Florida and Louisiana.

One problem, from the start, was to reconcile the slight convergence of lines running true north with the desire for squareness. From a glance at the globe it is clear that north-south longitude lines (meridians) converge to a point at each pole. When surveyors extended such lines, initially six miles apart, a few hundred miles north, the lines converged and no longer enclosed six-mile squares.

The solution, first put into practice in 1804 in what is now southern Indiana, was to make periodic corrections for this effect. The survey in each newly opened region was to be based on an east-west ''base line'' and north-south ''principal meridian.'' Lines marking out the square counties of the checkerboard would be drawn parallel to these reference lines. But at a certain distance north of the base line, where the spacing between meridian lines had shrunk substantially below six miles, the meridian lines were to be offset, restoring the six-mile spacing.

Thus in Dubuque, on the eastern border of Iowa, there is no offset in the north-

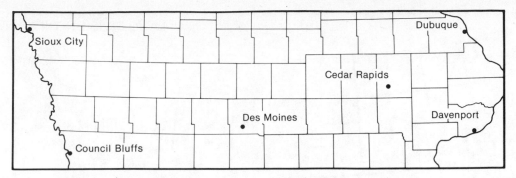

County boundaries in Iowa show offsets in north-south lines needed to allow for northward convergence of the meridians. The principal meridian was in the east, hence the offsets increase to the west.

south county lines, since that is close to the principal meridian, but to the west the offsets became increasingly great, reaching four miles at Sioux City on the western boundary of the state. The effect is sometimes evident from the air in doglegs on the roads that follow county lines.

The great American checkerboard, therefore, is actually a number of separate checkerboards slightly offset from one another. Where a regional base line passes through a city, as with the San Bernardino Base Line that skirts Los Angeles to the north or the one that traverses Boulder, Colorado, it may serve as a local street— "Baseline Road."

The Romans, when initiating a survey in their colonies, also used a base line (the Decumanus Maximus) and principal meridian (Cardo Maximus). The starting point, where these lines crossed, was the Umbilicus. Square-sided surveys were used by the Chinese 3,000 years ago, but it seems more likely that Jefferson was influenced by the Romans, who in the second century B.C. referred to the square units in new surveys as centuria—much like Jefferson's "hundreds." The centuria block pattern is still evident in the countryside near Padua and in other parts of the Po Valley.

Subdividing the land into squares was familiar to Jefferson's fellow committee member, Hugh Williamson, a delegate from North Carolina, who had taken a medical degree at Utrecht in Holland where polders—lands reclaimed from the sea—were often blocked out in this manner.

Before the Revolution square-shaped tracts were allocated in several of the original thirteen colonies, although never in the universal manner of the national survey and without its north-south, east-west rigidity. When Charles II gave William Penn what is now Pennsylvania, making him the largest landholder in America, Penn sought unsuccessfully to sell off the land in neat squares. In that highly uneven country this did not appeal to buyers. While Maine was still a district of Massachusetts, however, parts of its southern and coastal areas were surveyed in rectangles and disposed of by lottery. In 1820, when Maine became a state, Massachusetts retained title to some eight million acres there and offered to sell them to Maine for about four cents each. Maine refused. Further square-sided surveys were then conducted so that each state could identify and sell off its holdings.

In imitation of the national system, rectangular divisions were imposed in much of

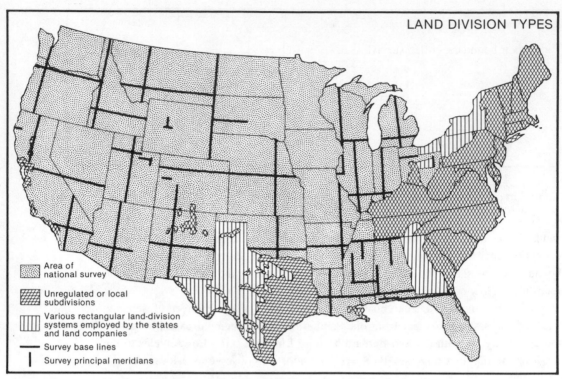

LAND DIVISION TYPES

Area of national survey

Unregulated or local subdivisions

Various rectangular land-division systems employed by the states and land companies

Survey base lines

Survey principal meridians

(Agricultural Research Service, U.S. Department of Agriculture)

western Tennessee and Kentucky after Andrew Jackson and Governor Shelby of Kentucky, as government agents, bought the land—now often referred to as the Jackson Purchase—from the Chickasaw Indians in 1818.

Nevertheless, the prevailing pattern of settlement and land division in most areas settled before the Revolution was far less ordered, as is evident in field patterns throughout the region. Sometimes land was allocated to entire communities or sects, who then did their own subdividing. There was relatively severe population pressure on the land as wave after wave of immigrants reached New England and New York, which, for sailing ships, were relatively close to Europe. Although the earliest settlements had been farther south—the Spanish in 1565 at St. Augustine, Florida, and the English in 1607 on the James River of Virginia—further settlement there was slow. The agriculturally rich coastal plain of Georgia was settled last. In 1800 only about 23 percent of the present state had been occupied. As its land claimants migrated westward, new counties were laid out and, like those of western Kentucky and Tennessee, tended to be square-sided.

Although Spanish influence never penetrated deeply into Florida it left its mark in the irregular land divisions of Spanish settlements in parts of Texas, coastal California, and the upper Rio Grande Valley from Santa Fe, New Mexico, north into Colorado. A typical grant by the King of Spain was four square leagues (about twenty-seven square miles). A village with gridiron streets was placed within it, as indicated in an 1849 map of Los Angeles (originally the Pueblo de Nuestra Señora de Los Angeles). Usually in the center was a plaza occupying four blocks of the grid around which were the church, customhouse, granary, and, sometimes, a governor's palace (as in Santa Fe). Nearby tracts were allocated as "ranchos" for cattle raising. Today their boundaries often survive as town lines, property borders, roads, or power lines, and their Spanish origins are still reflected in place names.

A very different imprint—the stamp of feudal Europe—was placed on the landscape by French settlers along bayous near the mouth of the Mississippi, along the Saint Lawrence River and east into the northern tip of Maine. As dramatically visible from the air, the land is divided into long, extremely narrow strips that often run inland from a riverbank, providing access to water transport for each. The practice was derived from the classic "seigneurial" system under which the land was assigned to a seigneur or feudal lord who then parceled out strips to individual farmers. The long, narrow fields minimized the number of times a farmer had to turn his plow. Narrowness of the strips may also have arisen from repeated division of the land to accommodate succeeding generations of sons. This type of agriculture is said to have been brought over by pioneers from Normandy. Canada and Acadia were settled by the French a century before they moved into Louisiana. The British, however, sent back to France all the Acadians they could catch after an armada of more than one hundred British ships and almost 15,000 men captured Louisbourg on Cape Breton Island in 1758. Although France, in 1762, was forced to cede Louisiana west of the Mississippi to Spain, 1,600 of the displaced Acadians colonized the delta region. It soon became part of the United States, but descendents of these colonists—known as Cajuns—continue to farm their long strips of land and have retained a separate cultural identity from those in New Orleans of direct French descent. While most of western Canada followed the lead of the United States by dividing the land into blocks of thirty-six square mile sections, French settlers along the Red River in Manitoba have left a pattern of strip-farming in the midst of the checkerboard.

When Texas entered the Union in 1846 a special provision of the annexation agreements allowed the state to retain title to public lands there. These were generally surveyed into mile squares, as in the national system. Their sale, for example, paid for construction of the state capitol, and, as noted earlier, the land grants proved so rich in oil that the state universities are among the wealthiest on earth.

The use of such grants on the federal level proved a powerful tool in support of development and education. As early as the Land Ordinance of 1785 it was specified that Section 16 in each township of thirty-six sections be allocated to the state for use in supporting schools. Additional grants were subsequently made for universities, hospitals, and asylums, culminating in an 1862 act providing for the creation of land-grant colleges for teaching and research in agriculture and mechanics as well as military instruction. Most ultimately evolved into major universities teaching a full range of subjects.

Wholesale grants were made to railroad and canal builders, not only providing a right-of-way but also land on either side for development. For twenty miles to each side of a route across California alternate 640-acre sections were deeded to the railroad. This created a patchwork pattern of land ownership that, for example, now impedes efficient administration of national forests in those areas.

Through much of the first half of the nineteenth century there was a bitter debate on

The traditional French pattern of strip farms along Bayou Lafourche in Assumption Parish, Louisiana. Floods have built levees along the river six to eight miles wide and twenty feet high nearest the bayou, which is almost as high as their crests. Homesteads are along the bayou. (U.S. Department of Agriculture)

whether to make grants to individuals on the scene or to entrepreneurs back in the cities. Pioneers would settle land, often at great risk to themselves and their families, only to learn that the land had been allocated to some distant party. This was partially resolved by the Homestead Act of 1862, which made it possible for someone to acquire land for a small fee after residing on it for a certain time and making improvements. By then most of the land east of the Mississippi had been spoken for

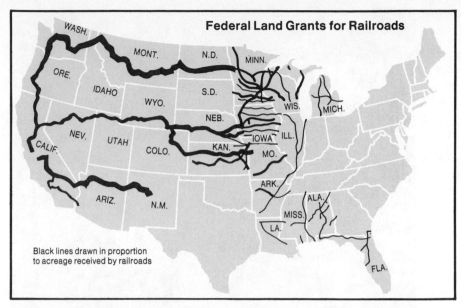

Land grants allocated to stimulate railroad development. Allocations shown are only approximate since the actual grants were in blocks. (Bureau of Land Management)

and the discovery of gold in California helped inspire a great westward migration.

The journey, for thousands, began in St. Louis, where now stands the towering Gateway Arch and where, across the Mississippi River, had been the great Indian city of Cahokia. Between A.D. 900 and 1300 Cahokia was a community of more than 30,000—the largest on the continent until surpassed by Philadelphia in 1800. It was built by a civilization whose ceremonial mounds are still evident in many parts of the Mississippi drainage area. It is no coincidence that a great modern city stands across the river from this ancient one. There is usually a reason why cities arise at certain locations, such as the confluence of rivers. Detroit, Cincinnati, Minneapolis, San Diego, Los Angeles, Tucson, and Santa Fe are all on the sites of former Indian settlements chosen for geographic reasons. The same applies to highways. When in 1775 Daniel Boone cleared the Wilderness Trail through the Cumberland Gap between Virginia and Kentucky, hoping to establish the latter as a fourteenth colony, he followed a trail used for centuries by the Cherokees, who repeatedly attacked his party. The trail, which became a major route for westward migration, was unrelated to the Cumberland Road (or National Road), built from 1811 to 1837 as the first federal highway, leading from Cumberland, Maryland, to Vandalia, Illinois, along what is now U.S. 40.

From St. Louis the pioneers followed closely the route of Interstate 70, crossing the Missouri River at Independence Landing, near the present site of Kansas City. Beyond there the route split into the Oregon Trail, trending northwest to join the valley of the Platte River (and Interstate 80) at Fort Kearney in Nebraska, and the fabled Santa Fe Trail that ran southwest.

In a single day as many as 800 wagons and 10,000 oxen are said to have passed Fort Kearney, as the pioneers hastened to complete the slow journey during summer

Scotts Bluff on the Oregon Trail. (William Keller, National Park Service)

months. At night they herded their livestock inside a circle of wagons whose wheels were chained to those of the wagons on either side, forming a strong bulwark against Indian attack. The Oregon Trail (and parallel Mormon Trail) followed Interstate 80 and U.S. 30 westward across Nebraska, then turned more northerly along U.S. 26 to pass Scotts Bluff at the western end of the state. The 800-foot bluff was a welcome landmark for the pioneers after their long trek across flat land. On the prairie they did not follow a fixed track and in most areas the trail has long since vanished, but at Scotts Bluff nearby badlands channeled the wagons into a single track through Mitchell Pass and there, in Scotts Bluff National Monument, one can walk for a mile along deep ruts still visible more than a century later. The trail continued to Casper, Wyoming, and on to South Pass at the south end of the Wind River Range.

Although South Pass, marking the continental divide, was one of the best-known landmarks on the trail, it was not sharply defined. When, in 1842, John C. Fremont led his surveying expedition to the pass with Christopher (Kit) Carson as his guide, he recorded: "We left our encampment with the rising sun. As we rose from the bed of the creek, the snow line of the mountains [the Wind River Range] stretched grandly before us, the white peaks glittering in the sun. . . . The ascent has been so gradual, that, with all the intimate knowledge possessed by Carson, who has made this country his home for seventeen years, we were obliged to watch very closely to find the place at which we had reached the culminating point."

It was four years later that Fremont led troops into Los Angeles, then a Mexican town largely populated by American colonists from the East, and seized it for the United States. As along other arid parts of its route, the Oregon Trail is still in evidence where South Pass is crossed by Wyoming Route 28. Farther west the trail splits, the Oregon Trail continuing northwest into the Snake River valley of Idaho and

Oregon, the south spur leading to Salt Lake City and California.

Because much of the Santa Fe Trail is across arid land with little vegetation, some sectors, as on the Oregon Trail, can still be seen. Examples in Kansas include the vicinity of Black Jack Park in Baldwin and between U.S. 56 and Old City Lake west of Council Grove. Five miles west of Dodge City and one mile west of a historic marker on U.S. 50 tracks are visible north of the highway.

In the Oklahoma panhandle ruts survive where the trail passed Camp Nichols, thirty-six miles west of Boise City, and in New Mexico they can be seen at several locations along U.S. 85 between Watrous and Wagon Mound (the scene of repeated Indian ambushes) and at Fort Union National Monument northwest of that highway. From there the trail followed the route of Interstate 25 into Santa Fe over Glorieta Pass.

As the pioneers trekked westward, so did the surveyors. In the 1820's Senator Thomas Hart Benton of Missouri (great uncle of the painter with the same name) sought to make his state gateway to booming colonization of the West. He persuaded Congress to appropriate $10,000 for surveying a road along the Santa Fe Trail and $20,000 to secure rights-of-way across what was still Mexican territory, including gifts to appease the Indians. He envisioned the route as "a highway between nations." Pioneers on both the Santa Fe and Oregon trails (the latter established in the early 1840's) were marching into lands of uncertain sovereignty. In 1818 Britain and the United States had ambiguously agreed on "joint occupation" of the Oregon region.

Eventually 78 percent of the continental United States, apart from Alaska, had been blocked out in checkerboard fashion. So arbitrary a division of the landscape has been criticized on several grounds. It ignored natural boundaries—rivers, ridge crests, and the like. It discouraged land use compatible with the terrain, be it a swamp or rocky hillside best suited as a woodlot. The air traveler, looking down on such a landscape, can see the ghosts of streambeds crossing the landscape in sinuous disregard of the regimentation.

Actually, where the terrain demanded it, common sense has often triumphed over regimentation. Township lines may follow the grid, but fields conform more to the landscape. Another criticism has been that the checkerboard was antisocial in that it scattered homesteads across the landscape instead of clustering them in villages from which, in the European manner, roads radiated to the farmlands like spokes of a wheel. Whatever the merits of this argument a few decades ago, it has lost its force with advent of the automobile and television. The checkerboard resident is little more isolated than his countryman in the East.

As pointed out by the geographer John Fraser Hart, of the University of Minnesota, the eastern village formerly suited the Puritan tradition: "The New Englander was just as concerned about the morals of his neighbor as he was about his own, and it obviously was more difficult for either to be corrupted when they were living side by side in constant vigilance." Today the Puritan tradition has largely vanished and homes in the eastern states are becoming almost as scattered as those in the West.

33 METROPOLITAN EXPLOSIONS

A continuing revolution is taking place in how Americans live. Its manifestations surround the motorist, but it is from the air that the sweeping changes are most evident. Evolution of metropolitan areas from the original core cities to the multi-centered urban-suburban complexes of today can be traced as planes approach and leave many airports.

A few of the oldest cities, such as Boston and New York, have original cores of narrow, twisting streets that evolved from cow paths and roads of the earliest settlements. What most strikes visitors from abroad, however, is the grid pattern that dominates almost all American cities. Its origin is a century earlier than that of the rural checkerboard derived from the vision of Thomas Jefferson. In 1682 William Penn drew up a plan for Philadelphia in which streets (named for trees and flowers) were to run inland from the Delaware River, crossed at right angles by numbered streets parallel to the river.

Grid patterns were not entirely new. Excavation of the ancient city of Mohenjo-Daro in northwest India has shown that such a street plan was used as early as 2800 B.C. The Greeks and Romans laid out their colonial cities in this manner, possibly because straight avenues made it easy to move troops rapidly to centers of internal unrest or to the encircling battlements to fight off external attack. Twisting, narrow streets, as in the Casbah of Algiers, lend themselves to conspiracy and revolt.

Nevertheless, the "Philadelphia plan," copied from coast to coast with local variations, is a special characteristic of the American scene. The cores of even such old cities as Savannah and Baltimore are laid out in grids that are strikingly uniform when seen from the air. In a few cases the grid, instead of being north-south and east-west, is aligned with a dominant local feature, such as the Mississippi River in the cases of both Minneapolis and Saint Paul. Younger cities, like Chicago, which grew on land already forming part of the national checkerboard, fit their street patterns into those squares. The growth of Chicago was phenomenal. In 1850 its population was 30,000 and a century later it had almost reached 4.5 million.

Penn's plan for Philadelphia provided for a central square at the corner of Broad and High streets, formed by cutting out rectangular corners from each of the four blocks facing it. It was to be flanked by "Houses for Publick Affairs," he wrote, such as an Assembly Building, State House, market, and school. Not until the nineteenth century was the towering City Hall built in the square's center, but meanwhile the practice of placing an imposing building—usually a courthouse—in the central square of the county seat had become common across the country, particularly between the Appalachian Mountains in the East and Iowa, Missouri, Arkansas, and Texas in the West.

Originally the boundary between city and country was relatively sharp, although not so much so as with the walled cities of the Middle Ages. The earliest suburbs were refuges for poor people and for undesirable activities, such as slaughterhouses, warehouses, noxious industries, and houses of ill-repute—still a characteristic of suburbs in some developing countries. As early as Roman times, however, the wealthy sought to escape urban congestion by flight to their villas, and in the nineteenth century a similar exodus was inspired by the view that life in the country, free from urban corruption and pollution, was more healthy both spiritually and physically. Country towns offered a serene life, and democracy there was practiced on the simpler town-meeting level.

The earliest American suburbs were probably occupied by those who could afford a horse and buggy and pay stable fees while at work in the city. Greenwich Village in New York City is said to have originated as such a community. A larger exodus from the cities was made possible by the rapid development of rail lines. The first began carrying passengers in 1830, and by the end of that decade railways were serving a number of cities. This was also the height of the romantic movement that had swept into the United States from Europe. As in the poems of William Wordsworth, the art criticism of John Ruskin, and the paintings of the Hudson River school, it extolled the beauties of nature in contrast to the squalor of cities.

The result was the design of outlying suburbs calculated to exploit natural beauty, with parks, parkways, and sinuous street patterns to avoid the regimentation of street grids. The heritage of this effort to escape the monotony of straight streets and row houses is evident as one flies over the suburbs of every American city.

The man chiefly credited with introducing such residential planning was Andrew Jackson Downing, son of a nurseryman in Newburgh, New York, and an early leader of the Romantic Gothic Revival in America. His influence can still be seen in Llewellyn Park, designed by his disciple, Alexander Jackson Davis and built in the 1850's on a 400-acre tract west of New York in rural New Jersey, now engulfed in the suburb known as West Orange.

Llewellyn Haskell, head of a large chemical firm in New York, sponsored the project to provide homes for businessmen and intellectuals sympathetic with the romantic movement. He proposed that they could commute to the Hudson River, a short ferry ride from New York, on a newly completed railroad. Llewellyn Park, a maze of sinuous streets (whose rustic names—Wildwood Avenue, Tulip Avenue, Trefoil Avenue—became typical of American suburbs) was built on both sides of a fifty-acre green strip, the Ramble, open to all residents. It was within walking distance of the railroad station.

Downing's most ambitious scheme was to design a park to be built down the center

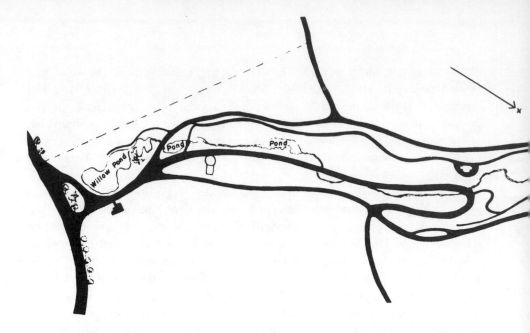

of New York's Manhattan Island. In this he was joined by a young English architect, Calvert Vaux, and Frederick Law Olmsted, apparently the first American to call himself "landscape architect," who had just completed a walking tour through the picturesque countrysides of Britain and Europe.

Their efforts were tragically interrupted when Downing was still a young man of thirty-seven. On July 28, 1852, he, with his wife and mother-in-law, boarded the Hudson River steamer *Henry Clay* for a trip from Albany to New York. The ship fell into a race with another vessel, the *Armenia,* and its fireboxes were apparently so heavily stoked that it caught fire off Yonkers and ran aground. The passengers, cut off at the stern by flames, began jumping overboard. Downing was seen on an upper deck throwing chairs to those in the water but was later found drowned.

It was, therefore, Olmsted and Vaux who built Central Park (and formed a lasting partnership). Word of the park's beauty spread across the country and commissions poured in. The firm (with most of the credit going to Olmsted) designed Prospect Park in Brooklyn, Riverside and Morningside parks in Manhattan, Fairmont Park in Philadelphia, Belle Isle Park in Detroit, the grounds around the Capitol in Washington, and Mount Royal Park in Montreal. It also mapped out parks for Boston, Buffalo, and San Francisco.

Olmsted was inspired by the same love of romanticism manifest in Llewellyn Park, carrying the concept of rustic suburbs and curving streets to many parts of the country. His most important effort in that regard was the planning of Riverside, a proposed suburb of Chicago on the Des Plaines River. It had been made a stop on a newly built, double-track line of the Chicago, Burlington and Quincy Rail Road.

To Olmsted the environs of Chicago were anything but attractive and he was determined to set this right. In his prospectus for the project, submitted to the developers on September 1, 1868, he wrote:

> Owing partly to the low, flat, miry and forlorn character of the greater part of
> the country immediately about Chicago, and the bleak surface, arid soil, and

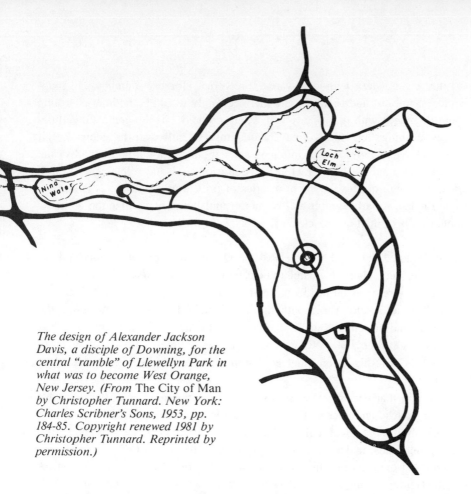

The design of Alexander Jackson Davis, a disciple of Downing, for the central "ramble" of Llewellyn Park in what was to become West Orange, New Jersey. (From The City of Man *by Christopher Tunnard. New York: Charles Scribner's Sons, 1953, pp. 184-85. Copyright renewed 1981 by Christopher Tunnard. Reprinted by permission.)*

exposure of the remainder to occasional harsh and frigid gusts of wind off the lake ... the city, as yet, has no true suburbs or quarters in which urban and rural advantages are agreeably combined with any prospect of long continuance.

Suburbs built up to that time, he said, were extensions of city street plans, with all the regimentation that made them monotonous and ugly. Straight streets and speeding (horse-drawn) traffic he regarded as symbols of hectic modern life. He wished the residents of Riverside to ride their carriages at a leisurely rate. He went on:

In the highways, celerity will be of less importance than comfort and convenience of movement, and as the ordinary directness of line in town-streets, with its resultant regularity of plan would suggest eagerness to press forward, without looking to the right hand or the left, we should recommend the general adoption, in the design of your roads, of gracefully-curved lines, generous spaces, and the absence of sharp corners, the idea being to suggest and imply leisure, contemplativeness and happy tranquility.

The ideal suburb, Olmsted believed, retained as much rural flavor as possible, with houses set back from the road with attractive planting. His warning to the Riverside developers of how ugly suburban streets could be, written more than a century ago, evokes visions of modern counterparts:

Line a highway...with coal-yards, breweries, forges, warehouses, soap-works, shambles, and shanties, and there certainly would be nothing charming about it. Line it with ill-proportioned, vilely-colored, shabby-genteel dwelling-houses, pushing their gables or eaveboards impertinently over the sidewalk as if for the advertising of domestic infelicity and eagerness for public sympathy, and it would be anything but attractive to people of taste and refinement. Line it again with high dead-walls, as of a series of private mad houses, as is done in some English suburbs, and it will be more repulsive to many than the window-lighted walls of the town blocks.

Olmsted designed the winding streets of the Druid Hills area of Atlanta and the Richmond, Virginia, suburb that came to be called Sherwood Park. The stamp of his efforts at rusticity remains on residential parts of Tarrytown, New York, Pinehurst, North Carolina, and Palo Alto, south of San Francisco, where he designed the railroad station and presented Leland Stanford with the layout for the university that bears his name. Olmsted's plans for two other university towns—Ithaca, New York, and Berkeley, California—were shelved but may have inspired those that were carried out.

An innovation that became typical of suburban developments was the quest for privacy through dead-end streets. These were featured in Olmsted's 1891 design for Roland Park, Baltimore. Such culs-de-sac are now common in suburbia and, in a maze of curving roads, make it even more difficult for the visitor to find an address.

After Olmsted died in 1903 his firm continued the tradition, as in its design for Forest Hills Gardens, completed in 1912 in New York's borough of Queens. It was built for the Russell Sage Foundation as a model for ideal middle-class housing. Sinuous streets were not an Olmsted monopoly. David Hotchkiss used them in his 1856 plans for Lake Forest, on Lake Michigan north of Chicago (beneath the most common aircraft approach to O'Hare Airport).

Affluent suburbs sprang up along the rail lines radiating from large cities, such as the famous "Main Line" running west from Philadelphia and the lines radiating northwest from Chicago. In 1869 Alexander T. Steward bought 8,000 acres of Long Island farmland near New York to build a model community, now known as Garden City. Pierre Lorillard, heir to a tobacco fortune and owner of 7,000 acres alongside the railway up the Ramapo Valley, present route of the New York State Thruway northwest of New York, founded Tuxedo Park there in 1886 as an exclusive residential enclave.

Only limited areas, however, enjoyed rail service. Following experiments with steam-driven street conveyances, horse-drawn streetcars had emerged in the 1850's as the most practical. Their lines soon reached several miles into the countryside, opening up new residential areas.

With the invention in 1884 of an electric motor suitable for propelling railway cars and, three years later, of an overhead power system, electric streetcars began to replace the horse-drawn trolleys, and the suburban explosion gained momentum. In Brooklyn streetcars became such a hazard to pedestrians that the name "Trolley Dodgers" was adapted for that city's baseball team (later shortened to "Dodgers").

Suburbs sprang up along streetcar lines radiating from the cities like spokes of a wheel.

Then, as the century drew to a close, there was an extraordinary boom in construction of interurban electric rail lines that ran on their own rights-of-way instead of streets. It was stimulated by invention in 1897 of a control system in which an entire train of self-propelled cars could be driven by a single motorman. A 14-mile line between Portland and Oregon City went into operation in 1893. Hourly limited-stop service between Cleveland and Detroit was initiated in 1904. By 1916 there were 15,580 miles of trackage in the interurban systems, being extensive in Michigan, Indiana, and particularly in Ohio, where only four towns of more than 5,000 population were without service. The trains ran far faster than streetcars and offered severe competition to the long-haul steam lines, for their electric motors enabled them to start and stop more swiftly, making possible more closely spaced stations.

Although areas between the streetcar and railroad lines remained largely farmland, clusters of housing and shops sprang up around each of the station stops, much as has happened around new stations on Washington's Metro system. The interurban lines also offered services now taken over by trucks, such as same-day delivery of perishable produce from rural to urban areas.

Although we think of Los Angeles, with its teeming freeways, as "the ultimate automobile city," no metropolis has been more strongly influenced by the interurbans. Its dispersed character is due largely to rail systems built from the late 1860's until 1910, when they were unified by Henry Edmunds Huntington into the Pacific Electric Railroad.

The city, in fact, evolved through a succession of transport systems. In the days of horse-drawn locomotion it took two days to travel from the little pueblo of Los Angeles to Santa Monica—today a freeway trip lasting only minutes. By the 1870's, as canals brought water into the arid Los Angeles Basin, new communities began evolving around the horse-drawn streetcar lines that crisscrossed the region. In Ontario, between Los Angeles and Riverside, mules hauled the cars up the long slope of Euclid Avenue, then, as the cars coasted on the return journey, the mules rode flatcars attached in the rear.

In 1869 the city's first railway linked downtown Los Angeles with Wilmington and San Pedro Bay. When the Southern Pacific began building its transcontinental rail line from San Francisco to Yuma and the East, it appeared that it would bypass the still-infant city of Los Angeles. The tracks from San Pedro, however, offered a route for bringing in rails and other ship-borne construction material. In return for its use the Southern Pacific agreed to come over Soledad Pass and through Los Angeles. With construction of the two-mile breakwater at Point Fermin, begun in 1899, San Pedro Bay became the world's largest man-made harbor.

Meanwhile the Pacific Electric Railway was spreading in all feasible directions, laying track into open country, across farms and orange groves. President Nixon's father was motorman on the lines to Whittier and Yorba Linda until he hit an automobile. It was said that wherever the railroad's Big Red Cars whistled, "whole cities arose." As its lines reached out to Santa Monica, San Fernando, Burbank,

Pasadena, Pomona, Long Beach, and Newport Beach, speculators raced to acquire land ahead of their advance. In 1887, when the population of Los Angeles was nearing 100,000, Horace Wilcox, a prohibitionist, developed a suburb that he hoped would serve the world as a model of sobriety and godliness. He gave it a suitably rustic name: Hollywood. In 1909 Harry Chandler, publisher of the *Los Angeles Times,* bought up 47,000 acres of suburban land, and within a few years it had all been subdivided into new communities. The British architect Reyner Banham, in his book on Los Angeles, credits the rail system with giving that city its special dispersion, rather than the freeways of today, which largely follow the old rail routes. This history has left large open areas throughout the region, thus enabling the city—even near its core—to accommodate an ever-burgeoning population of parking lots, malls, drive-ins, shopping centers, subdivisions, and freeways. As Banham puts it, the supercity's scattered nuclei stand isolated as "clusters of towers in a sea of single family dwellings."

At the turn of the century the interurban railways seemed irresistible to investors. Yet, as pointed out by Mildred M. Walmsley of Western Reserve University, "no American industry in which so much capital was invested was shorter lived and paid fewer corporate returns to investors." The nemesis of those rail lines was the automobile. As long as commuters remote from stops on rail or streetcar lines were dependent on walking or a buggy to get to and from work, the suburbs grew slowly, but the development of new private conveyances, such as the steam car (400 of which were in use by 1870), presaged radical changes to come.

At the start of this century Ransom E. Olds began turning out large numbers of Oldsmobiles and they were so successful that from 1904 to 1908 another 241 automobile makers went into business. In that last year Henry Ford began producing the Model T's that brought private cars within reach of millions. It became possible to commute even when living a considerable distance from a railroad station or trolley line and areas between the radiation spokes began to fill with housing.

By now many of the steam railroads, to compete with the interurban systems, had converted local lines to electricity. The interurbans, in an effort to improve business, promoted development of amusement parks and other recreation facilities along their lines. The Toledo-to-Cleveland Lake Shore Electric offered more than a score of such attractions. But the interurbans were doomed. Bus lines were more flexible and private cars often enabled people to commute door-to-door. By 1939 most of the interurban systems had gone out of business and their thousands of miles of track were abandoned. Much of it was sold as scrap to meet the needs of industry during World War II, and in 1961 the last surviving line of the Pacific Electric Railway, from Los Angeles to Long Beach, was shut down, although ironically Los Angeles is now preparing to build Metro Rail, a new rapid-transit system.

In 1921 opening of the Bronx River Parkway, running north from New York City, with landscaping, limited access, and restriction to private automobiles, set a precedent soon to be widely followed, notably in the extensive parkways developed in the New York area by Robert Moses. Prewar construction of the Arroyo Seco Parkway linking Los Angeles with Pasadena anticipated evolution of that region's dominant freeway system. After World War II that parkway became the Pasadena Freeway, first link in the system of superhighways that spread throughout the Los Angeles Basin and finally became part of an interstate highway system spanning the continent from coast to coast.

As the highways evolved, so did tourism. In the 1920's "tin can" tourists camped along the roads and ate canned food, leading to the birth of "motor courts," overnight cabins, and finally the elaborate motels of today.

In 1923 a little noticed but historic development occurred in a planned suburb outside Kansas City. It was the construction of Country Club Plaza, the first complete shopping center. It was not, however, until a decade or two after World War II that shopping centers came into their own and suburbia acquired its multi-nucleated character of today.

Furthermore, the hiatus in home construction and childbearing during the war years was followed by a building boom and baby boom. Veterans of the war and the war years, enriched by savings and encouraged by federal loans, sought homes of their own. In 1946 a developer named William J. Levitt began mass-producing homes selling for less than $9,000 on a large tract in Nassau County, Long Island, within commuting range of New York. The result was Levittown, a planned community of 65,000 residents with communal swimming pools, playgrounds, schools, social centers—and shopping centers. Levitt acquired another 5,000 acres of farmland in Pennsylvania midway between Philadelphia and Trenton, New Jersey, near the giant new Fairless Works of United States Steel. By the end of the 1950's this Levittown was home for 80,000. Near Los Angeles Lakewood Village was built to house 100,000. A pattern of development had been set that was copied (usually on a smaller scale) all over the country. "New cities" were built, such as Reston, Virginia, near Washington's Dulles International Airport, Columbia in Maryland, or Irvine Ranch near Los Angeles.

A more recent development has been the "superregional mall," such as the one in Schaumburg, Illinois, a short distance northwest of O'Hare Airport. It is said to be the world's largest, with 4 major department stores, 230 smaller shops on three levels, 10,800 parking spaces, over 100,000 daily visitors, and annual sales approaching $200 million. Tysons Corner Mall near the Capital Beltway in the Virginia suburbs of Washington, D.C., is another example.

Meanwhile industries have been moving away from the cities, being more dependent on freeways than on water power, seaport facilities, or railroads. In the countryside they find lower taxes and cheaper land for a fresh start in modernization. High-technology industries have sprung up along superhighways within reach of academic centers of advanced research, such as Route 128 circling Cambridge and Boston or California's Bay Freeway that runs south from San Francisco and passes near Stanford University. The stretch is known as Silicon Valley because of the extensive use of that substance by electronics industries.

Because of tax advantages, better living, and improved communications (including heavy use of computer links), many corporations have moved their headquarters from the central cities to attractive locations in the suburbs. The result has been dramatic

Levittown on Long Island. (*The New York Times*)

transformation of such communities as Greenwich and Stamford in Connecticut or White Plains in New York's Westchester County. The Long Lines Department of the American Telephone and Telegraph Company has moved even farther afield—to rural Bedminister in New Jersey.

Employees in such enterprises tend to find homes nearby. They are rarely drawn into the city that forms the nucleus of that metropolitan area. Their local community offers most of what they need in the way of cultural activity and services—medical, legal, financial, or otherwise. Computers enable banks, if state laws permit, to scatter branches throughout a region, all linked to a central accounting system.

Just as developments in horizontal transport—streetcars, trains, and automobiles— determined the evolution of suburbia, so were cities reshaped by the development of vertical transport. In 1859 an electric elevator was installed in New York's Demarest Building, demonstrating that shortness of breath no longer set a limit on how many stories could be piled, one on top of another, on a small piece of real estate. This, combined with the use of metal frames, inaugurated the skyscraper era. The sixty-story Woolworth Building, designed by Cass Gilbert in Gothic style, was completed in New York in 1913 and was the world's highest until completion of the Chrysler and Empire State buildings in 1930 and 1931. Just as cathedral spires once signaled the presence of European cities from far across the surrounding countryside, so today do the clustered skyscrapers of virtually every American city.

A radical transformation has also been taking place around major airports. They

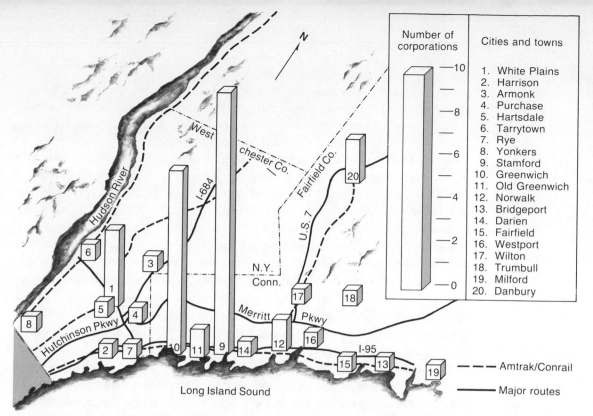

Exodus from New York to Fairfield and Westchester counties of headquarters for corporations on the Fortune *list of top 1,000, as of the end of 1978. (From* Contemporary Suburban America *by Peter O. Muller. Englewood Cliffs, N.J.: Prentice-Hall, Inc., 1981, p. 151. Adapted by permission of the publisher.)*

were originally built in open country where land was cheap but have become surrounded by towering hotels, interweaving freeways, and flat-roofed distribution warehouses with tractor trailers lined up along their sides in close ranks to receive or deliver goods. Shopping centers and other services have sprung up along highways leading to the airports, contributing to further decentralization of metropolitan areas.

Beyond the outer fringes of the suburbs surrounding such eastern cities as New York, Philadelphia, Baltimore, and Washington is a belt of "gentleman farms" with white-fenced fields for raising prize cattle or for fox hunting. This zone, however, is being penetrated by freeways—and hence by developers. As in the days of streetcar lines, suburbia is spreading along such radial spokes of the metropolitan system, but much farther into the countryside. More Americans now live in suburbs than in cities or rural areas, but it is becoming increasingly difficult to define "rural." Despite earlier migration of displaced farm workers to the cities, rural areas have been gaining in population, partly because of the flight to "exurbia" and the establishment there of retirement communities. The 1980 census showed that the population had become far more dispersed and it documented dramatic growth of the Sun Belt cities at the expense of old industrial centers of the Northeast. During the previous decade New York City lost 10.4 percent of its population and Houston grew by 29.2 percent. Growth of the southern suburbs was even more spectacular. Those around Houston expanded 71.2 percent.

The evolution of suburbia has segregated the population into remarkably uniform enclaves. Someone who scans the scene below on takeoff from any major airport, no matter how far from home, can usually see a community almost indistinguishable from his own. As pointed out by Peter O. Muller, a social geographer at the University of Miami, there has been a "sorting" of the population in terms of economic level. As incomes rose, people sought out "better" neighborhoods and the population became segregated according to income (and, in early days, in terms of ethnic background). Almost a quarter of Americans change their address each year, and they can move from one suburban community to one on the opposite coast that is essentially identical in its social, cultural, and economic character.

The process of urban-suburban development has also led to extreme polarization of districts within cities—particularly old ones such as New York and Boston. Ghetto areas like New York's South Bronx have become a national disgrace, resembling bombed-out cities. In 1980 a quarter of the Boston population was on welfare and the situation in New York was much the same. "Gentrification"—invasion and rehabilitation of low-income areas by settlers from neighboring, more affluent districts—is creating additional tension.

Although the centralized city of the past has spread into a multi-nucleated metropolis, urban renewal has led to an extraordinary rebirth of core areas in cities that have sought to make their centers attractive to shoppers, tourists, and convention planners. They have built "interior landscapes"—monumental meccas for shopping, entertainment, and conferences. In such cities as Baltimore and Toronto department stores, theaters, shops, garages, restaurants, miniparks, and hotels—sometimes with towering central atria and glassed-in elevators—are linked by aerial walkways or underground arcades. In Minneapolis thirty downtown blocks are laced together by glassed-in "skyways." In Calgary the elevated sidewalks are known as "plus fifteens" because they are more than fifteen feet above street level. Texas cities have put them underground as refuges from summer heat. In Boston, Baltimore, and New York decaying waterfronts have been rehabilitated into enticing tourist attractions.

In medieval times European cities sought to outdo one another in the magnificence of their newly built cathedrals. To some extent American and Canadian cities are engaged in similar constructive rivalry.

34 WATERED LANDSCAPES

Like giant green coins lined up in neat rows on the tawny landscape, center-pivot irrigation systems have become a remarkable feature of the western states—especially from Nebraska through eastern Colorado to the Texas Panhandle—as well as in the Pacific Northwest, California, central Minnesota, Georgia, and northern Florida. Each circle is periodically sprinkled by a pipe, typically a quarter-mile long, slowly swinging in a circle. The pipe is supported by self-propelled towers at intervals along its length.

In this way semiarid land formerly useful only for pasture, hay, or marginal farming can now produce bumper crops of corn, sugar beets, wheat, potatoes, and sorghum. The University of Nebraska has found that pasture in the Sand Hills region of that state normally producing a maximum of 27 pounds of beef per acre yearly can yield about 800 pounds with center-pivot irrigation. Several hundred such systems occupy the Sand Hills area between the Niobrara and Elkhorn rivers. So striking is the pattern formed by these ranks of green disks that in 1973 and 1974 they were repeatedly used for navigational reference by the orbiting *Skylab* astronauts as they sailed by 270 miles overhead.

Watering in this manner is particularly well suited to the Sand Hills, since delivery in the conventional way via furrows would be ineffective. The land is so sandy that the water almost immediately sinks below root level. The center-pivot sprinkler can spread the water lightly and frequently, keeping the roots moist, rather than in one large dose most of which is lost. Fertilizers or weed killers can be mixed with the water in a manner that not only intensifies crop growth but also permits controlled application instead of heavy dosage, which may contaminate groundwater. More conventional methods of irrigation are still the practice in much of the country, but close to a million and a half acres of American farmland are now irrigated in this manner.

The system was patented in 1952 by Frank Zybach, a farmer near Strasburg, east of Denver. Usually seven or more towers, each about eight feet high, support a pipe into which water is pumped from a central point, which often is also the well site. The motors propelling each tower are driven by the pressure of water flowing through the pipe or by electricity. The well pumps are frequently diesel-powered, and, all told, such irrigation uses up about ten times more energy per acre than conventional tillage, planting, cultivation, and harvesting.

The triumph of the system is the manner in which the pipe is kept straight as it swings in a circle. The outermost tower sets the pace, moving at roughly walking speed. When the control system at each tower senses that the next tower outward from it is getting ahead and the pipe is beginning to bend, it speeds up to maintain the alignment. Each sprinkler outward along the pipe has more reach to cover the larger area for which it is responsible.

As is evident from the air, most circles are the same size, a quarter mile in radius to fit neatly into the quarter-section, 160-acre squares of the great checkerboard. A few are twice as wide with pipes supported by twenty towers. Center-pivot systems are also flexible enough to function in rolling terrain. In some cases their towers climb up and down slopes as great as 30 degrees. Land that was too hilly or sandy for irrigation can therefore be farmed.

Several oddities will become apparent to the observant air traveler. One is that while most of the circles fit neatly inside each square of the checkerboard, some are sliced off where a road skirts them. The circles, so to speak, are "squared" on one or more sides. This is possible because some pivot systems are fitted with an outer section that can be swung back and turned off for part of the rotation period. Conversely, this makes it possible partially to fill in the corners of a square lot. Where there is a homestead within the quarter section, preventing the pipe from sweeping a complete circle, a pie slice remains unirrigated and is used for pasture or some other purpose.

An excellent water-saving method is drip irrigation (also called trickle irrigation) in which perforated plastic tubing is laid along crop rows. The technique, developed in Israel, makes it possible to deliver water at the optimum rate, exactly where needed, and with minimal loss to evaporation. Whereas more than half the water sprinkled by center pivot systems can be lost to evaporation, particularly on a windy day, the efficiency of drip irrigation can approach 100 percent. In 1960 only 40 acres of American farmland were being watered in this manner. By 1983 this had risen to 600,000 acres—still only a small percentage of the acres under cultivation. Nevertheless, on rocky slopes in California's San Diego County the method was doubling avocado yields with 50 percent less water than needed for conventional irrigation. Farther north, in the San Joaquin Valley, a tomato farmer reported that the drip method increased his per-acre yield from forty-six to fifty-eight tons. The method is not confined to row crops. In Arizona high cotton yields are being obtained from fields where the perforated tubes have been buried six to eight inches underground. The method is probably the most economical of water use but is expensive, with installation costs of $1,000 or more per acre, and the perforations tend to clog, requiring elaborate filtering and back-flushing systems.

Signs of more conventional forms of irrigation can be seen on almost any flight across the West. Rectangular green fields along streambeds in otherwise arid areas show where river water is being put to use. In Utah, where rivers emerge from the Wasatch Range that forms a wall along the east margin of the basin once occupied by

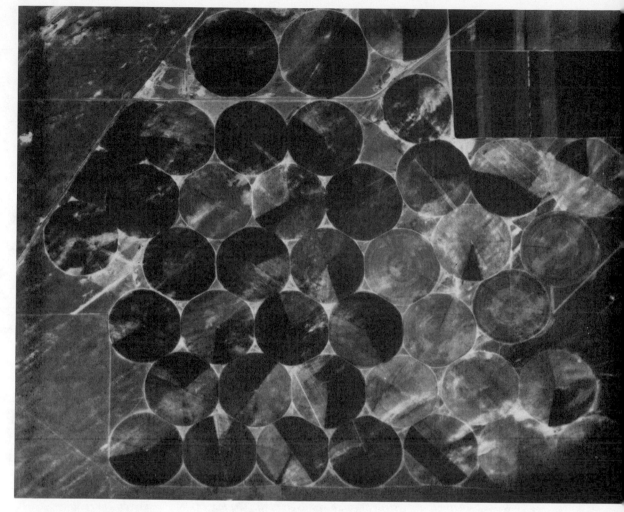

Center-pivot irrigation in the State of Washington. (Soil Conservation Service, U.S. Department of Agriculture)

Lake Bonneville, not only fertile fields but also communities have grown up, such as Salt Lake City, Provo, and Ogden. Such "oases" occur in other parts of the world, notably Central Asia and North Africa, where rivers fed by high mountain snows or rains make possible local irrigation of a desert.

The eastern flanks of the Rocky Mountains and Cascades, on the other hand, are in a "rain shadow" since the prevailing westerlies have already been drained of their moisture in crossing mountains. Water for communities east of the Rockies is carried from west to east through several tunnels.

Where, in the Southwest, green fields are remote from any river, the water may come from wells drawing on deposits of "fossil water" left over from the pluvial periods that formed Lake Bonneville and Lake Lahontan thousands of years ago. Because this water contains almost no residual carbon 14—the radioactive form of carbon—it is clear that for thousands of years it has received little or no replenishment

Circular fields under center-pivot irrigation, viewed with an imaging radar carried by the space shuttle Columbia *in November 1981, cover much of this sandy area south of the Platte River system in southwest Nebraska. The larger circles water an entire square-mile section. The rest cover quarter sections. Enders Reservoir and tributaries of the Republican River are in the lower center. (NASA/Jet Propulsion Laboratory)*

from the earth's surface. Carbon 14 is produced by cosmic rays high in the atmosphere and then gradually decays. If water (which normally contains some carbon dioxide, including carbon 14) is isolated from carbon 14 replenishment for thousands of years, little of that form of carbon remains.

Other irrigation draws on underground reservoirs that are partially replenished by rainfall, but not at the rate of withdrawal. If the rate continues, the reservoirs will eventually be exhausted. Meanwhile, as the water table drops, farmers are forced to drill deeper, install more powerful pumps, and spend more on pumping energy.

When the ancestral Rocky Mountains and their successors eroded, their debris, as gravel, sand, and silt, spread east of the mountains to form deep, water-permeable reservoirs the most widespread of which is known as the Ogallala aquifer. In some areas its thickness exceeds 1,000 feet. It is estimated to hold as much water as Lake Huron—and none of it evaporates. This is the resource drawn upon by more than

150,000 wells from Nebraska through eastern Colorado, the southeast corner of Wyoming, western Kansas, the Oklahoma and Texas panhandles, and the eastern edge of New Mexico. At the end of 1981 Nebraska had registered 68,348 irrigation wells in that state alone.

The tapping of this water, following the introduction of center pivot irrigation, has helped transform the High Plains region. The latter now includes almost a quarter of all irrigated land in the United States and, in contrast to its barren, dusty past, produces much of the country's grain and almost half of its grain-fed cattle. Water levels in parts of the Ogallala and other High Plains aquifers, however, have dropped alarmingly. In Grant and Stanton counties of Kansas the water table reportedly fell more than 100 feet between 1950 and 1975. In parts of Colorado, from 1964 to 1976, it fell 40 feet. In 1981 it was reported that in western Texas the water was being extracted eighteen times faster than it was being replenished. The water table in parts of Kansas and Texas was already 500 feet underground. The Sand Hills region of Nebraska is more fortunate in that the deposit there is relatively shallow and abundant. Some wells steadily produce 900 gallons an hour. But even there the water table has been sinking, particularly in the southwest corner of the state. Seasons of heavy

Distribution of Ogallala Formation
in Great Plains

rain help replenish the aquifers, but only about 4 percent of the rainfall percolates down that far.

To stem the depletion some states, such as Colorado, have enacted stringent limits on the drilling of new wells. In Arizona's areas of most rapid development no new farmlands can be irrigated, and irrigation cannot be resumed where it has been suspended. Proceeds of a new tax on irrigation pumps are used to buy land and take it out of irrigation. While violations of the Arizona law can be treated as a felony, under some circumstances, there is widespread belief that incentives and persuasion will be more effective than enforcement. Furthermore, the news is not all bad. A study of water resources in the High Plains, authorized by Congress in 1976, made it clear that while some areas were hard hit, serious depletions were localized. Nevertheless, it seemed likely that in some areas there would have to be a return to dry-land agriculture.

No state has been more transformed by irrigation than California. In 1981 more than ten million acres of its land were being watered—22 percent more than in Texas, its nearest rival in that regard. The state's central valleys that raise most of its produce were relatively dry when the first settlers arrived. Water, however, was available from two major sources: the Sierra Nevada, which forms a wall of mountains to the east, and the Colorado River, which skirts the southern tip of the state as it enters the Gulf of California.

As moist air blowing in from the Pacific is forced upward by the Sierra Nevada it cools, condenses into clouds, and deposits snow or rain on those mountains, whence numerous streams flow into the Great Valley of California, between the Sierra

Nevada on the east and the Coast Ranges on the west. Its northern half is drained by the Sacramento River and its southern half by the San Joaquin River, both of which then join and empty into San Francisco Bay.

The water of these rivers has been tapped to supply much of the state's agriculture. Nowhere is their effect more evident than in the rice-growing areas fed by waters impounded behind Shasta Dam on the Sacramento River and Oroville Dam on the Feather River, a tributary of the Sacramento.

In contrast to rice-growing in Asia or Africa, where lines of barefoot planters wade across flooded paddies, the rice is sown by airplanes that also spread herbicides and fertilizers. The fields are leveled with the aid of a rotating laser beam on a mast. Tractor-drawn scrapers keeping an electronic eye on the laser beam are guided by an on-board computer that sets the blade height to achieve just the right degree of slope. The field must drain readily yet slope so slightly that it can be kept under two to four inches of water during the growing season. Several scrapers are often guided simultaneously by a single laser.

The fields are bounded by sinuous levees that follow the subtle contours of the land. They, too, may be heaped up by twin-disk plows under laser control. The land is plowed and prepared when dry, then flooded. Seed is soaked for a day or more before being air-dropped so that it will sink immediately. Twenty to thirty days before harvest time the land is drained and allowed to dry enough to support the heavy harvesting machinery. The crops are usually rotated, with wheat or barley periodically replacing rice, or the land is left fallow for a while.

The productivity of these fields is extraordinary: 6,450 pounds of rice per acre in contrast to the world average of 2,360 pounds. Only 7 man-hours are needed for such a crop whereas more than 300 man-hours is typical in Asia and Africa. Arkansas produces more rice than California, but the per-acre yields are not as great.

The soil of the California valley is ideal for rice culture because its clay content slows the downward seepage of water, allowing fields to remain flooded from planting time in early May until they are drained before the autumn harvest. After the harvest, in former years, the air traveler would see numerous fires as the rice straw was being burned to kill any infestations of stem-rot fungus, but this has been at least partially curtailed to reduce air pollution.

Rice growing is also possible in some areas along the west side of the San Joaquin Valley—the southern part of the Great Valley—thanks to a project that pumps water into a canal leading there from the Sacramento River. Previously water for irrigation was available only on the east side of the valley, close to the Sierras, and it is there the view from aloft shows the closely packed farms and populous towns that indicate an area of intensive farming. West of the San Joaquin River that divides the valley the fields are large and settlements are sparse.

In low-lying, poorly drained parts of the valley irrigation water from higher ground has seeped down-slope and risen to the surface after picking up salts en route. When

Levees in rice fields near Stockton, California, curve to follow subtle contours. (Economic Research Service, U.S. Department of Agriculture)

the water evaporates, the salt remains. An estimated half-million acres have become so salty that crops are severely reduced. In Pakistan such an effect of irrigation has come close to destroying the food-producing capacity of that country's Indus Valley, and some historians believe it accounts for the fall of the ancient Mesopotamian civilization that flourished between the Tigris and Euphrates rivers.

The land can be recovered if drainage channels are dug and enough water is delivered to carry off the salt. This has been done in some parts of the San Joaquin Valley, but in 1980 the Council on Environmental Quality warned that salinization and reversion to desert "could spread to large stretches of this rich valley during the next thirty years."

Waters from the Colorado River have made California's arid Imperial Valley a bountiful source of winter vegetables. The Salton Sea is to the north. The All American Canal crosses the lower part of this Landsat image, just north of the Mexican border. There is less irrigation south of the border. (NASA)

Along the Colorado River this type of salt contamination, plus evaporation from the long lakes formed by dams on the river, has made the lower part of the river so salty that a $350-million desalting plant had to be built near Yuma, Arizona, to reduce the salt content to the level required by a treaty with Mexico before the water crosses the border. The All American Canal, built just north of the Mexican border to irrigate the Imperial Valley, carries much of the Colorado River water that remains from upstream diversions. Mexico then uses virtually all that is left and only a trickle reaches the river's mouth.

Of all the irrigated regions of California none stands out so boldly when viewed from above as the highly productive Imperial Valley, set in the desert country between the Salton Sea and the Mexican border. When the Colorado River, over millions of years, excavated the Grand Canyon and other parts of its course, the resulting sediment was laid down across the north end of the Gulf of California, filling the Imperial Valley and forming a giant dam across the upper part of the Gulf. The area that was cut off dried up, leaving as a remnant the Imperial Valley and the Salton Sink, filled in 1904 by inadvertent diversion of a Colorado River flood to form the Salton Sea. Now that sea is kept from drying up by seepage from the irrigation systems.

Parts of the Imperial Valley are 225 feet below sea level, and fears have been expressed that it might again be flooded if the hump of sediment to the south, holding back the waters of the Gulf of California, is breached by an earthquake along extensions of the San Andreas Fault crossing that "dam." Meanwhile, however, irrigation and intensely sunny days throughout the year enable the valley to keep American kitchens stocked with fresh lettuce, melons, tomatoes, and peas. The agricultural counties of California now provide the nation with a quarter of such produce, and, despite its salt problems, the San Joaquin Valley alone accounts for more than any state except Iowa, Texas, and Illinois.

To meet the increased water demands of the Southwest, additional canals are proposed or under construction, such as the $2-billion Central Arizona Project, a system of canals and tunnels designed to deliver water from the already overexploited Colorado River to the thirsty heartland of Arizona. This will carry water that otherwise might flow to California through the All American Canal or the great Colorado River Aqueduct system. The latter, 672 miles long, supplies the Los Angeles area via 92 miles of tunnel, 395 miles of huge pipe, 29 miles of siphon, and five pumping stations. The anticipated diversion to Arizona has led Californians to debate, rather heatedly, plans for a Peripheral Canal 43 miles long and costing about $6 billion to carry water from northern California to the California Aqueduct. The latter runs from the Sacramento River delta, northeast of San Francisco, to the area north of Los Angeles. As it is, California has the most elaborate irrigation system on earth, with 70 percent of its available surface water in the north and 77 percent of the demand in the south. In addition to the systems already named the venerable Los Angeles Aqueduct—built between 1908 and 1913—carries to that city water draining off the east side of the Sierras and into the Owens River valley. If the projected California State Water Project is carried out, it will eventually be possible to move water from the humid northern parts of the state as far south as the Mexican border.

35 THE WAR TO SAVE
THE LAND

Aerial perspectives of American farmland bear witness to a great revolution in land use—one that has demonstrated what can be done through a combination of persuasive leadership, voluntary action, and economic pressure. On closer inspection, however, it becomes clear that the revolution has not gone far enough and that topsoil is being swept away at an intolerable rate.

A few decades ago farmed landscapes would have looked completely different. Furrows were long and straight, regardless of the slope of the land. In large areas of the West ominous bright spots showed where dark topsoil had been washed or blown away.

While George Washington, Thomas Jefferson, and James Madison were concerned over the effects of erosion, the effort to save the land—which, under new pressures, has again become critical—was largely initiated through the evangelism of one man: Hugh Hammond Bennett, a soil specialist in the U.S. Department of Agriculture. In the late 1920's, increasingly alarmed at the deterioration of American soils, he paced the corridors of Washington bureaucracy, stumping for soil conservation. His circular, *Soil Erosion: a National Menace,* did not create much of a stir when it appeared. The nation was in a boom period. The only response by Congress, in 1929, was to allocate a modest $160,000 to establish ten stations for study of the erosion problem. They were set up under Bennett's direction in association with agricultural experiment stations or land-grant colleges in various states.

Then twin catastrophes hit the American farmer: the Great Depression and the dust storms of the 1930's. Congressmen who had ignored Bennett's warnings found the windowsills of their Capitol Hill offices coated with yellow dust from Kansas, Oklahoma, and Texas. In 1933 President Franklin D. Roosevelt named Bennett director of the Soil Erosion Service in the Department of the Interior, and two years later that agency was transferred to the Agriculture Department as the Soil Conservation Service.

Among Roosevelt's emergency measures was creation of the Civilian Conservation Corps, or CCC, which put three million unemployed to work in the forests and farmlands. By 1936 there were 450 CCC camps and an army of young men available

Terracing in Iowa. (Soil Conservation Service, U.S. Department of Agriculture)

for Bennett's demonstration of erosion control. Under expert guidance they dammed and planted gullies, set out tree seedlings, converted fields to contour plowing, and on steeper slopes heaped up ridges along lines of equal elevation to catch eroded soil and form terraces. There were 141 demonstration areas in forty-one states, trying out new grasses, new crop rotations, and other farming practices. Farmers were invited to see the advantages for themselves, but it became clear that demonstration projects alone would not change the deeply entrenched habits of millions.

A committee appointed by Henry A. Wallace, then Secretary of Agriculture, decided that only grass-roots organization of the farmers could bring about the needed revolution. It recommended that after July 1, 1937, all erosion control on private land be undertaken through locally constituted "soil conservation associations."

This resulted in drafting of the Standard State Soil Conservation Districts Law to be used, it was hoped, by each state as a model for its own legislature. Those chiefly responsible for this historic document were M. L. Wilson, Assistant Secretary of Agriculture, who had been a farmer and county agent in Montana, and Philip M. Glick, assistant solicitor in the Department of Agriculture.

Once a state had enacted legislation permitting organization of soil conservation districts, the initiative would rest with the farmers themselves. The first step would be a petition from twenty-five or more local landowners for the establishment of such a district in their area. It then could not come into being unless a majority of the local farmers and ranchers voted for it. The districts would be run by supervisors, also elected locally, but would receive generous technical help from the federal Soil Conservation Service.

In his foreword to this model law Wallace said: "The nation that destroys its soil destroys itself. The soil is indispensable. Heedless wastage of the wealth which nature has stored in the soil cannot long continue without the effects being felt by every member of society."

Of the 610 million acres of arable land in the country, he said, 100 million had been rendered useless or severely damaged, and erosion was threatening another 100 million acres. "The land already essentially ruined by erosion aggregates an area equal to all the land in two of the large midwestern agricultural states," he added. Early in 1937 Roosevelt forwarded the draft to each state governor with a letter that repeated Wallace's warning: "The nation that destroys its soil destroys itself."

In that first year twenty-two states adopted such laws and by 1947 all forty-eight states as well as Alaska, Hawaii, Puerto Rico, and the Virgin Islands had done so. The first conservation district was set up, appropriately, in Bennett's home county in North Carolina. By the 1980's there were some 3,000 of them covering 2.2 billion acres—96 percent of American farm, forest, and range land. Almost two million landowners had signed cooperative agreements with the districts. The resulting revolution in use of the land is evident on virtually any flight path across the American landscape.

It came about through a delicately balanced relationship among the federal government, state governments, and organized farmers. The Soil Conservation Service provided expert advice and funded much of the research. The states paid the farmers a substantial part of the cost of their conversions to new practices. From the farmers themselves came unpaid leadership. In 1980 there were some 17,000 locally elected or appointed men and women in these roles.

The pattern of federal support for research into more scientific and productive ways to use the land had been established much earlier, as farmers began their great migrations westward. Within a six-week period in 1862 Abraham Lincoln signed three landmark bills: one created the Department of Agriculture; the second was the Homestead Act; the third was the Land Grant College Act, under which states were able eventually to set up sixty-five universities. As Don K. Price of Harvard University has put it, from the land-grant colleges "grew the experiment station, the extension program, and the whole system of policy which has let the federal government play a more effective role in the agricultural economy than the government of any supposedly socialist state."

To achieve such basic changes in American farming practice the emphasis has been on education and economic incentives. Nevertheless, more than half the states authorized their districts to enact ordinances for enforcement. They are not often applied, partly because of manpower shortages. Conversions have been achieved by offering financial assistance only to those who comply. This is known as the "green ticket" approach, as opposed to the "red ticket" of compulsion. Although the districts operate essentially on democratic principles, as Hugh Hammond Bennett put it, "our American way has always provided a method whereby an unwilling few can be required to accede to certain actions taken by the majority.''

In Iowa an effort by the Woodbury County Soil Conservation District to force two farmers to comply with its regulations was carried to the Supreme Court of Iowa in 1979. The court ruled in favor of the district, saying, in part, ''The state has a vital interest in protecting its soil as the greatest of its natural resources, and it has a right to do so. . . . While this imposes an extra financial burden on defendants, it is one the state has a right to exact. The importance of soil conservation is best illustrated by the state's willingness to pay three-fourths of the cost. . . . A law does not become unconstitutional because it works a hardship.''

The land-use patterns that have emerged from the revolution in farming are not only striking but sometimes resemble abstract works of art. This is particularly true of contour plowing. The furrows lie along lines of equal elevation to prevent their becoming erosion channels. They look from the air like contour lines on a topographic map, except that the lines are broken up by fields of different color or shading. The effect is emphasized where strips of more easily eroded row crops (such as corn, with much bare soil between rows) are alternated with strips of close-growing ''catch crops'' (such as wheat, oats, barley, alfalfa, or grasses) that tend to capture soil washed down from the next higher strip.

Depending on the time of year the strips may be highlighted by their contrasting colors: green (corn, cotton, grass, or young grains), yellow (ripening cereal grains), or brown (newly plowed). Sometimes a grassy ribbon may be seen following a twisting path across a field. Such ''grass waterways'' have been planted where natural drainage of the field would otherwise erode a gully.

A holdover from the days of horse-drawn plows is the ''envelope'' pattern seen in relatively rectangular fields where the terrain is level and contour plowing is unnecessary. With a team of horses it was difficult to reverse direction at the end of each furrow. It was easier to plow parallel to each of the four sides of the field, starting at the outside and working toward the center. This necessitated making only right-angle turns at the corners instead of complete reversals. A field plowed thus acquires a pattern similar to that formed by the edges of back flaps on letter envelopes, as shown in the aerial view on page 332. What was advantageous for the plowman driving his team still has merit for the tractor driver.

Also striking from the air are the field shelterbelts of the West. In 1932, while campaigning for the presidency in the windswept dust bowl, Franklin D. Roosevelt conceived of planting millions of trees to form windbreaks in that region. As a result, from 1935 to 1942 more than 222 million were planted, usually in belts one hundred feet wide composed of from ten to fifteen rows. Typical shelterbelts were a half-mile long and oriented east-west to protect crops from hot southerly winds. They were planted in a 1,000-mile zone from the eastern Dakotas to northwest Texas. Many still stand out boldly as one looks down on the landscape, but often their trees are getting scrawny and no longer provide much protection. Furthermore, with dust storms of the 1930's almost forgotten, many financially pressed farmers have bulldozed them to free land for new crops and added income. Some belts have been cut to clear the way for center-pivot irrigation, whose very long pipes rotate in circles, and farmers have been encouraged to plant new, circular belts to enclose such fields. Little affected by

The same farmland near Chestnut Level, Lancaster County, Pennsylvania, seen from the air in 1937, and in 1977 after the introduction of contour stripping. State Route 72 is the main road cutting across the area. (U.S. Department of Agriculture)

the tree cutting have been the plantings that protect farm homesteads, usually north and west of each site to face the winter winds and also to relieve the bleakness of a treeless plain.

Another dramatic pattern on the dry, windblown High Plains is produced by strip-cropping. The strips typically run north and south, at right angles to the prevailing westerlies. This region was little farmed until early in this century, after a hardy winter wheat introduced from Turkey in 1874 proved well adapted to the dry climate. As a result the Great Plains now raise 60 percent of the nation's wheat and over 30 percent of its cattle, thanks in large measure to "dry land farming" in which alternate strips of land are left uncultivated for a year to allow time for the land to regain its moisture and for plowed-under crop residues to decay and enrich the soil. While the strips vary in width (they are typically 350 to 600 feet wide and a mile or so long) they are often uniform over wide areas, making the landscape resemble great swatches of striped fabric.

Further transformations in the plains states followed the drought and high winds of the mid-1950's. Damage in much of the region exceeded that of the dust bowl period, and in 1956 President Eisenhower signed an act creating the Great Plains Conservation Program. Farmers and ranchers in the ten affected states were urged to undertake costly and time-consuming changes in their land use. Some 60,000 enrolled in the

Near Stockton, California, suburbia has invaded farmland, partially surrounding fields ploughed in the "envelope" manner described on page 330. (Economic Research Service, U.S. Department of Agriculture)

program. The federal government paid as much as 80 percent of the cost. More than twenty-two million acres were converted to strip-cropping, nine million acres were planted in grass, seventeen million acres of range were reseeded, and 110,000 miles of windbreaks were planted. This has helped stem erosion, but much of the land is still ill-prepared to resist future onslaughts of wind, such as one in 1977 that blew away ten tons of topsoil per acre from parts of Texas and New Mexico.

In that year the Soil Conservation Service conducted the most thorough survey of soil erosion ever carried out in the United States. Assuming that the land could not long tolerate losing more than five tons per acre yearly (a coating slightly thinner than a dime), it was found that in 1977 erosion exceeded this level on 27 percent of American cropland. On 10 percent of it the rate was more than double the tolerable amount, and in the Southwest the percentage was even higher. These estimates did not include the effects of wind and of gully formation. Erosion is particularly severe in the loess-covered region along the Mississippi River and in west Tennessee, where annual losses of 150 tons per acre have been measured on some farms. By 1979 it was estimated that sixty-one million acres in the West were yearly being denuded of more than 14 tons per acre—almost three times the allowable rate.

A prime contributor to these high rates has been conversion to row crops—chiefly corn and soybeans—which leave the land between rows bare and vulnerable. From 1967 to 1977 the area planted in row crops increased 27 percent. Close-grown crops rose a modest 4 percent. Hay and pasture declined by 40 percent. Furthermore, much of the new planting in corn and soybeans was on readily eroded slopes. On about half the land planted to those crops in central Iowa and Illinois the slopes ranged from 6 to 12 percent.

Not all the eroded soil goes down rivers to the Gulf of Mexico. Particularly in northern states bulldozed by the ice sheet the soil accumulates in depressions left by the ice, rather than flowing to the rivers. High land, however, still loses its precious topsoil, and the low land is little improved by added layers.

The shift to soybean-corn rotation has been dramatic. The traditional rotation was corn-oats-hay, but this has been replaced on many farms. It took a century for the soybean, a native of Asia, to adjust to American conditions, but it is an ideal crop, not only because of its many uses but also for its deep roots. These enable the plant to resist droughts and the roots carry nodules of nitrogen-fixing bacteria that refertilize soil heavily depleted by the corn. The United States has changed from being the world's chief importer of soybeans to the largest exporter of that crop. The beans were originally raised for human consumption and are a constituent of many super-market products. Modern technology, however, has found more than a hundred other applications for them, as in the manufacture of plastics, adhesives, fire-fighting foams, and waterproofing compounds. The meal remaining after oil extraction is used as cattle feed.

Much of the increase in corn-soybean cultivation has been to take advantage of new foreign markets. After decades when surplus crops and low grain prices encouraged farmers to leave some land in pasture or idle, grain demands by the Soviet Union, China, and other countries, combined with continuing population growth at home, led to greatly increased planting. During the 1970's cultivated land in the United States

increased more than 60 percent. Crops harvested from one out of every three acres in 1979 were exported. This helped make up for the country's excessive imports, but as John F. Timmons, professor of economics and an agriculture specialist at Iowa State University, has put it: "We are, in effect, exporting our soil and water quality in the form of food and feed grain."

To stem this loss several forms of "no tillage" or "minimum tillage" are being tested. Under these systems the land is never plowed. Instead its surface is mechanically loosened enough to permit coverage of the seed. Weeds may be suppressed with chemicals, and fertilizers may also be applied. Where row crops are planted, residues of the previous crop are often used to keep down weeds between rows. The ground, held by the roots of former growth, is resistant to erosion. Tests, for example, have shown an annual loss on a tilled soybean field of 13.1 tons per acre whereas with no tillage it was 0.16 tons. Energy input, where tillage is eliminated in raising corn or soybeans, is cut between 7 and 18 percent, which helps make up for the reduced yield. The practice, however, has such disadvantages as proliferation of various pests in untilled soil and increased stream pollution from heavy use of fertilizers and pesticides. Nevertheless, in 1982 the Department of Agriculture estimated that one quarter of American cropland would not be plowed that year, and it appeared that by the end of the century almost half of it would be under the no-tillage system.

A small percentage of farmers in the corn belt have reverted to old-fashioned "organic" farming, raising crops on a commercial scale without either chemical fertilizers or pesticides. A study of 174 such farmers, described in 1981, found that

most had previously been conventional farmers, using chemicals, and thus were not members of the "back-to-the-land" movement. Corn yields were 10 percent lower than with fertilizer and soybean crops were 5 percent lower. While the practice eliminates pollution of local streams, it demands cultivation that exposes the land to water action.

A growing threat to agricultural production has been the loss of prime farmland to residential subdivisions, shopping centers, factories (with their huge parking lots), airports, strip mining, power lines, reservoirs for hydroelectric power or flood control, and freeways (which can gobble up thirty-six acres per mile). Between 1956 and 1975 almost two million acres were taken over for the interstate highway system.

Early housing developers built on rugged land bypassed by the farmers, but more recently extensive prime farmland has been covered with housing. This trend, plus erosion, threatens America's production of food and fiber. "In my lifetime," said Bob Bergland, Secretary of Agriculture in the Carter administration, in an appeal for curtailment of this trend, "we've paved over the equivalent of all the cropland in Ohio."

In 1979 the U.S. Department of Agriculture and the President's Council on Environmental Quality, with support from ten other federal agencies, launched a National Agricultural Lands Study. It found that more than 40 percent of new housing, including prefabricated and mobile homes, was being built on rural land. Only one in ten rural residents was living on a working farm. About three million

In a mere dozen years (between 1953, above, and 1965) suburbia took over this area of citrus groves near Ventura, California. (Economic Research Service, U.S. Department of Agriculture)

acres of potential agricultural land were being lost each year—twelve square miles a day. Of this, one million acres was in actual cultivation. In Florida, from 1966 to 1977, the loss was 1,160,000 acres. As stated by Lester Brown, president of the Worldwatch Institute in Washington, D.C., and an authority on world food supplies, "In the extreme case of Florida—source of half the grapefruits in the world and a quarter of the oranges—all the prime farmland will be put to other uses by the end of the century if current trends continue."

In a 1982 rallying cry the American Farmland Trust, with Norman A. Berg, former head of the Soil Conservation Service, and other prominent conservationists on its advisory committee, said that if the current trend continued through the next decade, the country will face "an irreversible national and international crisis of unprecedented scope—a crisis that will have a dire effect on the quality of your life, the cost of living, the quality and quantity of food that will be available to you, and on America's international relations."

A more optimistic assessment was presented in 1983 by Sandra S. Batie of Virginia Polytechnic Institute and State University and Robert G. Healy of the Conservation Foundation in Washington. They noted in *Scientific American* that while roughly a third of farmland in the Northeast and Southeast was removed from cultivation between 1939 and 1978, much of it was not for shopping centers and the like but reverted to forest. Even allowing for continued withdrawals, they proposed that enough added land could probably be brought under cultivation to meet the increased demands anticipated by the end of this century.

Meanwhile efforts are being made through zoning laws, tax incentives, and other measures to curb the loss of farmland. At the same time long-term experiments in erosion reduction are under way, such as the STEEP (Solutions to Environmental and Economic Problems) project in which scores of agricultural specialists in Washington, Oregon, and Idaho are testing various minimum tillage strategies. But what is needed, according to M. Rupert Cutler, a former Assistant Secretary of Agriculture, is rekindling "a new Bennett-style evangelism" to complete the job of saving the American land.

36 WHAT GROWS WHERE AND WHY

While mountain building, wind, and water have shaped the American landscape, much of it is colored by the crops being grown there. Productivity of the land that has made Americans among the best-fed people of the world is evident from coast to coast. The aerial views have an extraordinary tale to tell of ingenuity, enterprise, and adjustment to ever-changing conditions.

Those responsible for these achievements are a diverse crowd in the crops they raise and the way they do it. They range from the corn-hog farmers of Ohio and Indiana to the "beans-corn-Miami" farmers of Illinois, the dairy farmers of Wisconsin to the "suitcase" or "sidewalk" farmers of the Great Plains.

In the broadest sense the crop regions can be divided into seven areas: the corn belt, extending from western Ohio to eastern Nebraska; the dairy belt, farther north from New York to Minnesota; the belt from the Carolinas to Texas traditionally devoted to cotton but widely converted to other crops; the tobacco country of the Carolinas, Kentucky, and neighboring states; the wheat region from the Dakotas south to Texas; the cattle country to the west of that; and the citrus-fruit- and nut-growing areas of California, the Gulf Coast, and Florida.

Thanks in part to loess deposited during the ice ages, the corn belt, centered in Iowa, was blessed with some of the world's most productive land. Within that region there is considerable variation in how the corn is used. The greatest profit, per acre, comes from converting corn into meat by feeding it to hogs. On a corn diet a hog is ready for market in about six months. Raising hogs, however, is a year-round job. A farmer with much land to cultivate finds it difficult to handle hogs as well. The corn-hog region is therefore focused on Ohio and Indiana, where land was settled early and holdings are small.

The Iowa farmer, with more land—particularly if he has pasture—is more likely to fatten cattle during the winter and concentrate on his crops in summer. In the fall he buys scrawny cattle raised on western ranches and weighing about 650 pounds. By spring planting time they weigh more than 1,000 pounds and are ready to be slaughtered.

If the farm is very large, like those on the Grand Prairie of central Illinois, the

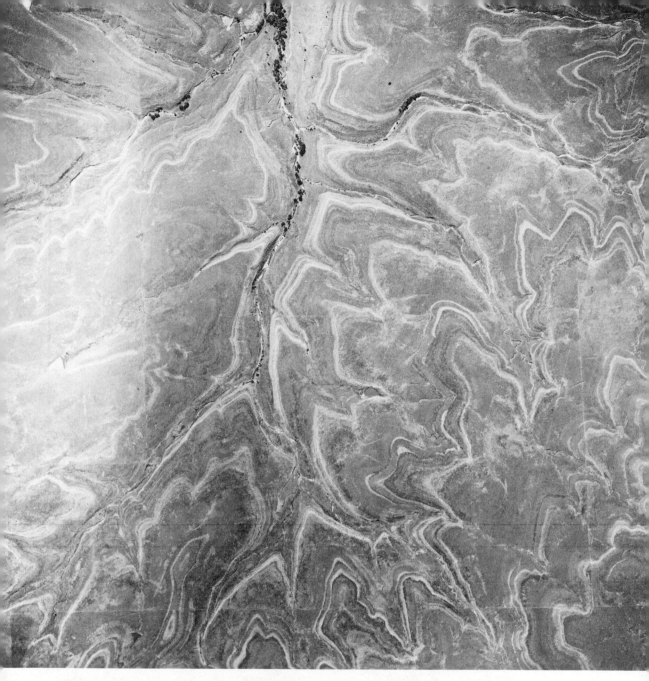

The Flint Hills in eastern Kansas, six miles north of Grenola. (U.S. Department of Agriculture)

farmer may concentrate entirely on crops to be sold: corn, usually rotated with soybeans. The holdings are large because the need for draining the land delayed settlement. The drainage, when finally done, was a major enterprise and the entrepreneurs sold off the land in big lots. A number of those who farm this region close up shop in winter and head south, causing their neighbors to refer to them as B.C.M. (for beans-corn-Miami) farmers.

In the dairying region north of the corn belt summers are cooler and corn is less apt to reach full maturity. Instead it is chopped up for silage to be fed to milk cows. The

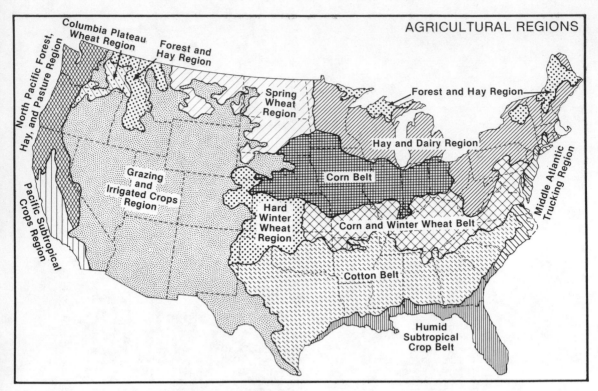

Columbia Plateau Wheat Region
Forest and Hay Region
North Pacific Forest, Hay, and Pasture Region
Spring Wheat Region
Forest and Hay Region
Hay and Dairy Region
Corn Belt
Middle Atlantic Trucking Region
Pacific Subtropical Crops Region
Grazing and Irrigated Crops Region
Hard Winter Wheat Region
Corn and Winter Wheat Belt
Cotton Belt
Humid Subtropical Crop Belt

(U.S. Department of Agriculture)

landscape is dotted with silos and fields tend to be smaller and more square than in the corn belt. Such fields are better suited to the control of grazing and breeding cattle. In the corn belt long, narrow fields mean fewer turns for cultivating and harvesting machinery.

To the west, where the plains are too dry for other crops unless irrigated, wheat dominates except where the land is rough and used for raising range cattle to be shipped elsewhere in the fall for fattening. That is the case, for example, in the Flint Hills of eastern Kansas, whose valleys, seen from the air, display strange chevron stripes where erosion has cut through flat-lying layers of white, flinty limestone interbedded with layers of gray shale.

Farms in the wheat country are very large and their "sidewalk" and "suitcase" farmers may no longer live on them. Suitcase farmers own parcels several hundred miles from their homes. They protect themselves by working large and widely separated tracts of land, hoping that all of them will not be stricken by drought in the same year. To the south—for example, in Kansas—they plant winter wheat, sown in the fall to be ready for harvest in late spring or early summer. To the north—as in the Dakotas—they sow wheat in the spring. Each holding need be visited only twice a year for planting and for harvest. The farmer, with his costly machinery for plowing, planting, or harvesting, moves north with the advancing season, keeping his investment in productive use longer than if he operated in a single climate zone. A survey in Sully County, South Dakota, has shown 15 percent of the farmers in this category.

From the air traces of the homesteads that once stood on the land may be seen, but the farmers themselves live far to the south, where the climate is friendlier.

In contrast to the suitcase farmers are the sidewalk farmers who own parcels within a radius of perhaps fifty miles in a region whose closely spaced county roads make their scattered fields readily accessible. They find it more pleasant to live in a nearby town than on any of those lonely lots. A survey in Toole County, in north-central Montana, has shown 30 percent of the farmers living in this manner. For some an added motivation is the absence on their farmland of potable drinking water.

As farming has become more highly mechanized, very large farms, requiring large capital investments, have become the most economical, and this has led to the emergence of "agribusiness" in which a corporation, rather than an individual farmer, tills the land. This is especially true for crops that are processed close by, such as wine grapes, citrus fruits, frozen vegetables, and breakfast cereals. Small farmers have complained that the land-grant colleges and other centers of agricultural research, through their success in developing crops suited to machine harvesting and shipment, are favoring big farmers and corporate farms. This was reflected in a 1972 report, *Hard Tomatoes and Hard Times*, issued by the Agribusiness Accountability Project, a public interest group in Washington, D.C.

Mass-production technology is increasingly being applied—privately or by corporations—to the fattening of range cattle on "drylots" where no grass grows under the hooves of steers standing shoulder-to-shoulder. Instead of being shipped to the corn belt they may be fattened by the hundreds or even tens of thousands near sources of other forms of feed. Drylot farms can be identified from the air because they are broken up into numerous corrals, each about the size of a half-acre house lot, crowded with forty to eighty head of cattle. In the more automated enterprises a feed trough runs the length of a fence on one side of each corral, extending under the fence so cattle on the inside can eat from it and a self-unloading truck can drive down the outside, steadily dumping feed into the trough.

In southern areas, as a substitute or supplement for corn, cottonseed residues are used. In the North some feed is derived from sugar-beet pulp. In the East the cattle may be fed residues from Florida fruit concentration plants. Grape pulp from wineries provides feed on the West Coast. Other exploited by-products include: spent mash from distilleries, almond hulls, peanut meal, olive meal, as well as residues from processing fruits and vegetables. Milo maize, a sorghum now widely grown in place of cotton, is used extensively in west Texas, whose combined feedlots fatten close to a million cattle at a time.

The Imperial Valley of California, using by-products of its intensive farming, has a score of feedlots, each handling at least 3,500 cattle. The largest can feed more than 30,000 head. In earlier days it was all a man could do to handle 100 steers.

The same mass-production techniques are applied to dairying, particularly near large cities, where land is too costly for pasturing but markets are close. Near Los Angeles some farms raise more than 50 cows per acre—almost as many as on an entire Wisconsin farm. Milking is done in a "walk-through" barn. Being close to the port of Los Angeles the farmer can use concentrated feeds from abroad, such as copra meal from the Philippines and pineapple residues from Hawaii. In the 1950's, as suburbia spread into the countryside southeast of Los Angeles, several communities, such as Dairy Valley, Cypress, and Dairyland, incorporated themselves to provide zoning regulations, tax structures, and other provisions favorable to dairying. By 1960 Dairy Valley had 53,000 cows on 241 farms. Since then, however, developers have taken over areas the farms used for waste disposal and this has created problems. A single drylot farm can produce as much sewage as a city of 15,000 people, and relations with the neighbors have been strained by wafting odors and cattle noises. Feedlots for dairy cattle are to be seen, as well, near major cities in the East.

In the southern tier of states from the Carolinas to Texas it was long said that "cotton is king," but this is far less true today. In Georgia abandoned cotton farms reverted to timber, but since the 1970's some land has again been cleared for such crops as soybeans, peanuts, and pecans. President Jimmy Carter awakened the nation to the fact that peanuts are now the chief crop in southwest Georgia and this is true, as well, in neighboring parts of Alabama.

In some areas, however, erosion has taken a severe toll. The Black Belt Prairie that extends from east-central Alabama into west-central Mississippi got its name from its black, lime-rich soil. It was ideal for cotton. But today much of the black soil has washed away, and the region is mainly used for pasture. Looking down on some sections of the cotton belt one can see where snaking terraces, laboriously constructed to stem the tide of erosion, extend into overgrowth where cotton fields have been abandoned.

On the terraces of Arkansas, formed in the Mississippi Valley between former ice ages when the world oceans were thirty or forty feet higher than now, rice has become a major crop and flooded fields are scattered across the landscape during the growing season. In Georgia, at the start of the last century, virgin forests of gum-cypress were cleared on deltas of the Savannah, Ogeechee, and Altamaha rivers to make way for rice plantations. The rectangular dike systems are still visible from the air, but the flooded fields are now maintained as winter refuges for waterfowl.

South of the cotton belt the landscape becomes increasingly dominated by pine forests that provide pulp for paper mills as well as turpentine, pitch, and other resinous products known traditionally as "naval stores."

Throughout the Southeast, as elsewhere, the geometric patterns of orchards and citrus groves are easily recognized from high altitudes. In Florida the orange and grapefruit plantations often belong to retired businessmen who bought them as an investment. They are worked by citrus-packing companies that cultivate, fertilize, spray, prune, and harvest the grove from a central complex of sheds for machinery, storage of supplies, and a radio tower for communications with field crews. One such enterprise may handle several hundred groves covering thousands of acres. The owner, who is charged for the services and credited with a share of the profits, may never see the grove. Florida also competes with California as a supplier of vegetables. During spring and fall the rich muck around Lake Okeechobee is heavily exploited for production of sweet corn, lettuce, celery, and radishes. From a plane approaching West Palm Beach across the lake, one can also look down on huge tracts planted in sugarcane.

In the San Joaquin Valley of California one sees groves of figs, olives, peaches,

A New Jersey orchard. (Soil Conservation Service, U.S. Department of Agriculture)

and plums, as well as vineyards that produce raisins and much of California's wine. Farther north, along the Oregon coastal plain, are orchards of filberts (hazelnuts). The apples for which Washington is famous come largely from the valleys of the Columbia and Wenatchee rivers east of the Cascade Mountains and the orchard country extends down into Oregon's Willamette Valley.

Such orchards tend to lie in the same climate zone as dairy farms. In Wisconsin cherries dominate the long, tapering Door Peninsula on the west side of Lake Michigan. Along the opposite shore is the so-called Michigan fruit belt with apples, peaches, pears, and cherries. New York, in addition to its many orchards, is second only to California in grape production, with extensive vineyards along Lake Erie at the western end of the state and near the Finger Lakes. Peach orchards extend as far south along the East Coast as Georgia, but deciduous fruit trees require a frosty winter to complete their dormancy cycle, and this sets a limit on how far south such fruits can be grown.

In the humid belt extending one hundred miles inland from the Gulf of Mexico and including northern Florida, frosts are too rare for such fruits as peaches and too frequent for citrus fruits. In that zone tung trees imported from China have become an important crop. The trees produce seeds whose oil is used to make linoleum, oilcloth, and other products.

Other regions have proven particularly well suited to certain crops. In North Dakota and Minnesota flax is raised for seeds that produce linseed oil and for fiber that goes, not usually into linen (its traditional use), but into cigarette paper and money. The rich soil of the glacial lake bed around Saginaw Bay, one hundred miles north of Detroit, is ideal for sugar beets. The bluegrass region of north-central Kentucky is famous for the horses raised on the pastures where tall grasses are tinted blue when they blow in the wind. The grass prospers in part because of lime and phosphate in the soil derived from the underlying karst formations.

To the south of Kentucky, in the hilly region of central Tennessee, farming is largely confined to narrow ridge crests and short, narrow valleys, or hollows, with the slopes heavily wooded. Fields therefore tend to be long, narrow, and winding. A favorite crop is lespedeza, which can grow on soil poorer than that required by most pasture crops. It is a warm-climate legume with nitrogen-fixing nodules on its roots that enrich the soil. Its name apparently is derived from V. M. de Zespedes, governor of east Florida under Spanish rule. Lespedeza is also grown along the Gulf Coast.

In New England a remarkable feature of the Connecticut River valley is fields roofed with white cheesecloth to protect the tobacco crop from excessive sunlight. The tobacco leaves, after being dried in the long barns typical of that valley, are used to wrap cigars. As recently as 1955 large areas of the valley gleamed white with shade tobacco coverings, but by then the tobacco companies had found a cheaper way to produce cigar wrappers, forming a slurry from pulverized leaves of less sensitive tobacco species and baking them on sheets. By 1981 the 13,700 acres of tobacco planted in the valley in 1955 had dwindled to 3,200.

In the last century the opening of rich farmlands to the west led farmers to abandon rocky New England, and extensive areas there have reverted to forest. Only stone walls crisscrossing the forest floors bear witness to the labors of those who pioneered the land. Much of the Northeast has also become part of exurbia.

Nevertheless, as in other parts of the country handy to city markets, farmers produce vegetables or flowers (sometimes in long greenhouses), dairy products, eggs, and chickens. As in drylot cattle feeding, the production of eggs and chickens has become a highly automated business. Some farms turn out more than a million chickens a year.

New Jersey calls itself the Garden State because of its intensive production of vegetables—canned, frozen, or fresh—chiefly in the region east of Philadelphia and Camden, although it is chiefly Florida and the irrigated valleys of California that keep American supermarkets stocked with fresh vegetables throughout the winter.

37 THE PANORAMAS ABOVE

There are few, if any, structures of nature more awesome than a soaring thunderhead, particularly if one flies among such menacing giants when they are discharging lightning. Clouds and the play of light upon them, as in rainbows, parhelia, and—most fascinating of all—the glory, are an integral part of the American scene. Like meanders they are not unique to this continent, but as is the case with more local features of the scenery, they are far more interesting if understood.

Clouds, being produced by different, well-defined processes, fall into categories. But no two are alike and therein lies part of their beauty. Not only are they infinitely variable, but they are also eternally changing.

The most spectacular, seen from either aloft or the ground, are the towering anvil clouds that rise above fully developed thunderstorms and nudge the stratosphere. Soaring air currents inside the storm sometimes exceed sixty miles per hour and can lift the rounded thunderheads higher than normal flight altitudes, into strong horizontal winds, usually from west to east, that sweep their tops into the tapering point of an anvil. The thunderhead updrafts are driven by energy that is produced as rain within them condenses, releasing latent heat that makes the air warmer and more buoyant than the surrounding air. At the top of the storm these soaring cloud turrets encounter dry air. Some cloud droplets evaporate, cooling the cloud, which sinks back again. Turrets are therefore constantly rising and sinking.

While updrafts that build the towering clouds make it rough going for aircraft that penetrate them, at least equally hazardous are "downbursts" of cold air dropping out of the storms near the ground. In recent years at least three airline crashes during takeoff or landing have been blamed on such sudden downdrafts.

Puffy, fair-weather clouds form in rising currents of warm air, but on a far smaller scale. A plowed field warmed by the sun may be enough to set the process in motion. The rising air is initially clear, but expands as the air pressure decreases at higher elevations. This lowers its temperature until the saturation level, or dew point, of water vapor in the air is reached, whereupon the vapor condenses into cloud droplets. The cloud continues soaring until the droplets evaporate. Sometimes, as far as one can see in all directions, the fair-weather clouds are flat on the bottom as though cut

off by some mysterious process. Their bottoms mark the lowest level where condensation can occur in the rising air.

The featureless cloud sheets that cover the sky from horizon to horizon, often shedding steady rain or snow, are produced by uniformly rising air, commonly where a body of warm air—a "warm front"—is pushing over a narrow wedge of cold air near the ground. A slow-moving cold front can also cause such a rise of warm air, but a fast-moving cold front produces a narrow line of showers or thunderstorms.

Aircraft climbing or descending between ground level and 30,000 feet may pass through a succession of cloud layers with clear air between each. They usually occur in cyclonic systems, where air is spiraling inward toward a center of low pressure and rising air. The spiral flow throughout the Northern Hemisphere is counterclockwise (being in the opposite direction south of the equator). Such systems, hundreds of miles wide, tend to move across the continent from west to east. A diversion for air travelers unable to see the ground is to trace such a system with the aid of that day's weather map. To someone on the ground, the first indication that a cyclonic system is approaching may be high, wispy streaks of cirrus cloud (formed of tiny ice crystals rather than droplets).

Left: A major storm over southeast Colorado, photographed from Denver. (Charles Semmer, National Center for Atmospheric Research)

Right: Hurricane Gladys photographed from Apollo 7, *rotating counterclockwise as it crossed the Gulf of Mexico toward Florida.* (NASA)

A particularly unstable situation may develop, especially during spring afternoons over the Great Plains and Mississippi Valley. A mass of cold polar air that has crossed the Rockies and has remained aloft, instead of hugging the ground like most cold fronts, rides over warm humid air moving north from the Gulf of Mexico. Warm air pushes upward in a rapid overturning process that generates violent thunderstorms and, frequently, tornadoes.

Strikingly lens-shaped clouds are sometimes produced when clear air passing over a mountain is lifted enough to condense its water vapor. Downwind of the mountain the air drops back to its original elevation, the droplets evaporate, and the air becomes clear again. The result is a cloud that seems to hang motionless over the mountain like a silvery cap. The mountaineer who assumes from this that there is no wind on the summit is in for an unpleasant surprise.

More common are elongated clouds that form in the same manner over a range of mountains, or even hills, and are then repeated in a succession of roll-shaped clouds downwind. The mountains set up a wave motion in the flowing air that produces a succession of clouds as the air repeatedly rises to higher elevation. Ranks of such clouds may extend for a hundred miles or more in the lee of a mountain range. Sometimes, when one flies over parallel ranges such as those in the Appalachians, the ranges are mimicked in the sky by a succession of long clouds hanging over each one.

A form of wave motion high in the atmosphere responsible for severe jostling of airliners is known as clear-air turbulence or CAT. It has been blamed for several aircraft accidents and is insidious because, being in the clear air that prevails near the bottom of the stratosphere, it does not normally produce cloud structures that can serve as a warning. On rare occasions, however, one can see cloud tops resembling a uniform succession of breaking waves. These are so-called Kelvin-Helmholtz waves produced by turbulence between air masses moving in opposite directions or at different speeds relative to one another. It is suspected that such conflicting air motions are responsible for CAT. The latter occurs not only downwind from mountains but in the border region between the lower part of the atmosphere, or troposphere, and the stratosphere above it. Wind velocities at that level sometimes reach 200 miles per hour. Such a "jet stream" may form at elevations ranging from 30,000 to 50,000 feet, depending on latitude and season. Yet only a few thousand feet higher there may be only light winds, producing the relative air motions or "shear" responsible for CAT.

Cap cloud over Mount Shasta in northern California. (John S. Shelton)

Cloud "streets" form in parallel rows, but unlike the long clouds that arise in the lee of mountains, they are aligned with the wind instead of across it. Furthermore, the "streets" are formed of puffy little clouds, rather than the dense rolls of mountain-lee clouds. They originate from the same rising warm-air currents that produce other fair-weather clouds but within a rather shallow layer of the atmosphere. Hence they form primarily over flat regions, such as the Great Plains or the ocean, where surface features do not perturb the uniformity of air circulation within the cloud-producing layer.

While a variety of processes cause clouds to form in long, parallel avenues, an illusion common to them all, when observed from the ground, is that the avenues seem to converge toward the horizon. It is a perspective effect like that when a highway seems to narrow in the distance.

Those riding an airliner above a cloud deck are apt to open a book or watch the movie, unaware of the wonder that may be visible below—a "glory" or small rainbow enclosing the plane's shadow. The glory is a vision that has terrified mountaineers and fascinated physicists. When the plane's shadow is cast onto a cloud layer or fog bank whose water droplets are of fairly uniform size, sunlight coming from directly behind the viewer's head is scattered almost directly backward, but at angles that differ slightly, depending on the wavelength of the light. Thus sunlight is split into its component colors, forming a tiny, multicolored ring that encircles the shadow. The innermost ring, like that in a regular rainbow, is violet and the outermost is red. On rare occasions several circles of rainbow colors form, one inside the other.

The glory often sits, like a glowing spearhead, at the front end of the long, narrow shadow cast by the plane's contrail. The shadow of the plane is superimposed on a bright region inside the circle of color. The vision can be awesome on a descent, the glory getting bigger and bigger until the plane plunges into it.

The term "glory" is also sometimes applied to the halo painted around the head of a holy person in both oriental and occidental religious images, and this may derive from the experience of those who, on a mountain summit above a cloud bank, see what seems an enormous human—or superhuman—shadow image projected onto the cloud, its head surrounded by a many-colored halo.

For centuries such apparitions were associated with witchcraft and the supernatural. It put the stamp of Satan on the Brocken, highest summit of the Hartz Mountains just east of the border between East and West Germany. The "Brocken Specter" observed from the mountaintop when a cloud bank lay opposite a sunset or sunrise was greatly feared. It was believed that on the eve of May 1, the feast of Saint Walburga, the witches of the world gathered there to dance and worship the devil. The superstitious peasants called it *Walpurgisnacht* and affixed crosses to livestock stalls, lest the witches carry off their animals.

A glory can sometimes be seen from the heights along the Big Sur coast of California. In his book *Big Sur and the Oranges of Hieronymus Bosch* Henry Miller describes such an experience: "If it be shortly after sunup of a morning when the fog has obliterated the highway below, I am then rewarded with a spectacle rare to witness. Looking up the coast . . . the sun rising behind me throws an enlarged shadow of me into the iridescent fog below. I lift my arms as in prayer, achieving a

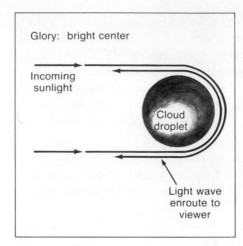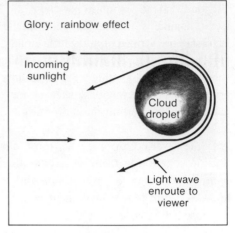

Optics of the glory: The brilliant white center is formed by rays of all wavelengths returning along the path of incoming sunlight (left). Much the same effect is produced by tiny beads in reflective paint. Rays that do not return directly along the incoming route (as shown right) travel slightly different distances as they circle the droplets in opposite directions. Therefore, when they meet again for the return trip, they can suppress or reinforce one another, depending on wavelength. This sorts out the colors, forming the rainbow.

wingspan no god ever possessed, and there in the drifting fog a nimbus floats about my head, a radiant nimbus such as the Buddha himself might proudly wear.''

Actually the specter is no larger than the person whose shadow is cast. It probably looks huge because the mind subconsciously assumes the shadow is much more distant and therefore ''sees'' it as big. The same effect is thought to explain why the image of the moon appears deceptively large near the horizon.

The optical effect that produces a glory can also lead the observer to believe he or she enjoys divine favoritism. If several people are standing side by side, each will see the halo around his or her own head and not that of anyone else. Each can feel privately blessed. Likewise, while all passengers on the side of an aircraft away from the sun may observe a glory (with the plane, rather than their heads, in the center), each will see one produced by a different constellation of droplets.

When ordinary rainbows are seen from the air they form a complete circle or two concentric circles. The manner of their production differs from that responsible for a glory, which is smaller. The rainbow is produced by drops that bend and reflect light waves back at an angle of roughly 42 degrees from their direction of arrival. The red waves, being longest, are bent the most, forming the outer ring. Waves of shorter wavelength are bent less, violet being the least affected. The effect is to produce a series of concentric rings in rainbow colors (the sequence of colors in the outer ring being reversed). The light waves producing a glory make a U-turn around each droplet, returning back toward the light source. This special feature of the glory, in which light waves travel around the curved surface of the droplet, is a phenomenon not well known even among physicists. It accounts for the brightness of the central bull's-eye area onto which the plane's shadow is cast.

Light waves circling droplets slightly to one side of this central area return to the

Anvil cloud forming at a very high altitude over North Dakota. (Carol Unkenholz, courtesy Richard S. Scorer)

viewer in a manner that sorts out the colors. The part of a wave that circles the droplet in one direction and returns toward the observer travels a slightly different distance from the part that goes around the droplet via the opposite route. When they meet for the return journey they can either reinforce one another, where wave crest meets wave crest, or cancel each other where crest meets trough—the process known as interference. Which wavelength (that is, color) is reinforced in this manner depends on the difference in distance traveled by light circling the droplets in opposite directions. This, in turn, depends on how far the droplets are to one side of the central area. It is this that sorts out the colors in rainbowlike sequence. Where several concentric glories are seen, the outer ones are apparently produced by light waves that have made more than one trip around the droplet. To produce a glory, billions of droplets are required, but there are plenty in a cloud or fog bank. The angle at which a droplet sends back a certain color depends on its size, and therefore the droplets must be of uniform size, otherwise neighboring droplets would produce different colors, canceling the effect.

A related phenomenon is the halo often seen around the sun or moon. It is produced by the tiny ice crystals in high cirrus clouds. Typically such a ring is 22 degrees of arc in radius, the light (in this case from behind) having been bent that much by the six-sided crystals. Sometimes there is an outer ring 46 degrees in radius produced by a less efficient form of light bending. Sometimes only those parts of the halo to either side of the sun or moon are visible, producing ''mock suns'' or ''sun dogs.'' These are parhelia. While they are most common in the frigid skies of the polar regions, this writer, approaching New York City on the Long Island Expressway, has seen magnificent, long-lasting examples.

The cloud types and celestial phenomena described above are only a selection of the more dramatic ones to be seen in American skies. An Icelandic visitor to the East Coast once complained to me that the environment in which most Americans live, hemmed in by trees and buildings, hid the grandest of all panoramas—the sky. He longed for relatively treeless Iceland. There is no doubt that for those who cross the Great Plains, as for travelers across the sea, it is overhead that the grandeur lies.

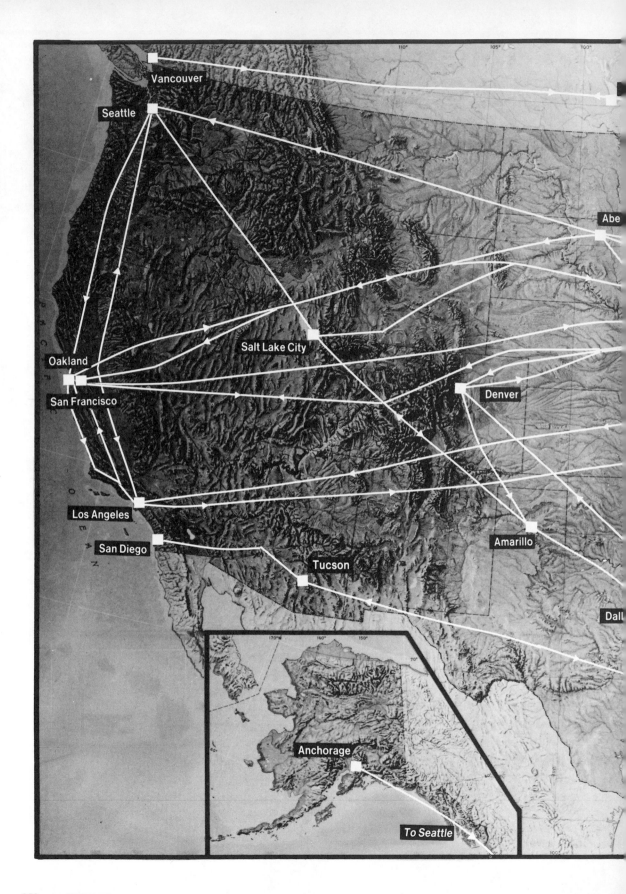

The Most Frequently Traveled Air Routes

ITINERARIES

The following are checklists, with occasional chapter references, for features along some of the more heavily traveled air routes. Flights, however, sometimes use alternate routes. West of the Mississippi westbound flights may avoid the jet stream; eastbound flights may seek it out. Wide-bodied aircraft in the West may fly direct routes under inertial guidance, but these often are close to the charted routes. Airport approach and departure paths are not described in the checklists, as they vary depending upon runways in use. Not listed are features appearing on many routes, such as river meanders, areas of intensive center-pivot irrigation, ice age relicts across the north-central states, and the checkerboard of the Great Plains. Where no routing in the opposite direction is shown, the route is usually the same in both directions. The sequence is therefore presented as a list that can also be read from the bottom up. The routes are shown on the preceding two pages.

ANCHORAGE TO SEATTLE

Reverse of Seattle–Anchorage route.

ATLANTA TO CHICAGO

Brevard Zone west of Atlanta; across south end of Blue Ridge (Chapter 4);
Across Great Appalachian Valley; Chattanooga to west;
Tennessee River; TVA impoundments (Chapter 25);
Cumberland Plateau;
East Tennessee strip mining (Chapter 31);
East side of Mammoth Cave karst region in Kentucky (Chapter 30);
Ohio River at Louisville, Kentucky;
Indianapolis to east;
Lafayette, Indiana.

ATLANTA TO MIAMI

Gainesville to east;
Circular karst ponds (Chapter 30) and old beach lines, far inland;
Lakeland;
Phosphate strip mines and slime ponds south of Bartow and east of Tampa/Saint Petersburg (Chapter 31);
West of Lake Okeechobee and over Everglades (Chapter 27).

ATLANTA TO NEW YORK
(Kennedy Airport)

Follows Houston–New York route.

ATLANTA TO NEW YORK
(LaGuardia Airport)

Spartanburg/Greenville, South Carolina;
Richmond, Virginia;
East of Washington and Philadelphia.

BOSTON TO NEW YORK
(LaGuardia Airport)

Northwest corner of Rhode Island;
Across Lake Char Fault (Chapter 5) at Danielson, Connecticut;
Hartford–Waterbury–Danbury–South Salem, New York.

CHICAGO TO ATLANTA

Terre Haute, Indiana;
Kentucky-Tennessee strip-mining zone (Chapter 31);
TVA coal-fired power plant west of Bowling Green, Kentucky—largest when built;
Nashville, Tennessee;
Cumberland Plateau (Chapter 4);
Tennessee River TVA impoundments (Chapter 25);

Great Appalachian Valley east of Chattanooga;

South end of Blue Ridge;

Across Brevard Zone at Atlanta (Chapter 4).

CHICAGO TO DENVER

Joliet;

Across Mississippi River at Rock Island, Illinois;

Des Moines, Iowa;

Across Missouri River north of Omaha, Nebraska; loess hills east of river (Chapter 29);

Along Platte River to Columbus, Nebraska;

At North Platte, across Platte River and Oregon Trail (Chapter 32); Sand Hills of Nebraska to north (Chapter 29);

Along, but south of, South Platte River to Sterling, Colorado, and Denver.

CHICAGO TO LOS ANGELES

Same route as Chicago–Denver to central Nebraska;

Across Oregon Trail (Chapter 32) at Lake C. W. McConaughy on North Platte River;

Across Front Range north of Fort Collins, Colorado (Chapter 15);

Medicine Bow Mountains;

Across Park Range at Rabbit Ears Pass;

Green River, north of Canyonlands (Chapter 12);

Capitol Reef; Waterpocket Monocline to south (Chapter 13);

Bryce Canyon;

Grand Canyon to south;

Lake Mead;

Hoover Dam on Colorado River (Chapter 25), Las Vegas to north;

Across southern Basin and Range Province (Chapter 13); Mojave Desert to north.

CHICAGO TO NEW ORLEANS

West of Kankakee;

Champaign/Urbana;

Centralia, Illinois;

Across Mississippi River at Cape Girardeau,

Missouri (Chapter 24);

Along Mississippi to Memphis; oxbows and curving features (Chapter 24);

South of Memphis along Bluff Hills that drop abruptly to flood plain on west (Chapter 29);

Jackson, Mississippi;

Along Pearl River to Lake Ponchartrain.

CHICAGO (Midway or O'Hare airports) TO NEW YORK (Kennedy Airport)

Kalamazoo, Michigan;

Detroit to north;

Across Lake Erie to Erie, Pennsylvania;

Chautauqua, New York;

Susquehanna River and anthracite coal fields near Wilkes-Barre (Chapter 4);

Delaware River north of Water Gap.

CHICAGO (Midway or O'Hare airports) TO NEW YORK (LaGuardia Airport)

South Bend, Indiana;

Toledo, Ohio;

Southern tip of Lake Erie;

Cleveland to south;

Oil City and original Pennsylvania oil fields (Chapter 4);

Susquehanna River at Milton;

Williamsport to north;

Delaware Water Gap to north;

Across New Jersey.

CHICAGO TO PORTLAND

Same as Chicago–Seattle route between Chicago and Sioux Falls, South Dakota;

Oahe Reservoir on Missouri River in South Dakota (Chapter 25);

North end of Powder River coal basin in Montana;

Along Yellowstone River at Billings, Montana;

Boulder batholith south of open-pit mine at Butte (Chapters 18 and 31);

Between Clearwater and Salmon River Mountains of Idaho batholith;

Hells Canyon, Wrangellia Terrane, on Idaho-Oregon border (Chapter 10);

North of Wallowa Mountains, also part of Wrangellia Terrane;

Past Pendleton, Washington, along Columbia River, route of Spokane floods (Chapter 21) and outlet of flood basalts (Chapter 20);

The Dalles, terminus of Oregon Trail (Chapter 32);

Columbia River Gorge across Cascade Range;

Mount Adams and Mount Saint Helens to north; Mount Hood to south.

CHICAGO TO SAN FRANCISCO

Dubuque, Iowa;

Sioux City, Iowa;

Sand Hills of Nebraska (Chapter 29);

Across Oregon Trail and North Platte River south of Scotts Bluff (Chapter 32);

Cheyenne, Wyoming;

Medicine Bow Mountains (Chapter 16);

Uinta Mountains to north; over Dinosaur National Monument and Green River (Chapter 17);

Across Basin and Range Province including Wheeler Peak, 13,063 feet, on Utah-Nevada border (Chapter 13);

Between Mammoth Lakes on south and Mono Lake volcanic area (Chapter 13);

Multicolored salt basins in San Francisco Bay (Chapter 31).

CHICAGO TO SPOKANE AND SEATTLE

Mississippi River at Dubuque, Iowa (Chapter 24);

Fort Dodge, Iowa, in zone formerly covered by Des Moines ice lobe (Chapter 28);

Sioux Falls, South Dakota;

Aberdeen, South Dakota;

Oahe Reservoir on Missouri River (Chapter 25);

Miles City, Montana;

South of Great Falls;

Across former bed of Lake Missoula, source of the Spokane floods, in valleys south of Flathead Lake (Chapter 21);

Across Idaho batholith via Coeur d'Alene mining district (Chapter 18);

Spokane, Washington;

Scablands, cut by Spokane floods; Grand Coulee (Chapters 20, 21);

Cascade Range north of Mount Rainier (Chapter 19).

DALLAS TO DENVER

Ardmore, Texas;

Oklahoma City to east;

Liberal, Kansas;

Across high plains past Lamar, Colorado.

DALLAS/FORT WORTH TO NEW YORK

Route to Kennedy Airport almost the same as Kennedy to Dallas;

Route to LaGuardia:

Red River beyond Texarkana;

Greenville, Mississippi, on Mississippi River (Chapter 24);

Birmingham, Alabama;

Atlanta, Georgia;

Via Atlanta–New York (LaGuardia) route.

DALLAS TO SEATTLE

Reverse of Seattle–Dallas route.

DENVER TO CHICAGO

Akron, Colorado;

Hayes Center, Nebraska;

Across Platte River and Oregon Trail (Chapter 32) between North Platte and Kearney, Nebraska;

Across Missouri River between Omaha, Nebraska, and Sioux City, Iowa; loess hills on east side of river (Chapter 29);

Across Des Moines River and former area of Des Moines ice lobe north of Des Moines (Chapter 28);

Across Mississippi River at Dubuque, Iowa.

DENVER TO DALLAS

Along Front Range past Colorado Springs to

Pueblo (Chapter 15);
Across high plains to Amarillo, Texas, on
Llano Estacado (Chapter 12);
Along Red River past Wichita Falls, Texas.

FORT LAUDERDALE

See Miami

FORT MYERS, FLORIDA TO WASHINGTON

Reverse of Washington–Fort Myers route.

HOUSTON TO NEW YORK

Eastward along coast;
Mississippi River at New Orleans (Chapter
24);
Mobile, Alabama;
Montgomery, Alabama;
Atlanta, Georgia; Brevard Zone skirts city
on west (Chapter 4);
Between Brevard Zone and Carolina Slate
Belt, past Greenville, South Carolina, and
Lynchburg, Virginia (Chapter 4);
Charlottesville, Virginia, to west;
Via Washington–New York route.

HOUSTON TO SAN DIEGO

Austin;
Fort Stockton and west Texas oil fields
(Chapter 31);
El Paso; south end of Rio Grande rift (Chap-
ter 14);
Tucson, Arizona; open-pit copper mines
nearby (Chapter 31);
Gila River to Gila Bend;
North of Cerro del Pinacate lava field (Chap-
ter 13);
Across Colorado River at Yuma;
Along All American Canal south of Imperial
Valley; dune fields to north and south
(Chapters 11, 25, 29, 34, and 36);
Coast Ranges.

LOS ANGELES TO CHICAGO

Reverse of Chicago–Los Angeles route.

LOS ANGELES TO NEW YORK

Palm Springs;
Joshua Tree National Monument;
Colorado River Aqueduct from Lake Havasu
(Chapter 25);
Colorado River at Parker Dam;
Prescott, Arizona;
Along Mogollon Rim at Sedona (Chapter 12)
with San Francisco Peaks to north (Chap-
ter 13);
Meteor Crater (Chapter 23) and Painted Des-
ert;
Gallup, New Mexico;
Valles caldera and Los Alamos to south;
Rio Grande rift (Chapter 14);
Taos; open-pit molybdenum mine to north in
Sangre de Cristo Mountains;
Along part of Santa Fe Trail in Oklahoma
panhandle (Chapter 32);
Beyond Wichita: Flint Hills of Kansas
(Chapter 36);
Lake of the Ozarks and Ozark Mountains to
the south (Chapter 30);
Strip coal mines on Kansas-Missouri border
(Chapter 31);
Junction of Missouri and Mississippi rivers
at St. Louis;
Cincinnati, Ohio, to north;
Across Ohio River;
Strip coal mines near Charleston, West Vir-
ginia;
Across Blue Ridge at south end of Skyline
Drive (Chapter 4);
Charlottesville;
South of Washington;
Over Cape May, New Jersey, and ocean to
Kennedy Airport.

LOS ANGELES TO SAN FRANCISCO

Santa Barbara;
Across Santa Ynez Mountains, part of the
Stanley Terrane (Chapter 10) and other
Coast Ranges;
Paso Robles and up Salinas Valley to Salinas
and Monterey Bay; Santa Lucia Range on
left; Gabilan Range, part of Salinia Ter-
rane, on right (Chapter 11);

Santa Cruz;
Across Santa Cruz Mountains and San Andreas Fault to San Francisco Bay.

LOS ANGELES TO SEATTLE

Reverse of Seattle–Los Angeles route.

MIAMI TO ATLANTA

Everglades and Lake Okeechobee (Chapter 27);
Karst ponds near Orlando (Chapter 30);
Along Saint Johns River, barrier islands to east (Chapter 30);
Jacksonville;
Across Coastal Plain to fall line at Macon, Georgia (Chapter 4);
Across Charlotte Belt and Inner Piedmont to Brevard Zone at Atlanta.

MIAMI TO NEW YORK (Kennedy Airport)

Reverse of New York (Kennedy)–Miami route.

MIAMI TO NEW YORK (LaGuardia Airport)

Reverse of New York (LaGuardia)–Miami route as far as Richmond, Virginia;
East of Washington;
Via Washington–LaGuardia route.

NEW ORLEANS TO CHICAGO

Follows Chicago–New Orleans route as far as Memphis;
Along Mississippi River;
East of St. Louis;
Springfield, Illinois.

NEW YORK (LaGuardia and Kennedy airports) TO ATLANTA

Same as route to Houston as far as Pulaski in Appalachian Great Valley in southwest Virginia;
Along Brevard Zone (Chapter 4) past Spartanburg/Greenville, South Carolina.

NEW YORK (LaGuardia Airport) TO BOSTON

Long Island Sound to New Haven, New London, Providence;
Out over Massachusetts Bay at Scituate;
Many Boston Harbor islands are drumlins (Chapter 28).

NEW YORK (Kennedy Airport) TO CHICAGO (Midway or O'Hare airports)

Trenton, New Jersey;
Susquehanna River north of Harrisburg;
Across Appalachian folds and Appalachian Plateau (Chapter 4);
Coal fields north of Pittsburgh;
Cleveland to north;
Fort Wayne, Indiana.

NEW YORK (LaGuardia Airport) TO CHICAGO (O'Hare Airport)

Along the New York–New Jersey border;
Across Appalachian folds, Delaware River;
Wilkes-Barre anthracite coal fields (Chapter 4) to south;
Elmira, Finger Lakes (fjords) to north;
From Dunkirk, New York, across Lake Erie;
London, Ontario, to north;
Flint, Michigan, Lansing, Michigan, to south;
Across Lake Michigan.

NEW YORK TO DALLAS/FORT WORTH

Same as New York–Houston route as far as Front Royal, Virginia;
Southwest across Blue Ridge;
Meandering Shenandoah River in Appalachian Great Valley (Chapters 4 and 24);
Across Valley and Ridge Province;
Pine Mountain overthrust on left (Chapter 4);
Strip mines on west side of Appalachians before Nashville (Chapter 31);

Memphis on Mississippi River (Chapter 24);
Little Rock on Arkansas River.

NEW YORK TO HOUSTON

Parallel to but west of New York (LaGuardia)–Washington route;
Dulles International Airport to east;
Along Blue Ridge and Appalachian Great Valley to Roanoke, Virginia;
Pulaski, Virginia;
Pine Mountain overthrust (Chapter 4) between Pulaski and Knoxville, Tennessee; many TVA impoundments (Chapter 25);
Great Smoky Mountains on left at Knoxville;
Chattanooga, Tennessee;
Birmingham, Alabama;
Meridian, Mississippi;
Bluff Hills drop abruptly to flood plain before crossing Mississippi River north of Baton Rouge, Louisiana (Chapters 24 and 29);
Sabine River at Orange, Texas;
Neches River near Beaumont.

NEW YORK TO LOS ANGELES

Lancaster, Pennsylvania;
Harrisburg and multiple water gaps where Susquehanna River cuts through Appalachian folds to the north (Chapter 4); across the river near Three Mile Island;
Contour strip farming (Chapter 35);
North of Chambersburg and Gettysburg battlefields;
Ohio River at Wheeling, Ohio;
In eastern Ohio county lines and some roads run east of true north, dating from initial phase of national survey (Chapter 32);
Cambridge, Ohio; strip mine twelve miles to the south;
At Columbus: the Scioto River, which flows south but was channel of the north-flowing Teays River (Chapter 28);
Indianapolis;
Mississippi River south of Hannibal, Missouri;
Along Missouri River before Kansas City;
West of Kansas City the Oregon and Santa Fe trails diverged (Chapter 32);
Topeka, Kansas;

Spanish Peaks, prominent twin volcanoes in Colorado, to south shortly before crossing Sangre de Cristo Mountains south of Blanca Peak (Chapter 15);
San Luis Valley, Great Sand Dunes to north;
Shiprock, New Mexico (Chapter 13);
Across Black Mesa in northeast Arizona; Peabody Coal Company strip mine;
Across southern end of Echo Cliffs monocline (Chapter 12) at Tuba City;
Along south rim of Grand Canyon;
Lake Mojave on the Colorado River;
Southern Basin and Range Province (Chapter 13); along San Bernardino and San Gabriel mountains.

NEW YORK (Kennedy Airport) TO MIAMI

Atlantic City, New Jersey;
Cape May;
Along Delmarva Peninsula;
Across mouth of Chesapeake Bay to Norfolk, Virginia;
Wilmington, North Carolina;
Over water;
Along barrier islands from east of Palm Beach to Miami (Chapter 27).

NEW YORK (LaGuardia Airport) TO MIAMI

Atlantic City, New Jersey, to east;
Dover, Delaware;
Across Chesapeake Bay to Patuxent, Maryland;
Fall Line at Richmond, Virginia (Chapter 4);
Coastal Plain; occasional Carolina "bays" (Chapter 30); to Wilmington, North Carolina;
Over water;
Along barrier islands from east of Palm Beach to Miami (Chapter 27).

NEW YORK TO PHOENIX

Same as New York–Los Angeles routing as far as northern New Mexico, then southwest across Arizona;
Across Roosevelt Lake, Roosevelt Dam (Chapter 25) near Phoenix;

Superstition lava field east of the city.

NEW YORK TO SALT LAKE CITY

Reverse of Salt Lake City–New York route.

NEW YORK TO SAN FRANCISCO

Buffalo, south of Niagara Falls;
London, Ontario;
Southern tip of Lake Huron;
Saginaw, Michigan;
Lake Michigan;
Green Bay, Wisconsin;
Formerly glaciated region in Wisconsin and
   Minnesota (Chapter 28);
Mississippi River at Minneapolis;
Oahe Reservoir on Missouri River in South
   Dakota (Chapter 25);
Black Hills to south; Devils Tower National
   Monument to north;
Gillette, Wyoming; strip mines (Chapter 31);
Big Horn Mountains in Wyoming;
Wyoming basins (Chapter 16); humped lay-
   ers of Little Dome exposed like an onion
   cross section;
Gannett Peak in Wind River Range (Chapter
   17);
Red Rock Pass north of Great Salt Lake,
   where Lake Bonneville broke through
   (Chapter 21);
Across Basin and Range Province in Ne-
   vada;
Lateral moraines flanking Green Creek on
   east side of Sierra Nevada (Chapter 28);
East wall of Sierra Nevada north of Mono
   Lake craters (Chapter 13); Yosemite;
Small patch of Cache Creek Terrane near
   Sonora (Chapter 10);
Modesto;
Colored salt ponds in San Francisco Bay
   (Chapter 31).

NEW YORK TO TORONTO

Middletown, New York;
Along Delaware River forming New York–
   Pennsylvania border;
Binghamton, New York;
Rochester, New York, with many drumlins

to the east (Chapter 28);
Across Lake Ontario.

NEW YORK (LaGuardia Airport) TO WASHINGTON (National Airport)

Along Watchung Mountains (Chapter 7),
   west of Newark;
New Brunswick; first hints of Appalachian
   folds to west; break on horizon is Delaware Water Gap;
Philadelphia to east;
Extensive contour strip farming (Chapter 35)
   on both sides of Susquehanna River south
   of Lancaster; triple domes of Three Mile
   Island nuclear plant upstream on right;
Approach down Potomac River passes over
   the long, narrow building of the David
   Taylor Model Basin where the navy tests
   hull designs; approach up the Potomac
   passes Naval Research Laboratory on
   right with dish antenna on roof.

PHOENIX TO NEW YORK

Reverse of New York–Phoenix route.

PORTLAND TO CHICAGO

Reverse of Chicago–Portland route.

SALT LAKE CITY TO NEW YORK

World's largest open-pit mine southwest of
   the city (Chapter 31);
Across Wasatch Range along Mormon Pio-
   neer trail to Fort Bridger;
Green River, Wyoming, at north end of
   Flaming Gorge Reservoir, where Powell
   began his journey (Chapter 17);
Uinta Mountains to the south;
Oil fields nearby in Rock Springs area
   (Chapter 31);
Across Wyoming basins (Chapter 16);
   open-pit uranium mine near Jeffrey City to
   north;
Pathfinder Dam and reservoir on North
   Platte River (Chapter 25);
Along that river to Casper, Wyoming;

Across Black Hills to Rapid City, South Dakota;
Along remaining San Francisco–New York
route.

SAN DIEGO TO HOUSTON

Reverse of Houston–San Diego route.

SAN FRANCISCO TO CHICAGO

Reverse of Chicago–San Francisco route.

SAN FRANCISCO TO LOS ANGELES

Along coast to Monterey; Big Sur; San Luis
Obispo;
Along Santa Ynez Mountains to Santa Bar-
bara (Chapter 11);
Along coast to Los Angeles.

SAN FRANCISCO TO NEW YORK

Sacramento;
Placerville gold mining area to south (Chap-
ter 31);
Sierra Nevada at Donner Pass; Lake Tahoe
to south;
Reno; Walker Lake to north; across Carson
Sink (sometimes flooded);
Across Basin and Range Province (Chapters
10 and 13); two open-pit mines at Battle
Mountain, Nevada (Chapter 31);
Gannett Peak in Wind River Range, Wyo-
ming;
Little Dome, whose humped layers have
been exposed like an onion cross section
(Chapter 16);
South end of Big Horn Mountains (Chapter
17);
Gillette, Wyoming; strip mines for coal in
Powder River basin;
Black Hills; Rapid City on east edge;
Badlands National Monument east of Rapid
City, South Dakota (Chapter 21);
Fort Randall Reservoir on Missouri River
(Chapter 25);
Sioux Falls;
Mississippi River where joined by Wiscon-
sin River at Prairie du Chien;
Locally unglaciated region before Madison,
Wisconsin (Chapter 28);
Drumlin fields, moraines, glaciated terrain
between Madison and Milwaukee, exten-
sive dairying (Chapters 28 and 36);
Across Lake Michigan and Michigan Penin-
sula to Detroit;
Across Lake Erie to Chautauqua, New York;
Appalachians in northern Pennsylvania;
Susquehanna River between Scranton and
Wilkes-Barre;
Across northern New Jersey.

SAN FRANCISCO TO SEATTLE

Reverse of Seattle–San Francisco route.

SEATTLE TO ANCHORAGE

Vancouver Island, west of Vancouver;
Queen Charlotte Islands to west, Coast
Mountains of British Columbia to east;
all these islands are part of Wrangellia
Terrane (Chapter 10);
Alexander Archipelago to east, part of Alex-
ander Terrane; across south end of straight
250-mile fjord (Chapter 10);
Saint Elias Mountains to east: Mount Logan
(highest, 120 miles away), Mount Saint
Elias, (100 miles); Bering Glacier on coast
(Chapter 28);
Prince William Sound, Kenai Peninsula to
west; Prince William Terrane.

SEATTLE TO CHICAGO

Reverse of Chicago–Seattle route as far as
Aberdeen, South Dakota;
Southwest corner of Minnesota;
East of Mason City, Iowa: formerly covered
by Des Moines ice lobe (Chapter 28);
Mississippi River north of Dubuque.

SEATTLE TO DALLAS

Across Cascade Range south of Mount Rainier;
Across Columbia River near McNary Dam;

Wallula Gap to north (Chapter 21);
Pendleton, Oregon;
Across Hells Canyon (Chapter 10);
Along Snake River Plain, route of Oregon
Trail, from Boise, to Twin Falls, Idaho
(Chapters 20 and 32);
Riverbed scoured by Bonneville flood at
Twin Falls (Chapter 20);
Great Salt Lake (Chapter 20);
Southwest of Salt Lake City, world's largest
open-pit mine (Chapter 31);
Across Wasatch Range and south of Uinta
Mountains (Chapter 17);
Grand Junction and Colorado National
Monument;
Black Canyon of Gunnison River (Chapter
17);
Between Sawatch Range and San Juan
Mountains (Chapter 15);
San Luis Valley; Rio Grande; south of Great
Sand Dunes National Monument (Chap-
ters 14 and 29);
Sangre de Cristo Mountains;
Along Santa Fe Trail east of the mountains
(Chapter 32);
Amarillo, Texas;
Along Red River to Wichita Falls.

SEATTLE TO LOS ANGELES

Across Columbia River at Portland, Oregon,
path of lava floods and Spokane flood
(Chapters 20 and 21);
Along Cascade Range volcano chain (Chap-
ter 19); Mounts Rainier, Adams, Saint
Helens, Hood, etc., to east;
Across Cascade chain north of Klamath
Falls;
Crater Lake to west;
Upper Klamath Lake and Klamath Falls;
Lava Beds National Monument in northern
California (Chapter 19);
Mount Shasta and Lassen Peak to west;
Down Great Valley past Stockton, Califor-
nia; Sierra Nevada to east.

SEATTLE TO SAN FRANCISCO

Entire route west of and parallel to Cascade
Range (Chapter 19);
Olympia, Washington;

Columbia River at Kelso;
Portland to east;
Along Willamette River to Eugene, Oregon;
Rogue River near Medford, Oregon;
Klamath River northwest of Yreka, Califor-
nia;
Klamath Mountains (Chapter 10);
Clair Engle Lake and Trinity Dam to east;
Along Coast Ranges west of Sacramento
Valley and over Yolla Bolly Middle Eel
Wilderness (Chapter 10);
Clear Lake east of Ukiah;
Sonoma and Marin counties.

TORONTO TO NEW YORK

Reverse of New York–Toronto route except
final leg crosses Brewster, New York.

TORONTO TO VANCOUVER

Sault Sainte Marie at east end of Lake Supe-
rior; on east-bound flights four or five
Great Lakes visible;
Across Lake Superior and Isle Royale to
Thunder Bay;
Large open-pit mine near Atikokan;
Lake of the Woods, many other lakes;
Winnipeg, Manitoba; across former bed of
Lake Agassiz south of Lake Winnipeg and
Lake Manitoba (Chapter 21);
Brandon, Manitoba;
Regina and Moose Jaw, Saskatchewan;
Medicine Hat, Alberta;
Near Lethbridge, Alberta, many flood-
scoured gorges (Chapter 21) and loess
hills (Chapter 29);
Across Front Range of Rocky Mountains;
Waterton Lakes National Park; Glacier
National Park in United States to south;
deep valleys cut through Lewis Thrust to
younger rocks beneath (Chapter 18);
Near Alberta–British Columbia border,
many coal mines; landslide buried a min-
ing town;
Cranbrook, British Columbia, at south end
of Rocky Mountain Trench (Chapter 18);
Kootenay Lake, Nelson Range, and Nelson;
Lower Arrow Lake on Columbia River;
Penticton at south end of Okanagan Lake;
Across Cascade Range (Chapter 19), Mount

Garibaldi to north, Mount Hood to south;
Along Fraser River.

VANCOUVER TO TORONTO

Reverse of Toronto–Vancouver routing.

WASHINGTON TO FORT MYERS, FLORIDA

Richmond, Virginia;
Along Piedmont from Raleigh, North Carolina, to Columbia, South Carolina;
Carolina "Bays" beyond the Fall Line to southeast (Chapter 30);
More bays before crossing Savannah River between Savannah and Augusta, Georgia;
Lake City, Florida;
Lakeland; phosphate strip mines and slime ponds (Chapter 31).

WASHINGTON (National Airport) TO NEW YORK (LaGuardia Airport)

After takeoff, usually a fine view of L'Enfant's plan for Washington;
Up Chesapeake Bay; Baltimore on left—its street plan is a grid, even in older part of the city (Chapter 33);
Dike encloses polygonal settlement basin embracing both Hart and Millers islands northeast of Baltimore, used for dredged spoil;
Army's Aberdeen Proving Ground on left;
Chesapeake and Delaware Canal on Intracoastal Waterway links north end of the bay with Delaware River (Chapter 27);
Wilmington and Philadelphia on left;
Trenton; McGuire Air Force Base, and Fort Dix on right;
Exercise tracks on horse farms;
Past Sandy Hook (Chapter 27) and out over New York Bay.

REFERENCES

Listed below are some of the books that were most useful in preparation of this book, as well as some that might be helpful to readers. Not included are standard geologic textbooks and the more technical source material. As noted below, some states publish highway guides for specific routes. The Bureau of Mines publishes visitor guides to mining and mineral operations by regions. They are available from the Superintendent of Documents, U.S. Government Printing Office, Washington, D.C. Local geologic guides are often available at national parks and national monuments. Regional geological maps are published by the states and the U.S. Geological Survey as are geological highway maps by the American Association of Petroleum Geologists, P.O. Box 979, Tulsa, Oklahoma. Mountain Press Publishing Company, P.O. Box 2399, Missoula, Montana, publishes roadside geology guides for Arizona, northern California, Colorado, the northern Rockies, Oregon, Texas, and Washington. For those seeking detailed flight routes the Mark Map Co., 20 South Havana Street, Aurora, Colorado, publishes *The Captain's Atlas* in separate editions for high- and low-altitude routes.

GENERAL REFERENCES

Duffus, Robert L. *The Santa Fe Trail*. Albuquerque: University of New Mexico, 1972; Franzwa, Gregory M. *The Oregon Trail Revisited*. Gerald, Missouri: Patrice Press, 1978; Hart, John Fraser. *The Look of the Land*. Englewood Cliffs, New Jersey: Prentice-Hall, 1975; Hunter, Louis C. *A History of Industrial Power in the United States, 1780-1930*, vol. 1. Charlottesville: University of Virginia Press, 1980; Leatherman, Stephen P., ed. *Barrier Islands from the Gulf of St. Lawrence to the Gulf of Mexico*. New York: Academic Press, 1979; Leatherman, Stephen P. *Barrier Island Handbook*. Charlotte, North Carolina: Coastal Publications, 1982; Marschner, F. J. *Land Use and Its Patterns in the United States*. Agricultural Handbook No. 153, Washington, D.C.: U.S. Department of Agriculture, 1959; Muller, Peter O. *Contemporary Suburban America*. Englewood Cliffs, New Jersey: Prentice-Hall, 1981; Pattison, William D. *Beginnings of the American Rectangular Land Survey System, 1784-1800*. Columbus: Ohio Historical Society, 1970; Prest, V. K. *Canada's Heritage of Glacial Features*. Ottawa: Geological Survey of Canada Misc. Report 28, 1983; *Scenic Wonders of America*. Pleasantville, New York: Reader's Digest, 1973; Shelton, John S. *Geology Illustrated*. San Francisco: W. H. Freeman and Co., 1966; Short, Nicholas M., Lowman, Paul D., Jr., Freden, Stanley C., and Finch, William A., Jr., *Mission to Earth: LANDSAT Views the World*. Washington, D.C.: National Aeronautics and Space Administration, 1976; Wones, David R., ed. *Proceedings: "The Caledonides in the USA" I.G.C.P. Project 27: Caledonide Orogen, 1979 meeting, Blacksburg, Virginia.* Blacksburg: Virginia Polytechnic Institute and State University, 1980; Wood, Elizabeth A. *Science From Your Airplane Window.* New York: Dover Press, 1975.

STATE-BY-STATE REFERENCES

ARIZONA: Nations, Dale, and Stump, Edmund. *Geology of Arizona.* Dubuque, Iowa: Kendall/Hunt Publishing Co., 1981. The Arizona Bureau of Mines, University of Arizona, Tucson, has published several guides to state and federal highways.

CALIFORNIA: Howard, Arthur D. *Geologic History of Middle California.* Berkeley: University of California, 1979 (paperback).

FLORIDA: Hoffmeister, John Edward. *Land From the Sea—The Geologic Story of South Florida.* Coral Gables: University of Miami, 1974; Douglas, Marjory Stoneman. *The Everglades: River of Grass,* revised edition. St. Simons Island, Georgia: Mockingbird Books, 1974.

GEORGIA: Wharton, Charles H. *The Natural Environments of Georgia.* Atlanta: Georgia Department of Natural Resources, 1978; Griffin, Martha M. *Geologic Guide to Cumberland National Seashore.* Atlanta: Georgia Geologic Survey, 1982.

HAWAII: Macdonald, Gordon A., Abbott, Agatin T., and Peterson, Frank L. *Volcanoes in the Sea—The Geology of Hawaii,* second edition. Honolulu: University of Hawaii Press, 1983.

IOWA: Prior, Jean Cutler. *A Regional Guide to Iowa Landforms.* Iowa City: Iowa Geological Survey Educational Series 3, 1976.

KANSAS: Buchanan, Rex, ed. *Kansas Geology—An Introduction to Landscapes, Rocks, Minerals and Fossils.* Lawrence: University of Kansas Press, 1984.

MASSACHUSETTS: Kaye, Clifford A. *The Geology and Early History of the Boston Area of Massachusetts—A Bicentennial Approach.* Geological Survey Bulletin 1476, Reston, Virginia: U.S. Geological Survey, 1976; Strahler, Arthur N. *A Geologist's View of Cape Cod.* Garden City, New York: Natural History Press, 1966; Oldale, Robert N. *Geologic History of Cape Cod.* Reston, Virginia: U.S. Geological Survey, 1980.

MINNESOTA: Ojakangas, Richard W., and Matsch, Charles L. *Minnesota's Geology.* Minneapolis: University of Minnesota, 1982.

MISSOURI: Vineyard, Jerry D., et al. *Springs of Missouri.* Rolla: Missouri Department of Natural Resources, 1982.

NEBRASKA: Franzwa, Gregory M. *The Oregon Trail Revisited,* second edition. Gerald, Missouri: Patrice Press, 1978.

NEW HAMPSHIRE: Billings, Marland P. *The Geology of New Hampshire.* Concord, New Hampshire: Department of Resources and Economic Development, 1980.

NEW MEXICO: Riecker, Robert E., ed. *Rio Grande Rift: Tectonics and Magnatism.* Washington, D.C.: American Geophysical Union, 1979.

NEW YORK: Roseberry, C. R. *From Niagara to Montauk—The Scenic Pleasures of New York State.* Albany: State University of New York, 1982; Schuberth, Christopher J. *The Geology of New York City and Environs*. Garden City, New York: Natural History Press, 1968.

OHIO: *Guide to the Geology Along U.S. Route 23 Between Columbus and Portsmouth*. Educational Leaflet No. 11, Columbus: Department of Natural Resources, 1979.

PENNSYLVANIA: Geyer, Alan R., and Bolles, William H. *Outstanding Scenic Geological Features of Pennsylvania*. Harrisburg: Pennsylvania Geological Survey, 1979 (State Book Store, P.O. Box 1365, Harrisburg 17105). The state's departments of Education and of Environmental Resources publish geologic guides to interstate highways 80 and 81 as well as pamphlets on numerous geologic features.

TENNESSEE: Wilson, Robert Lake. *Guide to the Geology Along the Interstate Highways in Tennessee*. Tennessee Division of Geology, 1981. Published by the *Lewisburg Tribune*, Lewisburg, Tennessee.

UTAH: Lohman, S. W. *The Geologic Story of Canyonlands National Park*. Geological Survey Bulletin 1327, Reston, Virginia: U.S. Geological Survey, 1974; Hansen, Wallace R. *The Geologic Story of the Uinta Mountains*. Geological Survey Bulletin 1291, Reston, Virginia: U.S. Geological Survey, 1969.

VIRGINIA: Gathright, Thomas M., II. *Geology of the Shenandoah National Park, Virginia*. Charlottesville: Virginia Division of Mineral Resources, 1976.

WASHINGTON: McKee, Bates. *Cascadia—The Geologic Evolution of the Pacific Northwest*. New York: McGraw-Hill, 1972; Baker, Victor R., and Nummedal, Dag. *The Channeled Scabland*. Washington, D.C.: National Aeronautics and Space Administration, 1978.

WISCONSIN: Paull, R. K., and Paull, R. A. *Geology of Wisconsin and Upper Michigan*. Dubuque, Iowa: Kendall/Hunt Publishing Co., 1977.

INDEX

Disaster Falls, 124
Dismal Swamp, 279
Dixwell, John, 43
Domes, 6-7
  gneiss, 32
Domino effect, in gorge formation, 171
Dorf, Erling, 119, 120
Downbursts, air, 345
Downing, Andrew Jackson, 307-08
Dragline, mine, 287
Drumlin, 253-55
  see also specific site(s)
Dry land farming, 332
Drylot farms, 341-42
Dunes, 235-36
  see also specific name(s)
Dustbowl, 330

Earth, 169
Earthquake Lake, 131
Earthquakes. *See specific site(s), state(s)*
East Coast, 228-32, 234-37
  ocean and, 228-32, 234-37
  rivers near, 213-14
  sea level, along the, 234
  volcanic activity along, 41-45
  see also specific state(s)
Eastern States
  farming in, 341-42
  strip mining in, 287
  see also specific state(s)
East Rock (Connecticut), 43
Eaton, Gordon P., 96
Eisenhower, Dwight D., 332
Elbert, Mount, 109
Emmons, Samuel Franklin, 121, 126
Emperor Seamounts, 52-53
Enforcement of soil conservation, 329-30
Entrenched meanders, 200-12
Envelope plowing pattern, 330
Environmental Protection Agency, U.S. (EPA),
  233-34
Environmental Quality, Council on, 325
Erosion, 222-24
  coastal, 235-42
  control, 328-33
Eskers, 251-55
Europe, 56, 234, 256
Evans, Mount, 107
Everglades, 238
Everglades National Park, 238
Evolution
  animal, 114-17
  of Cascades, 141-51
  of Coast Ranges, 141-51
  mammal, 116-17

Fall, Albert B., 292-93
Fall line, 14
Farallon Plate, 66, 69, 88-91
Farmers, 330-31
  gentlemen, 315
  sidewalk, 341

  suitcase, 340-41
Farming, 338-44
  dairy, 338-42
  dry land, 332
  drylot, 341
  erosion, 342-43
  landscape, 327
  organic, 334-35
  revolution, 330-32
  technology, 341-42
  see also Crops, Farmers, Farmland
Farmland
  conservation, 327-37
  erosion, 333
  see also Farming
Father Damien, 183
Faults, 96
Field shelterbelts, 330-31
Finger Lakes, 259
First Watchung Mountain, 43
Fish and Wildlife Service, U.S., 233-34
Flaming Gorge, 123
Flamingo (Florida), 238
Flint, Richard Foster, 164, 170
Flint Hills (Kansas), 340
Flood plain, 208
Floods, 168-74, 200-05
  Ice Age, 160-74
  lava, 152-59
Flood tides, 235
Florida, 36-40, 238
  barrier islands and, 235, 237
  Big Cypress Swamp, 238-41
  coastal ridge, 237
  Everglades, 238
  farming in, 342
  farmland loss in, 337
  fauna in, 238-41
  Flamingo, 238
  karsts in, 276
  Key Largo limestone, 237-38
  Lake Okeechobee, 238
  Marco Island, 242
  Miami Beach, 234
  mines in, 290
  Pamlico Shoreline, 237
Florida Bay, 238
Florida Keys, 237-38
Foote, A. E., 192
Ford, Henry, 219, 312
Ford, John, 86
Fordham gneiss, 6, 32
Forest Hills Gardens, 310
Fort Kearney (Nebraska), 303
Fort Peck Dam, 218
Fossilized desert, 83-84
Fossils, 36
  trilobite, 21-22, 81
  un-American, 32
  in Wrangellia, 62
Fossil water, 319
Fowke, Gerard, 256

Hoover Dam, 215-18
Horizontal transport, development of, 314-15
Hotchkiss, David, 310
Hot spot, Pacific, 53, 175-91
  motion of, 52-54
Housatonic Mountains, 15
Housatonic River, 33
Hudson Bay, 245
Hudson River, 10, 259
Hudson River Palisades, 7, 42-43, 259-60
Hunter, Louis C., 213-14
Huntington, Henry Edmunds, 311
Hurley, Patrick M., 36
Hutton, James, 163
Hydroelectric power, 214

Ice, 243-64
Ice Age, 164, 237
  dunes, 270-71
  floods, 160-74
Ice Age National Scientific Reserve, 259
Ice fronts, 246-47
Iceland, 7
Ice sheets, 231, 232
Ickes, Harold, 216
Idaho, 51-52, 154-56
  Bitterroot Range, 139
  Blackhawk Mountain slide, 131
  Clearwater and Salmon River mountains, 139
  Coeur d'Alene, 140
  Craters of the Moon, 158
  Devil's Orchard, 158
  Hells Canyon, 62, 170
  Lewis and Clark Line, 140
  Red Rock Pass, 170
  Snake River Plain, 156, 158-59
  Twin Falls scablands, 170
Illinois, 297
  Chicago, 271, 306
    suburbs, 308-09
  Grand Prairie, 338-39
  mines in, 288
  rivers buried in, 255-56
  state plan, 296-97
Impact craters, 99, 192-99
Imperial Valley, 326, 341-42
Indiana, 194, 298
  Fort Wayne, 298
  as karstlands, 273-75
  mines in, 288
  sinkholes in, 275
Indiana Dunes, 270-71
Industry, 282-93
  relocation of, 313
Inner Gorge, Grand Canyon, 80-81
Inner Piedmont, 22-23
Interurban railways, 311-12
Intracoastal Waterway, 227
Inwood marble, 33

Iowa
  corn belt, 338-40

Des Moines lobe, 250
  loess hills, 267
  mines in, 288
  soil conservation in, 330
Iridium, 116
Iron, 34-35, 43, 223, 285-87
Irrigation systems, 215, 317-23
  center-pivot, 317-18
  conventional forms, 318-19
  drip (trickle), 318
  wells, 321-22
  see also irrigation systems under specific
    state(s)
Irving, Washington, 158-59
Islands, 227
  migration, 234
  see also specific name(s)
Ixtacihuatl volcano, 141-42

Jackson, Andrew (Stonewall), 16, 294-300
Jackson Hole, 127
Jackson Purchase, 300
Japan, 55
Jefferson, Thomas, 294-97, 299
Jeffersonian township plan, 294-99
Jetstream, air, 347
Johnston, David A., 144, 146
Jones, David L., 57
Jones Beach (New York), 241
Jurassic Period, 224

Kaibab limestone, 82
Kalamazoo Moraine, 250
Kames, 252-53
Kansas
  coal mines in, 288
  farming in, 340
  Flint Hills, 340
  oil fields in, 292-93
  Santa Fe Trail, 305
  water table, 321
  winter wheat, 340-41
Karst formations, 273-81
Katabatic winds, 265
Katahdin, Mount, 32
Kauai island, 189-91
Kaye, Clifford A., 255
Kehew, Alan E., 171
Kelvin-Helmholtz cloud waves, 348
Kennecott Copper Corporation, 283
Kent, Dennis V., 36
Kentucky, 18
  coal production of, 287-90
  farming in, 344
  karstlands in, 273-75
  Mammoth Cave, 273
  mines in, 288, 290
Kettleholes, 251
Kettle Moraine State Forest, 259
Key Largo limestone, 237-38
Kiawah Island, 227
Kilauea volcano, 177-78